J A Z Z
O N   F I L M

THE COMPLETE STORY OF THE
MUSICIANS & MUSIC ONSCREEN

B Y   S C O T T   Y A N O W

Backbeat Books
San Francisco

Published by Backbeat Books
600 Harrison Street, San Francisco, CA 94107
www.backbeatbooks.com
email: books@musicplayer.com

An imprint of CMP Information
Publishers of *Guitar Player*, *Bass Player*, *Keyboard*, and *EQ* magazines

CMP
United Business Media

Distributed to the book trade in the US and Canada by
Publishers Group West, 1700 Fourth Street, Berkeley, CA 94710

Distributed to the music trade in the US and Canada by
Hal Leonard Publishing, P.O. Box 13819, Milwaukee, WI 53213

Text Design and Composition by Maureen Forys—Happenstance Type-O-Rama
Cover Design by Jim Shinnick and Noel Eckert
Front Cover Photo: ©Bettman/CORBIS

Library of Congress Cataloging-in-Publication Data

Yanow, Scott.
    Jazz on film : the complete story of the musicians & music onscreen / by Scott Yanow.
        p. cm.
    Includes bibliographical references and index.
    ISBN 0-87930-783-8 (alk. paper)
    1. Jazz—History and criticism. 2. Motion pictures—Reviews.
    3. Motion pictures—Catalogs. I. Title.

ML3508.Y39 2004
781.65'09—dc22

                    2004015615

Printed in the United States of America

04 05 06 07 08   5 4 3 2 1

Contents

Introduction

*F*or me, a lifetime of listening to and enjoying jazz began with a Hollywood film, **The Five Pennies**. When I was ten, I thoroughly enjoyed seeing the 1959 movie on television. It depicts the life of cornetist Red Nichols as played by Danny Kaye in semi-fictional but very entertaining fashion, with Louis Armstrong having one of his best roles. My favorite scene is still when Red Nichols, having made a drunken fool of himself, quickly recovers and comes out of the audience to battle Armstrong successfully on an exciting version of "Battle Hymn of the Republic." It is a magical moment.

Even at the time, I knew that Danny Kaye didn't really play cornet, and I wondered how the band could play such a tricky arrangement flawlessly without anyone even calling out the key. After I fully immersed myself in jazz at the age of 16, I searched record stores fruitlessly, trying to find a version of Red Nichols playing "Battle Hymn" in the 1920s; it does not exist since he did not play it regularly until the late 1940s. I was also disappointed to discover a version of the song "The Five Pennies" by Nichols from the '20s that had nothing in common with the memorable tune from the film, which was written by Sylvia Fine (Kaye's wife) 30 years later.

I never forgot the "Battle Hymn" scene in the movie and was even involved in a re-creation of sorts. At 22, I played alto sax in a 1920s-type group called the Fly-by-Night Jazz Band. The drummer in the group, George Metz, knew about Captain Jack's in Glendale, a neighborhood bar that had a piano but usually just played the radio for its drinking customers. One night we sent ahead our pianist Bob Mitchell, who urged the owner to turn off the radio and listen. From a distance of two blocks away, he could hear our group playing "St. James Infirmary," quietly at first but coming closer and closer. By the time we entered the bar, the customers were excited and cheering. We circled the room, settled near the piano, and had ourselves a regular gig. Throughout that adventure, I thought of Red Nichols/Danny Kaye and the excitement of jazz that was depicted in that one scene.

With the inevitable passing of so many jazz greats during the past 40 years, today's jazz fans can only experience the music and presence of such masters as Louis Armstrong, Duke Ellington, Coleman Hawkins, Lester Young, Billie Holiday, Charlie Parker, Dizzy Gillespie, John Coltrane, Ella Fitzgerald and Miles Davis on records or films. The bad news is that one cannot go out to a club and see Joe Williams or Mel Tormé. The good news is that a large percentage of jazz history is currently available on CD, and it is possible to see filmed performances by many of the immortals on television whenever one wants, thanks to the now-taken-for-granted proliferation of videocassettes and DVDs.

Up until now, the only general reference book that covered all styles of jazz on film has been David Meeker's invaluable *Jazz in the Movies*. Meeker did a fine job of listing all of the known film appearances by jazz musicians and singers. But that book is out of print, and a lot has happened since its publication in 1981. Although there have been some very good jazz film reference books dedicated to specific artists (most notably Dr. Klaus Stratemann's remarkably detailed works on Louis Armstrong and Duke Ellington), it was long overdue for a *Jazz on Film* book to be compiled that, in addition to the Hollywood films, shorts and documentaries, would include reviews of most of the videotapes and DVDs that have come out since the 1980s. Unlike the David Meeker book, *Jazz on Film* rates the films on a 1 to 10 basis, answering the question "Is it worth seeing?" I have included relevant details about what songs are performed and, where appropriate, the basic plot. Also, unlike audiences (though only a relative few featured jazz performances), and special music shorts. Some of the full-length films that featured jazz prominently include **The Big Broadcast**, **The Birth of The Blues**, **Syncopation**, **Sun Valley Serenade**, **Sweet and Lowdown**, **New Orleans**, **A Song Is Born**, **Young Man with a Horn**, **Pete Kelly's Blues** and such nostalgic and partly fictional biographies as **The Glenn Miller Story**, **The Benny Goodman Story**, **The Gene Krupa Story** and **The Five Pennies**. Many other films have appearances by jazz musicians in a small role, and it is a constant joy to discover those moments, such as the Coleman Hawkins quintet in **The Crimson Canary** or Benny Carter popping up in a scene of **The Snows of Kilimanjaro**. During the swing era when big bandleaders were national celebrities, it was not unusual for Harry James or Tommy Dorsey to be well featured in a Hollywood movie, and Louis Armstrong broke down some barriers with his film appearances even if he rarely had a chance to really show his acting abilities.

Although most all-Black films do not contain much jazz and were cheaply made, there are some exceptions, most notably **Hallelujah**, **Cabin in the Sky** and **Stormy Weather**, each of which had large budgets and were put out by major film companies. Of the low-budget productions, there are several films starring Louis Jordan and Cab Calloway and such surprises as **Paradise in Harlem** (with Mamie Smith and Lucky Millinder's Orchestra), **Boy, What a Girl** (with Sid Catlett and Slam Stewart) and **Sepia Cinderella** (which has two numbers from the John Kirby Sextet).

The musical shorts are almost always of great interest. There were many short subjects filmed during 1927–32 that feature legendary hot jazz bands and dance orchestras, but unfortunately a large percentage no longer exist. Among those that have survived and are essential are Duke Ellington's **Black and Tan**, Bessie Smith in **St. Louis Blues**, Louis Armstrong's somewhat bizarre **Rhapsody in Black**, **Pie Pie Blackbird** and **Smash Your Baggage**.

As the swing era began, shorts were made of many of the top orchestras. These usually consisted of three or four songs, with opening and closing instrumentals and two vocalists (one generally commercial) featured on the second and third numbers. Quite often the hotter numbers also showcased acrobatic dancers. The most remarkable short from the swing era is **Jammin' the Blues**, featuring Lester Young, Harry "Sweets" Edison and Illinois Jacquet in 1944. Shorts became less common in the 1950s and were largely extinct by the '60s.

Soundies

*I*n 1940, the Mills Novelty Company (the largest manufacturer of jukeboxes) and James Roosevelt (the son of President Franklin Roosevelt) formed Globe-Mills Productions to build and sell Panoram movie jukeboxes, machines that for a dime played three-minute single-song features called "Soundies." These shorts, produced by the Soundies Distributing Corporation of America during the next six years (most prolifically in 1941–42), showcase a wide variety of performers including many of the top swing stars. Filmed in a day with the music being prerecorded, the performances have the musicians and singers miming to the music (the same as in nearly all Hollywood films) and sometimes it is pretty obvious that they are not performing live. The visual element is often emphasized over the music (with a lot of interesting looking dancers), but the Soundies do give present-day viewers an opportunity to see some bands that rarely made it onto film. These visual jukeboxes were briefly popular, but the musicians union's recording strike of 1943–44 and World War II hurt the industry and in the long run relatively few bars and restaurants installed the Panoram machines.

Most of the more popular Soundies have been made available on videotapes and they are reviewed in this book. Here is a list of the remaining jazz-oriented Soundies, the ones that are more difficult to find:

Red Allen   **Mop, Crawl Red Crawl**

Ali Baba Trio   **E-Bob-O-Lee Bop, Your Feet's Too Big, Patience and Fortitude, If You Only Knew** (the latter two with trumpeter/singer Valaida Snow)

Harry Barris Trio   **Jivers' Holiday**

Ray Bauduc   **I'm Just a Lucky So and So, The Man with the Weird Beard, Shine on Your Shoes**

Will Bradley   **Jack and Jill, Basin Street Boogie, I'm Tired of Waiting for You, Deed I Do, Rickety Rickshaw Man, Who Dunnit, When You and I Were Young Maggie**

Les Brown   **If There Were Girls Like You in the Army, Once Over Lightly, Is It Love or Is It Conscription** (the latter two featuring Doris Day)

Una Mae Carlisle   **Tain't Yours, I'm a Good Good Woman, I Like It Cause I Love It**

Bob Chester Orchestra   **B-I-Bi, Wait 'Til the Sun Shines Nellie**

Larry Clinton   **Whatcha Know Joe, The Night We Met in Honomu, Chant of the Jungle, Deep Purple, Semper Fidelis, My Buddy, Smiles**

King Cole Trio   **Oh-H-E-E My My**

Bob Crosby   **Abercrombie Had a Zombie, Merry-Go-Round, Jazzy Joe, Hong Kong Blues** (with Hoagy Carmichael)

Dorothy Dandridge   **Yes, Indeed** (with the Spirits of Rhythm)**, Easy Street, Congo Clambake, Blackbird Fantasy**

Dardanelle Trio   **I Don't Know Enough About You, Backtrack, Happy Cat**

Jimmy Dorsey   **Oh Look, Man That's Groovy, La Rosita, A Whole Bunch of Something, Tired of Waiting for You, My Sister and I**

Sonny Dunham   **Sleepy Lagoon, The Lamplighter's Serenade, At the Club Savoy,**

Put-Put-Put Your Arms Around Me, Sadie Hawkins Day, Watch the Birdie, Heavenly Hideaway

Cliff Edwards Jeannie with the Light Brown Hair, Minnie My Mountain Moocher, Paddlin' Madeline Home, The Devil and the Deep Blue Sea

Harry "the Hipster" Gibson 4-F Ferdinand, Harry the Hipster

Adele Girard Harp Boogie

Glen Gray's Casa Loma Orchestra Just a Prayer Away, Low Gravy, Stars in Your Eyes, A Friend of Yours, Jonah, Savage

Tiny Grimes Swingin' in the Groove, Never Too Old to Swing, T.G. Boogie Woogie, Romance Without Finance

Jane Harvey It's a Pity to Say Goodnight

Erskine Hawkins Hot in the Groove

Milt Herth Trio Dark Eyes

Les Hite The Devil Sat Down and Cried, What to Do, Pudgy Boy, That Ol' Ghost Train

Bob Howard Hey Tojo Count Yo' Men, Dinah

International Sweethearts of Rhythm Jump Children, That Man of Mine, She's Crazy with the Heat

Cee Pee Johnson Swing for Your Supper, Jungle Jig (the latter two with Dorothy Dandridge), Jump in, Let's Go, You Can't Fool About Love

Louis Jordan The Outskirts of Town

Stan Kenton Jammin' in the Panoram, Reed Rapture, Jealous, I'm Gonna Love that Guy (with June Christy), I'm Homesick That's All, Eager Beaver

John Kirby Tweed Me

LeDonne Trio Hotsy Totsy, I'd Love to Be a Cowboy

Dr. Henry "Hot Lips" Levine Ja-Da, When My Sugar Walks Down the Street

Johnny Long When I Grow Too Old to Dream, Whatcha Know Joe, Swingin' at the Séance, My Girl Loves a Sailor, Caterpillar Shuffle, Let's Get Away from It All, Boogie Man, Chop Sticks, The Long and Short of It, Maria Elena, He Holds My Hand, It Just Be Jelly, Junior, Hanover Hangover, Watch Out, It's a Sin to Tell a Lie

Matty Malneck Orchestra The Coffee Song, Swingin' with William, Bumble Bee Hop, Carmen

Wingy Manone Vine Street Blues, The Saints Go Marching in, Sing, Sing, Sing, Juke Box Joe's, Rhythm on the River, Deacon Jones, I Lost My Sugar in Salt Lake City

Joe Marsala Don't Be a Baby Baby, Millennium Jump, The Boy and the Girl from North and South Carolina, Southern Comfort

Lucky Millinder Because I Love You (with Mamie Smith), Harlem Serenade, Big Fat Mama, I Want a Man

Roy Milton's Orchestra Ride On Ride On (with June Richmond), 47th Street Jive

Ozzie Nelson Orchestra Somebody Else Is Taking My Place, I'm Looking for a Guy Who Plays Alto and Baritone and Doubles on a Clarinet and Wears a Size 37 Suit, Loretta, Ozzie Nelson Blues

Mary Osborne Trio Tabu, Rhumba Rebop

Tony Pastor Corn on the Conga, Oh Marie, Doin' the Ratamacue, Good Morning Mr. Zip-Zip-Zip, Let's Do It

Les Paul Trio Dark Eyes, Nellie Gray, Don't Cry Baby

Ben Pollack   The Hut-Sut Song, Loch Lomond, The One I Love Belongs to Somebody Else, He Took Me for a Sleighride, I Only Want a Buddy, Kiss the Boys Goodbye, War Dance for Wooden Indians, A Little Jive Is Good for You, The Wife of the Man on the Flying Trapeze

Alvino Rey and the Four King Sisters   The Irish Washerwoman, Tying Apples on a Lilac Tree, St. Louis Blues, The Call of the Canyon, Chop Fooey, Java Jive, Cielito Lindo

June Richmond   Joseph 'n' His Brudders, We're Stepping Out Tonight, Baby Don't You Love Me Anymore, My Bottle Is Dry, Time Takes Care of Everything, Who Dunit to Who

Bill "Bojangles" Robinson   By an Old Southern River

Gene Rodgers   My My Ain't That Somethin', Big Fat Butterfly

Cecil Scott   I'm Making Believe, Don't Be Late, Contrast in Rhythm, Mr. X. Blues

Bobby Sherwood   I Know Somebody Who Loves You, In Love with a Song, Jive, Little Gypsy, Twelfth Street Rag, Last Night's Gardenias, What the Country Needs

Noble Sissle   Sizzle with Sissle, Joe Joe, Everybody's Jumpin' Now

Charlie Spivak   Hop, Skip and Jump, 'Leven Thirty Saturday Night

Kay Starr   I'm Secretary to the Sulta, Stop that Dancin', Up There

Maxine Sullivan   Case o' the Blues (with Benny Carter's orchestra)

Claude Thornhill   Count Me in, America I Love You, Where Has My Little Dog Gone, Somebody Nobody Loves

The Three Peppers   Mary Had a Little Lamb, Ain't She Pretty, Take Everything, Rhythm Sam

Liz Tilton and Matty Malneck's Orchestra   Just the Other Day

Skeets Tolbert   Blitzkrieg Bombardier, Corn Pone, Tis You Baby

Mel Tormé and the Mel-Tones   Dance Baby Dance, Indiana, Lullaby of Broadway, Juanita

Movies:

1960 to the Present Day

*I*t took some time, but Hollywood's depiction of jazz musicians gradually has become more realistic, evolving from the stereotypes of the swing and beatnik eras. While **Lady Sings the Blues** (1972) is a very messy and inaccurate depiction of the life of Billie Holiday and **Cotton Club** (1984) is at best fanciful, **Paris Blues** (1961), **Round Midnight** (1986) and **Bird** (1988) are closer to the truth (even if **Bird** fudges the facts in spots) and Spike Lee's **Mo' Better Blues** (1990) often rings true.

Although the subject is beyond the boundaries of this book, it should be noted that jazz has been a prominent part of many movie soundtracks, starting in the 1950s. Although its tie-in to crime scenes and violence is often stereotyped, jazz has been used quite effectively in many films, from **The Wild One** (1954) and **The Man with the Golden Arm** (1955), to the television series **Peter Gunn** (1958), **Richard Diamond: Private Detective** (1957–60), **M Squad** (1957–60) and **Mr. Lucky** (1959), not to mention most of Woody Allen's films.

While the rise of MTV and music videos has not affected jazz much (jazz videos made for television rarely ever get aired and mostly remain unavailable), the development of videocassettes in the 1980s and DVDs in the 1990s has resulted in a real boom for jazz viewers. There has been a large proliferation of jazz documentaries during the past few decades, many of which are reviewed in this book. The best ones allow the music to speak for itself part of the time, while the worst ones have endless talking and too little music. The most extensive jazz documentary ever, Ken Burns's **Jazz** (2001), is unfortunately a real mess with scores of errors, many significant omissions, speculation often substituting for facts and a general fictionalization of both jazz's past and the present scene. But many of the other documentaries that are now available on video and DVD are definitive, adding to the legacy of jazz on film.

The jazz world has been waiting for many years for some much-promised film biographies, particularly ones on Chet Baker and Miles Davis. But the chances are good that the most valuable and priceless footage will always be of the real thing.

Ruth Etting

*R*uth Etting never became a movie star, but she was one of the most popular of the female singers active during 1926–36 before she went into an early retirement. Although never an improvising jazz singer, she sang superior songs, had a cry in her voice when she bent notes and swung. She was in 41 shorts and four full-length films, all of which are of some interest. Of the latter, Etting is uncredited in **Palmy Days** (1931), has a minor role (singing "No More Love") in the Eddie Cantor movie **Roman Scandals** (1933), is in **Gift of Gab** (1934), and sings "Keep Romance Alive" in the Wheeler and Woolsey comedy **Hips Hips Hooray** (1934). Her 41 shorts (which usually are around ten minutes in length) are **Ruth Etting** (1928), **Paramount Movietone** (1928), **Melancholy Dame** (1928), **Glorifying the Popular Song** (1929), **Favorite Melodies** (1929), **The Book of Lovers** (1929), **Ruth Etting** (1929), **Roseland** (1930), **One Good Turn** (1930), **Broadway's Like That** (1930), **Words and Music** (1931), **Stage Struck** (1931), **Season's Greeting** (1931), **Radio Salutes** (1931), **Old Lace** (1931), **Freshman Love** (1931), **Artistic Temper** (1932), **A Regular Trouper** (1932), **A Modern Cinderella** (1932), **A Mail Bride** (1932), **Knee Deep in Music** (1933), **I Know Everybody and Everybody's Racket** (1933), **Crashing the Gate** (1933), **California Weather** (1933), **Bye-Gones** (1933), **Along Came Ruth** (1933), **Mr. Broadway** (1933), **A Torch Tango** (1934), **Southern Style** (1934), **The Song of Fame** (1934), **Hollywood on Parade** (1934), **Hell Bent for Love** (1934), **Derby Decade** (1934), **Bandits and Ballads** (1934), **Turned Out** (1935), **Ticket or Leave It** (1935), **An Old Spanish Onion** (1935), **No Contest** (1935), **Sleepy Time** (1936), **Melody in May** (1936) and **Aladdin from Manhattan** (1936). In addition, Ruth Etting's life is portrayed in semifictional form by Doris Day in **Love Me or Leave Me** (1955).

A Listing of the Key Artists

To avoid repetition, listed below are most of the key jazz musicians/vocalists and their instruments. This way it will not be necessary to mention in every one of their film appearances that Louis Armstrong plays trumpet, Benny Goodman is a clarinetist and Nat King Cole is a pianist/singer.

Cannonball Adderley *Alto*	Chick Corea *Piano, keyboards*	Herbie Hancock *Piano*
Nat Adderley *Cornet*	Eddie "Lockjaw" Davis *Tenor*	Coleman Hawkins *Tenor*
Henry "Red" Allen *Trumpet*	Miles Davis *Trumpet*	Joe Henderson *Tenor*
Lawrence Brown *Trombone*	Wild Bill Davison *Cornet*	Billy Higgins *Drums*
Cat Anderson *Trumpet*	Barrett Deems *Drums*	Earl Hines *Piano*
Ivie Anderson *Vocals*	Paul Desmond *Alto*	Milt Hinton *Bass*
Louis Armstrong *Trumpet, vocals*	Eric Dolphy *Alto, flute, bass clarinet*	Art Hodes *Piano*
Buster Bailey *Clarinet*	Jimmy Dorsey *Alto, clarinet*	Johnny Hodges *Alto*
Charlie Barnet *Tenor*	Tommy Dorsey *Trombone*	Lena Horne *Vocals*
Count Basie *Piano*	Harry "Sweets" Edison *Trumpet*	Freddie Hubbard *Trumpet*
Louie Bellson *Drums*	Teddy Edwards *Tenor*	Alberta Hunter *Vocals*
Barney Bigard *Clarinet*	Roy Eldridge *Trumpet*	Milt Jackson *Vibes*
Art Blakey *Drums*	Duke Ellington *Piano*	Illinois Jacquet *Tenor*
Wellman Braud *Bass*	Ziggy Elman *Trumpet*	Ahmad Jamal *Piano*
Lawrence Brown *Trombone*	Bill Evans *Piano*	Harry James *Trumpet*
Ray Brown *Bass*	Gil Evans *Arranger, piano*	Freddie Jenkins *Trumpet*
Dave Brubeck *Piano*	Art Farmer *Flugelhorn, trumpet*	Elvin Jones *Drums*
Gary Burton *Vibes*	Bud Freeman *Tenor*	Jo Jones *Drums*
Cab Calloway *Vocals*	Jimmy Garrison *Bass*	Jonah Jones *Trumpet*
Conte Candoli *Trumpet*	Stan Getz *Tenor*	Louis Jordan *Alto, vocals*
Harry Carney *Baritone*	Dizzy Gillespie *Trumpet*	Barney Kessel *Guitar*
Benny Carter *Alto*	Tyree Glenn *Trombone*	Kenny Kirkland *Piano*
Ron Carter *Bass*	Paul Gonsalves *Tenor*	Lee Konitz *Alto*
Big Sid Catlett *Drums*	Benny Goodman *Clarinet*	Gene Krupa *Drums*
Doc Cheatham *Trumpet*	Dexter Gordon *Tenor*	Billy Kyle *Piano*
Buck Clayton *Trumpet*	Stephane Grappelli *Violin*	John Lewis *Piano*
Billy Cobham *Drums*	Freddie Green *Guitar*	Shelly Manne *Drums*
Cozy Cole *Drums*	Sonny Greer *Drums*	Wingy Manone *Trumpet, vocals*
Nat King Cole *Piano, vocals*	Fred Guy *Banjo, guitar*	Branford Marsalis *Tenor, soprano*
Richie Cole *Alto*	Bobby Hackett *Cornet*	Wynton Marsalis *Trumpet*
Ornette Coleman *Alto*	Bob Haggart *Bass*	Les McCann *Keyboards, vocals*
John Coltrane *Tenor, soprano*	Jimmy Hamilton *Clarinet*	Jimmy McPartland *Cornet*
Eddie Condon *Guitar*	Lionel Hampton *Vibes*	Jay McShann *Piano, vocals*

Thelonious Monk   *Piano*
James Moody   *Tenor, flute*
Gerry Mulligan   *Baritone*
Ray Nance   *Cornet, violin, vocals*
Tricky Sam Nanton   *Trombone*
Red Norvo   *Vibes*
Kid Ory   *Trombone*
Walter Page   *Bass*
Joe Pass   *Guitar*
Les Paul   *Guitar*
Oscar Peterson   *Piano*
Buddy Rich   *Drums*
Max Roach   *Drums*
Sonny Rollins   *Tenor*
Jimmy Rushing   *Vocals*
Pee Wee Russell   *Clarinet*

Charlie Shavers   *Trumpet*
Artie Shaw   *Clarinet*
Arvell Shaw   *Bass*
Woody Shaw   *Trumpet*
George Shearing   *Piano*
Wayne Shorter   *Tenor, soprano*
Zoot Sims   *Tenor*
Bessie Smith   *Vocals*
Jess Stacy   *Piano*
Rex Stewart   *Cornet*
Joe Sullivan   *Piano*
Buddy Tate   *Tenor*
Jack Teagarden   *Trombone, vocals*
Clark Terry   *Flugelhorn, vocals*
Juan Tizol   *Valve trombone*

Mel Tormé   *Vocals*
McCoy Tyner   *Piano*
Joe Venuti   *Violin*
Miroslav Vitous   *Bass*
Fats Waller   *Piano, vocals*
Cedar Walton   *Piano*
Earl Warren   *Alto*
Ben Webster   *Tenor*
Dickie Wells   *Trombone*
Cootie Williams   *Trumpet*
Joe Williams   *Vocals*
Tony Williams   *Drums*
Teddy Wilson   *Piano*
Jimmy Witherspoon   *Vocals*
Phil Woods   *Alto*
Trummy Young   *Trombone*

What Is Purposely Missing from the First Three Sections

- Films and cartoons with jazz soundtracks but no onscreen performances
- Nonmusical acting roles by musicians and singers
- Obscure television performances that will probably not be issued anytime soon

There might be a second edition of *Jazz on Film* in the future. Comments, corrections, updates and omissions are very welcome. I can be contacted at Scottyanow@aol.com.

Review Section One:

Videos and DVDs

 After Hours/Jazz Dance
(1998, 49 minutes, Rhapsody Films)

Two unrelated jazz shorts are reissued in full on this DVD. **Jazz Dance** from 1954 is a real oddity, featuring an all-star Dixieland band playing at a dance before a noisy and preoccupied audience, which includes a couple of professional dancers who are obvious ringers. Jimmy McPartland leads the aggregation, which also includes trombonist Jimmy Archey, Pee Wee Russell, pianist Willie "The Lion" Smith, bassist Pops Foster and drummer George Wettling. The band plays such crowd pleasers as "Ballin' the Jack," "Royal Garden Blues," "Jazz Me Blues" and of course "The Saints." **Jazz Dance** brings listeners back to a time when drunken college students and former followers of the big bands used to go out to listen to boisterous Dixieland.

    After Hours from 1961 was a television pilot that was never sold. Although the announcing is a bit too hep, the music is often quite exciting. Coleman Hawkins plays "Lover Man" while joined by pianist Johnny Guarnieri, Milt Hinton and Cozy Cole. Roy Eldridge just happens to drop by the nightclub in time to play "Sunday." "Just You, Just Me" swings hard, while "Taking a Chance on Love" has singer Carol Seedens sitting in. Taken individually, **After Hours** rates a 9 and **Jazz Dance** a 6.

 Ahmad Jamal: In Concert
(2002, 57 minutes, Music Video Distributors)

Filmed at the 1981 Midem Jazz Festival, Ahmad Jamal directs his trio (with bassist Subu Adeyloa and drummer Crosley Payton) through "Appreciation," "Morning of the Carnival" and the funky one-chord vamp "One." The second half of the tape has also been included in the DVD **Gary Burton: Live**, which is the preferred purchase. Burton on vibes performs the complex "Bogota," "Autumn Leaves" and another version of "One" with the trio while sitting out on an unidentified number. In general the music is overlong and, although Jamal looks happy to be performing with Burton, the results are less exciting than expected.

 Airto & Flora Purim—The Latin Jazz All-Stars
(1988, 60 minutes, View Video)

Filmed at the 1985 Queen Mary Jazz Festival, the performance by singer Flora Purim and percussionist/drummer Airto Moreira finds them playing with three percussionists, three horns (including some prominent playing from trumpeter Jeff Elliot), bass and keyboardist Kei Akagi. An opening instrumental is followed by Airto singing and playing the birimbao and a section in which Airto is joined by the Batacaje Dance Troupe (consisting of percussionists and a few gymnastic dancers). A long vamp precedes Purim's entrance; the singer is seen wearing a flamboyant outfit worthy of Sun Ra. Purim sings quite well on four numbers (her voice was in its prime) although the individual compositions are not particularly memorable. She mixes together folk melodies, fusion, electronics and adventurous sound explorations. Guest tenor saxophonist Joe Farrell has a long solo on "Shoulder" and is aboard for the closer, Chick Corea's "Light As as a Feather." This well-photographed set will be of strong interest to the fans of Flora Purim and Airto although it falls short of essential.

Alberta Hunter: My Castle's Rockin'
(1992, 60 minutes, View Video)

This hour-long documentary, written by Chris Albertson, covers the remarkable life of Alberta Hunter. She is seen performing at Barney Josephson's Cookery (accompanied by pianist Gerald Cook and a bassist) while in her eighties, singing "My Castle's Rockin'," "Rough & Ready Man," "Darktown Strutters Ball," "Downhearted Blues," "I've Got a Mind to Ramble," "I'm Having a Good Time," "Handy Man" and "The Love I Have for You," songs that are perfectly integrated into her life story. She is also seen in her one movie appearance, performing the anti-racism song "Black Shadows" in the British film **Radio Parade of 1935**. Throughout **My Castle's Rockin'**, Hunter talks about her life, while Billy Taylor provides the narration. She was born in Memphis in 1895, ran away from home to go to Chicago as a teenager, and by 1917 was singing at the Dreamland with King Oliver. Hunter became one of the earliest of the blues singers to record, appeared on Broadway, and in 1927 moved to Europe where she starred in *Showboat* opposite Paul Robeson and worked in the 1930s as a sophisticated cabaret singer. After returning to the U.S. shortly before World War II began, Hunter became very active in the USO, performing in Asia and later on in South Korea during the Korean War. In 1956 her career was slowing down and she abruptly changed course, becoming a nurse at the age of 61. She lied about her age (saying she was 49) and, other than a couple of records in 1961, she was out of music for 20 years. In 1977 she was involuntarily retired from the hospital where she worked, at what her superiors thought was five years past the retirement age of 65; she was actually 82. Within a short time she was persuaded by Barney Josephson (who owned the Cookery) to return to music and her final seven years were triumphant. Alberta Hunter passed away in 1984 at the age of 89, more famous than she had been in the 1920s. Her unique story is definitively told on this DVD.

All Girl Bands *(1993, 61 minutes, Storyville)*

During the 1930s and '40s, scores of all-female groups and orchestras performed in the United States. Many were mere novelty bands, allowing customers to gape at the odd sight of women in gowns playing trombones, but some were on a higher level. This video is quite valuable for it has the best film appearances of Ina Ray Hutton's Melodears and the International Sweethearts of Rhythm. Hutton, a glamorous singer who conducted her orchestra quite colorfully and was also a talented tap-dancer, had an excellent band even if none of her sidewomen ever became famous. The ensemble is featured during their appearance in the 1935 film **Star Reporter** and as the centerpiece of a pair of ten-minute shorts from 1936–37, **Accent on Girls** and **Swing Hutton Swing**. The best numbers are "Truckin'," "Suzy Q" and "Melodear Swing." The obscure Lorraine Page Orchestra sounds pretty strong on a Soundie version of "Sweet Sue" with the singers Six Hits and a Miss in the spotlight. Rita Rio's Mistresses of Rhythm are featured on a quartet of two-to-three minute shorts from the early '40s, each of which has one song. "I Look at You" is unusual in that it features the future Hollywood actor Alan Ladd as a singer, "Flying Feet" has some acrobatic dancing from Anita Jacobi before singer/dancer Rio (a Latin version of Ina Ray Hutton) struts her stuff, and "Sticks and Stones" has Rito interacting with a male quartet. Best of the quartet is "Feed the Kitty" which mostly features the excellent if now forgotten band. Considered the greatest all-female band of the time, the International Sweethearts of Rhythm only recorded four songs during their existence, but fortunately in 1946 they were filmed for a trio of three-song shorts (**The International Sweethearts of Rhythm**, **How About that Jive** and **Harlem Jam Session**), all of which are on this videocassette, so it is possible to watch them for 23 minutes. Fronted by singer Anna Mae Winburn, the band has a particularly strong tenor soloist in Viola Burnside, Tiny Davis sings, plays trumpet and jokes around on **How About that Jive**, and the band sounds a little boppish in spots on **Harlem Jam Session**. The legendary group declined after 1946 and slipped away into history.

 ### Antonio Carlos Jobim: An All-Star Tribute
(1995, 60 minutes, View Video)

Just a year before his death in 1994, the great Brazilian composer Antonio Carlos Jobim's musical legacy was celebrated at a filmed concert from Brazil that has been reissued on this DVD. Shirley Horn sings and plays piano on "Once I Loved," pianist Gonzalo Rubalcaba is featured on "Agua de Baker" and "Ofha Maria" and Joe Henderson, who would soon record a Jobim tribute album (on which the composer was originally supposed to appear), stars on "O Grande Amor." Jon Hendricks (backed by Herbie Hancock and Ron Carter) sings "No More Blues" and vocalist Gal Costa is quite charming on "A Felicidade" and "So Todas Fassem." Jobim himself appears on the last few numbers: "Iquais a Voce," "Luiza," "Wave" and "The Girl from Ipanema" (the latter also features Costa and Hendricks). Although weak, Jobim was clearly happy about this concert, which was his last significant public appearance.

 ### Archie Shepp: I Am Jazz…It's My Life
(1990, 52 minutes, Rhapsody Films)

Avant-gardist Archie Shepp talks about the African roots of jazz and its revolutionary purpose. He also recites a couple of poems and performs on tenor and soprano with pianist Siegfried Kessler, bassist Wilbur Little, both Don Mumford and Clifford Jarvis on drums, and percussionist Cheikd Tidiane Fall.

 ### Art Blakey: A Jazz Messenger
(1987, 78 minutes, Rhapsody Films)

This is a rather fascinating documentary that traces Art Blakey's career and life during a one-year period. Trumpeter Terence Blanchard and altoist Donald Harrison were getting ready to leave Blakey's Jazz Messengers so the drummer is seen auditioning a variety of younger musicians. Several of his alumni comment on the importance of their period with the Jazz Messengers (including tenor saxophonist Benny Golson, trombonist Curtis Fuller, altoist Bobby Watson and Wynton Marsalis), Blakey jams with tenor saxophonist Courtney Pine, backs dance groups and continually discusses his philosophy of both jazz and life. There are so many interesting scenes in this documentary that one wishes that Blakey had been followed around as extensively during the previous 40 years too.

 ### Art Blakey's Jazz Messengers
(2002, 61 minutes, TDK Mediactive)

This DVD has a set by Art Blakey's Jazz Messengers as played at Umbria Jazz '76 on July 20, 1976. At the time the Messengers consisted of the leader, trumpeter Bill Hardman, tenor saxophonist David Schnitter, pianist Mickey Tucker and bassist Cameron Brown. While Hardman plays in a hard bop style, Schnitter's solos are more intense and explorative. The quintet performs "Backgammon," "Along Came Betty," "Uranus," "Blues March," "All the Things You Are" and "Gypsy Folk Tales" in spirited if not classic renditions.

 ### Art Blakey and the Jazz Messengers: Live at Ronnie Scott's
(2002, 57 minutes, Music Video Distributors)

From February 21, 1985, Art Blakey is featured leading a particularly strong version of the Jazz Messengers that consists of trumpeter Terence Blanchard, altoist Donald Harrison, Jean Toussaint on tenor, pianist Mulgrew Miller and bassist Lonnie Plaxico. There are three brief and forgettable interview sections along with fine renditions of "On the Ginza," "I Want to Talk About You" (a feature for Harrison that unfortunately cuts off right before its conclusion), "Two of a Kind" and the uptempo blues "Dr. Jackle." Surprisingly there are no drum solos on this set, which is of greatest interest for showing how Blanchard and Harrison sounded in 1985.

The Art Ensemble of Chicago— Live from the Jazz Showcase
(1990, 50 minutes, Rhapsody Films)

The Art Ensemble of Chicago (trumpeter Lester Bowie, Roscoe Mitchell and Joseph Jarman on many reeds, bassist Malachi Favors and drummer Don Moye) was always one of the most visual of the avant-garde jazz groups. Utilizing a wide array of both conventional and "little" instruments, wearing unusual outfits, and displaying the ability to both freely improvise and use aspects of earlier jazz styles, at their best the Art Ensemble of Chicago put on very memorable shows. Fortunately the band was in top form on November 1, 1981, when they performed the continuous set that is on this video. The music ranges from percussion displays and a jam through "I Got Rhythm" chord changes (featuring Bowie) to a bit of funk and some New Orleans parade rhythms. The eight selections on this definitive DVD (which is the best all-round film of the group) include "We-Bop," "New York Is Full of Lonely People," "New Orleans" and "Funky AECO."

Art Pepper: Notes from a Jazz Survivor
(1999, 50 minutes, Shanachie)

This documentary from 1982 was filmed shortly after Art Pepper's autobiography *Straight Life* came out. The altoist is refreshingly honest about his life as a saxophonist, junkie and petty thief. He is seen playing with his quartet (pianist Milcho Leviev, bassist Bob Magnusson and drummer Carl Burnett) at Pasquale's in Malibu, California, but none of the performances are complete (the searing ballad "Patricia" comes the closest), and all of the songs eventually have him talking over the music. However, Pepper's storytelling and opinions are consistently fascinating, as are those of his third wife, Laurie Pepper (who largely made his successful comeback possible). Pepper talks about his heroin addiction, his relationship with Laurie, his childhood, his life of crime, his first two wives, the time in prison and various other topics. There are some painful spots along the way but not a boring

moment, and one wishes that this DVD were twice as long, with a complete song or two.

 ### Back to Balboa Highlights: The Kenton Discussions
(1991, 90 minutes, GOAL Productions)

During May 30–June 2, 1991, a 50th anniversary celebration took place, celebrating Stan Kenton's debut as a bandleader. In addition to four days of music, there were panel discussions featuring the key survivors of Kenton's many bands. Many funny and insightful stories were told, and fortunately it was all filmed. The 12 hours of panels have been edited down to the best 90 minutes. This tape allows one to see such legends as Jimmy Lyons (founder of the Monterey Jazz Festival, who was an early Kenton booster), Howard Rumsey, Bob Gioga, Gene Norman, Anita O'Day, Buddy Childers, Pete Rugolo, Bob Cooper, Milt Bernhart, Jack Costanzo, Laurindo Almeida, Eddie Bert, Shorty Rogers, Bud Shank, Manny Albam, Chris Connor, Pete Candoli, Conte Candoli, Bill Holman, Lee Konitz, Vic Lewis, Lennie Niehaus, Bill Perkins, Marty Paich, Hank Levy, Gabe Baltazar, Jiggs Whigham, Carl Saunders, Steve Huffstetter and others telling the Stan Kenton story. There are many spontaneous and heart-warming moments along the way. The love that all of the participants had for Kenton and his music is obvious.

 ### Banu Gibson & New Orleans Hot Jazz
(1993, 53 minutes, Banjou Productions)

One of the major classic jazz singers since the 1980s, Banu Gibson consistently features an inspired repertoire full of standards and obscurities from the 1920s to the early '40s. Gibson leads her New Orleans Hot Jazz Band, a sextet that includes three top horn players and pianist/arranger David Boeddinghaus. This video is a bit different, for Gibson and her group are accompanied by the Skagit Valley Symphony Orchestra and they essentially put on a pops concert. There are some hot moments although the strings do get in the way at times and a few more "bonus," a 1972 television appearance (possibly on Johnny Carson's **Tonight Show**) that has Rich sounding quite fiery on "On Green Dolphin Street."

Buddy Rich: The Lost West Side Story Tapes
(2001, 54 minutes, Hudson Music)

Filmed during the same session that resulted in the DVD **Channel One Suite** (April 3, 1985), this set was actually lost for many years, believed destroyed in a fire. After it was discovered in 2000, it was soon put out on DVD and proved to be even better than **Channel One Suite**. Steve Marcus, pianist Bill Cunliffe, trumpeter Michael Lewis and altoist Mark Pinto are the main soloists, with bassist Dave Carpenter adding to the power of the rhythm section. The set ("Mexicali Rose," "Willowcrest," "'Round Midnight," "Cotton Tail," "New Blues," "Tee Bag," "The Red Snapper," "West Side Story Suite") is particularly strong with "Tee Bag" being a feature for the trio. The 67-year-old drummer is

The world's greatest drummer, Buddy Rich was well documented throughout much of his career. Several DVDs feature his big bands of the '70s and '80s.

stunning on "West Side Story Suite," taking two spectacular solos although he does look a bit tired when it is over. In addition, this DVD has a variety of bonus cuts, including comments from daughter Cathy Rich, Buddy's wife Marie, various family members, producer Gary Reper and grandson Nick Rich.

Buddy Rich Memorial Scholarship Concert—
Tape One *(1989, 64 minutes, DCI Music Video)*

On October 14, 1989, a concert was held at the Wiltern Theatre in Los Angeles featuring the Buddy Rich big band and six guest drummers, with the proceeds going toward a scholarship for drummers. The music has been released on two videotapes. Tape One, after a verbal introduction by Cathy Rich (Buddy's daughter), has two songs apiece with Louie Bellson ("Wind Machine" and "Carnaby Street"), Gregg Bissonette ("In a Mellotone" and "Time Check") and Dennis Chambers ("Sister Sadie" and "Dancing Men"). All three drummers fare quite well, with Bellson's long solo on "Carnaby Street" taking honors while Chambers sounds the closest style-wise to Rich. The other main soloists are trumpeter Bobby Shew and Steve Marcus. This tape (and the first half of the concert) concludes with a drum battle by Bellson, Bissonette and Chambers that is a bit too long.

Buddy Rich Memorial Scholarship Concert—
Tape Two *(1989, 64 minutes, DCI Music Video 054)*

The second set from the October 14, 1989, concert is in the same format as the first. Dave Weckl sits in with the Buddy Rich big band for "Mercy, Mercy, Mercy" and "Bugle Call Rag," Vinnie Colaiuta swings on "Ya Gotta Try" and "Big Swing Face" and Steve Gadd sounds impressive on "Keep the Customers Satisfied" and "Just in Time." In addition to Steve Marcus and Bobby Shew, several other sidemen get solos, including altoist Eric Marienthal (on "Keep the Customers Satisfied") and pianist Matt Harris. Colaiuta, Gadd and Weckl conclude the concert with an unaccompanied drum trio that works out pretty well. In addition, Cathy Rich sings "That's Enough" with her husband Steve Arnold on drums with the Rich band. Buddy Rich once again appears twice, both taken from his 1968 television series with his big band. Buddy Greco sits in on piano for "The Rotten Kid" (altoist Ernie Watts is among the soloists) and "Mexicali Rose" receives a light-hearted treatment.

🎵 Burning Poles *(1991, 60 minutes, Mystic Fire)*

Cecil Taylor deserves to be well documented on film. This live DVD falls short due to Taylor spending an excessive amount of time reciting and singing his strange poetry. Once he settles down at the piano and plays with bassist William Parker, drummer Tony Oxley and percussionist Henry Martinez, the film wakes up though one had to be quite patient to make it that far. Taylor's playing is thunderous, atonal and quite forbidding, with his sidemen effectively hanging on throughout the storm.

🎵 Calle 54 *(2000, 106 minutes, Miramax)*

This tribute to Latin jazz put together by Fernando Trueba is one of the greatest jazz films ever produced and is essential for all jazz libraries. There is a brief segment in Spanish (with English subtitles) before each song that features an artist, usually at home. Otherwise the music speaks for itself. There is one inspired performance after another and the photography is superb. Paquito D'Rivera (on alto and clarinet) performs the episodic "Panamericana" with a group that includes trumpeter Diego Urcola, a rhythm section, bandoneon, a tres guitar, three bata players and vibraphonist Dave Samuels. Pianist Eliane Elias performs "Samba Triste" with her trio (which includes bassist Marc Johnson). Pianist Chano Dominguez interacts with a flamenco dancer and a singer for "Oye Como Viene." Trumpeter Jerry Gonzalez's Fort Apache Band (with altoist Joe Ford, pianist Larry Willis and bassist Andy Gonzalez) plays hard bop on "Earth Dance." "From Within" has some outstanding piano from Michel Camilo in a trio with bassist

Alphonso Johnson and drummer Horacio "El Negro" Hernandez. Tenor saxophonist Gato Barbieri is typically passionate on "Bolivia." Tito Puente shows off his restaurant and then leads his band (which includes flutist Dave Valentin, saxophonist Mario Rivera and pianist Hilton Ruiz) on "New Arrival," playing both timbales and a bit of vibes. One of the high points of this remarkable film is seeing Chucho Valdes's solo piano version of "Caridad Amaro," alternating tenderness with some explosive virtuosic runs. Another memorable performance is Chico O'Farrill conducting an orchestra (with trumpeter Mike Mossman and Chico's son pianist Arturo O'Farrill) through his "Afro Cuban Jazz Suite." Pianist Bebo Valdes

A dozen inspired performances by the who's who of Afro-Cuban jazz are featured in the remarkable *Calle 54.*

not play bop but instead used Powell's reharmonized themes as the basis for their own post-bop improvisations. This DVD features Corea's quintet at two different European concerts, featuring trumpeter Wallace Roney, either altoist Kenny Garrett or (on the second date) tenor saxophonist Joshua Redman, bassist Christian McBride and drummer Roy Haynes. The performances ("Glass Enclosure," "Tempus Fugit," "Dusk in Sandi," "Bud Powell," "Oblivion," "I'll Keep Loving You," "Un Poco Loco"), which consist of six Powell songs plus Corea's "Bud Powell," are actually a bit dull in spots though Corea has some fine solos. Fred Johnson takes a guest vocal on "Bud Powell." The best moments are during "Oblivion" when Roney and Redman trade off and light some sparks.

Chick Corea Elektric Band—Inside Out
(1990, 32 minutes, GRP)

With the rise of MTV and rock music videos, there were a few attempts to make jazz videos in the early '90s in a similar vein. Chick Corea's Elektric Band (with Corea on electric keyboards, altoist Eric Marienthal, guitarist Frank Gambale, electric bassist John Patitucci and drummer Dave Weckl) is featured on four of the six pieces that were also released as the CD **Inside Out**. The music ("Inside Out," "Kicker," "Child's Play" and the four-part "Tale of Daring") is the same as on the CD (leaving out "Make a Wish" and "Stretch It"), but one cannot be sure if the band is really playing the music live. The production, which on one song shows kids who are allegedly Corea's musicians as children (they are not), is rather cheesy, using a few dancers on one number and meaningless clips of a city throughout "Tale of Daring." Worse yet, these particular selections are quite forgettable and, although the playing is excellent, the melodies were not destined to catch on.

Chris Barber: Music from the Land of Dreams Concert *(1986, 83 minutes, Storyville)*

British trombonist Chris Barber has led one of the top trad jazz bands since 1954, a group that since its beginnings has featured trumpeter Pat Halcox. The band is well showcased on this 15-song concert from Stockholm, Sweden, from April 13, 1986. In addition to Barber and Halcox, the group includes clarinetist Ian Wheeler, John Crocker on tenor and alto, guitarist Roger Hill, banjoist Johnny McCallum, bassist Vic Pitt and drummer Norman Emberson, all longtime members. There are many fine moments along the way with clean and coherent ensembles, riffing behind soloists and enough variety to keep one continually interested. Among the highlights are an uptempo "Do What Ory Says," a spirited "Precious Lord Take My Hand," features for Halcox on "Some of these Days" and "Buddy Bolden's Blues," and a couple of blues that have spots for guitarist Hill and Wheeler on harmonica. In addition, three songs ("Just a Little While to Stay Here," "Just a Closer Walk with Thee" and "When the Saints Go Marching In") have the band wearing parade uniforms and the rhythm section switching to baritone horn, tuba, snare drum and bass drum. The occasional vocals (including some fine scatting on "Ice Cream") are purposeful and enjoyable. All in all, this video shows how strong and entertaining a band Chris Barber has always had.

Chris Barber: On the Road
(1988, 50 minutes, Storyville)

Considering that all but one of the performance clips on this documentary are taken from Chris Barber's **Music from the Land of Dreams Concert**, which is available in full in the above video, this release is of limited interest. The British trombonist was interviewed in 1988 and his comments about the difficulties of constantly touring, his musical beginnings, musical tastes and his tips for keeping a band together are quite interesting. But eliminate the performance clips and this would be a ten-minute tape. It is a pity that selections from other time periods were not included too, for there is little reason to acquire this video.

Chuck Mangione: The Feeling's Back
(72, minutes, 1998, Chesky)

After more than a decade off the scene, the popular flugelhornist Chuck Mangione made a brief comeback in the late '90s. This DVD, centered around the recording of his debut CD for the Chesky label, finds Mangione still in fine form, largely unchanged musically from his *Feels So Good* days. His band (flutist Gerry Niewood, keyboardist Cliff Korman, guitarist Jay Azzolina, David Finck or Kip Reid on bass, drummer Paulo Braga and percussionist Café) performs a variety of light and melodic originals ("Mountain Flight," "Consuela's Love Theme," "Leonardo's Lady," "Fotografic," "Quase," "Aldovio," "Once Upon a Love Time," "Maracangalha") plus "Manha de Carnaval" and "La Vie en Rose."

 ### The Clark Terry Quartet
(1992, 46 minutes, Storyville)

Clark Terry, pianist Duke Jordan, bassist Jimmy Woode and drummer Svend Norregaard are featured performing six songs at the Club Montmartre in Copenhagen, Denmark, on April 7, 1986. Terry is in typically exuberant form for a program that includes four Duke Ellington songs ("In a Mellotone," "Mood Indigo," "Just Squeeze Me," "Satin Doll") and two standards ("God Bless the Child" and "Lady Be Good"). Highlights include Terry's doubletime solo on "Mood Indigo" (which includes some unexpected song quotes) and his warm rendition of "God Bless the Child." CT and Woode sing "Just Squeeze Me" together, and "Lady Be Good" is mostly a feature for Terry's scatting. The results overall are enjoyable if not overly memorable.

 ### Clark Terry: Live in Concert
(2001, 84 minutes, Eagle Entertainment)

Filmed for **BET on Jazz**, this set from the Santa Lucia Jazz Festival is probably from 2001. The great flugelhornist Clark Terry is heard in excellent form, leading a quintet that also includes altoist Donald Harrison, pianist Anthony Wonsey, bassist Curtis Lundy and drummer Victor Lewis. The younger sidemen clearly enjoyed playing with CT, who constantly gets them to smile with his typically good-humored music ("Quicksand," "Elijah," "Moten Swing," "Love Love Love," "St. Lucia Blues," "All Blues," "My Gal," "Take the 'A' Train," "Bye Bye Blackbird"). There are a couple of attempts (mostly successful) at sing-alongs and a few short Terry vocals (including on the humorous blues "My Gal"), but mostly the musicians dig in and play, with Terry's sidemen adapting themselves well to his music. As a bonus, there is also an 11-minute interview with Clark Terry in which he discusses his beginnings, Count Basie, teaching Quincy Jones, working for NBC and various other topics.

 ### Classic Drum Solos and Drum Battles
(2001, 55 minutes, Hudson Music)

This DVD and its follow-up certainly live up to their names. There are seven unaccompanied drum solos (mostly excerpts from longer performances) and five drum battles, so this program is primarily for drum fanatics. Featured are Sonny Payne (1959), Sam Woodyard (1962), Joe Morello (a 1961 version of "Take Five"), Art Blakey (1965), Rufus Jones (a remarkable solo in 1965), Louie Bellson (1969) and Buddy Rich (who cuts everyone on a 1978 solo). The drum battles match Buddy Rich with Jerry Lewis in a humorous collaboration from 1955, Gene Krupa with Cozy Cole (from the 1957 Timex special), Krupa, Lionel Hampton and Chico Hamilton (1958), Elvin Jones, Art Blakey and Sunny Murray (1968) and Rich with Ed Shaughnessy (1978). As a bonus track, the trailer for **The Gene Krupa Story** is included, and it is possible (by clicking a few buttons) to have Peter Erskine commenting on each of the drummers.

 ### Classic Drum Solos and Drum Battles Volume 2
(2002, 73 minutes, Hudson Music)

This DVD is similar in format to the first volume, with a variety of drum solos and "battles" mostly being shown

Pictured here in 1966, altoist Ornette Coleman is featured improvising a soundtrack in the intriguing *David, Moffett & Ornette*.

singer live at the North Sea Jazz Festival. Bridgewater is in prime and enthusiastic form, the repertoire is excellent ("I'm a Stranger Here Myself," "Youkali," "This Is New," "Here I'll Stay," "The Saga of Jenny," "Lost in the Stars," "Interlude," "Bilbao," "Alabama Song") and the band (pianist/organist Thierry Eliez, guitarist Louis Winsberg, bassist Ira Coleman, drummer Andre Ceccarelli, percussion Minino Gabriel Garay, saxophonist/flutist Danielle Scannapieco, trumpeter Nicolas Felmer and trombonist Phil Abraham) knows the material well. So why the low rating? For unclear reasons, the sound quality is echoey and abysmal, making Dee Dee and the band sound like they were playing in a wind tunnel. It is a real pity because the photography is flawless and the music is important. This DVD is worth acquiring due to its historic value, but let the buyer beware!

 DeJohnette/Hancock/Holland/Metheny
(2001, 98 minutes, Pioneer)

This DVD is a straight performance film taken from two concerts both performed on June 23, 1990, at Philadelphia's Mellon Jazz Festival. Herbie Hancock (mostly on electric keyboards) and guitarist Pat Metheny are the solo stars, though bassist Dave Holland and drummer Jack DeJohnette also get their spots. All four musicians in this supergroup contributed some originals ("Shadow Dance," "Indigo Dreamscapes," "Nine over Reggae," "Solar," "Silver Hollow," "The Good Life," "Blue," "Hurricane," "The Bat," "Cantaloupe Island") and the styles range from post-bop to fusion with a bit of pop/jazz.

 Dexter Gordon: More Than You Know
(1996, 52 minutes, Blue Note Video)

The Dexter Gordon Story would make for a memorable movie since the tenor saxophonist had three major comebacks along with a half-century career full of colorful events. This relatively brief documentary tells his story mostly through Gordon's own words (he was interviewed on film many times) and excerpts of his playing, some of which are fairly long. Gordon covers most of the important events of his life although the 1948–63 period is skipped through very quickly. There are also brief (and generally familiar) interviews with bassist Niels Pedersen, Phil Woods, Steve Lacy, Woody Shaw (the latter three taken from the film **Jazz in Exile**), photographer Francis Paudras and filmmaker Bertrand Tavernier, but it is the way that the Gordon clips are weaved together that really makes this film worth watching. There are also brief excerpts of some of Gordon's musical heroes performing (including a priceless clip from a 1958 television show of Coleman Hawkins and Lester Young trading off) and films of Gordon playing an uptempo blues, "Loose Walk," "King Neptune," "Soy Califas," "More than You Know," "Fried Bananas" and "'Round Midnight."

 Dexter Gordon Quartet:
Jazz at the Maintenance Shop
(1993, 58 minutes, Shanachie)

This one-hour set, filmed and televised by Iowa Public Television in 1979, features Dexter Gordon three years after he triumphantly returned to the United States. Gordon is in excellent form here, performing lengthy versions of "On Green Dolphin Street," "Polka Dots and Moonbeams" and "Tanya—The Girl Upstairs" with pianist George Cables, bassist Rufus Reid and drummer Eddie Gladden. His talking to the audience is typically delightful and Gordon's long solos never seem to run out of ideas.

 ### Dexter Gordon Quartet:
Jazz at the Maintenance Shop
(1995, 58 minutes, Rhapsody Films)

A second one-hour show featuring the same Dexter Gordon Quartet in 1979, this video is the equal of the other one except that Gordon says relatively little to the enthusiastic crowd. He performs extended renditions of an uptempo "It's You or No One," his minor blues "The Panther," "Alone Together" (on which he switches from his usual tenor to soprano and sounds quite effective) and the blues "Back Stairs." Gordon's tenor solo on the latter is the high point of this fine performance tape.

 ### Diana Krall: Live in Paris
(2002, 113 minutes, Eagle Vision)

At the time that this concert was filmed, Diana Krall was the most famous living jazz singer. This DVD is quite jazz-oriented with many piano solos from Krall and spots for guitarist Anthony Wilson. Krall is joined by Wilson, bassist John Clayton and drummer Jeff Hamilton as her core group. Some numbers have percussionist Paulinho Da Costa and acoustic guitarist John Pisano helping out,

Diana Krall shows throughout *Live in Paris* that she is a swinging and inventive jazz pianist in addition to being a distinctive singer.

and nine songs add the Orchestre Symphonique European & Paris Jazz Band (conducted by either Alan Broadbent or Claus Ogerman). The orchestra is mostly used sparingly, and there are many heated jams for the quartet on the standards ("I Love Being Here with You," "All or Nothing at All," "Let's Fall in Love," "The Look of Love," "Maybe You'll Be There," "'Deed I Do," "Devil May Care," "Cry Me a River," "I've Got You Under My Skin," "East of the Sun," "I Get Along Without You Very Well," "Pick Yourself Up," "'S Wonderful," "Love Letters," "I Don't Know Enough About You," "Do It Again," "A Case of You"). As bonuses, two okay Krall videos ("The Look of Love" and "Let's Face the Music and Dance") and rehearsal footage of three songs are included. Throughout the swinging set, Diana Krall is heard at her best and shows that, in addition to her singing, she's a pretty good pianist too.

 ### Diane Schuur & the Count Basie Orchestra
(1987, 51 minutes, GRP Video)

On February 25, 1987, the Count Basie Orchestra under the direction of Frank Foster teamed up with singer Diane Schuur in a successful collaboration. The CD is excellent and the resulting DVD is even a little better due to the inclusion of opening and closing instrumentals ("Splanky" and "Jumpin' at the Woodside"). Otherwise the Basie band (which includes trumpeters Sonny Cohn and Byron Stripling, veteran bass trombonist Bill Hughes, Foster, Eric Dixon and Kenny Hing on tenors, pianist Tee Carson, bassist Lynn Seaton and drummer Dennis Mackrel) is very much in the background. Rhythm guitarist Freddie Green is seen in one of his very last gigs since he passed away four days later. As for Diane "Deedles" Schuur, she is clearly inspired by the setting and sings at her best. She is featured on "I Just Found Out About Love," "Until I Met You," "Travelin' Light," "Travelin' Blues," "Only You," "A Touch of Your Love," "I Loves You Porgy," "You Can Have It," "We'll Be Together Again," "Everyday I Have The Blues," "Climbing Higher Mountains" and "Deedles' Blues."

 ### Dizzy Gillespie Dream Band
(1982, 120 minutes, Wellspring)

About the time of Dizzy Gillespie's 65th birthday, his musical legacy was celebrated on this PBS special. Among the guests who help Dizzy celebrate are Gerry Mulligan (featured on "Groovin' High"), Max Roach, Milt Jackson, John Lewis, Jon Hendricks and altoist Paquito D'Rivera, with such songs as "Manteca," "Night in Tunisia," "Hot House" and "Salt Peanuts" being performed with plenty of spirit and drive. Although Dizzy's trumpet playing was a little past its prime, he is mostly inspired throughout this enjoyable film.

 ### Dizzy Gillespie: Live in Montreal
(2002, 57 minutes, Image Entertainment)

This 1981 concert features Dizzy Gillespie with a rather sparse trio consisting of guitarist Ed Cherry, electric bassist Michael Howell and drummer Thomas Campbell. Unfortunately the material is quite weak, consisting of two unidentified funky numbers, "The Truth" and "Blues of Dizzy" in addition to "A Night in Tunisia." Gillespie plays okay (particularly for this late in his career), but there is not much for the band to work with. The bass solo on "A Night in Tunisia" seems endless and Dizzy sings during much of "Blues of Dizzy."

 ### Dizzy Gillespie: A Night in Chicago
(1993, 53 minutes, View Video)

Although this DVD comes from near the end of Dizzy Gillespie's career (probably 1989), the trumpeter is in surprisingly good form. He heads a quintet also including baritonist Sayyad Abdul Al-Kahbyyr, pianist Walter Davis Jr. (who passed away the following year), electric bassist John Lee and drummer Nassyr Abdul Al-Kahbyyr. The music is full of happy spirits with Gillespie trying out some of his dance steps over the funky rhythms played on "Swing Low, Sweet Cadillac." Dizzy plays muted on his ballad feature "Embraceable You," baritonist Al-Kahbyyr takes a torrid yet rhythmic solo on "Nature Boy," and

Gillespie and Davis share "'Round Midnight." The funky calypso "Fiesta Mojo" has the baritonist hitting some screeching high notes and the whole band is featured on a lengthy rendition of "A Night in Tunisia." This fine DVD ends with a short excerpt of "Dizzy's Scat," which runs over the closing credits and has Gillespie showing off his virtuosic scatting.

 ### Django: A Jazz Tribute
(1995, 28 minutes, View Video)

Despite its title, the participation of Babik Reinhardt (Django's son) and the fact that Bireli Lagrene as a young teenager used to sound just like Django, this brief tape is not really a tribute to Django Reinhardt. The guitar duo of Lagrene and Reinhardt perform four songs ("Birelli's Original," "Nuages," "Action," "Bacera"), which, other than "Nuages," are post-bop rather than swing. The playing is strong (both guitarists take turns soloing and backing each other) although the newer tunes are not particularly memorable. A real Django tribute would have been much more interesting. As it is, this tape is recommended mostly to Lagrene fans.

 ### Don Cherry: Multikulti
(1995, 57 minutes, View Video)

Don Cherry, who became well known in the late '50s as Ornette Coleman's trumpeter and as an important free jazz stylist, traveled the world exploring other countries' folk music later in life. By then, Cherry played flute, keyboards and various exotic instruments as much as he did his pocket trumpet, so his trumpet chops declined a bit. This performance film from the early '90s (Cherry died in 1995) teams the multi-instrumentalist with tenor saxophonist Peter Apfelbaum, bassist Bo Freeman and Joshua Jones on drums and tablas for five group originals and Thelonious Monk's "Bemsha Swing." The music is colorful and spirited even if not flawless, with Cherry's trumpet playing a bit erratic and hesitant. However, he worked well with Apfelbaum, and the open-minded players do come up with plenty of fresh ideas, making the potentially esoteric music seem quite accessible.

 ### Don Menza Quintet: Live in New Orleans
(1991, 60 minutes, Leisure Video)

Don Menza has long been an explosive tenor saxophonist, most famous for his feature on "Channel One Suite" with Buddy Rich's big band in the late '60s. Menza gets to stretch out quite a bit on this hour-long performance tape, which has just three songs: "Another Who," "Faviana" and "Cedar's Blues." Menza teams up with veteran trumpeter Sam Noto, pianist Cedar Walton, bassist Tony Dumas and drummer Ralph Penland for some spirited and sometimes fiery straightahead jazz.

 ### Duke Ellington 1929–1943
(1991, 55 minutes, Storyville Films)

This valuable videotape has four Duke Ellington shorts and two of his orchestra's appearances in Hollywood films. **Black and Tan** from 1929 was Ellington's earliest appearance on film. This short features Freddi Washington as a singer with a heart condition who dances with Duke's band in a show to help ensure its success even though it risks her health. Along the way there are a few versions of "Black and Tan Fantasy" (including a priceless duet version of Ellington with trumpeter Arthur Whetsol), a couple of renditions of "Black Beauty" and brief bits of "The Duke Steps Out," "Cotton Club Stomp" and Flaming Youth." Along with Whetsol, the Ellington orchestra includes Freddie Jenkins, Cootie Williams, Tricky Sam Nanton, Juan Tizol, Barney Bigard, Johnny Hodges, Harry Carney, Fred Guy, Wellman Braud and Sonny Greer. Although this short has some racial stereotypes, particularly the two characters who try to repossess Duke's piano, Ellington is portrayed as being distinguished and intelligent—a real breakthrough for Blacks in films. "Old Man Blues" from **Check and Double Check** (1930) is the Ellington orchestra's lone instrumental

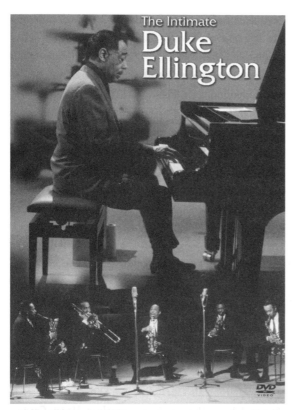

Duke Ellington is featured on this DVD without his orchestra, playing with an octet and excelling as a pianist.

choruses) on a minor blues. High points of the show are Ellington's renditions of "Mood Indigo" and an extended version of "Take the 'A' Train" that never quite resolves; Duke's sly smile shows that he did this on purpose, leaving the listener wanting more.

 ### Duke Ellington's Sacred Concerts
(1999, 79 minutes, Image Entertainment)

Filmed in 1999 as part of Duke Ellington's centennial celebration, this concert features the Lausanne Big Band with an eight-voice choir, trumpeter Jon Faddis, drummer Adam Nussbaum and singers Michele Hendricks and Allan Harris. The music is comprised of the best selections from Ellington's three sacred concerts ("In the Beginning, God," "Ain't But the One," "Tell Me It's the Truth," "Heaven," "Praise God," "The Lord's Prayer," "The Shepherd," "David Danced," "Come Sunday," "My Love," "Freedom," "Meditation," "Praise God and Dance"). The Swiss band does a fine job of re-creating the Ellington sound, particularly the pianist, baritonist and clarinetist. Faddis emulates Cat Anderson in spots and does a close impression of Cootie Williams on "The Shepherd." The two lead singers are in excellent form and the choir is perfect for this setting. Listeners who enjoy Ellington's sacred music will find much to savor on this expertly conceived set.

 ### Dynasty: The Jackie McLean Quintet
(1989, 58 minutes, Triloka Video)

This video is a filmed version of an exciting CD from altoist Jackie McLean, a live recording from November 5, 1988. McLean is joined by his son Rene McLean on tenor, soprano, flute, and alto, pianist Hotep Idris Galeta, bassist Nat Reeves, and drummer Carl Allen. The altoist plays at his most intense and creative and is heard at the peak of his powers, particularly on a dramatic version of Burt Bacharach's "A House Is Not a Home." The other selections ("Bird Lives," "Dance Little Mandissa," "Five," "J. Mac's Dynasty," "Knot the Blues," "Third World Express," "King Tut's Strut") are almost at the same level, consistently burning with passion.

 ### Earl Hines & Coleman Hawkins
(1986, 28 minutes, Rhapsody Films)

This black-and-white film from 1965 starts out with Earl Hines, bassist George Tucker and drummer Oliver Jackson performing "But Not for Me," "I'm a Little Brown Bird Looking for a Blue Bird" (which Hines sings) and "Fine and Dandy." The playing is excellent although the camera work is sometimes overly artsy and difficult to sit through. Things settle down technically and the heat goes up when Coleman Hawkins makes the group a quartet on "Just One More Chance" and a hard-swinging "Crazy Rhythm."

Eastwood After Hours
(2001, 106 minutes, Warner Home Entertainment)

At Carnegie Hall on October 17, 1996, Clint Eastwood was honored the way he most prefers, with an all-star jazz concert. Eastwood plays piano on the final medley of "Parker's Mood" and "CE Blues." The Carnegie Hall Jazz Band (under the direction of Jon Faddis) and strings perform with such major soloists as trumpeter Roy Hargrove, altoists Charles McPherson and James Moody, tenors Flip Phillips, James Rivers, Joshua Redman and James Carter, pianists Barry Harris, Kenny Barron and Jay McShann, bassists Christian McBride and Peter Washington, drummers Kenny Washington and T.S. Monk, violinist Claude Williams (featured on "San Antonio Rose") and singers Jimmy Scott, Gary LeMel and Kevin Mahogany plus the Kyle Eastwood Quartet. Some of the songs performed ("Misty," "The First Time Ever I Saw Your Face," "Hootie's Blues," "San Antonio Rose," "This Time the Dream's on Me," "Satin Doll," "Doe Eyes," "Jitterbug Waltz," "Take Five," "Claudia's Theme," "Tightrope," "The Good, the Bad and the Ugly," "Rawhide," "Misty," "Straight No Chaser," "'Round Midnight," "I See Your Face Before Me," "Cherokee," "Laura," "I Didn't Know What Time It Was," "Parker's Mood," "These Foolish Things," "Lester Leaps In," "After Hours," "C.E. Blues") had been used in the past in Clint Eastwood films, while others are bebop favorites. "Lester Leaps In," which has solos from Hargrove, Redman, Rivers, Carter, Phillips, McPherson and Moody, is a highlight. The DVD also includes a ten-minute featurette that tells the story behind the concert.

 Eddie Jefferson: Live from the Jazz Showcase
(1990, 50 minutes, Rhapsody Films)

On May 9, 1979, Eddie Jefferson (the founder of vocalese) was shot to death in Detroit. Just two days earlier, he was filmed performing at Chicago's Jazz Showcase with a group also including Richie Cole, pianist John Campbell, bassist Kelly Sill and drummer Joel Spencer. Although he had no way of knowing that his life was almost at an end,

his filmed set actually acts as a retrospective of his career. Jefferson performs "Jeannine," "A Night in Tunisia," "Trane's Blues," "I Cover the Waterfront" (based on a James Moody solo), "So What," "I Got the Blues," "When You're Smiling," "My Baby Has Gone Away," "Body and Soul," "How High the Moon," the humorous "Bennie's from Heaven," the famous "Moody's Mood for Love," "Summertime" and "Freedom Jazz Dance." There is also an opening instrumental by Cole. Sixty at the time, Jefferson was still in his creative prime. If one can somehow forget what would happen just two days later, this definitive film is enjoyable.

 Eddie "Lockjaw" Davis, Volume One
(1991, 49 minutes, Storyville)

This video and Volume Two feature the great tenor Eddie "Lockjaw" Davis performing at the Jazzhus Stuketter in Copenhagen, Denmark, in 1985, less than two years before his death from cancer. Davis, who is heard throughout at the peak of his powers, is teamed with pianist Niels Jorgen Steen, bassist Jesper Lundgaard and drummer Ed Thigpen. Lockjaw's every note is passionate and distinctive. He sounds quite inspired, causing his sidemen (most notably Thigpen) to constantly smile. The quartet starts off with a hard-swinging "Take the 'A' Train" (which is oddly enough the last song of one of the sets) and then jams on an uptempo "Just Friends," "Out of Nowhere," "The Shadow of Your Smile," the video's lone ballad "If I Had You" and Davis's medium-tempo blues "Light and Lovely." An exciting performance.

Eddie "Lockjaw" Davis, Volume Two
(1991, 41 minutes, Storyville)

This video is almost the equal of the first volume, featuring the same quartet digging into "'S Wonderful," "Shiny Stockings," "Meditation," "I Can't Get Started" (check out Lockjaw's cadenza) and "Don't Get Around Much Anymore." The rhythm section is fluent and swinging, sounding pleased to be playing with Eddie "Lockjaw" Davis, in Love," "Mona Lisa," "In the Good Old Summertime," "The Day that I Met You," "Lazy-Hazy Crazy Days of Summer," "Rambling Rose") is comprised of ballads and middle-of-the-road pop arrangements, with occasional contributions from the Cliff Adams Singers. On "It's Only a Paper Moon," "Sweet Lorraine" and "Let There Be Love," Cole also plays piano and is joined by trumpeter Reunald Jones (who mostly plays muted), guitarist John Collins, bassist Charlie Harris and drummer Leon Petties, but this touch of jazz is just a temporary and nostalgic departure. Nat Cole's voice sounds in prime form throughout.

 The Evolution of Solo Jazz Piano—Part 1: Traditional Styles
(1990, 50 minutes, Advance Music)

This video and the second part have a plot. The highly versatile pianist Bill Dobbins performs an original based on "All of Me" in the style of a couple dozen different pianists. For part one, he sticks to pre-bop styles and shows how it might have been played by Scott Joplin, Jelly Roll Morton, James P. Johnson, Willie "The Lion" Smith, Earl Hines, Fats Waller, Teddy Wilson, Duke Ellington, Art Tatum, Meade Lux Lewis, Pete Johnson and Jimmy Yancey. From ragtime and stride to swing and boogie-woogie, Dobbins traces the evolution of jazz and brings back the style of the 12 masters.

 The Evolution of Solo Jazz Piano—Part 2: Modern Styles
(1990, 50 minutes, Advance Music)

For the second of two videos, pianist Bill Dobbins performs his original based on "All of Me" in the styles of Thelonious Monk, Bud Powell, Oscar Peterson, Erroll Garner, Lennie Tristano, Bill Evans, Clare Fischer, Jimmy Rowles, Cecil Taylor, Chick Corea, Keith Jarrett and Richie Beirach. Although one can complain about who is missing (McCoy Tyner is the most obvious absentee), Dobbins's ability to assume the musical identities of these very different players and improvise in their styles is quite impressive. Both videos are well worth searching for by fans of jazz piano styles.

 Fats Waller: The Centennial Collection
(2004, 18 minutes, Bluebird)

Released to celebrate the centennial of pianist/singer Fats Waller's birth, this package has a CD containing 20 Waller studio recordings (nothing too rare) and a medley from a radio show. In addition, there is an 18-minute DVD that includes Waller's four Soundies from the 1940s (**The Joint Is Jumpin'**, **Ain't Misbehavin'**, **Honeysuckle Rose**, **Your Feet's Too Big**) and his segment from the 1935 film **King of Burlesque** that has him singing, playing piano and clowning around during "I've Got My Fingers Crossed." In addition, a 1983 cartoon titled "Your Feet's Too Big" uses the Waller song as the soundtrack for a tale of an elephant with gigantic feet. This DVD is enjoyable overall, but it is a pity that it does not also include Waller's two other movie appearances from **Hooray for Love** and **Stormy Weather** for then it would be the complete Fats Waller on film, and still not exceed a half hour.

 Five Guys Named Moe
(1990, 55 minutes, Vintage Jazz Classics)

Many of the very best performances by Louis Jordan and his Tympany Five are included among the 21 selections on this collection. All but a version of "Choo Choo Ch'Boogie" taken from the 1960 television special **The Swingin' Singin' Years** date from 1943–46. Some of the selections are Soundies, including eight that are also available on **Harlem Roots Vol. 2: The Headliners**. Other numbers are taken from Jordan's films of the era, including some that are also on **Louis Jordan and His Tympany Band**. In each case, the numbers qualify as "the best of Louis Jordan," featuring him with groups that include Eddie Roane or Aaron Izenhall on trumpet and sometimes pianist Wild Bill Davis. This fairly definitive Louis Jordan videotape shows why the altoist/singer/entertainer, who was such an important bridge between swing and R&B, was so popular. Songs include "Five Guys Named Moe," "Caldonia," "The Green Grass Grows All Around," "If You Can't Smile and Say Yes," "Let the Good Times Roll,"

"That'll Just About Knock Me Out," "Beware," "Tillie," "Ration Blues," "Fuzzy Wuzzy," "That Chick's Too Young to Fry," "Jumpin' at the Jubilee," "Honey Chile," "Texas and Pacific," "Choo Choo Ch-Boogie," "Salt Port, West Virginia," "Reet, Petite and Gone," "Don't Worry 'Bout that Mule," "Ain't That Just Like a Woman," "Buzz Me" and "Is You Is or Is You Ain't Ma Baby."

 ### Flip Phillips' 80th Birthday Party
(1996, 118 minutes, Arbors)

During the weekend of March 24, 1995, Arbors Records had a giant jazz party that celebrated the 80th birthday of veteran tenor Flip Phillips. This DVD documents the event and has 11 full-length performances. Phillips was interviewed a little bit about his life and his comments are spliced between some of the songs, but otherwise the nearly two-hour tape consists of the live jams. The camerawork is a bit primitive since most of the time only one camera was used, and there are instances where one cannot see the main soloist. However, the music is superior and, if thought of as a labor of love (and watched with tolerance), the results are worth it. Thirty all-stars are featured throughout. "Tenor Madness" and "Spanish Eyes" have Phillips, clarinetist Buddy DeFranco, trumpeter Randy Sandke, tenor saxophonist Scott Hamilton, trombonist Carl Fontana (who takes solo honors particularly with two unaccompanied choruses on "Tenor Madness"), altoist Phil Woods, guitarist Herb Ellis, pianist Derek Smith, bassist Sean Smith and drummer Butch Miles, and that is just the start. "Nuages" has Phillips joined by four guitarists (Ellis, Howard Alden, Billy Bauer and Bucky Pizzarelli) with Pizzarelli displaying the most creative ideas. "Rosetta" and "Hindustan" feature a reunited version of "Soprano Summit," with Bob Wilber on soprano, clarinetist Kenny Davern, pianist Dick Hyman, bassist Milt Hinton, drummer Tony DeNicola and Pizzarelli; "Hindustan" is the best all-around performance of the tape. A spirited version of "When You're Smiling" has fine playing from trumpeter Joe Wilder, clarinetist Peanuts Hucko, both Dan Barrett and George Masso on trombones, pianist Ralph Sutton, guitarist Bauer, bassist Bob Haggart and drummer Jake Hanna. "Constantly" features the two trombones with the same rhythm section while Wilder is showcased on "Am I Blue." "Allen's Alley" is a bit bebopish with trumpeter Jack Sheldon, flugelhornist Clark Terry, Woods, DeFranco, Alden, pianist Dave McKenna, bassist Michael Moore and drummer Joe Ascione, while "Mean to Me" is a silly vocal duet by Terry and Sheldon. For the grand finale, a 19-minute version of "Jumpin' at the Woodside" has all 14 horns taking a couple of choruses, plus Ellis and Alden on guitars, Smith and Hyman on pianos, Hinton and Smith on basses, and Miles and Ascione on two sets of drums. Musically if not visually, this videotape is a dream for fans of mainstream straightahead jazz.

 ### 40 Years of MJQ *(1995, 58 minutes, View Video)*

This video was released to celebrate the 40th anniversary of the Modern Jazz Quartet, which took place in 1992 (if one does not count their seven-year "vacation" of 1974–81). Pianist John Lewis, vibraphonist Milt Jackson and bassist Percy Heath are joined by drummer Mickey Roker (who was subbing for the ailing Connie Kay). The classic group performs "Three Windows" (a medley from Lewis's soundtrack to the film **No Sun in Venice**), "Sketch," "Alexander's Fugue," "Adagio from Concierto de Aranjuez" and "A Day in Dubrovnik." Since the band's hits are not here and the music is sometimes a bit classical-oriented, this video is not definitive, but the musicians do play quite well.

 ### Gary Burton: Live
(2002, 57 minutes, Music Video Distributors)

The music on this performance DVD was recorded at the Midem Jazz Festival in Europe on January 26, 1981. Gary Burton is first featured with the Hum Trio, a French unit consisting of pianist Rene Andreger, bassist Pierre Michelot and drummer Daniel Humair. Burton is outstanding

DVD is not definitive, but it gives today's listeners a sampling of the musical magic that Washington was able to create, and shows how he could expertly work a crowd.

 ### Grover Washington, Jr.: Standing Room Only
(2001, 57 minutes, Image Entertainment)

Grover Washington, Jr., who helped popularize R&B-oriented jazz (rhythm and jazz), sounds enthusiastic during this 1990 concert from Atlantic City. His backup group (two keyboards, guitar, electric bass, drums and percussion) is pretty anonymous although they do their job well in backing the great saxophonist. Washington plays alto on "Winelight," soprano on an easy-listening version of "Nice and Easy," tenor on "Take Me There," soprano on the straightahead "Blues for DP," tenor on "Time Out of Mind," alto on "Let It Flow" and all three of his horns during a nine-song, ten-minute medley ("Inner City Blues," "Mercy Mercy Me," "Where Is the Love," "Knucklehead," "Black Frost," "Santa Cruisin'," "Just the Two of Us," "Feels So Good," "Sausalito").

 ### GRP All-Star Big Band
(1992, 59 minutes, GRP Video)

This is a band that greatly defied expectations. Organized by pianist Dave Grusin, the group (seen here on January 12, 1992) features most of the top artists from the label he co-ran with Larry Rosen, GRP. What is particularly unusual is that there were a large number of crossover and pop/jazz musicians involved, yet the music is essentially hard bop of the 1960s performed by a big band. The lineup of musicians consists of trumpeters Randy Brecker, Arturo Sandoval and Sal Marquez, trombonist George Bohanon, saxophonists Eric Marienthal, Nelson Rangell, Bob Mintzer, Ernie Watts and Tom Scott, either Dave Grusin, David Benoit, Russell Ferrante or Kenny Kirkland on piano, bassist John Patitucci, drummer Dave Weckl, percussionist Alex Acuna, guitarist Lee Ritenour, vibraphonist Gary Burton, clarinetist Eddie Daniels and flutist Dave Valentin. One certainly would not expect that

personnel to be playing these ten standards ("Sister Sadie," "Airegin," "Maiden Voyage," "Donna Lee," "I Remember Clifford," "Blue Train," "Spain," "Seven Steps to Heaven," "Manteca," "The Sidewinder"), but the band swings the charts (by Michael Abene, Grusin, Scott, Ferrante, Mintzer, Benoit and Chick Corea) quite expertly and solos very credibly in the hard bop style, even Marienthal, Rangel and Scott.

 ### Gypsy Guitar: The Legacy of Django Reinhardt
(1992, 52 minutes, Shanachie)

This is an enjoyable and informative film that pays tribute to the influence and musical legacy of Django Reinhardt with a variety of performances and short interviews. One gets to see such performers as Babik Reinhardt (Django's son), Bireli Lagrene, Boulou and Elios Ferre, the Gypsy Kids, the Stochelo Rosenberg Trio (featuring Jimmy Rosenberg), Serge Krief and Gary Potter all playing Django's music. Included along the way are such songs as "All Love," "Nuages," "Anouman," "Nuits de St. Germain des Pres," "Douce Ambiance," "Djangology," "Minor Swing," "Miroirs" and "Melodie au Crepescule." The interviews are interesting, the many sites shown are picturesque and one comes away from this film thinking that every guitarist in Europe sounds like Django Reinhardt!

 ### Harlem Roots Vol. 1: The Big Bands
(1988, 57 minutes, Storyville)

Storyville has released in their **Harlem Roots** series four videotapes filled with some of the very best Soundies dating from 1941–47. **The Big Bands** is particularly strong for it has all of the Soundies of Duke Ellington, Cab Calloway and Count Basie plus four of Lucky Millinder's. The 1941–42 Ellington band performs **I Got It Bad** (a feature for Ivie Anderson), **Bli Blip** (which has the dancing and nonsense singing of Marie Bryant and Paul White), **Flamingo** (featuring Herb Jeffries and a couple exotic dancers) and a spirited rendition of **Hot Chocolate** (which would soon be renamed **Cotton Tail**) with

Ben Webster and Whitey's Lindy Hoppers. Best of the five is **C Jam Blues**, a superior Soundie with solos from Ellington, Ray Nance (on violin), Rex Stewart, Webster, Tricky Sam Nanton, Barney Bigard and Sonny Greer; Junior Raglin is on bass. Cab Calloway shows why he was considered such a charismatic and colorful performer with his crazy singing, dancing and conducting on his Soundies. During these performances from 1942 and 1945 his band includes such notables as Jonah Jones, pianist Bennie Payne, Milt Hinton, Cozy Cole, altoist Hilton Jefferson and (in 1945) Ike Quebec on tenor. Other than two numbers featuring singer Dotty Saulter, Calloway is the main focus throughout, making some sense out of **Foo a Little Boogaloo** and performing **Walkin' with My Baby** (that particular Soundie is not in very good shape), **Blowtop Blues, I Was Here When You Left Me, We the Cats Shall Hep Ya, Blues in the Night, The Skunk Song** (with trombonist Tyree Glenn helping with the singing), **Minnie the Moocher** and **Virginia, Georgia and Caroline**. Count Basie also filmed two Soundies, but both are near-classics featuring Jimmy Rushing. **Take Me Back Baby** has Rushing as a saxophonist who falls asleep onstage and dreams that he is singing the blues to his girlfriend. A hot version of **Air Mail Special** at a dance contest has the bulky Rushing outlasting his competition in humorous fashion. The band at the time included Buck Clayton, Harry "Sweets" Edison, Dickie Wells, the tenors of Don Byas and Buddy Tate, Freddie Green, Walter Page and Jo Jones, all of whom can be seen. This valuable video concludes with four numbers from Lucky Millinder's band: the lightweight "Hello Bill" (featuring the leader's vocal), "I Want a Big Fat Mama" and two excellent features for Sister Rosetta Tharpe's singing ("Four or Five Times" and "Shout Sister Sister").

 Harlem Roots Vol. 2: The Headliners
(1988, 51 minutes, Storyville)

Three of the most likable and talented Black jazz entertainers of the early '40s are featured on this superior tape of Soundies. Singer/pianist/composer Fats Waller made four Soundies in 1941 and they are all included. **Honeysuckle Rose, Your Feet's Too Big, Ain't Misbehavin'** and an appropriately riotous **The Joint Is Jumpin'** feature Fats and his Rhythm (trumpeter John Hamilton, Gene Sedric on tenor and clarinet, guitarist Al Casey, bassist Cedric Wallace and drummer Slick Jones) along with singer Myra Johnson. Louis Armstrong and his big band in 1942 (with pianist Luis Russell, guitarist Lawrence Lucie and Sid Catlett) perform "When It's Sleepy Time Down South," "Shine," "I'll Be Glad When You're Dead, You Rascal You" and "Singin' on Nothing." Velma Middleton (who dances on two numbers) and trombonist George Washington vocalize on "Singin' on Nothing." Although racial stereotypes fill these clips, Armstrong is in fine form, particularly on "Shine." But the best music is on ten Louis Jordan Soundies filmed during 1942–44: **Five Guys Named Moe, Honey Chile, G.I. Jive, If You Can't Smile and Say Yes, Fuzzy Wuzzy, Tillie, Caldonia, Buzz Me, Down, Down, Down,** and **Jumpin' at the Jubilee.** Jordan is seen and heard in prime form, his singing is witty and musical, and his band is quite hot, with plenty of solos from the leader on alto and tenor and the underrated trumpeter Eddie Roane. Even the dancers are excellent, so Jordan's Soundies were comparatively first-class productions.

 Harlem Roots Vol. 3: Rhythm in Harmony
(1988, 54 minutes, Storyville)

From the jazz standpoint, this tape is of lesser interest although the music on this collection of Soundies is of excellent quality. Five different vocal groups, each consisting of four male voices, are featured. The Mills Brothers are seen in 1942 and 1944 when they were in a transitional period, evolving from a remarkable ensemble that expertly imitated instruments into a more conventional but commercially successful vocal quartet. With the exception of the closing **Paper Doll**, which features some dancing by Dorothy Dandridge, the performances are pretty straightforward. **Caravan** and **Rockin' Chair** are taken a capella (as is **Paper Doll**), while **Up the Lazy River**, **Till Then**, **Cielito Lindo** and **You Always Hurt the One You Love** have the Mills Brothers (actually three siblings plus their father by then) backed by an acoustic guitarist. The Delta Rhythm Boys show a great deal of versatility in their seven numbers, most notably on the amusing **Rigoletto Blues** (which has them satirizing classical music), **Just a Sittin' and a Rockin'** and **Take the "A" Train**. They are also in fine form on **Dry Bones**, **I Dreamt I Dwelt in Harlem**, **Jack, You're Playing the Game** and the odd **Snoqualomie Jo Jo**. The Deep River Boys are moderately religious on **Shadrack**, but quite secular during the spirited **Toot that Trumpet**. The Charioteers romp on **Darktown Strutters Ball** while the Jubilaires are excellent on **Preacher and the Bear**, **Noah** and the catchy **Brother Bill**. Fans of vintage swinging vocal groups will want this collection.

 Harlem Roots Vol. 4: Jivin' Time
(1988, 60 minutes, Storyville)

Thirteen different performers are featured on 22 selections during this worthy collection of Soundies. The Nat King Cole Trio (with guitarist Oscar Moore and bassist Johnny Miller) swings on **Got a Penny, Benny**, **Come to Baby Do** and **Errand Boy for Rhythm**. Henry "Red" Allen's group (with trombonist J.C. Higginbotham and altoist Don Stovall) performs the novelties **Drink Hearty** and **House on 52nd Street** and romps on **Count Me Out** although the dancers get a bit distracting on the latter. Bob Howard sings, plays stride piano and mugs on **Shine** and **She's Too Hot to Handle**. Altoist/singer Skeets Tolbert is excellent on **No, No Baby**. The Musical Madcaps, with Joe Carroll singing/scatting like Leo Watson and holding a trumpet, wear outlandish costumes but play spirited music on **Rhythm of the Rhythm Band**. A trumpeter/singer billed as Dallas Bartley but actually Walter Fuller (formerly of the Earl Hines Orchestra) performs **Cryin' and Singin' the Blues** and **Sendin' Joe**.

The wonderful actress Dorothy Dandridge sings and dances on the classic **Zoot Suit** and **A Jig in the Jungle**. Sister Rosetta Tharpe performs **Lonesome Road** with Lucky Millinder's Orchestra, the obscure but talented singer Mabel Lee is fine on **Chicken Shack Shuffle** and **The Cat Can't Dance**, and Bill "Bojangles" Robinson sings a bit and shows off some of his tricky dance steps on **Let's Scuffle**. June Richmond displays a strong voice on **Hey Lawdy Mama** and **Mr. Jackson from Jacksonville**, singer Vanita Smythe is excellent on **They Raided the Joint**, and Edna Mae Harris (along with a male singer) wraps up the tape with the novelty **Tain't No Good**. Overall this volume gives viewers a strong cross-section of the Black talent that was active in the mid-'40s.

 Harry Connick, Jr.: New York Big Band Concert
(1993, 60 minutes, Sony Video)

On this live DVD, Harry Connick, Jr., and his big band alternate standards with his originals ("Sweet Georgia Brown," "Don't Get Around Much Anymore," "Recipe for Love," "Bare Necessities," "They Can't Take That Away from Me," "You Didn't Know Me When," "He Is, They Are," "With Imagination," "We Are in Love," "It Had to Be You," "Just Kiss Me," "All of Me," "Paramount Fanfare"). The music on this date swings, the leader is charming, and the overall results are entertaining.

 Harry Connick, Jr.: Only You
(2004, 144 minutes, Columbia Music Video)

Filmed in Quebec City, singer/pianist Harry Connick, Jr., is featured at a concert with his big band and a small string section. Originally a one-hour PBS special, an additional 30 minutes of music have been added to the show plus a full hour of bonus material. The show is entertaining and full of variety ("Save the Last Dance for Me," "For Once in My Life," "Good Night My Love," "It Might as Well Be Spring," "We Are in Love," "The Very Thought of You," "You Don't Know Me," "Bourbon Street Parade," "One More Time," "Sweet Georgia Brown," "I Still Get Jealous," "Other

Hours," "My Blue Heaven," "Only You," "I'm Walkin'," "Come by Me"). Sometimes Connick croons in front of the orchestra à la Frank Sinatra, at other times he sings while accompanying himself on piano, and there are some instrumental stretches. The music includes older standards, tunes from the 1960s and a few of Connick's originals. Highlights include his playing on "It Might as Well Be Spring" (which starts out as a trio piece), Connick's singing on "We Are in Love," "The Very Thought of You" and "I Still Get Jealous," his flashy solo piano version of "Sweet Georgia Brown" and a fun rendition of "Bourbon Street Parade." Among the featured sidemen are tenors Jerry Weldon and Ned Goold, trombonists John Allred and Lucius Barbarin and trumpeter Leroy Jones. In addition to the concert, there is a lengthy interview with Harry Connick, Jr., that is of some interest, some behind-the-scenes footage about the making of the concert, and opportunities for Connick's sidemen to reminisce a bit.

 Harry Connick, Jr.: Singin' and Swingin'
(1990, 45 minutes, Sony Video)

This set features Harry Connick, Jr., singing and playing with his trio when he was 22. As he shows on the video-tape, he had charisma from an early age, performing such numbers as "Do You Know What It Means to Miss New Orleans," "Stompin' at the Savoy," "Where or When," "I Could Write a Book," "Don't Get Around Much Anymore," "It Had to Be You" and his own "Recipe for Love."

 Harry Connick, Jr.: Swinging Out Live
(1991, 77 minutes, Sony Video)

Harry Connick, Jr., and his 16-piece big band (which includes guitarist Russell Malone, Ned Goold on tenor and a pair of high-note trumpeters in Dan Miller and Roger Ingram) are in spirited form during a Dallas concert. Connick starts off rehearsing "Nice Work If You Can Get It" with his rhythm section and then during the concert puts on a varied program ("Don't Get Around Much Anymore," "I Could Write a Book," "All I Really Need Is the

Girl," "Avalon," "Something's Got to Give," "Free for Now," "Recipe for Love," "How Deep Is the Ocean," "We Are in Love," "It Had to Be You," "It's Alright with Me," "The Saints," "Do You Know What It Means to Miss New Orleans"). In addition to his singing, there are many examples of Connick's likable piano playing (including some romping blues) and his charming ad-libs to the audience. This is the most rewarding of the four Connick videos.

 Herb Ellis: Detour Ahead—
An Afternoon with Herb Ellis
(1998, 60 minutes, Vestapol)

This hour-long film on Herb Ellis alternates between live performances and very brief interviews. Ellis performs "I Want to Be Happy," a blues, "The Days of Wine and Roses," "Sweet Georgia Brown," "Body and Soul," "Georgia on My Mind," "Danny Boy," "John Brown's Body" and "Wave." Unfortunately all of the songs are warhorses, and the renditions are overly relaxed and never exciting. Ellis is usually joined by rhythm guitarist Terry Holmes, either Norm Cochran or Jack Hannah on bass, either Tommy Perkins or Ernie Durawa on drums and pianist Sonny Gray. "Georgia on My Mind" (on which Ellis is the only soloist) and "Wave" team him with Tal Farlow and Charlie Byrd, but unfortunately the latter fades out. There are also brief testimonials from some of the guitarist's contemporaries (including Byrd, Ray Brown, Benny Golson, Benny Green, Al Grey, Lionel Hampton, Gene Harris, Jon Hendricks and Hank Jones), but they say nothing of importance other than the fact that they like his playing. Surely there must be some worthwhile tales to be heard and inspiring performances to be seen, but this well-meaning documentary lacks both.

 Herbie Hancock: Future2Future Live
(2002, 104 minutes, Columbia, Legacy Video)

Herbie Hancock, although sticking to acoustic piano during much of this live DVD (from Los Angeles' Knitting

Ivo Perelman: Live in New York
(1991, 59 minutes, Video Artists International)

A powerful and intense tenor saxophonist inspired both by Albert Ayler and Brazilian music, Ivo Perelman really stretches out on his performance tape from an October 16, 1990, performance at the Knitting Factory. In just under an hour, he performs three numbers ("Slaves of Jo," "Nesta Rua" and "The Carnation and the Rose"), joined by pianist Geri Allen, bassist Fred Hopkins, drummer Andrew Cyrille, percussionist Mino Cinelu, Elson Nascimento on bass drum, and guest singer Flora Purim. Perelman has a liking for children's melodies and that is felt in places, but most of the fiery music is free and passionate, with the passionate tenor not being shy to be very expressive on his horn.

 Jack Sheldon: In New Orleans
(1989, 60 minutes, Leisure Video)

Trumpeter/singer Jack Sheldon has long been overdue to be filmed running through his hilarious if tasteless monologues. Unfortunately this DVD is not that, but it does feature some fine playing and singing by Sheldon in a quintet with pianist Dave Frishberg, guitarist John Pisano, bassist Dave Stone and drummer Frank Capp. Frishberg is featured singing on his "I Was Ready," John Pisano plays some nice guitar on "Corcovado," and otherwise the full group romps on "Yo' Mama," "Don't Get Around Much Anymore," "Historia de un Amor," "The One I Love," "Rosetta" and "The Joint Is Jumpin'."

 Jack Teagarden: Far East Tour 1958–59
(1989, 60 minutes, Teagarden Video)

This documentary put together by Joe Shouler ties together two shorts, a television appearance and home movies, all pertaining to Jack Teagarden's four month tour of Asia during 1958–59. During that period of time Teagarden and his sextet (trumpeter Max Kaminsky, clarinetist Jerry Fuller, pianist Don Ewell, Stan Puls and later Lee Ivory on bass, and drummer Ronnie Greb) visited such countries as Thailand, Cambodia, Vietnam, Afghanistan, Ceylon, Malaya, Hong Kong, India, Burma, Singapore, South Korea and finally Japan. After Joe Shouler makes an introduction of the material, the 15-minute short **Jack Teagarden in Thailand** is shown. Although the narration is in Thai and much of the footage features the musicians touring the country and sightseeing, they do perform fine versions of "St. Louis Blues" and "The Saints." After some color films taken by the musicians (with Teagarden heard talking a few months later in a radio interview), a short (in English) documents their stay in Cambodia without offering any live music. More home movies (with Teagarden talking from a hotel room), a newsreel from Vietnam (with versions of "Big Noise from Winnetka" and "Tiger Rag") and some private films from Malaya precede Mr. T. performing on Japanese television. Unfortunately he had become quite ill by then (he would recover after making it back to the U.S.), and is seen gamely making his way through "I've Got a Right to Sing the Blues" and "That's a Plenty" with his Dixieland sextet and performing "Stars Fell on Alabama," "Diane" and "Indiana" with a Japanese string orchestra. Jack Teagarden fans will want this video although more general fans will not find it quite so indispensable.

 Jackie McLean on Mars
(1986, 31 minutes, Rhapsody Films)

Although overly brief, this film (whose title has nothing to do with its content) is an excellent portrait of altoist Jackie McLean. Filmed in the early '80s, McLean is seen talking with his students about jazz, drugs, the difficulties of the music business and the joy of the music. There are glimpses of McLean playing, trumpeter Woody Shaw has a cameo appearance and the short documentary always holds one's interest. Pity that it is not twice as long.

 Jaco Pastorius: Modern Electric Bass
(1985, 90 minutes, DCI Music Video)

Instructional videos are not reviewed in this book because they are aimed primarily at student musicians, but this one is too historic to be left out. **Modern Electric Bass** is included because of electric bassist Jaco Pastorius's premature death at age 35 in 1987, and because of the performances on this video. Filmed in 1985, Pastorius explains his approaches to playing in an interview with session bassist Jerry Jemmott. He performs several solos along the way, duets with Jemmott and closes the tape by jamming for 20 minutes in a trio with guitarist John Scofield and drummer Kenwood Dennard. This video should greatly interest all fans of Jaco Pastorius, whether they play instruments or not.

 ### Jane Bunnett: Cuban Odyssey—
Spirits of Havana
(2002, 90 minutes, EMI Music Canada)

Canadian soprano saxophonist and flutist Jane Bunnett and her husband, trumpeter Larry Cramer, have visited Cuba many times. They have played and recorded with many of the top Afro-Cuban jazz and folkloric musicians, formed touring bands with some of the players and have been involved in helping the music schools gain new instruments. This documentary covers their 1999 visit to Cuba. Along the way, one sees Bunnett and Cramer interacting with local musicians (including the vocal/percussion group Los Munequitos), recording in a studio, talking with average Cuban citizens, visiting the gravesite of singer Merceditas Valdes, playing in concert, having a scare when it appeared that Bunnett's horns were stolen and delivering donated instruments to a top music school. A few bonus cuts add to the travelogue element of this generally intriguing documentary.

Jane Monheit: Live at the Rainbow Room
(2003, 102 minutes, N Coded Music)

Obviously a lot of work went into this DVD, which features 24-year-old singer Jane Monheit on September 23, 2002 performing at New York's prestigious Rainbow Room. Unfortunately, it appears that there was too much preparation. Monheit's natural beauty is buried a bit by

an excess of makeup; the same can be said for her singing. The opening number, a normally sweet and innocent version of "Over the Rainbow," finds Monheit's voice almost drowned out by an overblown arrangement for a 27-piece orchestra. The orchestra (conducted by Alan Broadbent) is only on five of the 20 songs, but even the other numbers (which often utilize pianist Michael Kanan, Ron Carter, drummer Kenny Washington, tenor saxophonist Joel Frahm and guitarist Rene Toledo) rarely live up to their potential. There is an excess of ballads and, although the range of material is wide ("Over the Rainbow," "Just Squeeze Me," "No More Blues," "Dindi," "More than You Know," "Since You've Asked," "It Might As Well Be Spring," "Tea for Two," "Hit the Road to Dreamland," "Love Has No Pride," "Once I Walked in the Sun," "Commecar de Novo," "Please Be Kind," "It Never Entered My Mind," "Turn Out the Stars," "Haunted Heart," "Cheek to Cheek," "Around Us," "Waters of March," "Some Other Time"), there are few moments of excitement or surprise. Monheit, who can improvise a bit, mostly comes across as a cabaret singer who bounces around excessively. She is best on a 6/4 rendition of "It Might As Well Be Spring" and a version of "Tea for Two" that is taken as a slow ballad. Her former singing teacher Peter Eldridge and Alan Broadbent also guest on piano. As a special feature, there is an eight-minute documentary that is a countdown to the concert, with comments from Monheit, N Coded Music president Carl Griffin, Broadbent and Ron Carter plus glimpses of the prior day's rehearsal. But as a permanent document, all of the preparation was just not worth the effort.

 ### Jazz—A Film by Ken Burns
(2000, 19 hours, PBS Home Video)

This should have been the greatest jazz documentary ever. The ten-part series is certainly the lengthiest and most expensive, and, with the experienced Ken Burns behind the project, it is not surprising that it looks nice and utilizes many colorful photos. It is well-intentioned

in its championing of Louis Armstrong and Duke Ellington, and many musicians were interviewed along the
way; Dave Brubeck and Milt Hinton fare particularly well.
But something went terribly wrong and the result is a
real mess.

By relying far too heavily on the commentary and
beliefs of Wynton Marsalis, Stanley Crouch and Albert
Murray, this documentary emphasizes the distant past at
the almost complete exclusion of the present. The ten
chapters are: **Gumbo (Beginnings–1917), The Gift
(1917–24), Our Language (1924–29), The True Welcome (1929–34), Swing: Pure Pleasure (1935–37),
Swing: The Velocity of Celebration (1937–39), Dedicated to Chaos (1940–45), Risk (1945–55), The Adventure (1956–60)** and **A Masterpiece by Midnight
(1960–present)**. West Coast cool jazz, Afro-Cuban jazz
and soul jazz are generally overlooked, there is no mention
of bossa nova or the Dixieland revival, the avant-garde
(once the story gets beyond John Coltrane and the Ornette
Coleman Quartet) is completely written off (with Branford Marsalis dissing Cecil Taylor), and fusion is treated as
a minor frivolity by Miles Davis that is not worth discussing. Other than a few quick snapshots, 1970–2000 is
passed by altogether. By neglecting post-1970 jazz, Burns
is able to create the impression that jazz died with Armstrong and Ellington. One commentator actually says that
in 1975 nothing much was happening in jazz, and viewers
are given the impression that today's jazz at its best is
merely a shadow of the past.

The number of mistakes is high, whether having a
piece of music from the wrong period of time depicting
an event, saying that Miles Davis first met Gil Evans in
1949 or claiming twice that Count Basie's arrival on the
jazz scene saved the jazz world from Glenn Miller (Basie
actually became famous two years before Miller). But,
nit-picking aside, the flaws are huge. Relatively little
music is actually heard except in brief excerpts with the
talking heads chitchatting virtually nonstop. Burns
emphasizes the civil rights struggle throughout the 19

hours, downplays the contributions of Whites to jazz
(other than Bix Beiderbecke and Benny Goodman), over-
emphasizes the fact that jazz is American music (very few
non-Americans are mentioned at all), and never gets tired
of putting the focus on Armstrong, Chick Webb and swing
music. Imagine spending 19 hours on the history of jazz
and including virtually nothing on Django Reinhardt, Nat
King Cole, Oscar Peterson, Stan Kenton, Erroll Garner, Joe
Williams, Carmen McRae, Wes Montgomery, Albert Ayler,
Weather Report, Pat Metheny, Betty Carter, Woody Shaw,
Chick Corea, Keith Jarrett, Joshua Redman, Diana Krall,
and dozens of others. Wynton Marsalis, who is shown
"singing" more than Ella Fitzgerald, Sarah Vaughan and
Dinah Washington combined, looks particularly foolish, at
one point playing his impressions of a Buddy Bolden solo;
Bolden never recorded!

It quickly becomes obvious while watching this endless
mess that Ken Burns actually knows very little about jazz.
In fact, many of the ideas expressed in this documentary
are similar to those previously included in **The Story of
Jazz**, a 1993 film mostly written by Chris Albertson.

Jazz—A Film by Ken Burns is analogous to a student handing in a fancy book report for school, a work
that looks impressive until one realizes that the student
never read the book.

Jazz Alley Vol. 1
(1999, 56 minutes, Storyville)

This video and the ones that follow have a pair of complete half-hour shows that Art Hodes hosted for a
Chicago educational radio station in 1968. All of the programs feature freewheeling playing from veteran all-
stars, with Hodes's piano and occasional commentary
adding to the music's value. The first half of this tape is
particularly intriguing for, in addition to Jimmy McPartland, Hodes, bassist Rails Wilson and drummer Harry
Hawthorne, Pee Wee Russell is heard at the end of his
career. His wife would soon pass away, whereupon Russell
essentially dropped out of music. However he is in good

form as is McPartland on "China Boy," "St. James Infirmary," "Oh Baby" and "Meet Me in Chicago." The fine trumpeter Doc Evans, who spent his life based in Minneapolis but did record on a regular basis, is showcased during the latter part of this tape in a trio with Hodes and drummer Bob Cousins. They perform "You Took Advantage of Me," "Singin' the Blues," "Once in a While," "Squeeze Me," "Buddy Bolden's Blues," "Wolverine Blues" and "Everybody Loves My Baby." Evans also gets to talk a bit with Hodes. This spirited tape is highly recommended to trad jazz collectors.

♪⁸ Jazz Alley Vol. 2
(1999, 58 minutes, Storyville)

The first show on this videocassette features Art Hodes leading a sextet that includes trombonist George Brunies, the underrated trumpeter Nap Trottier, clarinetist Jimmy Granato, bassist Truck Parham and drummer Monte Mountjoy. Their Dixieland versions of "I've Found a New Baby," "Blues," "Jazz Me Blues," "Farewell Blues" and a truncated "Tiger Rag" are not flawless but contain plenty of spirit. The second half of this volume is of greatest interest overall, for it showcases Bud Freeman with Hodes, bassist Rails Wilson and drummer Bob Cousins. After Hodes introduces the set with his "I Remember Chicago," the tenor saxophonist is in excellent form on "Sunday," "Sweet Sue," "You Took Advantage of Me," a slow one-chorus version of "Dinah," "Three Little Words" and a brief "Blues for Lemon." The latter show aired on October 2, 1968, and is one of the best existing films of Bud Freeman.

♪⁷ Jazz Alley Vol. 3
(1999, 56 minutes, Storyville)

Art Hodes heads a septet for the first half hour of this tape consisting of the fine (if unknown) trumpeter Smokey Stover, an over-the-hill but still rambunctious J.C. Higginbotham on trombone, clarinetist Tony Parenti, Eddie Condon (who strangely enough is on banjo rather than his usual rhythm guitar), bassist Rails Wilson and drummer Harry Hawthorne. The band plays "Ballin' the Jack" (Parenti gets two beats ahead of the band during his solo), "Someday Sweetheart," "Old Fashioned Love" and "Royal Garden Blues." Hodes and Stover take solo honors overall with Parenti redeeming himself on "Someday Sweetheart." Also on this third volume is a show from August 27, 1968, that showcases Barney Bigard in a quartet with Hodes, Wilson and drummer Bob Cousins. Bigard plays his usual repertoire ("Rose Room," "High Society," "Sweet Lorraine," "Perdido," "Blues," "C Jam Blues," "Caravan") plus a brief closing "When It's Sleepy Time Down South."

Other episodes in this valuable series that have not been reissued yet include two sets with Kenny Davern, Herb Hall, Butch Thompson and Benny Morton, a quartet outing with Davern, a blues-oriented program with Little Brother Montgomery and a session with Wingy Manone.

♪⁹ Jazz at the Smithsonian: Alberta Hunter
(1982, 60 minutes, Kultur Films)

The **Jazz at the Smithsonian** series (which is available on both DVD and VHS) features veteran musicians in 1982 performing for an hour before a large audience. Each film has a short interview segment and some background information provided by narrator Willis Conover, but is otherwise a performance film.

In the best entry in this series, 87-year-old Alberta Hunter (who is accompanied by pianist Gerald Cook and bassist Jimmy Lewis) is in outstanding form. Two years before her death, Hunter still sang with power, swing, charm and wit. Her repertoire ("My Castle's Rocking," "Downhearted Blues," "My Handy Man," "When You're Smiling," "Nobody Knows You When You're Down and Out," "Train to Glory," "Without a Song," "Darktown Strutters Ball," "Rough and Ready Man," "You Can't Tell the Difference After Dark," "Remember My Name") is full of vintage songs (other than the final number), but she makes these period pieces, standards and double-entendre tunes sound timeless.

Jazz at the Smithsonian: Art Blakey
(1982, 60 minutes, Kultur Films)

Art Blakey's Jazz Messengers in 1982 consisted of the leader, Wynton Marsalis (who was 20 or 21 at the time), Branford Marsalis on alto, tenor saxophonist Bill Pierce, pianist Donald Brown and bassist Charles Fambrough. They perform "Little Man," "My Ship" (a feature for the already impressive trumpeter), "New York" and a heated rendition of "Webb City."

Jazz at the Smithsonian: Art Farmer
(1982, 60 minutes, Kultur Films)

Flugelhornist Art Farmer is in fine form playing with pianist Fred Hersch, bassist Dennis Irwin and drummer Billy Hart. The quartet performs "Nancy with the Laughing Face," "Summer Song," "Blue Monk," "Firm Roots," "You Know I Care," "Red Cross," "Cherokee Sketches" and "Recorda Me."

Jazz at the Smithsonian: Benny Carter
(1982, 60 minutes, Kultur Films)

The ageless Benny Carter (75 at the time) jams a variety of standards ("Honeysuckle Rose," "On Green Dolphin Street," "Misty," "Take the 'A' Train," "Cotton Tail," "Autumn Leaves") with a group consisting of the underrated violinist Joe Kennedy, Jr., pianist Kenny Barron, bassist George Duvivier and drummer Ronnie Bedford. "Take the 'A' Train" is particularly rewarding, and Carter sounds as classy and swinging as usual.

Jazz at the Smithsonian: Bob Wilber and the Smithsonian Jazz Repertory
(1982, 60 minutes, Kultur Films)

Bob Wilber, as a young clarinetist and soprano saxophonist in the late '40s, was Sidney Bechet's protégé. For this 1982 concert, he pays tribute to his former teacher, featuring a group (trumpeter Glenn Zottola, guitarist Chris Flory, pianist Mark Shane, bassist Phil Flanigan and drummer Chuck Riggs) that would soon be renamed Bechet Legacy. The music is frequently exciting and quite joyful, being very much in the New Orleans tradition ("Down in Honky Tonk Town," "Swing Parade," "Coal Cart Blues," "China Boy," "Kansas City Man Blues," "Lad Be Good," "Polka Dot Stomp"), with "China Boy" being a high point. Sidney Bechet would have enjoyed sitting in with this group.

Jazz at the Smithsonian: Joe Williams
(1982, 60 minutes, Kultur Films)

The great singer Joe Williams, who is joined by pianist Kirk Stuart, bassist Keeter Betts and drummer Steve Williams, performs in concert in prime form. Williams performs spirited versions of his usual repertoire, including "Every Day I Have the Blues," "The Comeback," "Once in a While," "If It's the Last Thing I Do," "Same Old Story," "Everything Must Change," "Who She Do," "Alright, Okay You Win," "Stella by Starlight," "I Had Someone Else Before I Had You," "Save that Time for Me" and "Joe's Blues."

Jazz at the Smithsonian: Mel Lewis Jazz Orchestra
(1982, 60 minutes, Kultur Films)

The Mel Lewis Orchestra (formerly co-led by Thad Jones) at the time of this concert film included trumpeter Tom Harrell, tenor saxophonist Joe Lovano, baritonist Gary Smulyan, pianist Jim McNeely and bassist Marc Johnson in the personnel along with the drummer/leader. Among the songs that they perform (during a set of tunes written by either Herbie Hancock or Bob Brookmeyer) are "One Finger Snap" and "Dolphin Dance."

Jazz at the Smithsonian: Red Norvo
(1982, 60 minutes, Kultur Films)

For this concert, Red Norvo and guitarist Tal Farlow have a reunion (they had played together regularly over 30 years earlier) in a trio with bassist Steve Novosel. Norvo, who would retire a couple of years later, is inspired by Farlow's presence and sparks fly as they play off each other on "All of Me," "Cheek to Cheek" and "Fascinating Rhythm." "When You're Smiling" has the group becoming a quintet with the addition of pianist Norman Simmons and drummer Mike Sheppard, and the piano/bass/drums rhythm section accompanies singer Mavis Rivers on "Teach Me Tonight," "Wave" and "Just Friends." Rivers, who used to work for Norvo, is joined by her old boss on a happy version of "Pennies from Heaven."

Jazz at the Top: Remembering Bix Beiderbecke
(1995, 60 minutes, Rochester Area International)

This hour-long PBS television special was aired in August 1976. Several jazz musicians who knew Bix Beiderbecke (Jimmy McPartland, Joe Venuti and trombonist Spiegel Willcox) team up with a few more recent players (Russ Mussieri on clarinet and tenor, Dick Cary on alto horn and peckhorn, pianist Marian McPartland, bassist Major Holley and drummer Cliff Leeman) to perform a set of songs associated with Bix ("At the Jazz Band Ball," "Royal Garden Blues," "In a Mist," "China Boy," "Sweet Georgia Brown," "Candlelights," "Nobody's Sweetheart"). Venuti is wonderful to watch, Willcox gets in a few good licks, Jimmy McPartland was still in his prime, and Marian McPartland is showcased on the two piano pieces ("In a Mist" and "Candlelights").

Jazz Ball
(1996, 60 minutes, Republic Pictures Home Video)

Considering that this compilation of shorts from the 1930s (with a few from the '40s) was put together in 1956, this hour film is pretty decent. There is some unnecessary narration that unfortunately is often heard over the first part of many of the songs. However, a lot of music is stuffed into the 60 minutes, including performances from Cab Calloway ("Zah Zu Zah"), Rudy Vallee, Duke Ellington ("Rockin' in Rhythm," "Stormy Weather"

and "Bugle Call Rag"), the Mills Brothers ("I Ain't Got Nobody"), Red Nichols ("St. Louis Blues"), Ina Ray Hutton ("Truckin'"), Louis Armstrong ("Shine"), Russ Morgan ("Wabash Blues"), Louis Prima ("Chinatown My Chinatown"), Bob Crosby, Isham Jones, Henry Busse ("Hot Lips"), Bob Chester, Hal Kemp ("Swamp Fire"), Jimmy Dorsey ("Long John Silver"), Johnny "Scat" Davis, Peggy Lee ("It's a Good Day"), Lawrence Welk ("Ain't She Sweet"), Artie Shaw, and Sammy Davis, Jr., tapping with the Will Mastin Trio.

Jazz Band Ball
(1993, 60 minutes, Shanachie)

This is a remarkable DVD that collects 16 of the most important jazz clips from the 1925–1933 period. It begins with an excerpt of the Dorsey Brothers Band in 1929 (with trombonist Tommy and clarinetist Jimmy Dorsey) playing "Get Out and Get Under the Moon." The Duke Ellington instrumental ("Old Man Blues") from the 1930 film **Check and Double Check** is here. The Boswell Sisters are in delightful form on "Heebies Jeebies" from 1931. A pickup group led by drummer Chick Webb backs some dancers in 1929 on brief versions of "Sweet Sue" and "Tiger Rag." Louis Armstrong is featured on three exciting numbers from 1933 with a European band: "I Cover the Waterfront," a very memorable version of "Dinah" and "Tiger Rag." After decades of rumors, a newsreel that has cornetist Bix Beiderbecke playing with Paul Whiteman's orchestra (the only sound film ever discovered of Bix) was found. Unfortunately Beiderbecke really cannot be heard (he just leads the ensemble), but this rendition of "My Ohio Home" is worth seeing. Bill "Bojangles" Robinson is featured tap-dancing in 1932 on "Swanee River," there are some excerpts from Duke Ellington's first film (**Black and Tan**) and Charlie Wellman's little-known band plays "Alabamy Snow" in 1930.

And that's not all. An excerpt from a 1931 newsreel features Louis Armstrong (in his earliest film appearance) with his band playing short excerpts from "Chinatown,

My Chinatown" and "High Society." A long excerpt from Bessie Smith's lone film, **St. Louis Blues**, precedes a black-face singer/dancer (Tessie Maize on "Someday Sweetheart") and the superior 1928 dance band of Tommy Christian playing "Who Is It" and "Tommy Christian Stomp." After an unknown but hot band backs a couple of tap dancers in 1931 on "Whistle and Blow Your Blues Away" and "Mandy" and before Ruby Darby concludes the tape with 1930's "Tell the World He's Mine," Ben Bernie's Orchestra is seen in 1925 during what may be the earliest example of a jazz band in a sound film, playing a new song called "Sweet Georgia Brown." Jack Pettis is featured on C-melody sax. This DVD belongs in every serious jazz collector's library.

 Jazz Casual: Art Farmer/Jim Hall
(2000, 30 minutes, Rhino Home Video)

Ralph Gleason's **Jazz Casual** series in the 1960s resulted in over a couple dozen programs. Thirteen have been made available by Rhino Home Video, a dozen of which have also been packaged as three-packs, although those are all available individually as they are reviewed here. Among the shows that have not been reissued yet are programs featuring Louis Armstrong, Earl Hines, Muggsy Spanier, Turk Murphy, Joe Sullivan, the Modern Jazz Quartet, Bola Sete with Vince Guaraldi, Art Pepper, Charles Lloyd, Thad Jones and Mel Lewis, Paul Winter, Lambert, Hendricks and Bavan and the Duke Ellington Trio plus additional shows with Woody Herman.

After the breakup of the Jazztet (his sextet with Benny Golson), Art Farmer formed a quartet that included guitarist Jim Hall (fresh from Sonny Rollins's band), bassist Steve Swallow and drummer Walter Perkins. This particular show, which aired on January 10, 1964, has the group performing two vintage standards ("Change Partners" and "My Kinda Love") plus "Some Time Ago," Charlie Parker's "My Little Suede Shoes" and a very brief "Bags' Groove" (which fades out with the closing credits). Ralph Gleason also has a short interview with Farmer. The interplay between the lyrical leads (Farmer and Hall) is subtle if not overly exciting, but this set (along with all of the others in this valuable series) is well worth acquiring.

 Jazz Casual: Cannonball Adderley
(2001, 30 minutes, Rhino Home Video)

The 1961 Cannonball Adderley Quintet (with cornetist Nat Adderley, pianist Joe Zawinul, bassist Sam Jones and drummer Louis Hayes) performs excellent versions of Zawinul's "Scotch & Water," Eddie "Cleanhead" Vinson's "Arriving Soon" and Jones's "Unit Seven." The latter is the most rewarding jam although it is slightly interrupted near its end by Ralph Gleason's closing remarks. There is also a short discussion/interview in which Cannonball talks about the blues and how his band alters and augments the blues changes to make them more modern.

 Jazz Casual: Carmen McRae
(2001, 30 minutes, Rhino Home Video)

Carmen McRae was long one of Ralph Gleason's favorite singers; in fact, the journalist championed McRae before she was widely known. Her appearance on his **Jazz Casual** program (the video box says it is from 1968, but it looks more like 1963) teams McRae with pianist Norman Simmons, bassist Victor Sproles and drummer Walter Perkins. She is in fine form on "I'm Gonna Lock My Heart and Throw Away the Key," "Trouble Is a Man," "If You Never Fall in Love with Me," "'Round Midnight" and "Love for Sale" even if nothing all that memorable occurs. The show serves as a good souvenir for fans of Carmen McRae.

 Jazz Casual: Count Basie
(2001, 30 minutes, Rhino Home Video)

In this unusual entry in Ralph Gleason's **Jazz Casual** series, Count Basie is featured in the mid-'60s outside of the confines of his big band, playing in a quartet with rhythm guitarist Freddie Green, bassist Norman Keenan and drummer Sonny Payne. Basie is typically self-effacing in talking with Gleason and quite modest about his playing. Most of the selections are quite brief (including a tantalizing 25-second version of Fats Waller's "Handful of Keys") with Basie best on the blues "Twenty Minutes After Three," "As Long As I Live" and "If I Could Be with You."

 Jazz Casual: Dave Brubeck
(2000, 30 minutes, Rhino Home Video)

The classic Dave Brubeck Quartet with Paul Desmond, bassist Eugene Wright and drummer Joe Morello was featured in October 1961 in Ralph Gleason's **Jazz Casual** series. The group plays "Take Five" (which has fine solos from Desmond and Morello, but surprisingly none from the leader), a definitive and memorable rendition of "It's a Raggy Waltz," "Castilian Blues," a brief "Waltz Limp" and just a tiny bit of "Blue Rondo à la Turk" (over the closing credits). During an interview with Gleason, Brubeck talks about polytonality, polyrhythms and where he thinks the future of jazz is heading.

 Jazz Casual: Dizzy Gillespie
(2001, 30 minutes, Rhino Home Video)

There was a lot of potential for this particular show, but it falls short. Dizzy Gillespie and his 1961 quintet (Leo Wright on alto and flute, pianist Lalo Schifrin, bassist Bob Cunningham and drummer Chuck Lampkin) perform the obscure original "Norm's Norm," Benny Golson's "Blues After Dark" (the best overall performance with Schifrin's chordal solo taking honors), "Lorraine" and the Tocatta section from Schifrin's "Gillespiana." Gillespie is fairly restrained during the date, but was cutting loose on the last piece when the camera suddenly shifts to Ralph Gleason, who makes a few nonessential closing remarks. Surprisingly Gleason's interview with the trumpeter finds Dizzy less articulate than usual, talking a little about the blues, jazz musicians using originals and the advantage of learning a bit of piano. So although not without interest, this program is a bit of a disappointment.

 Jazz Casual: Gerry Mulligan
(2000, 30 minutes, Rhino Home Video)

From 1962, this program features baritonist Gerry Mulligan (who doubles on piano) leading a quartet also including valve trombonist Bob Brookmeyer, bassist Wyatt Ruther and drummer Gus Johnson. The musical magic between the two horns (who shared a similar musical personality along with a sly wit) makes this a worthwhile set. The quartet performs Mulligan's "Four for Three," "Darn that Dream," Brookmeyer's "Open Country" and the group's theme song "Utter Chaos."

 Jazz Casual: Jimmy Rushing
(2000, 30 minutes, Rhino Home Video)

This episode, filmed on September 26, 1962, is unusual for it features the great singer Jimmy Rushing not just on vocals but accompanying himself on piano. The music is both blues-oriented and a bit introspective and wistful. Rushing talks about his early days and his brand of blues, performing concise versions of "Goin' to Chicago," "Am I to Blame," "Good Morning Blues," "Trix Ain't Walkin' No More" and "How Long Blues" along with brief excerpts of "Baby, Don't You Tell on Me" and "See What Tomorrow Brings." The rather personal half hour is often touching.

 Jazz Casual: Jimmy Witherspoon and Ben Webster
(2000, 30 minutes, Rhino Home Video)

Blues/swing vocalist Jimmy Witherspoon often teamed up with Ben Webster in the early '60s. This set has plenty of room for both stars, who are joined by pianist Vince Guaraldi, bassist Monty Budwig and drummer Colin Bailey. Witherspoon (who is interviewed briefly by Ralph Gleason) sings "Money's Getting Cheaper," his trademark "Ain't Nobody's Business," "Outskirts of Town" and "Roll 'Em" while Webster is featured in fine form on two songs that he played regularly for over 30 years: "Cotton Tail" and "Chelsea Bridge."

Jazz Casual: John Coltrane
(2000, 30 minutes, Rhino Home Video)

Aired December 7, 1963, as an episode in Ralph Gleason's **Jazz Casual** series, this was apparently the only appearance by the John Coltrane Quartet on American television. Coltrane, McCoy Tyner, Jimmy Garrison and Elvin Jones perform stirring versions of "Afro Blue," "Alabama" and "Impressions." Other than a couple of minutes of talking by Gleason (Coltrane had declined to be interviewed), everything on this tape is available on the more comprehensive video **The Coltrane Legacy** (the better buy); otherwise the rating would have been a 10.

 Jazz Casual: Mel Tormé
(2000, 30 minutes, Rhino Home Video)

Filmed in the early '60s and aired in 1964, this episode of **Jazz Casual** features Mel Tormé with the Benny Barth Trio (drummer Barth, pianist Gary Lang and bassist Perry Lind). Tormé (who also plays a little bit of piano) is in typically fine form, performing "We've Got a World that Swings," his recent hit "Comin' Home Baby," "Sidney's Soliloquy," "Dat Dere," "When Sunny Gets Blue" and "Route 66." He is also quite informative in discussing jazz singing with Ralph Gleason even if Tormé says that he does not consider Mark Murphy to be a jazz singer; one imagines that his opinion on Murphy changed by the 1970s.

 Jazz Casual: Sonny Rollins
(2001, 30 minutes, Rhino Home Video)

This is one of the strongest episodes in this series. Shortly after Sonny Rollins came out of retirement in late 1961, he recorded "The Bridge" in a quartet with guitarist Jim Hall, bassist Bob Cranshaw and drummer Ben Riley. On March 3, 1962, the same group appeared on Ralph Gleason's show and their versions of "The Bridge," "God Bless the Child" and particularly "If Ever I Would Leave You" are quite memorable. In fact, the latter piece goes on for nearly 11 minutes (it fades after the closing credits) and near its conclusion the camera quickly

shifts to Gleason who quickly and awkwardly says a few closing words before the camera returns to Rollins. This show is probably the earliest existing film of the great Sonny Rollins.

 Jazz Casual: Woody Herman
(2000, 30 minutes, Rhino Home Video)

Woody Herman, who appeared on Ralph Gleason's **Jazz Casual** series three times, was the only musician to be on more than one of the shows. This set, which aired on May 24, 1963, features his Young Thundering Herd. "Molasses" is a strutting blues with a heated solo from tenor saxophonist Sal Nistico. Bill Chase's "El Toro Grande" also features Nistico along with some driving drumming from Jake Hanna. The ballad "Lonesome Old Town" gives trombonist Phil Wilson a chance to show off his giant range (starting with a screaming high note) and the closing "That's Where It Is" has spots for pianist Nat Pierce (who arranged all of the music), and the tenors of Nistico, Bobby Jones and Jacke Stevens. Herman takes a few short solos along the way on clarinet and, in a brief discussion with Gleason, talks enthusiastically about his band and his goals.

Jazz Festival Vol. 1
(1999, 61 minutes, Storyville)

In 1962, the Goodyear Tire Company sponsored five jazz performance films, each clocking in around 24 minutes. These showed up on television and in movie theatres as shorts. Along the way, the films have been issued a few times but never as definitively as on Storyville's two videotapes, which feature a greatly improved picture and sound, with two and a half of the shows on each tape.

Vol. 1 emphasizes Dixieland. The Louis Armstrong All-Stars (with Trummy Young, clarinetist Joe Darensbourg, Billy Kyle, bassist Billy Cronk and drummer Danny Barcelona) perform a definitive version of Satch's theme "When It's Sleepy Time Down South," "C'est Si Bon," and an exciting "Someday You'll Be Sorry." Although much of the music was pretty well set, the beauty of Armstrong's horn, his facial expressions while he sings and the joy of the music in general keep one smiling. Singer Jewel Brown is featured on an out-of-place "Jerry," Armstrong sings a sensitive version of "Nobody Knows the Trouble I've Seen," and it all concludes with "The Saints." Brown's overbearing backup singing is unintentionally funny on the latter.

The best of the five shows features the Eddie Condon All-Stars with Wild Bill Davison, trombonist Cutty Cutshall, clarinetist Peanuts Hucko, pianist John Varro, bassist Joe Williams (no relation to the singer), drummer Buzzy Drootin and Condon on rhythm guitar. While Condon is the leader, setting off the tempos and verbally introducing the songs, Davison is clearly the main star. On "Royal Garden Blues" Wild Bill looks very ready to play. Davison is showcased on "Blue and Broken Hearted" and he plays so emotionally and sarcastically (particularly at its conclusion) that Condon nearly laughs. Davison also stars on the uptempo "Big Ben Blues." Hucko is showcased on "Stealin' Apples," the slow blues "Little Ben Blues" gives each of the horns a chance to shine, and the show concludes with "Muskrat Ramble." The riffing, organized transitions and concise solos, along with Wild Bill's colorful playing, make this into a memorable set.

Also on **Vol. 1** are the three Dixieland numbers from a set by Bobby Hackett's Sextet ("Bill Bailey," "Struttin' with Some Barbecue," "The Saints") with trombonist Urbie Green, clarinetist Bob Wilber, pianist Dave McKenna, bassist Nabil Totah and drummer Morey Feld.

♪ ⑦ Jazz Festival Vol. 2 *(1999, 60 minutes, Storyville)*

The second of two videotapes that reissue all five of the 1962 short films sponsored by Goodyear Tires starts off with the Duke Ellington Orchestra. Cornetist Ray Nance has his usual spot on "Take the 'A' Train" and "Satin Doll" (featuring the leader on piano and bassist Aaron Bell) is uneventful. "Blow by Blow" has Paul Gonsalves taking a marathon tenor solo on an uptempo blues, while Johnny

Hodges is in the spotlight on "Things Ain't What They Used to Be." A medley of "VIP Boogie" and "Jam with Sam" is the high point of this set, with short spots for Harry Carney, clarinetist Jimmy Hamilton, trumpeter Harold Baker, Gonsalves, Lawrence Brown, altoist Russell Procope and trumpeters Bill Berry, Nance, Baker and Cat Anderson. This program concludes with the rhythm trio (Ellington, Bell and drummer Sam Woodyard) playing "Kinda Dukish."

Next is the second half of the Bobby Hackett show, featuring Hackett, Green, Wilber, McKenna, Totah and Feld on "'Deed I Do," "The Sentimental Blues" and a cooking "Swing that Music." Mike Bryan, who played guitar with Benny Goodman in the mid-'40s, served as executive producer for the series and led his own pickup band for one of the shows. With tenor saxophonist Georgie Auld, trumpeter Doc Severinsen, vibraphonist Harry Sheppard, pianist Derek Smith, bassist Jack Lesberg and drummer Mousie Alexander, Bryan and his group play three songs associated with Goodman's sextet ("Benny's Bugle," "7 Come 11" and "Air Mail Special") plus "Blues in G," Auld's "Ain't Got Time" and a feature for Auld on "Sweet Lorraine." Although the group plays well and it is interesting to hear Severinsen in this setting (his solos are heated but overly brief), this is the weakest of the five shows. However both of the **Jazz Festival** tapes (particularly **Vol. 1**) are worth getting.

♪ ⑤ Jazz in Exile *(1986, 58 minutes, Rhapsody Films)*

Many American jazz musicians who were living in Europe in the late '70s are featured in this generally intriguing documentary from 1978. There are on-camera interviews with Phil Woods, Richard Davis, Gato Barbieri, Gary Burton, Wilton Felder, Dexter Gordon, Steve Lacy, Freddie Hubbard, Chuck Mangione and McCoy Tyner along with brief performance clips of Elvin Jones's band, Steve Lacy's quintet, Carla Bley's JCOA ensemble, the Richard Davis Trio ("All Blues"), Randy Weston ("High Fly"), Dexter Gordon, Johnny Griffin and Phil Woods

("Last Night When We Were Young"). Unfortunately there is much more talk than music, but this film has its moments.

Jazz Legends: Mike Mainieri
(2003, 52 minutes, Music Video Distributors)

Although vibraphonist Mike Mainieri gets virtually all of the billing on the outside of this DVD, the better half of this reissue actually features Richie Cole's group. Both portions were issued as half of the Storyville videotapes **Jazz Life Vol. 1** and **Vol. 2** and were filmed in 1981 as half-hour British television shows produced by Ben Sidran. Altoist Richie Cole's quintet at the time featured the virtuosic, percussive and crazy pianist Bobby Enriquez, along with guitarist Bruce Forman, bassist Marshall Hawkins and drummer Scott Morris. Enriquez often steals the show, particularly on "Hi Fly" and "Yardbird Suite" as he bangs away (sometimes with his fists) on the piano, causing Forman to smile. Cole (not exactly a somber performer himself) keeps up with Enriquez and is showcased on "I Can't Get Started" and the R&B-ish "Punishment Blues." The second part of this release features fusion and post-bop music from vibraphonist Mike Mainieri's group (with tenor saxophonist Bob Mintzer, keyboardist Warren Bernhardt, bassist Eddie Gomez and drummer Omar Hakim). The three Mainieri originals ("Sarah's Touch," "Bamboo" and "Bullet Train") are not particularly memorable although the playing is strong, with the latter being a lengthy vibes/piano duet. But overall, this DVD should be acquired for the performances of Cole and Enriquez.

Jazz Life Vol. 1 (2000, 62 minutes, Storyville)

In the early 1980s, pianist/vocalist Ben Sidran produced a series of half-hour shows for British TV featuring bands performing in New York clubs. There is no narration at all, just music with introductions from the leader. **Vol. 1** of this two-tape series has a pair of separate minisets from the Village Vanguard that were filmed in 1981. Veteran tenor saxophonist Johnny Griffin (joined by pianist Ronnie Mathews, bassist Ray Drummond and drummer Kenny Washington) is quite explosive on the uptempo "Blues for Gonzi," his "A Monk's Dream" (which is appropriately Monkish) and the rapid "56" which is really raging. The second half of this video features Richie Cole's quintet (with pianist Bobby Enriquez, guitarist Bruce Forman, bassist Marshall Hawkins and drummer Scott Morris) and is the same performance released on the DVD **Jazz Legends: Mike Mainieri**. Both the Griffin and Cole sets are quite hyper, so **Jazz Life Vol. 1** (which is currently out of print) is for viewers with strong hearts.

Jazz Life Vol. 2 (2000, 55 minutes, Storyville)

The second of two tapes that reissue a pair of Ben Sidran's **Jazz Life** programs of the early '80s is a bit of a disappointment. The 1982 version of Art Blakey's Jazz Messengers (Blakey, Wynton Marsalis, tenor saxophonist Billy Pierce, altoist Branford Marsalis, pianist Donald Brown and bassist Charles Fambrough) was particularly strong, but their filmed set is forgettable. A brief version of "Fuller Love" (actually just the closing part) precedes "MX'B.C.," a piece that has throwaway solos from the three horns and Brown. "My Ship" is a lengthy ballad feature for Wynton Marsalis with the rhythm section, but he does little other than imitate Miles Davis and, although his technique at that early stage was obviously impressive, his solo is far from flawless. Other than a short and fairly free solo on "MX'B.C.," nothing much is heard from Branford Marsalis. The second part of the tape, featuring vibraphonist Mike Mainieri leading a group also including keyboardist Warren Bernhardt, the reeds of Bob Mintzer, bassist Eddie Gomez and drummer Omar Hakim, has been reissued on the DVD **Jazz Legends: Mike Mainieri**. Unfortunately that set is a bit dull despite some fine vibes/keyboards interplay on "Bullet Train," and overall this videotape is not essential.

Jazz on a Summer's Day
(1987, 84 minutes, New Yorker Video)

This documentary (available on DVD) of the 1958 Newport Jazz Festival is beautifully filmed in color. The camerawork wanders at times (a performance of "Blue Monk" by Thelonious Monk suddenly shifts away to a boat race), and there are more shots of the crowd than necessary. But almost despite itself, the film contains some very special musical moments. Most memorable is Anita O'Day's performance of a sensual "Sweet Georgia Brown" and a very heated, scat-filled "Tea for Two"; these ended up being the high points of the singer's career. Also featured are the Jimmy Giuffre 3 (with Bob Brookmeyer and Jim Hall) performing "The Train and the River," the Chico Hamilton Quintet (with Eric Dolphy), Eli's Chosen Six (trombonist Roswell Rudd is in the group), Sonny Stitt, the George Shearing Quintet, Dinah Washington with Terry Gibbs ("All of Me"), the Gerry Mulligan Quartet with Art Farmer, Big Maybelle, Chuck Berry, the Louis Armstrong All-Stars (with guests Jack Teagarden and Bobby Hackett) including a definitive "Rockin' Chair," and Mahalia Jackson. Sidemen along the way include pianist Wynton Kelly, Max Roach, Trummy Young, clarinetist Peanuts Hucko, Billy Kyle, guitarist Sal Salvador, bassist Henry Grimes, drummer Roy Haynes, pianist Jimmy Jones, Buck Clayton, tenorman Georgie Auld and Jo Jones.

 Jazz Scene USA—Cannonball Adderley Sextet/Teddy Edwards Sextet
(1994, 60 minutes, Shanachie)

In 1994, the Shanachie label released four videos, each of which consist of two complete shows from the legendary 1962 **Jazz Scene USA** series. This set and the Frank Rosolino/Stan Kenton tape have been reissued on DVD. Hosted by the always-hip Oscar Brown, Jr., these programs feature strong performances by working groups plus a short interview with the leader conducted by the genial Brown. On this DVD, Cannonball Adderley is seen leading his finest group, his sextet with Nat Adderley, pianist Joe

Zawinul, bassist Sam Jones, drummer Louis Hayes and Yusef Lateef on tenor, flute and oboe. Their versions of "Jessica's Birthday," "Primitivo," the as-yet unnamed "Jive Samba" and "Work Song" are concise but memorable. Tenor saxophonist Teddy Edwards is the dominant force during the second half of the program, heading a sextet also including trumpeter Freddie Hill and trombonist Richard Boone through five of his originals, including "Sunset Eyes."

 Jazz Scene USA—Frank Rosolino Quartet/ Stan Kenton & His Orchestra
(1994, 60 minutes, Shanachie)

The first half of this DVD has trombonist Frank Rosolino leading a quartet also including pianist Mike Melvoin, bassist Bob Bertaux and drummer Nick Martinis, performing a rapid "Yesterdays," "Mean to Me," "Lover Man," "Well You Needn't" and "Please Don't Bug Me." Rosolino is in excellent form and in high spirits. The tape concludes with a set from the Stan Kenton Orchestra featuring trumpeter Marvin Stamm, tenor saxophonist Don Menza and a mellophonium section, performing "Limehouse Blues," "Malaguena," "Maria," "Waltz of the Prophets" and "All the Things You Are." Both Rosolino and Kenton are briefly interviewed by Oscar Brown, Jr.

Jazz Scene USA—Phineas Newborn, Jr., Trio/Jimmy Smith Trio
(1994, 60 minutes, Shanachie)

This tape gives one a rare opportunity to see the brilliant pianist Phineas Newborn, Jr., playing in a trio with bassist Al McKibbon and drummer Kenny Dennis. Newborn performs three originals ("Theme for Basie," "New Blues" and "Blues Theme for Left Hand Only") plus "Lush Life" and a very rapid "Oleo." This video also includes a miniset by organist Jimmy Smith with his regular group (guitarist Quentin Warren and drummer Donald Bailey). Smith fools around a lot and the individual selections ("Walk on the Wild Side," "Mack the Knife," and a burning version of "The Champ") go on a bit too long although it is interesting to see the organist at this early stage. But get this video for Phineas Newborn.

 ### Jazz Scene USA—Shelly Manne and His Men/Shorty Rogers & His Giants
(1994, 60 minutes, Shanachie)

For this volume, two different West Coast jazz bands are featured at the tail end of the cool jazz era. Shelly Manne's quintet consists of Conte Candoli, tenor saxophonist Richie Kamuca, pianist Russ Freeman and bassist Monty Budwig. The playing is actually more memorable than the songs, which are the standard "Speak Low," Freeman's "Fantan" and two numbers from John Williams's score for the television series **Checkmate**: "The King Swings" and "The Isolated Pawn." Shorty Rogers's band has tenor saxophonist Gary LeFebvre (doubling on flute), pianist Lou Levy, bassist Gary Peacock and drummer Larry Bunker with Rogers sticking to flugelhorn. Their repertoire is stronger than Manne's since it consists of "Greensleeves," "Time Was," LeFebvre's bopish "The Outsider" and Rogers's witty blues "Martians Go Home."

While Shanachie did a fine job of releasing eight of the **Jazz Scene USA** programs, many more remain out of print. Among the ones that will hopefully surface someday are half-hour shows featuring the Curtis Amy-Paul Bryant quintet, Teddy Buckner, the Firehouse Five Plus Two, Pete Fountain, Paul Horn's quintet, the Jazz Crusaders, the Barney Kessel Trio, the Harold Land-Red Mitchell Quintet, the Les McCann Trio, Big Miller with the Russ Freeman Trio, the Modern Jazz Quartet, Mark Murphy, Ben Pollack's Pick-A-Rib Boys (a Dixieland sextet with Bob Wilber and Dick Cary), Lou Rawls, Vi Redd, the Bud Shank Quartet, the Cal Tjader quintet, Nancy Wilson and Oscar Brown, Jr., himself.

 ### Jazz Shorts *(1986, 30 minutes, Rhapsody Films)*

This tape has four short films from the 1980s that are of limited interest. **Honky Tonk Bud** features saxophonist Edward Wilkerson, Jr., and his group in an odd story with

John Toles-Bey as a rapping narrator. **Bird Lives** is animation set to the music of Charlie Parker, while **Daybreak Express** has a subway ride in New York with Duke Ellington's title cut as the soundtrack. Finally Gil-Scott Heron performs **Is that Jazz?** Overall, none of these shorts are too memorable, and they ultimately seem a bit pointless.

 ### A Jazz Story
(1999, 22 minutes, Maya Productions)

This fictional tale has a sweet story. Altoist Gary Bartz is playing a moody original ballad at a club when his old flame, singer Tamm E. Hunt, walks in with a young saxophonist, Bernd Stoll. After they greet each other, Hunt persuades Bartz to give Stoll a few lessons. Bartz teaches Stoll about life and emphasizes that he should express himself in his music, believe in his playing and know that it is most important to play for yourself. Hunt sings a blues at a club (she deserves to be much better known), and the two saxophonists play a few duets along the way during their lessons. When Bartz suddenly passes away, Stoll takes his place during his gig, putting the lessons that his mentor taught him to good use. This short film, written, produced and directed by Mevlut Akkaya, also has a little playing (but no lines) from pianist John Hicks, bassist Steve Kirby and drummer Victor Jones.

 ### Jazzvisions: All Strings Attached
(1991, 59 minutes, Polygram Video)

This special concert from 1986 teams four jazz guitarists influenced by rock and pop (John Abercrombie, Larry Carlton, Larry Coryell and John Scofield) with bop veteran Tal Farlow. Bassist John Patitucci and drummer Billy Hart accompany the five guitarists on "Autumn Leaves," "Misty," "My Romance," "All Blues" and Jobim's "Meditation." Since the guitarists are on Farlow's turf, it is not surprising that Tal is one of the stars, but Carlton fares quite well too. The series of **Jazzvisions** concerts from

Los Angeles' Wiltern Theater (including a Brazilian set by Ivan Lins, Djavan and Patti Austin that is not reviewed here) were released at the time simultaneously on CDs, LPs, videotapes and videodiscs and have since been reissued on DVDs.

 Jazzvisions: Echoes of Ellington Part 1
(1991, 59 minutes, Polygram Video)

The first of two videotapes taken from the same concert, this Duke Ellington tribute features trumpeter Randy Brecker, saxophonists Bill Evans and Tom Scott, guitarist Robben Ford, either Pete Jolly or Roger Kellaway on piano, bassist Andy Simpkins and drummer Ndugu Chancler. Dianne Reeves sings "Do Nothin' Till You Hear from Me" (a vocal duet with O.C. Smith), "I'm Just a Lucky So-and-So," and "I've Got It Bad." Kellaway takes "Prelude to a Kiss" as a piano solo, and the band jams "It Don't Mean a Thing," "Mood Indigo" and "Take the 'A' Train." Despite the unusual personnel, nothing that extraordinary occurs although the music is pleasing.

 Jazzvisions: Echoes of Ellington Part 2
(1991, 59 minutes, Polygram Video)

The same lineup of musicians appears on **Part 2** of this concert except that Dianne Reeves is absent. The repertoire is pretty predictable although the use of electric piano and R&B-ish solos on "It Don't Mean a Thing" and "Caravan" is a bit unusual. "Satin Doll" is given more energy than usual and "Rockin' in Rhythm" has Roger Kellaway and Pete Jolly battling it out on dueling pianos. The other musicians on the set are Randy Brecker, Tom Scott, saxophonist Bill Evans, Robben Ford, Andy Simpkins and Ndugu Chancler.

 Jazzvisions: Implosions
(1991, 59 minutes, Polygram Video)

For this concert (from December 5, 1986), an all-star group comprised of Randy Brecker, Frank Morgan, Ernie Watts, McCoy Tyner, Roger Kellaway, guitarist Eric Gale, bassist Stanley Clarke and drummer Peter Erskine are heard in top form on such standards as "Green Dolphin Street," "Lover Man," "Skylark," "Softly As in a Morning Sunrise" and "Will You Still Be Mine."

 Jazzvisions: Latina Familia
(1991, 59 minutes, Polygram Video

Tito Puente, Pete Escovedo and Sheila E. (who actually gets top billing due to her pop fame) perform stirring Latin jazz ("E Medley," "Revolt in Cell Bock 2," "Brasiliero," "Yesterday's Memories, Tomorrow's Dreams," "La Cuna," "El Rey Del Timbale," "Suenos De Los Toreros"). David Yamasaki contributes some rockish electric guitar and Puente is heard on timbales and vibes. The percussion battles between the three principals (plus Juan Escovedo) are exciting.

 Jazzvisions: The Many Faces of Bird
(1991, 59 minutes, Polygram Video)

In the best videotape of the series, Charlie Parker's music is played by four immortal altoists (James Moody, Bud Shank, Lee Konitz and Richie Cole) plus pianist Lou Levy, bassist Monty Budwig and drummer John Guerin. However, Bobby McFerrin, who comes out of the audience, ends up completely stealing the show. Among the more memorable numbers are "Billie's Bounce," "Confirmation," "Moose the Mooche," "Scrapple from the Apple" and "Yardbird Suite."

Jazzvisions: Rio Revisited
(1991, 59 minutes, Polygram Video)

The premiere bossa nova composer Antonio Carlos Jobim, his band and several vocalists (including Gal Costa) perform some of his best songs on this excellent concert videotape ("One Note Samba," "Desafinado," "Auga De Beber," "Dindi," "Wave," "No More Blues," "Two Kites," "Samba Do Soho," "Sabia," "Samba Do Aviao," "Waters of March," "Corcovado"). This is a must for fans of Brazilian jazz.

Jazz West Coast: The Legends Talk
(1994, 91 minutes, GOAL Productions)

During October 27–30, 1994, Ken Poston produced 18 concerts held mostly at the Holiday Inn Crowne Plaza in Redondo Beach and called Jazz West Coast, a celebration of jazz in Los Angeles, mostly centering on the 1950s. In addition, there were ten panel discussions featuring many important veterans from the era. The best 90 minutes from those ten hours are on this fascinating, sometimes touching and often humorous tape. Many of the 1950s alumni have since passed away, so it is a joy to hear them reminiscing and chuckling about their past adventures. The panels are titled *Central Avenue Revisited, Bebop Invades the West, L.A. Jazz in the '40s, The Stan Kenton Innovations Orchestra, The Lighthouse & The All Stars, Gerry Mulligan, The Record Companies, West Coast Jazz in the '50s, Continuing the Development,* and *The Composers & Arrangers.* Seen and heard along the way are Lee Young, Jack McVea, Buddy Collette, Ernie Andrews, Clora Bryant, Gerald Wiggins, Roy Porter, Teddy Edwards, Stan Levey, Russ Freeman, Gerald Wilson, Marshall Royal, Gene Norman, Buddy Childers, Bud Shank, Milt Bernhart, Don Bagley, Pete Rugolo, Pete Candoli, Howard Rumsey, Claude Williamson, Conte Candoli, Jimmy Giuffre, Gerry Mulligan, Roy Harte, William Claxton, Dave Pell, Dotty Woodward, Jimmy Bond, Pete Jolly, Larry Bunker, Bobby Troup, Lou Levy, Leroy Vinnegar, Larance Marable, Herb Geller, Jack Montrose, Bill Holman and Lennie Niehaus.

 ### Jazz Women *(1990, 28 minutes, Rosetta Records)*

When this brief videotape, which has nine performances from female singers and musicians, was released in 1990, all of the clips were rare. Since that time, more than half of these selections have become readily available elsewhere, but it still makes for a fine retrospective of pre-bop female jazzers. Included is Nina Mae McKinney with Eubie Blake's orchestra in 1932 singing "Everything I've Got Belongs to You," Helen Humes with the Count Basie Septet in 1951 performing "I Cried for You," Maxine Sullivan on a Soundie (**Some of these Days**), Ida Cox's only film appearance ("Woman's No Fool"), a Sister Rosetta Tharpe Soundie with Lucky Millinder's orchestra (**Lonesome Road**) and a Soundie apiece from Rita Rio's Mistresses of Rhythm, Ada Leonard's All-American Girl Orchestra, and the International Sweethearts of Rhythm. Best of all is Billie Holiday in 1950 with the Count Basie Septet performing "God Bless the Child" and the blues "Now Baby or Never."

 ### Jim Hall: A Life in Progress
(1999, 59 minutes, Rhapsody Films)

This documentary features guitarist Jim Hall in the recording studio making the Telarc CD **By Arrangement**. Hall sums up aspects of his life along the way, including discussing his beginnings, his associations with the Chico Hamilton Quintet, the Jimmy Giuffre 3, Sonny Rollins, Art Farmer and Paul Desmond, and such inspirations as Charlie Christian, Lester Young, Ben Webster and Freddie Green. Also seen talking about Hall are Pat Metheny, John Lewis, bassist Scott Colley, Chico Hamilton, Nat Hentoff, the guitarist's wife Jane Hall, Joe Lovano, drummer Terry Clarke, producer John Snyder, altoist Greg Osby and pianist Bill Evans (in a 1966 interview). Along the way there are some brief film clips and excerpts from most of the songs on Hall's **By Arrangement** set. Unfortunately none of the performances (which include spots for Tom Harrell) are close to complete, and most of the music is talked over so viewers never get to really hear for themselves why Jim Hall is such a highly respected guitarist.

 ### Jivin' in Be-Bop
(1992, 55 minutes, Storyville)

Relatively little of the bebop era was filmed, especially compared to the swing era. One of the very few exceptions was **Jivin' in Be-Bop**, a 1947 film featuring the

Dizzy Gillespie Orchestra as the house band. At the time the orchestra included James Moody (who unfortunately does not have a single solo in the film), John Lewis, Milt Jackson, Ray Brown, drummer Joe Harris, altoist Scoops Cary and the trumpeter/leader. **Jivin' in Be-Bop** was meant to be a variety film and it turned out to be a bit of a hodgepodge. There is no plot as the emcee Freddie Carter and Gillespie exchange dated puns and jokes between acts. Dizzy's big band is featured on camera for eight numbers: "Salt Peanuts," "Be-Baba-Leba," "Oop-Bop She Bam," "I Waited for You," "Crazy about a Man," "One Bass Hit," "He Beeped When He Should Have Bopped"

and "Things to Come." Each of those numbers is also on the Vintage Jazz Classics video **Things to Come**, reviewed elsewhere in this book. Helen Humes sings on "Be-Baba-Leba" and "Crazy about a Man," Kevin "Poncho" Hagood croons "I Waited for You," and Gillespie vocalizes during "He Beeped." In addition, Dizzy's orchestra is heard but not seen backing a variety of dancers on "'Shaw Nuff," "Dynamo A," "Ornithology," "Grosvenor's Square," "Ray's Idea" and "Bag's Boogie." The boogie-woogie duo of pianist Dan Burley and organist Johnny Taylor is featured on "Boogie in C" and two versions of "Hubba-Hubba Blues," also often backing dancers. The movie

Jivin' in Bebop saves for posterity the exciting 1947 Dizzy Gillespie Orchestra.

ends inconclusively, almost as if the low-budget production had run out of film. However, this version of **Jivin' in Be-Bop** uses a better print than most and it does allow one to see the innovative Dizzy Gillespie big band. But **Things to Come** is the better buy.

The Jo Stafford Show
(1991, 60 minutes, Vintage Jazz Classics)

Jo Stafford was always a fine singer, but she never attempted to sing jazz. Her tape is included in this book because of the appearances of Ella Fitzgerald. Stafford starts off by singing "The Gentleman Is a Dope" and the satirical "Tim-Tay-Shun" (during which she makes fun of hillbilly singers) in 1960. The remainder of the tape is taken from **The Jo Stafford Show** in 1961. In addition to Stafford, Rosemary Clooney sings "June Is Bustin' Out All Over" and "'Tis Autumn," while Mel Tormé is lost in the overproduced "County Fair." Fitzgerald swings on fine versions of "I Got a Right to Sing the Blues," "What Is this Thing Called Love" and "The Man that Got Away." This tape concludes with Fitzgerald and Jo Stafford singing a rather frivolous medley of 24 songs, most of which are extremely brief. Jo Stafford fans will want this tape, but jazz listeners will only find the Fitzgerald solo pieces of interest.

Joe Lovano: Jazz Standards—Solo Interpretations & Expressions
(2001, 31 minutes, JSL Records)

On April 1, 2001, tenor saxophonist Joe Lovano performed seven standards for the camera while at home. These unaccompanied solos ("Hot House," "Stella by Starlight," "Giant Steps," "Gallop's Gallop," "Star Eyes," "Along Came Betty," "Body and Soul") are really the equivalent of watching Lovano practice except that his solos are coherent and keep the melody in mind. Most of the numbers are four or five minutes apiece, with Lovano switching to his odd-looking straight alto on "Gallop's Gallop" and soprano on "Star Eyes." His improvisations

are purposeful and logical, but his DVD is mostly recommended to his most ardent fans.

Joe Pass: In Concert, Brecon Jazz Festival, 1991
(1995, 40 minutes, Vestapol)

In the early '70s, Joe Pass amazed many listeners with his unaccompanied solo guitar performances. Not only could he play ballads, but he could romp through "Cherokee" and "How High the Moon" while providing the melody, bass lines and harmony simultaneously. Not a tapper like Stanley Jordan, Pass mastered conventional technique and turned his guitar into a miniature orchestra. This solo concert from 1991 has Pass playing a medley from *Porgy and Bess* ("Summertime" and "It Ain't Necessarily So"), "They Can't Take That Away from Me," "Beautiful Love," "All the Things You Are," Dizzy Gillespie's "That's Earl Brother" and "Joe's Blues." As usual, he swings effortlessly and makes it all look so easy on this DVD.

Joe Williams: A Song Is Born
(1992, 57 minutes, View Video)

This enjoyable tape features jazz/blues singer Joe Williams performing in 1991 at the Paul Masson Winery, accompanied by George Shearing, bassist Neil Swainson and drummer Paul Humphrey. The combination of Williams and Shearing works quite well and the 72-year-old singer was still in his musical prime. He performs a strong set ("Just Friends," "I Let a Song Go Out of My Heart," "Nobody's Heart Belongs to Me," "Blues in My Heart," "Shake Rattle and Roll," "A Child Is Born," "Muddy Water," "Little Girl Blue," "Who She Do," "Sometimes I'm Happy," "Roll 'Em Pete," "Tenderly," "The Comeback") full of standards, ballads and (best of all) rollicking blues.

John Carter and Bobby Bradford: The New Music
(1986, 29 minutes, Rhapsody Films)

Clarinetist John Carter and cornetist Bobby Bradford were two of the leaders of the Los Angeles avant-garde from the mid-'60s until Carter's death in 1991. Both were underrated due to their decisions to live in L.A. (where they worked as teachers) and to perform such consistently esoteric music, although Bradford's comparatively mellow sound was a fine contrast to Carter's often-screeching flights. This historic if brief video has Carter and Bradford performing a pair of unaccompanied duets: "Circle" and "And She Speaks." The music still sounds forbidding and adventurous today despite Bradford's melodic nature.

John Coltrane—The Coltrane Legacy
(1985, 61 minutes, VAI Artists International)

Nearly all of the sound footage that exists of John Coltrane is on this DVD, which lets the music tell the story. Coltrane is seen playing his solo from "So What" with Miles Davis in 1959 (taken from the trumpeter's half hour TV special) and then is featured at great length on two complete half hour television shows. The remarkable tenor and soprano saxophonist teams up with Eric Dolphy (on alto and flute), McCoy Tyner, bassist Reggie Workman and Elvin Jones on a 1961 West German show produced by Joachim Berendt. The quintet performs "Every Time We Say Goodbye," an explosive version of "Impressions" and "My Favorite Things." Even with some erratic camerawork (a couple of times it appears that the cameraman is dozing off!), this is a priceless show. The second half of the video is all of the music from the classic Coltrane Quartet's appearance on Ralph Gleason's **Jazz Casual** series in 1964. Coltrane, Tyner, Jimmy Garrison and Jones are featured on intense renditions of "Afro Blue," "Impressions" and the melancholy "Alabama." This DVD is essential.

John Pizzarelli: Live in Montreal—The Big Band
(1992, 50 minutes, BMG Video)

Guitarist/singer John Pizzarelli and his trio are joined by a big band on this enjoyable concert DVD. Pizzarelli is as charming as usual and romps on the uptempo material, while not taking himself overly seriously on his vocal

numbers. The music ("Three Little Words," "My Blue Heaven," "You Stepped Out of a Dream," "I'm Hip," "I Know that You Know," "If I Had You," "Roslyn," "All of Me," "My Baby Just Cares for Me," "Sing Sing Sing," "Honeysuckle Rose," "Lady Be Good") mostly dates from the swing era, a period of time in which Pizzarelli's guitar is a comfortable fit. His fans will find much to enjoy during the cheerful concert.

A Joyful Noise
(2003, 60 minutes, Winstar Home Entertainment)

Sun Ra and his Arkestra (with singer June Tyson, tenor saxophonist John Gilmore and altoist Marshall Allen) are seen at the pyramids in Egypt, in Baltimore and in Philadelphia. Among the pieces they play in this erratic but intriguing documentary are "Astro Black," "Calling Planet Earth," "Organ Solo," "We Travel the Spaceways," "Ankh" and "'Round Midnight."

Keith Jarrett: Last Solo
(2002, 92 minutes, Image Entertainment)

From his Tokyo concert of January 25, 1984, Keith Jarrett freely improvises on "Tokyo '84 #1," "Tokyo '84 #2" and "Tokyo '84 Encore" in addition to performing a respectful version of "Over the Rainbow." The music is often beautiful although sometimes repetitive as it evolves from a ballad to a one-chord vamp, a very rhythmic section full of passion and then back to the original ballad mood. Jarrett's anguished facial expressions can be difficult to watch at times.

Keith Jarrett: Solo Tribute
(2002, 102 minutes, Image Entertainment)

Filmed on April 14, 1987, this concert by Keith Jarrett was his 100th performance in Japan. He is in typically brilliant form on 13 standards and his original "Sound" ("The Night We Called It a Day," "I Love You," "Things Ain't What They Used to Be," "I Loves You Porgy," "There Is No Greater Love," "'Round Midnight," "Solar," "Then I'll Be Tired of

You," "Sweet and Lovely," "The Wind," "Do Nothing Till You Hear from Me," "I Got It Bad," "Summertime"). Jarrett often acts as if the music was flowing through him, sometimes standing up while he plays and wriggling around. As usual, Jarrett's music is easier to listen to than to watch being created. He is particularly sensitive on the ballads (especially "The Night We Called It a Day," "I Loves You Porgy" and "The Wind"), and he creates some danceable soulful grooves on some of the other numbers.

 ### Keith Jarrett Trio: Live at Open Theatre East
(2001, 130 minutes, Image Entertainment)

Of the many Keith Jarrett DVDs, this is the most rewarding. Jarrett, bassist Gary Peacock and drummer Jack DeJohnette are featured on July 25, 1993, performing in Japan. Their repertoire is strong ("In Your Own Sweet Way," "Butch and Butch," "Basin Street Blues," "Solar," "If I Were a Bell," "I Fall in Love Too Easily," "Oleo," "Bye Bye Blackbird," "The Cure," "I Thought about You") and their renditions, though often quite lengthy ("Solar" is 26 minutes long), hold one's interest throughout. The audience is rightfully enthusiastic, forcing the trio to play three encores. The music is quite boppish and sometimes telepathic, for the musicians follow each other very closely. Recommended.

 ### Keith Jarrett Trio: Standards
(2001, 105 minutes, Image Entertainment)

This Tokyo concert from February 15, 1985, features Keith Jarrett, Gary Peacock and Jack DeJohnette performing two lengthy sets ("I Wish I Knew," "If I Should Lose You," "Late Lament," "Rider," "It's Easy to Remember," "So Tender," "Prism," "Stella by Starlight," "God Bless the Child") plus, as a bonus cut, the five-minute "Delaunay's Dilemma." The communication between the three musicians is always impressive and Jarrett leads the group through some surprising tempos and moods including an uptempo "If I Should Lose You," the gospelish "Rider" and the fiery "So Tender." Due to the pianist's constant moving around and facial expressions (which sometimes

make it look as if he is agony), some of this DVD is difficult to watch, so consume it all in small doses.

 ### Keith Jarrett Trio: Standards II
(2001, 91 minutes, Image Entertainment)

This DVD has two sets from October 26, 1986, by Jarrett, Gary Peacock and Jack DeJohnette ("You Don't Know What Love Is," "With a Song in My Heart," "When You Wish Upon a Star," "All of You," "Blame It on My Youth," "Love Letters," "Georgia on My Mind," "You and the Night and the Music," "When I Fall in Love," "On Green Dolphin Street," "Woody'n You") plus a nine-minute bonus cut ("Young and Foolish"). The music ranges from sensitive ballads to hard swinging with the high points being a wistful and tender version of "When You Wish Upon a Star" and a cooking rendition of "All of You."

 ### Ken Peplowski Quintet: Live at Ambassador Auditorium
(1994, 67 minutes, Concord Jazz)

This video is a filmed version of a Concord CD. The very fluent and swinging clarinetist and tenor saxophonist Ken Peplowski leads a quintet also featuring guitarist Howard Alden, pianist Ben Aronov, bassist Murray Wall and drummer Tom Melito. Veteran trumpeter Harry "Sweets" Edison (a welcome addition even though he was past his prime) is on three of the numbers. The repertoire, which has swing standards, some bop and a few basic originals ("Birk's Works," "Nuts," "I Don't Stand a Ghost of a Chance," "The Best Things in Life Are Free," "At Long Last Love," "Menina Flor," "I Brung You Finjans for Your Zarf," "Why Try to Change Me Now," "Exactly Like You"), works well with this group; Peplowski and Alden consistently inspire each other.

 ### Kenny Drew Trio: At the Brewhouse
(2001, 52 minutes, Storyville Films)

About a year before his death, pianist Kenny Drew (who spent the last 30 years of his life living in Europe) was filmed playing at the Brewhouse in England in a trio with bassist Niels-Henning Orsted Pedersen and drummer Alvin Queen. This performance from July 22, 1992, features Drew still in excellent form, digging into "My Shining Hour" (which is taken at a rapid pace), "You Don't Know What Love Is," "Oleo," "Bluesology," "In Your Own Sweet Way," "All Blues" and "Blues in the Closet." Pedersen has a few typically virtuosic bass solos and Queen is driving in support, but the main focus is on the 1950s-style bebop pianist.

 ### Kenny Drew Trio: Live
(1999, 52 minutes, Videoarts Japan)

Also filmed in 1992 at the Brewhouse in England, Kenny Drew, Niels-Henning Orsted Pedersen and Alvin Queen perform five lengthy numbers ("In Your Own Sweet Way," "It Might As Well Be Spring," "St. Thomas," "It Could Happen to You," "Hush-A-Bye"). Drew is powerful on "In Your Own Sweet Way," the interplay between the musicians is humorous on "St. Thomas" (before they start cooking), and "It Could Happen to You" is taken as a ballad. This videotape is equal in quality to **At The Brewhouse**.

 ### Kid Ory/Red Allen in Europe
(2002, 60 minutes, 30N-90W Records)

In 1959, Henry "Red" Allen joined Kid Ory's New Orleans jazz band, recording and visiting Europe. Their Paris concert from October 4, 1959, was televised and, although the picture is a bit blurry in spots, the music is excellent. At the time the group consisted of Ory, Allen, clarinetist Bob McCracken, pianist Cedric Haywood, bassist Squire Girsback and drummer Alton Redd. Surprisingly the best soloists that day were Haywood and McCracken. Ory plays percussively and with spirit as usual and, although Allen is fine, he should have been featured much more. The repertoire is typical of Ory's band ("Do You Know What It Means to Miss New Orleans," "Tiger Rag," "Aunt Hagar's Blues," "High Society," "Muskrat Ramble," "Sister Kate," "Royal Garden Blues," "Basin Street Blues," "Shine,"

"Do What Ory Says," "Without You"), and there is a short interview with Ory who briefly discusses his beginnings.

 ### The Ladies Sing the Blues
(1988, 60 minutes, View Video)

A variety of film clips, mostly taken from movies but also including a couple of Soundies and Snader Telescriptions, make up the 16 performances on this enjoyable DVD. There is an excerpt of Bessie Smith singing "St. Louis Blues," Ethel Waters is featured on "Darkies Never Dream" and "Quicksand," and Billie Holiday's performance of "Fine and Mellow" from **The Sound of Jazz** is also here. In addition, there are selections from Ida Cox ("When You Lose Your Money Blues"), Sister Rosetta Tharpe ("That Lonesome Road"), Connee Boswell ("Nobody's Sweetheart Now"), Dinah Washington ("Lean Baby" and "Only a Moment Ago"), Ruth Brown ("Have A Good Time"), Lena Horne ("The Man I Love" and "Unlucky Woman"), Sarah Vaughan ("You're Mine You"), Helen Humes with Count Basie's Septet ("I Cried for You") and Peggy Lee ("Why Don't You Do Right" with Benny Goodman plus "I Cover the Waterfront"). Rarest are the numbers by Connee Boswell, Dinah Washington and Ruth Brown.

 ### Lady Day: The Many Faces of Billie Holiday
(1991, 60 minutes, Kultur)

This definitive portrait of Billie Holiday (which is available on DVD) is everything that the movie **Lady Sings the Blues** is not, mainly factual. The hour special was produced for the **Masters of American Music** series on PBS and de-emphasizes Holiday's difficulties in her personal life for more of a focus on her musical career. With interesting comments from Carmen McRae, Milt Gabler, Harry "Sweets" Edison, Buck Clayton, Annie Ross and Mal Waldron, and expert use of film clips (although surprisingly not her 1951 appearance with the Count Basie Septet), the Billie Holiday story is told without resorting to legendary tales; the truth is fascinating enough. The editing is very good, as when Lady Day's recording of "Swing, Brother, Swing" is utilized for an exciting dance sequence. Although the narrative rushes a bit too quickly through Holiday's earliest years, the story covers all of the periods of her life quite well. In addition to some familiar film clips (including the great bulk of "Fine and Mellow" from **The Sound of Jazz**), there are a few rare numbers taken from television appearances of 1958–59 (very late in Holiday's life) including "Please Don't Talk about Me When I'm Gone," "Strange Fruit," "Don't Explain" and "What a Little Moonlight Can Do."

LaMont Johnson: Top of the Marc
(1998, 88 minutes, MasterScores)

Pianist LaMont Johnson, who is best remembered for having played with altoist Jackie McLean in the 1960s, recorded several dates for his own MasterScores label in the 1990s in addition to making this performance film. The concert is from February 15, 1998, before a live audience in Austin, Texas. Johnson, bassist Edwin Livingston and drummer J.J. Johnson interpret nine selections ("City

The premature death of Eric Dolphy, a remarkable altoist, bass clarinetist and flutist, is explored on *Last Date*.

Block Shout," "My Romance," "Calypso After Nine," "Edwin's Blues," "Tio's Hispano," "'Round Midnight," "All the Things You Are," "Song for My father," "What Is This Thing Called Love") with the drummer fine in support and Livingston taking occasional short solos, while the main focus is mostly on the pianist. LaMont Johnson plays quite well (particularly on "My Romance," the tango "Tio's Hispano" and "All the Things You Are") although this set is a bit dull to watch at times.

Last Date: Eric Dolphy
(1993, 92 minutes, Rhapsody Films)

This French documentary from 1991 is by Hans Hylkema with biographer Thierry Bruneau as the main interviewer and narrator; it is in both French (with English subtitles) and English. **Last Date** mostly focuses on multi-instrumentalist Eric Dolphy's last couple months of life when he left Charles Mingus's sextet in order to settle in Paris and play throughout Europe. Heard throughout the soundtrack are Dolphy's solos from his last sanctioned record, which was also posthumously called **Last Date**. The trio from that session (which includes pianist Misha Mengelberg and drummer Han Bennink) are interviewed in the same studio where the date took place. Part of the film traces Dolphy's career, including a visit to his family's home and brief interviews with Buddy Collette (who was one of his teachers), drummer Roy Porter, a neighbor and his aunt. Strangely enough, nothing is said about his period with Chico Hamilton, and the chronology of his activities during 1960–63 is never outlined. There are short and valuable interviews with Ted Curson, Richard Davis, Jaki Byard and Gunther Schuller although nothing from the musicians with whom he played during his stints with John Coltrane. A few excerpts from Scandinavian television shows feature Dolphy with the Mingus Sextet in Stockholm (April 12) and Oslo (April 13). The latter is available in complete form as a Shanachie videotape called **The Charles Mingus Sextet**, but the former is more obscure and deserves to be released. Several people (including Dolphy's fiancée, Joyce Mordecai) talk about his final days when life was full of great promise but his health was unexpectedly declining. He died on June 29, 1964, in Berlin from a diabetic coma that was misdiagnosed as drug abuse by German doctors; ironically, he lived a clean life. Eric Dolphy was 36. Although not perfect, this video sheds additional light on Dolphy's life and career.

 ### The Last of the Blue Devils
(2001, 90 minutes, Rhapsody Films)

This famous 1979 film by Bruce Ricker, reissued on DVD, has a reunion of Kansas City jazz veterans, most of whom played 40–50 years earlier with Walter Page's Blue Devils, Bennie Moten's orchestra, Count Basie, Andy Kirk and/or Jay McShann. On the minus side, the clips jump around quite a bit and are sometimes confusing, not really telling the story of Kansas City jazz that coherently. However, there are some great moments along the way. The reunion (from 1974 or '75) was held at the old Union Hall in Kansas City and, when Count Basie enters, meeting up with Jay McShann, Big Joe Turner and other veterans, it is a memorable moment. Musically, one wishes that more of the clips were complete. Best are when Turner is featured with McShann, both with a quartet and a big band full of local players. Turner is in top voice on two versions of "Piney

rhapsody films
THE LAST OF THE BLUE DEVILS

Left: Count Basie
Right: Jay McShann
as seen in
THE LAST OF THE BLUE DEVILS

333 W. 39th Street Suite 503
New York, NY 10018
212-629-6880 Fax 212-714-0871
contact@kino.com

Count Basie and Jay McShann are two of the many Kansas City veterans featured in *The Last of the Blue Devils.*

Brown Blues," an excerpt of "Shake, Rattle & Roll" and a spirited "Roll 'Em." McShann is featured on excerpts of "Jumpin' the Blues," "Hootie's Blues," "After Hours" and "One O'Clock Jump." The Count Basie Orchestra (with drummer Butch Miles and the always-present rhythm guitarist Freddie Green) performs "Moten Swing" (a feature for tenor-saxophonist Jimmy Forrest) "Jumpin' at the Woodside" (with Forrest and Eric Dixon battling it out on tenors), "Night Train" and a brief "One O'Clock Jump." There is also a jam session version of "Lester Leaps In" (again an excerpt) with solos from tenor saxophonist Paul Quinichette, trombonist Eddie Durham and altoist Charles McPherson, and brief musical moments from violinist Claude Williams, drummers Jo Jones and Baby Lovett and tap dancer Speedy Huggins. Also seen are drummers Jesse Price and Ernie Williams, altoist Buster Smith, bassist Gene Ramey and tenor saxophonist Budd Johnson. Former club owner Milton Morris does the best job of summing up the old days. As a bonus, in addition to the film, this DVD has 19 minutes of outtakes of Turner and McShann performing "Honey Hush," "Rose Garden," "Chains of Love" and an incomplete "Shake, Rattle & Roll." The overall production leaves one with a happy feeling although the editing and storyline could have been greatly improved.

⑧ Lee Konitz: Portrait of an Artist As Saxophonist
(1990, 83 minutes, Rhapsody Films)

One of the great jazz alto saxophonists, Lee Konitz has for decades retained a strong musical curiosity and an open-minded approach while displaying his own sound. During this fascinating documentary from 1988, Konitz talks about his career and music, and is seen teaching music students and performing at a rehearsal. His wit and intelligence come across very well, as does his personality and attitude toward life. In addition he performs six duets with pianist Harold Danko: "Stella by Starlight," "Struttin' with Some Barbecue" (quoting Louis Armstrong's famous solo from 1927), "Hi Beck," "Kary's Trance," "Subconscious-Lee" and "She's as Wild as Springtime."

The Legend of Teddy Edwards
(2001, 84 minutes, Image Entertainment)

Teddy Edwards was one of the great tenor saxophonists to emerge during the 1940s and was a major force for 55 years. Despite that, he was always greatly underrated due to his decision to spend most of his life living in Los Angeles. This film, which was put together by Mark Cantor and Kirk Silsbee two years before Edwards's death, does a fine job of correcting the historic neglect. Edwards is featured performing with his quartet/quintet (pianist Larry Nash, bassist Wendell Williams, drummer Gerryck King and sometimes trumpeter James R. Smith) on complete performances of "L.A. After Dark," "Regina," the boppish "Takin' Off" (a high point), "I'm So Afraid of Love" and "At the La Villa." In addition, Edwards's solo from a late '50s film clip of "Sunset Eyes" is included. The tenor was extensively interviewed for this DVD, and he discusses the universality of music, his early life, Central Avenue (which is shown a bit in some silent clips), kicking heroin in the early '50s, Charlie Parker, playing with Benny Goodman in the '60s and his current life. Surprisingly, nothing much is said of the legendary jam sessions with Dexter Gordon and Wardell Gray or of his other activities in the 1960s, '70s and '80s. Also adding comments are Dan Morgenstern, Kirk Silsbee, trumpeter Clora Bryant, Teddy Edwards, Jr., Ernie Andrews and the members of Edwards's quintet. At the end of the documentary are a few bonuses: a complete version of "It's All Right" by the quintet, Edwards reading his lyrics to "What Else Do You Want from Us" and reciting his poem "Paris Nights" while playing piano. This important DVD, which was made just in time, adds to the legacy of Teddy Edwards.

⑤ Legends of Jazz Drumming Part One, 1920–1950
(1996, 63 minutes, DCI Music Video)

Watching this video and the second part can be a bit frustrating. The history of jazz drumming during the 1920–50 period is summed up quite well by narrator Louie Bellson (with comments by Roy Haynes) and even non-drummers will find the narrative interesting. The problem is that, although many film clips are shown, virtually all of them are excerpts and quite often Bellson talks over part of the music. One gets glimpses of many of the great early drummers, but if the music were allowed to speak for itself more, this tape could have been essential. Seen along the way are Zutty Singleton, Paul Barbarin, Tony Sbarbaro, Sonny Greer, Chick Webb, Gene Krupa, Jo Jones, Big Sid Catlett, Dave Tough, Ray Bauduc, Ray McKinley, Cozy Cole, Louie Bellson, Buddy Rich, Kenny Clarke ("Strike Up the Band" with Lucky Thompson and pianist Patti Bown in a 1960 quintet), Max Roach, Shelly Manne and Art Blakey. Some of the dates given are wrong, and key musicians who are not drummers are often not identified.

♪④ Legends of Jazz Drumming Part Two, 1950–1970
(1996, 73 minutes, DCI Music Video)

The same comments about **Part One** in this series apply to this tape except, in addition to Bellson and Haynes, Jack DeJohnette comments and reminisces a bit. While the talking is interesting, it cuts into the playing time. The excerpts of performances feature Shelly Manne, Vernell Fournier (with Ahmad Jamal), a couple of seconds apiece of Chico Hamilton, Ed Thigpen, Jimmy Cobb and Sam Woodyard, Connie Kay (with the Modern Jazz Quartet), Joe Morello playing "Take Five" with Dave Brubeck, Art Blakey, Philly Joe Jones, Roy Haynes, Sonny Payne (taking a colorful solo on "Old Man River" with Count Basie in 1959), Mel Lewis, Elvin Jones, Jack DeJohnette and Tony Williams. It is a pity that complete performances were not included.

♪⑤ Legends of Jazz Guitar Volume 1
(1995, 60 minutes, Vestapol)

Vestapol has come out with three videotapes (all have been reissued on DVD) in their **Legends of Jazz Guitar** series, featuring bop-oriented jazz guitarists, primarily filmed in the 1970s and '80s. Because most of the performances by Herb Ellis, Barney Kessel, Charlie Byrd, Joe Pass and Wes Montgomery are also available on other tapes in more complete form, and due to the similarity of the styles, this series is at best a decent sampling of the idiom. Volume 1 features Wes Montgomery in 1965 on a British television show ("Twisted Blues," "Jingles" and "Yesterdays"), a pair of unaccompanied solos from Joe Pass ("Original Blues in G" and "Do Nothin' Till You Hear from Me") Barney Kessel ("Basie's Blues" and "The Shadow of Your Smile"), Herb Ellis ("Sweet Georgia Brown" and a medley of "It Might As Well Be Spring" and "Things Ain't What They Used to Be") and a collaboration by Ellis and Kessel ("A Slow Burn").

♪⑤ Legends of Jazz Guitar Volume 2
(1995, 60 minutes, Vestapol)

This DVD has ten performances by bop-oriented guitarists. Most interesting is 1969's "Blue Mist" because, in addition to Barney Kessel and Kenny Burrell, it has a rare filmed solo from Grant Green. Wes Montgomery is seen on two more numbers from a 1965 television show ("Full House" and "'Round Midnight") and otherwise there are selections from Joe Pass ("Original Blues in A" and "Prelude to a Kiss"), Kenny Burrell from 1987 ("Lover Man" and "My Ship"), Barney Kessel ("BBC Blues") and Charlie Byrd ("Jitterbug Waltz" and "Isn't It a Lovely Day"). As with Volume 1, most of these numbers (other than the cuts with Burrell) are available elsewhere.

♪⑤ Legends of Jazz Guitar Volume 3
(1995, 63 minutes, Vestapol)

This is the most wide-ranging of the three volumes in this series. Most interesting are the selections featuring Jim Hall, who plays "I'm Getting Sentimental Over You" and "Valse Hot" in 1964 (the latter also features flugelhornist Art Farmer) and a duet with pianist Michel Petrucciani in 1986 on "My Funny Valentine." Also somewhat rare is Pat Martino in 1987 playing "Do You Have a Name." However, the other performances, all of which feature Barney Kessel in different settings, are also available on other videotapes.

Kessel in 1969 performs a medley of "Manha de Carnaval" and "Samba de Orfeu," he jams "Lady Be Good" and "Flintstones Theme" with Herb Ellis, and the Great Guitars (Kessel, Ellis and Charlie Byrd) play a medley of "Nuages," "Goin' Out of My Head" and "Flying Home."

 ### Lennie Tristano Solo: The Copenhagen Concert
(2000, 41 minutes, Storyville)

The highly original pianist Lennie Tristano became semi-retired as a performer in the early '50s, preferring to work as a teacher and a guru for like-minded up-and-coming jazz musicians, but he made occasional recordings and appearances during the next 20 years. Tristano was seldom captured on film, making this set from October 31, 1965, a real rarity. The concert (performed at the Tivoli Gardens Concert Hall in Copenhagen, Denmark) was broadcast on Danish television, and it features Tristano playing solo piano on seven standards and two of his originals ("Darn that Dream," "Lullaby of the Leaves," "Expressions," "You Don't Know What Love Is," "Tivoli Gardens Swing," "Ghost of a Chance," "It's You or No One," "Imagination," "Tangerine"). Unfortunately the music is not as exciting as one would hope. Starting with a very abstract and dark rendition of "Darn that Dream" and continuing through the dense "Expressions" and a thoughtful "Ghost of a Chance," much of the music is taken out of tempo and emphasizes complex chord voicings. Only a relaxed "Lullaby of the Leaves" and "Tangerine" (the date's high point) show much spirit and swing, showcasing Tristano's powerful bass lines. Otherwise this is a rather introspective and downbeat session, interesting historically but not worth watching more than once or twice.

Leonard Maltin's Movie Memories— Soundies: Vol. 1, The 1940s Music Machine
(1990, 56 minutes, BMG Video)

Film critic and historian Leonard Maltin produced four CDs worth of Soundies from the 1941–46 period. The first volume is a bit of a grab bag, an introduction to the concept of Soundies. Maltin talks a bit about the idiom and then introduces the films, often two or three at a time. There are a few excerpts that show the diversity of what was filmed, but most of the Soundies are complete. Included on this tape are Louis Armstrong (**I'll Be Glad When You're Dead, You Rascal You**), Les Brown and a 17-year-old Doris Day (**My Lost Horizon**), Stan Kenton with future actress Cyd Charisse (**This Love of Mine**), Rita Rio and actor Alan Ladd (**I Look at You**), the Les Paul Trio and singer Carolyn Gray (**Shoo Shoo Baby**), Larry Clinton's 1943 band with an unidentified singer (**My Reverie**), the King Cole Trio (**Errand Boy for Rhythm**), Stan Kenton's big band with bassist Ed Safranski and trombonist Milt Bernhart (**Southern Scandal**), the Mills Brothers and Dorothy Dandridge (**Paper Doll**), Fats Waller (**Honeysuckle Rose**), Cab Calloway (**Minnie the Moocher**), Vincent Lopez (**Minute Waltz**), the Three Murtah Sisters (**Arthur Murray Taught Me Dancing in a Hurray**), Gray Gordon (**Scrub Me Mama with a Boogie Beat**) and Duke Ellington (**Cotton Tail**).

 ### Leonard Maltin's Movie Memories— Soundies: Vol. 2, Singing Stars of the Swing Era
(1990, 54 minutes, BMG Video)

Volume 2 in this excellent series focuses on vocalists and often reaches beyond jazz. Dick Hogan (**I Can't Get Started**), Lina Romay (**Don't Get Around Much Anymore**), Patricia Ellis (**I Thought about You**), Francis Langford (**Someday When the Clouds Roll By**), Lanny Ross (**The Night We Met in Honomu**), Marilyn Maxwell (**Tea on the Terrace**) and Buddy Rogers (**Dreamsville, Ohio**) would never be considered major jazz singers, but in general their Soundies hold one's interest. Of stronger significance jazz-wise are the Soundies with Glenn Miller's Modernaires (**Juke Box Saturday Night**), Jimmy Dorsey with Helen O'Connell (**All Reet**), Gene Krupa (**Thanks for the Boogie Ride**), Nick Lucas (**Tip Toe through the Tulips**), Hoagy Carmichael (**Lazy Bones**), the Delta Rhythm Boys (**Take the "A" Train**), Gray Gordon with

Meredith Blake (**Beat Me Daddy, Eight to the Bar**), Martha Tilton with Bobby Sherwood (**Love Turns Winter into Spring**), Liz Tilton with Matty Malneck (**Ah Yes, There's Good Blues Tonight**), the Dinning Sisters (**No Can Do**) and Stan Kenton with June Christy (**It's Been a Long, Long Time**).

 Leonard Maltin's Movie Memories—
Soundies: Vol. 3, Big Band Swing
(1990, 58 minutes, BMG Video)

The third volume in this series mostly features big bands, although some of the performances could have fit into the vocalists' tape. Leonard Maltin says a few words at the beginning and in a couple of interludes, but mostly lets the performances speak for themselves. Best among the clips are the much-reissued Gene Krupa performance of **Let Me Off Uptown**, Johnny Long's band doing their one hit **In a Shanty in Old Shanty Town**, Will Bradley with Ray McKinley romping on **Barnyard Bounce**, Count Basie's **Air Mail Special** and Stan Kenton with June Christy performing **Tampico**. This tape also includes Glen Gray (**Sentimental Journey**), Charlie Spivak (**Comin thru the Rye**), Tony Pastor (**Paradiddle Joe**), Larry Clinton (**Dipsey Doodle**), Les Elgart (**I May Be Wrong**), Sonny Dunham (**Skylark**), Ray Sinatra (a swinging **Boogie Woogie Upstairs**), Ozzie Nelson (**Wave-A-Stick Blues**), an out-of-place Rita Rey (**Pan-Americonga**), Cab Calloway (**Foo a Little Bally-Hoo**), Will Osborne (**Star Dust**), Jimmy Dorsey (**Bar Babble**) and a surprisingly jazz-oriented clip from Lawrence Welk (**Doing You Good**).

 Leonard Maltin's Movie Memories—
Soundies: Vol. 4, Harlem Highlights
(1990, 51 minutes, BMG Video)

The fourth and final volume of this valuable series includes some superior Soundies, although many of these are common and available elsewhere. Concentrating on Black performers, this tape has the King Cole Trio

and Ida James (**Is You Is or Is You Ain't My Baby**), Bill "Bojangles" Robinson (**Let's Scuffle**), the Mills Brothers (**Till Then** and **Up the Lazy River**), Cab Calloway (**Virginia, Georgia and Caroline** and **The Skunk Song**), Pat Flowers (**Scotch Boogie**), the Jubilaires (**Brother Bill**), Day, Dawn and Dusk (**Rigaletto**), the Delta Rhythm Boys (**Don't Get Around Much Anymore**), Maxine Sullivan (**Some of these Days**), Louis Jordan (**Tillie**), Dorothy Dandridge (**Cow Cow Boogie**), dancer Katherine Dunham (**Cuban Episode**), and Lucky Millinder with Sister Rosetta Tharpe (**Four or Five Times**). For some reason there is a medley of excerpts from Fats Waller's Soundies (rather than showing them complete), but at the tape's conclusion, Waller's **Ain't Misbehavin'** is seen (partly behind the closing credits).

 Les McCann & Eddie Harris: Swiss Movement
(1996, 45 minutes, Rhino Home Video)

At the 1968 Montreux Jazz Festival, the surprise hit was the set performed by the Les McCann Trio (which includes bassist Leroy Vinnegar and drummer Donald Dean) with tenor saxophonist Eddie Harris and trumpeter Benny Bailey (who had never previously played with McCann) sitting in as guests. Their versions of "Compared to What" (which has McCann's most famous vocal) and Harris's catchy "Cold Duck Time" became quite popular when the LP from the festival was released. Decades later, it was revealed that the classic set was filmed, and this video is the result. It has three of the original five songs from the album ("Cold Duck Time," "Kathleen's Theme," "Compared to What"), a number not originally issued until the music appeared on CD ("Kaftan") and, as a bonus, Eddie Harris performing his "Listen Here" with an unidentified group at the same festival. On the album, the crowd seems to go quite crazy during Bailey's exciting trumpet solo on "Cold Duck Time" and on the film, it is obvious why: Ella Fitzgerald had entered the hall and taken a seat right at that moment!

Les McCann: Live in New Orleans
(60 minutes, 1991, Leisure Video)

Les McCann and his "Magic Band" circa 1990–91 are featured on this video. Unfortunately, the songs ("I'm All Strung Out on You," "Bat Yam," "Just Like Magic," "Someday We'll Meet Again," "I Got Me a Lady—She Drives A Little Blue Volkswagen Car," "Compared to What") are not too memorable other than a remake of McCann's hit "Compared to What." The band (a quartet with Bobby Bryant, Jr., on saxophones, bassist Curtis Robinson and drummer Tony St. James) is decent, but not a standout. The music is funky and soulful, but a bit run-of-the-mill.

 Les Paul: Living Legend of the Electric Guitar
(1992, 60 minutes, BMG Video)

This video is in two parts. At first a narrator relates the Les Paul story, documenting Paul's career as a versatile guitarist, inventor and innovator with plenty of photos shown and a few brief excerpts of his playing. The bulk of this tape has the Les Paul Trio (with rhythm guitarist Lou Pallo and bassist Gary Mazaroppi) performing at Fat Tuesday's, with brief interview segments (often covering the same territory as the opening part of the film) between some of the songs. Paul is heard in excellent and good-humored form, stretching out on "How High the Moon," "Stardust," "Nuages," "Body and Soul," "Sweet Georgia Brown," "St. Louis Blues," "Exactly Like You," "Melancholy Baby," "Over the Rainbow" and "Avalon."

Les Paul & Friends: He Changed the Music
*(1988, 60 minutes, A*Vision)*

This HBO television special celebrates Les Paul's wide range of music with a live performance from the Brooklyn Academy of Music on August 18, 1988. The guitarist and his trio perform "Lover," and then Paul is joined (and sometimes replaced) by a variety of guest artists, most of whom are outside of jazz. Rock guitarist Eddie Van Halen shows off his virtuosity, B.B. King joins with Paul on "Every Day I Have the Blues," Carly Simon sings

"It Happens Every Day," and Steve Miller performs "God Bless the Child." Rita Coolidge does her best to fill in for Mary Ford on "Am I Blue" and "I'm a Fool to Cry," and the Paul trio plays nostalgic versions of "Over the Rainbow" and "It's Been a Long Long Time." David Gilmore wails on a blues, Stanley Jordan duets with Paul on "Georgia on My Mind," and Waylon Jennings drops by to sing "I Really Don't Want to Know." For the grand finale, the Stray Cats start "Blue Suede Shoes" and then welcome back all of the guitarists for a blues jam including Van Halen, King, Jordan and the guest of honor. Les Paul wraps up the hour with "How High the Moon." In general this show is fast moving and holds one's interest, emphasizing the importance that Les Paul's inventions and innovations had on the world of music.

 Let's Get Lost *(1989, 119 minutes, Novus Home Video)*

This intriguing if bizarre portrait of Chet Baker late in his life often misses the mark completely. Baker is portrayed by director/producer Bruce Weber as a washed-up singer who occasional plays trumpet, not as an excellent trumpeter who was still playing (if not singing) quite well despite his very erratic lifestyle. Baker is interviewed (for what it is worth) though the cat-fighting and anecdotes from his wife, ex-wives, girlfriends (both past and present) and Jack Sheldon are much more illuminating. Some of the scenes are obvious setups and quite ludicrous. One ends up feeling sorry for the family that Baker left behind. Baker performs a few numbers (including "My Funny Valentine," "Imagination" and "My One and Only Love") while mostly sounding in sub-par form. There are also excerpts from a few television and film appearances during the 1950s and '60s. Although some fans who really love Chet Baker will enjoy this film, it is largely a wasted opportunity.

Lionel Hampton: One Night Stand
(1994, 53 minutes, Video Artists International)

This video contains a 1971 television special that is ridiculously overcrowded with far too many performers, as if the producer was afraid that the show would lose the attention of viewers if it stayed in one spot for more than a minute. **One Night Stand**, which features vibraphonist Lionel Hampton and Mel Tormé as emcee, has a bewildering assortment of musicians and singers. Hampton and his big band play a brief original, Mel Tormé sings "Ridin' High," Dusty Springfield (!) is featured on "Ain't No Sunshine" and "Come Back to Me," and Gene Krupa performs "Sing, Sing, Sing" for one of his final times. After Mel Tormé croons the forgettable ballad "Cool Autumn Wind," Hampton performs the pop song "Traffic Light" with a vocal trio, a go-go dancer who struts her stuff on top of the piano and trumpeter Cat Anderson, who blasts out some screaming notes. Johnny Mercer with pianist Joe Bushkin and Tormé sings a medley of his hits, and the pop group Ocean performs "Put Your Hand in the Hand."

Chet Baker is portrayed during his final period in the somewhat bizarre documentary *Let's Get Lost*.

The most potentially interesting section is next, but is ruined by its brevity. Hampton leads an all-star group on "Ring Dem Bells" that includes Roy Eldridge, Tyree Glenn, Zoot Sims, Bushkin, Milt Hinton, Krupa and an unidentified guitarist. But other than Hampton's speedy two-fingered spot on piano, the solos are limited to one chorus apiece. Hamp, Krupa, Teddy Wilson and an unseen bassist play two choruses of "Undecided" and four of "How High the Moon." B.B. King pops by to sing one and a half choruses of a bluesy pop song and a half-chorus of "Every Day I Have the Blues." Tormé then leads Dusty Springfield, Johnny Mercer, B.B. King, Gene Krupa, Ocean and Hampton through a very odd "Story of the Blues," which is essentially a medley of songs having nothing to do with each other. "Flying Home" has Gerry Mulligan being largely wasted, and the whole shebang concludes with Krupa, Hampton, Tormé and Buddy Rich all trading off on drums; Mel Lewis is introduced, but is lost in the background. This show is quite a mess though interesting in its own odd way.

 Los Hombres Calientes: Live
(2004, 65 minutes, Basin Street Records)

One of the most exciting Afro-Cuban/Latin jazz bands, Los Hombres Calientes is co-led by the brilliant trumpeter Irvin Mayfield and conguero-singer Bill Summers. This DVD has highlights from their March 28, 2003, performance at the House of Blues in New Orleans. Performing before an enthusiastic dancing audience (which includes a couple of dancers who sometimes appear onstage with the band), Los Hombres Calientes plays a set of mostly riff-filled originals ("Vodou Hoodoo Babalu," "Foforo Fo Firi," "El Negro," "Latin Tinge," "Creole Groove," "New Bus Stop," "A Night in Tunisia"). These selections make up in their creative frameworks for what they lack as compositions (other than Dizzy Gillespie's "A Night in Tunisia"). In addition to the co-leaders, the group has an excellent horn section (trumpeter Leon Brown, trombonist Stephen Walker and tenor saxophonist Devin Phillips), each of whom get solo space on a couple numbers, and a rhythm section that includes Victor Atkins on piano and electric keyboards, Ronald Markham on organ and piano, electric bassist Edwin Livingston, and Ricky Sebastian and Jaz Sawyer on drums and percussion. There are some group vocals in spots, and Summers takes a few solos, both vocally and on percussion. After the first number, Summers, Mayfield and the president of Basin Street Records, Mark Samuels, talk a bit about how the band got started. There are also some clips of the band and local musicians in Cuba, Trinidad and Haiti, but the emphasis is on the fiery live show. Included as bonus features are a music video that is mostly a recut of "Vodou Hoodoo Babalu," some footage from their travels (including a steel band briefly playing "A Night in Tunisia") and a few teasers from other Basin Street acts performing live. The latter consists of excerpts from Jon Cleary ("When You Get Back"), Theresa Andersson ("Break Up"), Henry Butler ("The Game Has Just Begun"), Kermit Ruffins (the calypso "Skokiaan"), Irvin Mayfield ("The Denial"), Jason Marsalis ("The Upper Second Line") and Dr. Michael White ("Louisian-i-a"). One imagines that the full-length versions will be found in future DVDs.

 The Lou Rawls Show: With Duke Ellington
(1991, 48 minutes, View Video)

This tape is a straight reissue of an early '70s Lou Rawls television special. The music is quite dated with such pop tunes as "Tobacco Road," "Oh Happy Day" and "It Was a Very Good Year" joining a program of forgettable material. The only value to the set is that Duke Ellington (sans his orchestra) makes a guest appearance, playing "Satin Doll" with a studio orchestra and backing Rawls's singing on "Sophisticated Lady." Although interesting, it is certainly not enough of a reason to get the tape.

 Louie Bellson: And His Big Band
(1986, 55 minutes, View Video)

Louie Bellson heads an 18-piece big band for six songs in 1986, including "The Drum Squad," "Blues for Freddy"

and "Explosion." Bellson gets his share of solo space as does trumpeter Randy Brecker and tenor saxophonist Michael Brecker. Also notable in the orchestra (although not featured much) are trumpeters Lew Soloff and Benny Bailey, trombonist Jiggs Whigham, altoist Herb Geller and baritonist Howard Johnson. The music is fine, but no real surprises or excitement occur on this DVD and the performances are largely forgettable.

 Louis Armstrong: 100th Anniversary
(50 minutes, 2001, Passport Entertainment)

Although there is some narration by Paula Kelly and a few comments from Gerald Wilson and Red Holloway, this DVD makes no real attempt to tell the Louis Armstrong story. However, the performance clips, with three

The *100th Anniversary* DVD includes some rarely seen TV clips of Louis Armstrong during the '50s and '60s.

exceptions, are rare and they are usually shown complete. There is an excerpt from the 1932 short **I'll Be Glad When You're Dead, You Rascal You** (with Armstrong playing the title cut) and the Soundie versions of "I'll Be Glad When You're Dead" and "Swingin' on Nothing" have been reissued elsewhere. Much rarer are a rendition of "Now You Has Jazz" from a Bing Crosby television show (shortly after Satch and Bing filmed **High Society**), 1952 versions of "Birth of the Blues" (with Eddie Fisher) and "The Boppenpoof Song," a second "Birth of the Blues" (with Frank Sinatra), "Gabriel Blew His Horn" from a mid-'50s television show (with Trummy Young, Edmond Hall, Billy Kyle, Arvell Shaw and Barrett Deems) and "Hello Dolly" from 1966 (with Tyree Glenn, clarinetist Joe Muranyi, Kyle, bassist Buddy Catlett and drummer Danny Barcelona). The same group (with Buster Bailey on clarinet) is well featured on a 1965 special performing "Mack the Knife," "I've Got a Lot of Living to Do," "Struttin' with Some Barbecue," "Avalon" (a feature for Glenn on vibes) and "Ole Miss." Throughout, Armstrong is heard in excellent form (he was still hitting high notes in 1965), and this valuable DVD adds to the legacy of Louis Armstrong on film.

Louis Jordan and His Tympany Band
(1992, 76 minutes, Storyville)

This videotape has all of altoist/singer Louis Jordan's musical performances from three films in which he starred during 1946–48: **Beware** ("You Gotta Have the Beat," "How Long Must I Wait for You," "Hold On," "Long Legged Lizzie," "Good Morning Heartache," "In the Land of the Buffalo Nickel," "Got an Old Fashioned Passion for You," "Don't You Worry 'Bout that Mule," "Salt Pork, West Virginia," "Beware"), **Reet, Petite and Gone** ("Let the Good Times Roll," "Texas & Pacific," "Reet, Petite & Gone," "Wham Sam," "All for the Love of Lil," "The Green Grass Grows All Around," "I Know What You're Putting Down," "That Chick's Too Young to Fry," "Ain't that Just Like a Woman," "If It's Love that You Want That's Me") and **Look**

Out Sister ("Caldonia," "Jack You're Dead," "Got a New Ten-Gallon Hat," "Don't Burn the Candles at Both Ends," "We Can't Agree," "Boogie in the Barnyard," "You're Much Too Fat," "Turkey in the Straw," "I Got those Roamin' Blues," "Early in the Morning," "Look Out Sister"). The 202 combined minutes from the movies have been cut down to 76 minutes of pure music, with the lightweight plots taken out. Jordan was in prime form during this period, and he was very well featured in the films, with all of his selections complete and unhampered by dialogue or irrelevant action. There are 31 numbers in all (a few are quite brief) on this tape, making this set very complementary to other videos that feature Jordan's Soundies of the era. The performer's likable personality, ability to sing a wide variety of material (including tongue-twisting lyrics full of philosophical ideas) and his fine alto solos made him a very popular figure throughout the 1940s.

 ### Louis Prima: The Wildest
(1999, 80 minutes, Image Entertainment)

Louis Prima had a long and episodic career, as a New Orleans trumpeter, a comic Italian vocalist, leader of a swing band and one of the most popular attractions in Las Vegas starting in the mid-'50s. In Las Vegas, Prima combined New Orleans jazz, swing standards, early R&B, a shuffle beat, a rock 'n' roll sensibility, his wife Keely Smith's ballad vocals and his own zany Italian humor to form a unique blend of styles, foreshadowing retro swing of the 1990s. This DVD is full of priceless clips, some of which are fairly complete. There are comments from family members, associates, writers Bruce Raeburn and Will Friedwald, Keely Smith, tenor saxophonist Sam Butera, his older brother Leon Prima, Woody Herman and Prima's last wife Gia Maione. But it is the music that makes this a special film: "Way Down Yonder in New Orleans," "That Old Black Magic," "Basin Street Blues," "Chinatown, My Chinatown," "Oh Babe," "Night Train," "Caldonia," and a medley of "Just a Gigolo" and "I Ain't Got Nobody."

Machito: A Latin Jazz Legacy
(1987, 58 minutes, Icarus Films)

This documentary of the pacesetting Cuban bandleader Frank "Machito" Grillo does a very effective job of summing up both his life story and his musical legacy. There are some vintage film clips, street performances and comments from Ray Barretto, Dizzy Gillespie, Tito Puente and Dexter Gordon.

 The Making of Burning for Buddy, Part One
(1996, 83 minutes, DCI Music Video)

In May 1994, drummer Nick Peart organized a tribute to the late, great Buddy Rich. Peart and Cathy Rich (Buddy's daughter) brought back the Buddy Rich Orchestra, and during a two-week period recorded a song or two with 18 different drummers, resulting in a CD for Atlantic. The proceedings were also filmed, and the performances of 15 drummers with the big band have been released as two videotapes. This part begins with an archival clip of Buddy Rich taking a typically miraculous drum solo. None of the seven drummers featured on this tape come up to Rich's level (none ever did) although they have their moments. Peart is featured on "Cotton Tail" and also performing are Marvin "Smitty" Smith ("Ya Gotta Try"), Dave Weckl (a slower-than-usual rendition of "Mercy, Mercy, Mercy"), Kenny Aronoff ("Straight No Chaser"), Ed Shaughnessy ("Shawnee"), Steve Gadd ("Love for Sale") and Bill Bruford (whose original "Lingo" is out of place). Although tenor saxophonist Steve Marcus has a few solos as do a couple of other sidemen, the big band is mostly in the background, with the camerawork focusing on the drummers. Along the way the seven drummers plus Omar Hakim, Joe Morello, Billy Cobham, Simon Phillips, Steve Smith, Steve Ferrone, Rod Morgenstein and Rich's old friend Stanley Kay tell stories about discovering Rich, meeting him and what he meant to them as aspiring drummers, doing their best to describe his technical skills. This is a heartfelt tribute.

 The Making of Burning for Buddy, Part Two
(1996, 89 minutes, DCI Music Video)

The second of two videos centered around Nick Peart's tribute to the late Buddy Rich, this film has studio performances with the Buddy Rich Big Band featuring drummers Rod Morgenstern ("Machine"), Omar Hakim ("Slo-Funk"), Joe Morello ("Drumorello"), Steve Smith ("Nutville"), Matt Sorum ("Beulah Witch"), Simon Phillips ("Dancing Men"), Billy Cobham ("Milestones") and Steve Ferrone ("Pick Up the Pieces"). Along the way there are comments about Buddy Rich by Peart, Morgenstein, Bill Bruford, Kenny Aronoff, Ed Shaughnessy, Stanley Kay, Fred Gruber, Joe Morello, Steve Gadd and Dave Weckl although there is less storytelling than on Part One. The playing is fine, but the closing film clip of the remarkable Buddy Rich (from 1984 performing the last ten minutes of "Channel One Suite") easily takes honors.

 The Making of Burning for Buddy, Part Three
(1997, 61 minutes, DCI Music Video)

Due to the success of the original **Burning for Buddy** CD, Atlantic Records agreed to have Nick Peart organize and record an encore in 1996; two additional videotapes also resulted. For this project, Peart and Buddy Rich's daughter Cathy Rich decided that it would be a good idea to concentrate on more of the straightahead charts from the Rich Orchestra's repertoire. They talk about the sessions a bit, saxophonist Steve Marcus reminisces about his original meeting with the fiery drummer, and Peart comments on each of the guest drummers. Peart performs "One O'Clock Jump" with the Rich Orchestra, Steve Smith plays "Moment's Notice," Bill Bruford is excellent on the medium-tempo blues waltz "Willowcrest," Kenny Aronoff fares well on "Big Swing Face," and Steve Gadd is featured on "Basically Blues." In addition, Joe Morello plays "Take the 'A' Train" with tenor saxophonist Marcus in a quartet. But as good as everyone plays, Buddy Rich himself (seen at the beginning of this tape performing a solo in 1948 and concluding the hour with a stunning feature from 1981) once again takes honors. There was never a drummer on his technical level.

The Making of Burning for Buddy, Part Four
(1997, 61 minutes, DCI Music Video)

Taken from the same recording sessions as Part Three, this tape once again has Nick Peart commenting on each of the drummers who are featured and the arrangements for the Buddy Rich tribute. Cathy Rich also reminisces briefly on the project as does Steve Marcus. This time around five different drummers are showcased with the Buddy Rich ghost orchestra: Marvin "Smitty" Smith (the uptempo "Standing Up in a Hammock"), David Garibaldi ("Groovin' Hard"), Simon Phillips ("Goodbye Yesterday"), an enthusiastic Gregg Bissonette ("In a Mellow Tone") and Dave Weckl (the rapid "Time Check"). In addition, Buddy Rich opens the tape playing "If I Were a Bell" in 1984 with a trio and finishes it off with a stunning solo from 1985 on "West Side Story Suite."

The Manhattan Transfer: Vocalese Live
(2000, 80 minutes, Image Entertainment)

The Manhattan Transfer, arguably the premiere jazz vocal group since the 1970s, is capable of singing in nearly any style. The emphasis on these live performances from Tokyo (February 20 and 21, 1986) is on jazz since the Transfer had recently released their acclaimed *Vocalese* album. The quartet (Tim Hauser, Alan Paul, Janis Siegel and Cheryl Bentyne) is joined by their fine backup group (keyboardist Yoran Gershovsky, Dan Roberts on tenor and other reeds, guitarist Wayne Johnson, bassist Alex Blake and drummer Buddy Williams) on a particularly inspired set ("Four Brothers," "Rambo," "Meet Benny Bailey," "Airegin," "To You," "Sing Joy Spring," "Move," "That's Killer Joe," "The Duke of Dubuque," "Gloria," "Heart's Desire," "Birdland," "On the Boulevard," "Shaker Song," "Java Jive," "Blue Champagne," "How High the Moon," "Boy from New York City," "Ray's Rockhouse"). As can be ascertained from the titles, the first half of this program

is strictly boppish jazz, including a speedy rendition of "Airegin," Siegel singing Clifford Brown's "Joy Spring" solo on "Sing Joy Spring," and a rapid "Move." Things bog down a bit with a rather silly and overlong "Killer Joe." From that point on, the Manhattan Transfer runs through some of their earlier hits that cover doo wop, rock 'n' roll, pop and "Birdland." These renditions are excellent and "How High the Moon" (based on the Les Paul version) and "Ray's Rockhouse" end the set with some fine swinging. Overall, this is the Manhattan Transfer's definitive DVD so far.

The Marsalis Family: A Jazz Celebration
(2003, 124 minutes, Marsalis Music/Rounder Records)

The retirement of Ellis Marsalis from teaching served as a good excuse for this special concert (from August 4, 2001), which brings together the pianist with his four musical sons: trumpeter Wynton Marsalis, tenor and soprano saxophonist Branford Marsalis, trombonist Delfeayo Marsalis and drummer Jason Marsalis; bassist Roland Guerin completes the core group. The rhythm section starts off the show with "Surrey with the Fringe on Top" (with Guerin slapping his bass à la Milt Hinton) and the ballad "After." "Sultry Serenade" features Delfeayo, while "Cain and Abel" has Wynton and Branford in a pianoless quartet, showing that their interplay is still quite magical. Harry Connick, Jr., joins Ellis for an excellent piano duo version of "Caravan," and he sings "St. James Infirmary," joined by trombonist Lucien Barbarin. Connick also jams on "Limehouse Blues" with Barbarin and some musicians from his regular band (tenor saxophonist Ned Goold, bassist Neal Caine and drummer Arthur Latin II). The five Marsalises and Guerin finally share the stage for the hard bop original "Swingin' at the Haven," "Nostalgic Impressions," "Struttin' with Some Barbecue" and "Twelve's It." As an encore, Ellis plays solo piano on "The Party's Over." The bonus cuts are 33 minutes long, consisting of very interesting interviews with the Marsalises and Connick about each of the members of the Marsalis family. Although it is a pity that Wynton and Branford are not showcased more extensively (their improvised ensembles are quite exciting), this is a well-conceived and easily recommended DVD.

Marsalis on Music
(1995, 200 minutes, Sony Classical Film & Video)

This four-part series, which is available as one box or in four separate sets, has Wynton Marsalis teaching children about music and jazz in general. The chapters are **Listening for Clues** (dealing with the form and structure of music), **Sousa to Satchmo**, **Tackling the Monster** (how to practice) and **Why Toes Tap** (the importance of rhythm). Marsalis is joined along the way by the Tanglewood Music Center Orchestra, the Tanglewood Music Center Wind Band, cellist Yo Yo Ma and musicians from his regular groups. Although primarily of interest to music beginners, there are some insightful comments (and excellent playing) that should interest Marsalis fans.

Marty Krystall Quartet Plus One
(2000, 60 minutes, K2B2)

Filmed in someone's house, this is a straight performance film without any talking at all, although the personnel and the song titles are flashed on the screen. Marty Krystall is a high-powered and adventurous improviser who during the set mostly plays tenor but also takes two numbers on bass clarinet and one on soprano. He is joined by Hugh Schick (primarily on piano but also playing trumpet on two cuts), bassist Jack Bone, drummer Barry Saporstein and on a few numbers Brenton Banks on violin or piano. The repertoire is quite intriguing, since it consists of a variety of rare Herbie Nichols songs ("'Orse at Safari," "Hangover Triangle," "Beyond Recall," "Trio," "Wildflower"), Bizet's "Prelude and Aragonaise from Carmen," Thelonious Monk's "Evidence," Duke Ellington's "Black and Tan Fantasy" and Krystall's "Press Submit." The post-bop playing is excellent, but the balance is a little off since the piano, bass and violin are not loud enough in spots. The main reason to acquire this video is for Marty Krystall's passionate and inventive playing.

Max Roach: In Concert & In Session
(1990, 60 minutes, DCI Music Video)

This tape has two different projects released in full. First Max Roach is seen at the 1982 Kool Jazz Festival in New York performing six unaccompanied drum solos that emphasize his ability to construct logical improvisations and the potentially melodic nature of the drums. The second half is essentially a filmed press kit dealing with the Roach Quartet's **Chattahoochie Red** album, a project featuring tenor saxophonist Odeon Pope, trumpeter Cecil Bridgewater and bassist Calvin Hill. While the drum solos from the first part of this tape have their moments of interest, the "In Session" portion is a bit like watching an overlong commercial.

Maxine Sullivan: Love to Be in Love
(1990, 48 minutes, Jezebel Productions)

The gently swinging and subtle singer Maxine Sullivan is lovingly profiled in this documentary, much of which was filmed a couple of years before her death in 1987. She starts out singing her hit "Loch Lomond" in a group with tenor saxophonist Scott Hamilton and is seen at a recording session from December 1985 with Hamilton and pianist Dick Hyman, performing part of "Under a Blanket of Blue." As Sullivan talks about her early days, her life story is told through photos and film appearances. A clip from 1939's **St. Louis Blues** has her singing "Loch Lomond" again and she is also seen in the movie **Going Places** (interacting with Louis Armstrong), in her Soundie **Some of these Days** and during part of a late 1960s version of "I'm Gonna Sit Right Down and Write Myself a Letter" with trombonists Tyree Glenn and Bill Watrous. Marian McPartland reminisces about seeing the singer in England in the mid-'40s, and there are comments from Scott Hamilton and record producer Ted

Ono. A nearly complete version of "Georgia on My Mind" from a late period concert with Hamilton and Howard Alden is shown, as is part of "You Hit the Spot" from a record date with Hyman, Hamilton, bassist Major Holley and drummer Mel Lewis. There are also scenes of her during a European tour near the end of her life. Although it would have been better to have complete performances, perhaps expanding this documentary to 60 minutes, **Love to Be in Love** is an informative and enjoyable look at a talented swing singer.

 ### Meet the Bandleaders
(1984, 50 minutes, Swingtime Video 101)

In 1984, the Swingtime Video label came out with a series of videotapes titled **Meet the Bandleaders**, which usually feature several swing-oriented orchestras on each release. The material generally consists of performances from 1964–65 by the surviving big bands on performances made originally for a television series, playing before dancing audiences filled with middle-aged fans. In addition, several of the tapes include band shorts from the 1940s. Some of the collections are of little interest to jazz viewers and these will be skipped: Swingtime Video 103 (Tex Beneke, Ralph Flanagan, Les and Larry Elgart and Vaughn Monroe, all from 1965), Swingtime Video 106 (Lawrence Welk, Russ Morgan, Hal Kemp and Jan Garber), Swingtime Video 107 (Guy Lombardo) and Swingtime Video 109 (Hal Kemp, Johnny Long, Frankie Carle, Jan Garber and Art Mooney). In addition, Swingtime Video 113, which features a Stan Kenton performance from 1962, has been reissued in more complete form as **Stan Kenton** (Vintage Jazz Classics 2007). The nine most jazz-oriented tapes are reviewed here.

Swingtime 101 starts with Count Basie's orchestra in 1964 performing "One O'Clock Jump," "April in Paris," "Big Brother," "Git" (Leon Thomas takes the vocal), "I Can't Stop Loving You," "Jumpin' at the Woodside" and "This Could Be the Start of Something Big." Lionel Hampton is as excitable as ever in 1965 on "Airmail Special,"

"Broadway," "Cute" and "Hamp's Boogie Woogie." Duke Ellington's orchestra (also in 1965) performs the usual versions of "Do Nothing Till You Hear from Me," "Rockin' in Rhythm," "Satin Doll" and "Take the 'A' Train" plus the lesser known "Prowling Cat."

 ### Meet the Bandleaders
(1984, 50 minutes, Swingtime Video 102)

Most of the performances on this tape, which dates from 1965, emphasize nostalgia swing. Harry James provides the high points in a set that consists of "Caravan," "Ciribiribin," "Come Rain or Come Shine," "Green Onions," "I'm Beginning to See the Light," "Rainbow Kiss," "Shiny Stockings," "Take the 'A' Train" and "That's All." Featured are Corky Corcoran on tenor, trombonist Ray Sims, Buddy Rich and singer Cathy Carter. Otherwise this tape is of lesser interest. Ray McKinley leads the Glenn Miller ghost band through "Little Brown Jug," "Rhapsody in Blue" and "String of Pearls," Si Zentner's dance band plays two versions of their lone hit "Up the Lazy River" plus "Puddle Jumpin'," "Sentimental Journey" and "Without a Song," and trumpeter Ralph Marterie's orchestra performs melodic versions of "Just Friends," "Little Girl Blue" and "Tangerine."

 ### Meet the Bandleaders
(1984, 50 minutes, Swingtime Video 104)

One of the best tapes in this series, this set features four very different bands. Tex Beneke leads the Glenn Miller ghost band in 1946 (the short was originally called **Melody Time**) when the big band featured many alumni. The enthusiasm was still very much present as the large ensemble (which includes a full string section) performs "In the Mood," a medley, "American Patrol" and "The Woodchuck Song." Bobby Nichols is heard on trumpet. Clarinetist Jerry Wald, whose playing and band generally imitated Artie Shaw, sounds fine in a 1942 short that includes "Diga Diga Doo," "Mad about Him Blues," "Trains in the Night" and a vocal by Anita Boyer on "Wonder

Memories of Duke (1984, 85 minutes, A*Vision)

Duke Ellington's tour of Mexico (September 23–29, 1968) was documented and released in 1972 as the 45-minute film **The Mexican Suite**. After Ellington died in 1974, it was decided to take the original performances, rearrange parts of them and put in additional concert footage to transform it into a more substantial picture. Russell Procope and Cootie Williams were interviewed in 1978 and are shown watching parts of the earlier film, which in its new version is nearly twice as long. There is quite a bit of strong music on the video, with the repertoire consisting of "Satin Doll," a memorable medley of "Creole Love Call," "Black and Tan Fantasy" and "The Mooche," "Happy-Go-Lucky Local," "The Mexican Suite" (which would be rewritten and later emerge as "The Latin American Suite"), "It Don't Mean a Thing" (with a vocal by Trish Turner), "I Got It Bad," "Things Ain't What They Used to Be," "Mood Indigo," "Take the 'A' Train," "Sophisticated Lady" and "Do Nothing Till You Hear from Me." Among the main soloists, in addition to Williams and Procope, are Paul Gonsalves, Lawrence Brown, Johnny Hodges and Harry Carney.

 Michael Buble: Come Fly with Me
(2003, 63 minutes, Reprise)

Michael Buble, who was 28 in 2003, is a throwback to Frank Sinatra and Bobby Darin, his two biggest influences. This package has both an eight-song CD and a DVD. Buble clearly has a strong voice even if he lacks originality, but the editors of this DVD should be shot. The camerawork is incredibly busy and the picture skips around constantly during songs, alternating between color and black and white, jumping between the main stage performance and offscreen bits, and ruining every performance. Buble, backed by a nine-piece group, sounds okay, but this set ("Come Fly with Me," "For Once in My Life," "You'll Never Know," "Kissing a Fool," "Sway," "Mack the Knife," "That's All," "Fever," "How Can You Mend a Broken Heart," "The Way You Look Tonight,"

"Moondance," "My Funny Valentine") is very difficult to watch. Did the editors feel that having MTV-like action during the songs (rarely staying in one place for more than five seconds) would keep listeners from realizing how derivative Buble's singing is and the obvious nature of the arrangements? Between songs, the interludes are trivial and the many weak attempts at comedy are annoying. The bonus cuts on the video (studio versions of "The Way You Look Tonight," "For Once in My Life" and "Kissing a Fool") are more watchable since the camerawork is less frantic. Overall it is a pity because Michael Buble has a nice voice and seems to have a charming personality. Hopefully both will be better served on a future DVD.

Miles Davis: Live in Montreal
(1985, 59 minutes, Pioneer Films)

Miles Davis's group in 1985 consisted of guitarist John Scofield, soprano saxophonist Bob Berg, keyboardist Robert Irving III, electric bassist Daryl Jones, drummer Vince Wilburn and percussionist Steve Thornton. This DVD, recorded at the Montreal Jazz Festival on July 28, 1985, gives one a strong sampling of Davis's music at the time. The 14-minute "One Phone Call" is rockish, intense, grooving and noisy. Davis, Berg and a blazing Scofield all have their spots although the music is ensemble-oriented with the trumpeter in the lead. The pop ballad "Human Nature" is surprisingly happy with Davis playing muted and melodically. "Something's on Your Mind" is funky, "Time After Time" shows off Davis's tone, "Code M.D." returns to the original rock mood (sometimes the rhythm section is excessively relentless) and the playful "Jean Pierre" closes the performance.

Miles Davis: Live in Munich
(2002, 132 minutes, Pioneer Films)

The 1988 Miles Davis band (comprised of altoist Kenny Garrett, who also plays some flute and a brief amount of baritone, keyboardists Adam Holzman and Robert Irving

III, guitarist Joe "Foley" McCreary, electric bassist Benjamin Rietveld, drummer Ricky Wellman and percussionist Marilyn Mazur) performs a long set on this videotape. The repertoire ("Perfect Way," "The Senate," "Me & U," "Human Nature," "Wrinkle," "Tutu," "Time After Time," "Splatch," "Heavy Metal Prelude," "Heavy Metal," "Don't Stop Me Now," "Carnival Time," "Tomaas," "New Blues," "Portia") is Davis's usual show of the period. Much of it is rockish but there are some quieter moments, particularly "Human Nature" and "Time After Time." "New Blues" is a bit disappointing (Miles does not seem into the blues that night), and there are some meandering moments along the way. Next to Davis and Garrett, Marilyn Mazur takes honors, contributing three colorful solos. Of particular interest is an informal half-hour interview with the trumpeter that takes place at the end of the tape. He draws a picture while answering questions, states that jazz is more of an attitude than a music, says of leaving some of his former fans behind, "To create you have to be kind of selfish," and comments about his then-current sidemen, "I know who to pick to play this style." This may be the lengthiest on-camera interview of Miles Davis to be released thus far and in some ways it overshadows his performance with his band.

Miles Davis: Miles in Paris
(1990, 60 minutes, Warner Reprise Video)

Filmed on November 3, 1989, at the Paris Jazz Festival, this DVD has a brief interview segment and an excess of stop-action photography, but otherwise is a fine performance film of Miles Davis's group of the period. The trumpeter, altoist Kenny Garrett, keyboardist Kei Akagi, Foley and Benjamin Rietveld on basses, drummer Ricky Wellman and percussionist John Bigham perform "Human Nature," "Amandla," "Tutu," "New Blues" and "Mr. Pastorius." The latter two songs are best. Davis's band has a lighter feel than it did a few years earlier (with Foley's high-note bass playing taking the place of the rockish guitar) but still grooves in a similar fashion.

Miles Davis & Quincy Jones: Live in Montreux
(1998, 75 minutes, Warner/Reprise Video)

In the summer of 1991, just a few months before his death, Miles Davis made the surprise decision to revisit his past. For that year's Montreux Jazz Festival, he was persuaded by Quincy Jones to perform some of the music from his **Birth of the Cool** album and the three main records that he made with arranger Gil Evans: **Miles Ahead**, **Porgy and Bess** and **Sketches of Spain** ("Boplicity," "Maids of Cadiz," "The Duke," "My Ship," "Miles Ahead," "Gone, Gone, Gone," "Summertime," "Here Comes de Honeyman," "Pan Piper"). It is true that some of his solos were given to trumpeter Wallace Roney and altoist Kenny Garrett, but Davis plays surprisingly well throughout the historic set even if he is not at the level that he was three decades earlier. It does seem silly to give Jones co-billing for this concert since he just conducts the orchestra, which is drawn from both George Gruntz's Concert Jazz Band and the Gil Evans ghost band, but he was clearly fulfilling one of his dreams. This set was almost Miles Davis's final act and it served as his last hurrah.

Miles Davis Quintet: Live in Sweden
(2001, 34 minutes, Columbia/Legacy)

This extraordinary video will probably be difficult to obtain since it only had a limited release. As of this moment it is the third earliest example of Miles Davis on film, only preceded by his half-hour 1959 television special and a newsreel from 1957. Davis's 1965 quintet with Wayne Shorter, Herbie Hancock, Ron Carter and Tony Williams is featured on a continuous if brief four-song set. George Wein quickly introduces the group, and then they play an original, Shorter's "Footprints," an abstract "'Round Midnight" and a piece that sounds like Jimmy Heath's "Gingerbread Boy." The music constantly changes tempos and moods with Davis sounding quite effective, Shorter heard in brilliant form and Hancock successfully carving out a

Song, Brubeck's **The Jazz Ambassador**, Monterey's jazz education program and the passing of the torch from Jimmy Lyons to Monterey's current musical director Tim Jackson. But the promised "archival footage" is mostly excerpts from **Monterey Jazz Festival 75**, and the music is very secondary to the talking. Considering the many clips from other editions of the Monterey Festival that exist but are unavailable, this film (even with its interesting moments) is a bit of a disappointment.

The Moscow Sax Quintet: The Jazznost Tour
(1990, 57 minutes, View Video).

The Moscow Sax Quintet was founded by Vladimir Zaremba in 1987. Three years later they toured the United States and one of their concerts (from Northeastern University) is documented on this videotape. The group is comprised of five saxophonists (Zaremba and Oleg Ageyev on tenors, Alexandre Boychuk and Grennady Pakhtusov on altos and baritonist Vladimir Konibolotsky) plus a rhythm section. The group performs a fairly traditional bop/swing repertoire ("In the Mood," "Yardbird Suite," "Parker's Mood," "Four Brothers," "Your Eyes," "I Got Rhythm," "Smashing Thirds," "Smooth Sailing," "Donna Lee," "Waltz for Debby," "Crazy Rhythm," "Michelle," "Flight of the Bumble Bee") with Lyubov Zazullna taking the wordless scat vocal on "Smooth Sailing" in the style of Ella Fitzgerald. The highlights are the three a capella pieces (Fats Waller's "Smashing Thirds," "Waltz for Debby" and "Michelle"). There are also a few Supersax-like ensemble re-creations of Charlie Parker solos ("Yardbird Suite," "Parker's Mood" and "Donna Lee") and some worthy if not particularly distinctive individual improvisations. The overall results are pleasing and fairly interesting.

Mystery, Mr. Ra *(1984, 51 minutes, Rhapsody Films)*
Sun Ra and his Arkestra (with John Gilmore, Marshall Allen and June Tyson) are featured at a pair of Paris concerts performing a wide variety of material ("Along Came Ra," "Children of the Ra," "Blue Lou," "Nuclear War," "1984," "Cocktails for Two," "Love in Outer Space," "Astro Black," "Nuclear Walk," "Mystery, Mr. Ra," "Discipline 27") in typically colorful if very eccentric fashion.

New Orleans: Til the Butcher Cuts Him Down
(1986, 53 minutes, Rhapsody Films)

This film on veteran New Orleans trumpeter Punch Miller was almost made too late. It features him in 1971 talking a bit about his life and career. There is some music from the Olympia Brass Band ("Oh Didn't He Ramble" and "The Old Rugged Cross"), the Algiers Stompers ("Algiers Strut" and "Over the Waves") and the 77-year-old Miller in a group that includes cornetist Bobby Hackett ("Exactly Like You," "Eight, Nine and Ten," "You Can Depend on Me" and "That's My Home") at the New Orleans Jazz Festival. Miller, whose trumpet playing had long since become erratic, does his best throughout these numbers and sings with spirit. He passed away on December 2, 1971.

A Night in Tunisia *(1980, 27 minutes, View Video)*

This short film focuses on Dizzy Gillespie and his most famous original "A Night in Tunisia." The first half of the video has Gillespie (seen on piano and conga part of the time), Jon Faddis and Leonard Feather discussing the creation of the tune, while the latter part of the documentary is a 12-minute version of the song. Gillespie (back on trumpet), guitarist Ed Cherry, bassist Michael Howell and drummer Tommy Campbell are in decent form although this version is just okay, with only the blues section near the end sticking in one's mind.

Nina Simone: Live at Ronnie Scott's
(2003, 57 minutes, Music Video Distributors)

As a singer and pianist, Nina Simone was impossible to classify because she crossed through a variety of genres, including jazz, folk music, pop, R&B and soul. This hour-long DVD gives viewers a fairly definitive set by the unique Simone, a performance from November 17, 1985, with her only accompaniment being drummer Paul

Robinson. The program ("God, God, God," "If You Knew," "Mr. Smith," "Fodder in Her Wings," "Be My Husband," "I Loves You Porgy," "The Other Woman," "Mississippi Goddam," "Moon Over Alabama Medley," "For a While," "See-Line Woman," "I Sing Just to Know I'm Alive," "My Baby Just Cares for Me") also includes a few brief interviews between songs. Simone discusses her beginnings, early incidents of racism and the spiritual nature of music. Highlights of her set include "Be My Husband" (on which she does not play piano), a sensitive version of "The Other Woman" and her encore, "My Baby Just Cares for Me."

The 1962 Newport Jazz Festival 1962
(2003, 51 1/2 minutes, Music Video Distributors)

The black-and-white picture is sometimes blurry and primitively filmed, and occasionally the camera wanders away to street scenes, the beach and what could pass for a travelogue of Newport. But despite its faults, this film gives viewers a valuable look at some of the performers at the 1962 Newport Jazz Festival. The Oscar Peterson Trio (with Ray Brown and drummer Ed Thigpen) performs an unknown original and "Yours Is My Heart Alone." Lambert, Hendricks and Bavan sing "Come on Home" (each of the singers gets a solo section) and "Moanin'." Rahsaan Roland Kirk is seen playing his many horns as an ensemble and taking a flute solo on an excerpt from "Three for the Festival." The Clara Ward Gospel Singers perform a couple of rousing numbers including "The Saints." Unfortunately, all that is seen of the Newport All-Stars on "You Can Depend on Me" is a short excerpt, although there are solos from cornetist Ruby Braff and clarinetist Pee Wee Russell. Duke Ellington's orchestra is featured on the second half of "Rockin' in Rhythm" (Lawrence Brown, trumpeter Bill Berry and Ray Nance are seen), and Johnny Hodges is well featured on "Chelsea Bridge" and a fine version of "Things Ain't What They Used to Be." The best moments are from Count Basie's band. The orchestra performs a pair of blues ("I Needs to Be Bee'd With" with trombonist Quentin Jackson quite prominent and "Four, Five Six") and backs its former singer Jimmy Rushing on "I'm Coming Virginia." The high point of the DVD is a unique and classic performance of "Goin' to Chicago" which features Rushing and Joe Williams (Basie's two greatest vocalists) singing together.

Norman Granz Presents Duke Ellington at the Cote d'Azur with Ella Fitzgerald and Joan Miro
(1966, 64 minutes, Quantum Leap Group Limited)

Norman Granz produced this television special, available as a British videotape, which has Duke Ellington and his orchestra at a festival at Juan-Les-Pins with guest Ella Fitzgerald. Filmed July 27–28, 1966, the Ellington orchestra performs "The Opener," "Such Sweet Thunder," a medley of "Black and Tan Fantasy," "Creole Love Call" and "The Mooche," "The Old Circus Train Turn-Around Blues," "La Plus Belle Africaine" and "Things Ain't What They Used to Be." The usual Ellington sidemen (including a prominent Johnny Hodges plus Billy Strayhorn) are featured. Ellington and his trio also perform "Kinda Dukish" and "The Shepherd," and Ella Fitzgerald (with the Jimmy Jones Trio) sings "Satin Doll," "Something to Live For" and "So Dance Samba." Artist Joan Miro accompanies Ellington during part of his sightseeing.

On the Road Again *(1999, 50 minutes, Yazoo)*

In 1963, a group of musical archeologists went to the South to find and document talent. They filmed a wide variety of musicians in New Orleans, Houston, Nashville and elsewhere, covering blues, gospel, traditional music and just a little bit of jazz. Captured along the way were pianists Mance Lipscomb, Buster Pickens, and Whistlin' Alex Moore, blues greats Lightnin' Hopkins and Lowell Fulsom, steel guitarist Hop Wilson, guitarist Black Ace, the Blind James Campbell String Band and J.E. Mainer's family band, among others. The reasons that the tape is included in this book are that from New Orleans one gets to see the Eureka Brass Band playing a funeral, pianist Sweet Emma Barrett performing "I Ain't Gonna Give

Paris Reunion Band
(1988, 57 minutes, Proscenium Entertainment)

The Paris Reunion Band began in 1984 when British jazz critic Mike Hennessey put together an all-star group that included drummer Kenny Clarke. Although Clarke soon passed away, the band stayed together (with changing personnel) on and off for a decade. This video has the group performing in West Germany in 1988. The lineup is quite impressive, consisting of Woody Shaw, Nat Adderley, trombonist Curtis Fuller, Joe Henderson, Nathan Davis on tenor and soprano, pianist Walter Bishop, Jr., bassist Jimmy Woode and drummer Idris Muhammad. They perform four originals from group members ("Work Song," "The Man from Potter's Crossing," "Hot Licks," "Sweet Love of Mine"), Kenny Drew's "Tune Down" and the standard "Old Folks." This tape is particularly of value due to the participation of Shaw and Henderson, although each of the musicians is in excellent form on the advanced hard bop music.

 Pat Metheny Group: We Live Here—Live in Japan
(2002, 110 minutes, Image Entertainment)

This DVD was filmed on October 12, 1995. Guitarist Pat Metheny and each of his musicians (keyboardist Lyle Mays, bassist Steve Rodby, drummer Paul Wertico, percussionist Armando Marcal, David Blamires on vocals, flugelhorn, guitar, accordion and miscellaneous instruments, and Mark Ledford on vocals, flugelhorn, bass, vibes and percussion) are briefly interviewed individually between songs. The nearly two-hour performance ("Have You Heard," "And Then I Knew," "Here to Stay," "First Circle," "Scrap Metal," "Farmer's Trust," "Episode D'Azur," "Third Wind," "This Is Not America," "Antonia," "To the End of the World," "Minuano," "Stranger in Town") is colorful and unpredictable. The unclassifiable music is modern jazz that is open to the influences of folk, rock and pop. It is particularly intriguing how Blamires, Ledford and Marcel are used in the background as part of the

ensemble sound. The music ranges from fusion to the avant-garde, from quite passionate to very introspective, and shows that this was one of the stronger versions of the Pat Metheny Group.

 Pepper's Pow Wow
(1995, 57 minutes, Upstream Productions)

Jim Pepper was an important if underrated tenor saxophonist who was a pioneer in fusion (playing with guitarist Larry Coryell in the Free Spirits as early as 1965) and, most importantly, in mixing together his American Indian heritage with jazz. Most of this documentary was filmed before he was stricken with cancer in 1991, and Pepper is extensively interviewed about his life and career (including at a question-and-answer session with young students). There is plenty of music throughout the film (mostly taken from live appearances) although no complete performances. Pepper is heard playing and chanting his hit "Witchi Tai To," "Caddo Revival," "Comin' & Goin'," a couple of standards and a variety of originals. Pepper, his parents and various relatives talk about his early days, including his career as a child dancer, his struggles to find his own musical identity and the story behind "Witchi Tai To." There are also comments from drummer Bob Moses, tenor saxophonist Bert Wilson (who is a delight), singer Chris Hill, drummer Ed Schuller and pianist Mal Waldron in addition to a frail-looking Don Cherry speaking at Pepper's funeral in early 1992. The documentary whets one's appetite to hear more of Jim Pepper's music, but most of his recordings (including his album with Free Spirits) are quite scarce at the moment.

 Phil Woods: In Concert
(1988, 68 minutes, View Video)

The veteran altoist Phil Woods is in his usual hard-swinging form throughout his set with baritonist Joe Sudler's Swing Machine, a 17-piece orchestra. With the exception of pianist Uri Caine and bassist Tyrone Brown (both of whom have their names misspelled on the back cover), the personnel of the big band is obscure, but they are quite musical and tight. Woods is the main soloist, alternating bop standards with swinging originals ("Charles Christopher," "Watch What Happens," "Blues in Extacy," "Garr," "Untitled Original," "Groovin' High," "Willow Weep for Me," "Baja Laza," "Body and Soul," "Dedicated to Ollie") and playing consistently well.

Phil Woods: Jazz at the Maintenance Shop
(1993, 59 minutes, Shanachie)

Phil Woods is featured during this hour-long performance film leading his quartet of 1979, a group also including pianist Mike Melillo, bassist Steve Gilmore and drummer Bill Goodwin. Woods is in top form stretching out on "Song for Sisyphus," "A Little Piece," "Only When You're in My Arms," "Shaw Nuff" and "How's Your Mama" before an appreciative audience.

Phil Woods: Jazz in the Great Tradition
(1995, 58 minutes, Rhapsody Films)

Taken from the same engagement as Phil Woods's **Jazz at the Maintenance Shop**, this set also features him with Mike Melillo, Steve Gilmore and Bill Goodwin. The music is on the same level as the previous tape, showcasing the tight group on "Change Partners," "Body and Soul," "The Scene Is Clean," "Along Came Betty" and "How's Your Mama."

Piano Legends
(1987, 63 minutes, Video Arts International)

Chick Corea hosts this hour program, comprised of film clips (some rare, some a bit more common) that give listeners an opportunity to see some of the greatest jazz pianists. Represented are Earl Hines, Fats Waller, Meade Lux Lewis, Art Tatum, Oscar Peterson, Mary Lou Williams, Marian McPartland, Bud Powell, Thelonious Monk, Mal Waldron, John Lewis, Dave Brubeck, Duke Ellington, Count Basie, McCoy Tyner, Bill Evans, Keith Jarrett, Cecil Taylor and Corea himself, with the clips dating from 1941–86.

Playboy Jazz Festival, Vol. 1
(1991, 91 minutes, Musicvision)

Highlights from the 1984 edition of the Playboy Jazz Festival (held annually at the Hollywood Bowl) have been released on two videos. The first volume has selections from Maynard Ferguson, the Red Norvo Trio with Tal Farlow and Red Mitchell, Nancy Wilson with Art Farmer and Benny Golson ("I'll Remember April," "Save Your Love for Me," "I Thought About You"), Willie Bobo, Lionel Hampton and Grover Washington, Jr., with Pieces of a Dream ("Just the Two of Us").

Playboy Jazz Festival, Vol. 2
(1991, 91 minutes, Musicvision)

Most notable about the second video from the 1984 Playboy Jazz Festival is seeing the Manhattan Transfer and Weather Report team together for "Birdland." Also on this tape are numbers from Ornette Coleman's Prime Time, Wild Bill Davison, Sarah Vaughan ("Send in the Clowns"), the Dave Brubeck Quartet ("Take Five"), Dexter Gordon and Milt Jackson ("Bags' Groove").

Poncho Sanchez: A Night at Kimball's East
(1991, 60 minutes, Concord Picante)

Poncho Sanchez's spirited Latin jazz band performs a strong set of music ("Alafia," "Jumpin' with Symphony Sid," "Co Co May May," "Cinderella," "Cold Sweat," "Funky Broadway," "Half and Half," "Baila Mi Gente," "Yumbambe," "A Night in Tunisia," "Se Acabo Lo Que Se Daba," "Domitla") at San Francisco's Kimball's East. The program is similar to the group's CD of the same name and features Sanchez's regular band of the era (the leader on congas and vocals, trumpeter Sal Cracciolo, trombonist Art Velasco, Gene Burkert on alto, tenor and flute, pianist David Torres, bassist Tony Banda, Ramon Banda on timbales and Jose "Papo" Rodriguez on bongos). Fans of the popular group will enjoy this snapshot view of a typical night of Afro-Cuban rhythms, Latin dance music, R&B and jazz solos.

Portrait of Pee Wee Russell/Baby Laurence: Jazz Hoofer
(2004, 58 minutes, Rhapsody Films)

Two unrelated documentaries have been reissued on this DVD. **Portrait of Pee Wee Russell** is not so exciting. This 1998 film mostly focuses on the clarinetist's interest in painting during 1965–67, including utilizing a lot of silent footage of Russell mixing paint and creating pictures. Writer Dan Morgenstern talks about Pee Wee's life in somewhat rambling fashion (mostly relating familiar stories), and there are brief examples of Russell's playing (along with use of his music on the soundtrack) plus a taped interview of him talking about his painting. Perhaps some of the footage could be used for five minutes in a better documentary on Pee Wee Russell's life but this half-hour film is quite dull.

In contrast, **Baby Laurence: Jazz Hoofer** is an invaluable documentary. One of the great tap dancers, Baby Laurence is seen performing in the early '70s at an outdoor concert in Baltimore and at the New York Jazz Museum, demonstrating some remarkable dance steps. A professional since 1933, he talks about his early days, but is mostly featured delighting audiences with his demonstrations of the evolution of tap dancing, including re-creating the styles of Bill "Bojangles" Robinson and John Bubbles. Laurence is so full of energy and enthusiasm that it comes as a bit of a surprise at the film's conclusion when it is revealed that he died in 1974 from cancer at the age of 53.

So the Pee Wee Russell film gets a 3 and Baby Laurence gets an 8.

Rahsaan Roland Kirk: The One Man Twins
(50 minutes, Rhino Home Video)

Rahsaan Roland Kirk was a phenomenal performer and, as good as some of his records are, he was more remarkable live in concert. Unfortunately, relatively little film exists of Rahsaan, so this DVD of his June 24, 1972, concert at the Montreux Jazz Festival is quite valuable. It shows Kirk playing three saxophones at once and expertly juggling instruments on stage despite being blind. Kirk is joined by pianist Ron Burton, bassist Henry Pearson, drummer Robert Shy and percussionist Joe "Habao" Texidor for some typically miraculous performances. The opening "Improvisation" features Rahsaan harmonizing on two horns at once while backed only by Texidor's tambourine. "Balm in Gilead" (which is similar to Duke Ellington's "Black and Tan Fantasy") has Kirk alternating his New Orleans clarinet with some rollicking tenor. After a very expressive flute feature ("Seasons"), Rahsaan combines "Misty" and "I Want to Talk about You," climaxed by a remarkable cadenza on tenor. "Blue Rol No. 2" features Rahsaan playing recorder with his nose while blowing through his mouth simultaneously on flute, an impossible feat. He concludes the piece with some three-horn chording and then drives the audience to a frenzy on the lengthy "Volunteered Slavery." The DVD concludes with brief versions of "Serenade to a Cuckoo" and "Never Can Say Goodbye." Rahsaan Roland Kirk was in his own musical universe, and this video hints at his enormous potential.

Ralph Sutton and Ruby Braff: Ralph and Ruby Remembered
(2003, 115 minutes, Arbors Video)

Ralph Sutton (one of the greatest stride pianists ever) and cornetist Ruby Braff were friends for 52 years and played music together occasionally. This DVD has their only filmed appearances together: three sets from the Mid-America Jazz Festival in St. Louis (March 19–20, 1988) and a performance from March 18, 2001, at Arbors' March of Jazz Party. It will take viewers some time to get used to the primitive nature of the camerawork, as the music was documented by a single handheld camera. The first set in particular is a bit frustrating for sometimes one does not get to see the soloist. However, the camerawork improves as it goes along, often sticking with Braff as he wanders around the stage. It is worth it to be patient—Braff is in brilliant form during the 1988 selections, and Sutton, bassist Milt Hinton and drummer Gus Johnson also sound fine interpreting the well-known standards ("Jeepers Creepers," "Fine and Dandy," "Russian Lullaby," "Old Folks," "Keepin' Out of Mischief Now," "The Man I Love," "Body and Soul," "Poor Butterfly," "Rockin' Chair," "Thou Swell," "All by Myself," "Sugar," "I Can't Give You Anything but Love," "Tea for Two"). Among the highlights are a very slow version of "Fine and Dandy," Braff's glorious low notes on "Old Folks," Sutton on "Thou Swell" and a relaxed "All by Myself." The 2001 set has Braff and Sutton playing duets on "Tea for Two," a false start on "Gone with the Wind" and an excellent version of "Thou Swell." On "'Deed I Do" and "Dinah," Braff and Sutton are joined by cornetists Bryan Shaw and Randy Reinhart, trumpeter Randy Sandke, guitarist Jon

Stride pianist Ralph Sutton and cornetist Ruby Braff overcome a handheld camera to create musical fireworks.

Wheatley, bassist Nicki Parrott and drummer Sherrie Maricle. The many short solos and the riffing make these numbers quite lively. Since Sutton died later in 2001 and Braff passed away in 2003, these performances can never be duplicated; fortunately they were filmed.

 Randy Weston: Live in St. Lucia
(2003, 68 minutes, Image Entertainment)

Pianist Randy Weston is in very good spirits during this hour-long performance, playing six of his compositions ("African Cookbook," "The Shrine," "African Sunrise," "Little Niles," "The Three Pyramids & the Sphinx," "Blue Moses") with his quintet: veteran trombonist Benny Powell, T.K. Blue on alto, soprano and flute, bassist Alex Blake and Neil Clarke on African percussion. The opening number is overly long and there are times when the episodic music meanders a bit, but Weston's solo piano performance of "Little Niles" and the solos of Blake (who is featured on a duet with the pianist on "The Three Pyramids & the Sphinx") are always colorful. A bonus is a 13-minute interview with Weston in which he discusses his beginnings, his discovery of music in Africa and his musical beliefs.

The Rarest New Orleans Jazz
(2002, 58 minutes, 3ON-8OW Records)

This grab bag of clips, most of which deal with the New Orleans jazz revival movement of the 1960s, has some moments of interest but is quite erratic. The selections are taken from six different situations and three are actually silent movies. The Olympia Brass Band is seen playing at a parade in the 1960s with plenty of enthusiastic second-liners dancing away. Although the music fits the picture, it was actually added later, a version of "It Feels So Good" from the Young Tuxedo Brass Band. Of strong historic value are some silent home movies of trumpeter Bunk Johnson (probably the only footage that exists of him), clarinetist George Lewis, trombonist Jim Robinson, pianist Alton Purnell, bassist Slow Drag Pavageau and writer Bill Russell taken in Central Park around 1945. The musicians are seen fooling around a bit, and Bunk plays a few notes on his trumpet. The least interesting part of this videotape is "A Photo Gallery of New Orleans Musicians," a variety of still photos shown while a George Lewis record plays; the musicians are not identified. Sweet Emma Barrett's band of the late '60s (trumpeter Chuck Willis, trombonist Frog Joseph, clarinetist Cornbread Thomas, pianist Jeanette Kimball, banjoist Albert French and drummer Louis Barbarin) performs at a New Orleans club (possibly Preservation Hall), jamming a fine version of "Charleston"; the horn playing is excellent. Barrett had suffered a stroke a few years before, but she still felt compelled to sing "Bill Bailey" and "Ain't Gonna Give Nobody None of this Jelly Roll," also playing a little bit of piano with her right hand. Her contribution brings down the quality of the music. The band plays "Alabama Jubilee" over the closing credits. In addition, trumpeter Kid Thomas Valentine's band (with clarinetist Albert Burbank, trombonist Louis Nelson, tenor saxophonist Emanuel Paul, pianist Octave Crosby, banjoist Emanuel Sayles, bassist Joe Butler and drummer Alonzo Stewart) is featured on two occasions, probably in the early '70s. The band is quite primitive and frequently out of tune on "Just a Closer Walk with Thee," but does pretty well on "Tiger Rag." This tape concludes with the same band at a European concert, struggling on "Basin Street Blues" and "Just a Closer Walk with Thee," and jamming "Darktown Strutters' Ball" while joined by the Duke Ellington Orchestra; Duke looks a bit amused by it all.

Reed Royalty
(1992, 58 minutes, Video Artists International)

Branford Marsalis is the host during this hour-long survey of the history of the clarinet, soprano, alto and baritone in jazz. In addition to Marsalis (who plays an unaccompanied blues on soprano at the beginning and conclusion of the show), there are 25 performances, all excerpts, some of which are more common than others.

Although one wishes that the renditions were complete (and that this video was expanded to 90 minutes), the tape gives a brief history lesson. To the credit of the organizers, this set does not leave out the avant-garde leaders. The key missing players are Buddy DeFranco, Jackie McLean and Pepper Adams, but nearly all of the other significant musicians are here: Omer Simeon ("Panama" in 1958), Pee Wee Russell ("I May Be Wrong" from 1958), Artie Shaw (1939), Woody Herman (1945), Benny Goodman (1942), Harry Carney, Jimmy Hamilton and Russell Procope on clarinets (1951 on "Caravan" with Duke Ellington), Sidney Bechet (1951), Jimmy Dorsey ("Beebe" in 1940), Benny Carter ("Honeysuckle Rose" from 1974), Johnny Hodges ("Don't Get Around Much Anymore" with Duke Ellington in 1946), Willie Smith ("Sophisticated Lady" with Duke in 1951), Harry Carney (finishing "Sophisticated Lady" in 1964), Gerry Mulligan ("Line for Lyons" with his 1956 quartet), Charlie Parker (1951's "Hot House"), Sonny Stitt ("Parker's Mood" in 1964), Cannonball Adderley (a rare version of "'Round Midnight" from 1958), Phil Woods (1978), Lee Konitz (1958), John Coltrane (the last part of "My Favorite Things" from 1961), Eric Dolphy (mostly unaccompanied bass clarinet with Charles Mingus in 1964), Ornette Coleman (1966), Steve Lacy (1983), Anthony Braxton (a fiery solo from 1983), Jane Ira Bloom (1989) and Paquito D'Rivera (1990).

Remembering Bud Powell Live
(1997, 84 minutes, Image Entertainment)

In 1996, pianist Chick Corea toured with a special all-star group called "Remembering Bud Powell," resulting in a CD. During the same period he also filmed this live DVD. Corea is heard during a pair of concerts with trumpeter Wallace Roney, bassist Christian McBride, drummer Roy Haynes and either altoist Kenny Garrett or tenor saxophonist Joshua Redman. Rather than just jamming Powell's bop classics, Corea contributed new and modern arrangements to such songs as "Glass Enclosure," "Tempus Fugit," "Bud

Powell" (an original by Corea which here has Fred Johnson as a guest vocalist), "Oblivion," "I'll Keep Loving You" and "Un Poco Loco." The musicians swing hard on the often-tricky material, and Corea adds his wit to the potentially forbidding music.

 ### Renee Rosnes: Jazz Pianist
(1997, 45 minutes, Rhapsody Films)

The bulk of this videotape is a half-hour Canadian television portrait of modern mainstream pianist Renee Rosnes. She performs her uptempo original "Lexicon," her somber piece "The Ache of the Absence" (which becomes an intense modal waltz) and a comparatively lighthearted version of Thelonious Monk's "Eronel" with bassist Larry Grenadier and drummer Billy Drummond. Between songs, Rosnes talks a bit about her life and music. After the closing credits there are two additional songs in what is called "The Alternate Sessions": Alec Wilder's "Moon and Sand" and a somewhat eerie version of Jimmy Rowles's "The Peacocks."

 ### Rhythm and Blues at the Apollo
(1989, 56 minutes, Storyville)

The 19 selections on this filmed record of an all-star show at the Apollo Theatre in 1955 range from late-period swing and early '50s R&B to pre–rock 'n' roll. Some of the performances are of more interest to jazz viewers than others, but in general the show is enjoyable. Baritonist Paul Williams's sextet (with trumpeter Jimmy Brown and an unidentified but talented tenor saxophonist) is the house band. The headliners are Amos Milburn ("Rocky Mountain," "Bewildered," "Bad, Bad, Whiskey" and "Down the Road Apiece"), Martha Davis ("We Just Couldn't Say Goodbye," "Vipity Vop" and "Goodbye"), Big Joe Turner ("Oke She Moke She Pop" and "Shake, Rattle and Roll"), Ruth Brown ("Oh What a Dream," "Raining Teardrops from My Eyes" and "Mama, He Treats Your Daughter Mean"), Faye Adams ("Everyday" and "Somebody Somewhere"), the Clovers ("Fool,

Fool, Fool" and "Miss Fanny"), the Larks ("Without a Song") and Dinah Washington ("My Lean Baby") with trumpeter Jimmy Brown singing and featured on "My Love Is True." Many of the performances on this television special and those on the tape **Variety at the Apollo** were spliced together in different combinations (along with some Snader Telescriptions) to form 13 half-hour shows released in the 1950s as **Showtime at the Apollo**.

 ### Rick Fay and Friends: Live at the State
(1992, 98 minutes, Arbors)

The technical quality of this performance film is weak in that only one video camera was used and some of the musicians (particularly in the rhythm section) are often in the shadows. However, the quality of the music is quite high and generally compensates for the primitive nature of this video. Tenor and soprano saxophonist Rick Fay leads a top-notch trad septet also featuring trumpeter Jon-Erik Kellso, trombonist Dan Barrett, clarinetist Chuck Hedges, pianist Chuck Folds, bassist Bob Haggart and drummer Eddie Graham. The band performs 13 Dixieland and swing standards ("Way Down Yonder in New Orleans," "Who's Sorry Now," "I'm Coming Virginia," "Undecided," "Struttin' with Some Barbecue," "Beale Street Blues," "Butter and Egg Man," "Just One More Chance," "South Rampart Street Parade," "I Would Do Anything for You," "She's Funny that Way," "Big Noise from Winnetka," "Farewell Blues") during this long set, recorded on April 5, 1992, before an enthusiastic audience. In general Folds and Kellso take the most consistently rewarding solos, although all of the musicians are in fine form. Kellso is showcased on "I'm Coming Virginia," Barrett's pretty tone is featured on "Just One More Chance" and Hedges is in the spotlight for "She's Funny that Way." It is a particular joy seeing Haggart and Graham play "Big Noise from Winnetka." This is a good example of how these musicians sounded during the era at classic jazz festivals.

Robert Altman's Jazz
(1997, 75 minutes, Rhapsody Films)

Robert Altman's 1996 film **Kansas City** was a turkey on all levels. The plot was unoriginal and dull, none of the characters were sympathetic, and the overall story was pointless. Altman (with the assistance of Hal Willner) gathered together some of the top jazz musicians of the mid-'90s, dressed them in period outfits and had them perform at an endless jam session. Very little of the music was used in the film, most of the songs were cut down to just one chorus apiece and the musicians were wasted; none of the players had a single line of dialogue. The only good point to **Kansas City** is that, because so much footage was taken of the musicians, this video was released as compensation. One has to suspend critical judgment a bit because although the musicians (and the enthusiastic audience at the "Hey Hey Club") all look like it is 1934 and the repertoire is mostly from the era (although "Tickle Toe," "Harvard Blues" and "Pagin' the Devil" had not yet been written), the horn soloists generally sound like themselves. Despite attempts by others to match these musicians with past greats, Joshua Redman does not sound like Lester Young, Craig Handy does not emulate Coleman Hawkins and Kevin Mahogany (as a singing bartender) fails to sound like Big Joe Turner. To their credit, the rhythm section comes close at times (with Geri Allen cast as Mary Lou Williams), but one should forget all of that and just enjoy the music, which was apparently much too good for the movie. The lineup of musicians is quite impressive, since it consists of Joshua Redman, Craig Handy, James Carter and David Murray on tenors, altoists David "Fathead" Newman and Jesse Davis, clarinetist Don Byron, trumpeters Nicholas Payton, James Zollar and Olu Dara, trombonists Curtis Fowlkes and Clark Gayton, acoustic guitarists Russell Malone and Mark Whitfield, pianists Geri Allen and Kevin Mahogany, bassists Ron Carter, Christian McBride and Tyrone Clark, and a tireless Victor Lewis on drums.

There are some strong musical moments along the way ("Tickle Toe," "Indiana," "Solitude," "Blues in the Dark," "Prince of Wails," "Froggy Bottom," "Harvard Blues," "King Porter Stomp," "Lafayette," "Lullaby of the Leaves," "Piano Boogie," "Pagin' the Devil," "Moten Swing," "Queer Notions," "Yeah Man," "Closing Two-Bass Blues"), so overlook the 1934 references and just enjoy the performances.

 Ron Carter & Art Farmer: Live at Sweet Basil
(1992, 60 minutes, View Video)

In 1990, Ron Carter and Art Farmer were teamed together with Cedar Walton and Billy Higgins. This performance DVD has the quartet performing five group originals (two by Carter and one apiece from the other players) plus "My Funny Valentine." Although there are some brief interviews, the emphasis is on the music, which is generally low-key and swinging. Few memorable moments occur, but the musicians play up to their usual level on such numbers as "Art's Song," "When Love Is New" and "A Theme in 3/4."

 Ron Kobayashi: Live at Steamers
(2003, 84 minutes, Music Sweethearts Inc.)

Pianist Ron Kobayashi, bassist Baba Elefante and drummer Steve Dixon had played together as a trio for ten years at the time of this live DVD. Although two of their three recordings are more funk/pop-oriented, this program is mostly straightahead jazz ("There Is No Greater Love," "Waltz for Bill," "Soaring," "Watch What Happens," "Autumn Leaves," "Hang Time," "Highway 133," "Yesterdays," "Counter Culture," "I'll Remember April," "I've Got You Under My Skin," "Take the 'A' Train"). Kobayashi is in excellent form throughout the set and, although the frameworks are not too inventive (Baba Elefante has a bass solo on every song), the music is enjoyable if consumed in several sittings. In addition, the pianist's four originals (particularly "Waltz for Bill") are excellent. Singer Debbi Ebert is featured on "Watch What Happens," "Autumn Leaves," "I've Got You Under My Skin" and "Take the 'A' Train." The most intriguing arrangement is on "Yesterdays" where the trio alternates between 5/4 and 4/4 time. As a bonus, the three trio members and Ebert are briefly interviewed (for a total of five minutes) by Steamers' owner-manager Terence Love.

♪ The Rosemary Clooney Show: Girl Singer
(2004, 60 minutes, Concord DVD)

This hour-long DVD has Rosemary Clooney singing 18 songs taken from her 1956–57 television series ("Tenderly," "My Blue Heaven," "Lullaby of Broadway," "I Got It Bad," "Moonlight in Vermont," "They Can't Take That Away from Me," "Blues in the Night," "You Make Me Feel So Young," "Come on-a My House," "Mambo Italiano," "There Will Never Be Another You," "Hey There," "I've Got My Love to Keep Me Warm," "Taking a Chance on Love," "Love and Marriage," "Count Your Blessings," "I'll Be Seeing You," "Come Rain or Come Shine). She is accompanied by the unseen Nelson Riddle Orchestra, her husband José Ferrer sings a duet with her on "Love and Marriage," and on a few numbers she is assisted by the Hi-Los. Between many of the songs, there are insightful interview excerpts with her five children (Miguel, Maria, Gabriel, Monsita and Rafael Ferrer), her nephew George Clooney, her brother Nick Clooney and friend Michael Feinstein. Rosemary Clooney was technically not a jazz singer (she tended to stick to both the melodies and the words) but she has always been a favorite of jazz listeners. She always seemed to sing effortlessly, finding the middle of each note and putting plenty of understated feeling into each word. Clooney was a very natural singer who, like her close friend Bing Crosby, never looked like it was the slightest bit difficult to sing. In addition to the hour show/documentary, the bonus material includes a performance of "Chicago" from her television series, comments by Feinstein on each of the songs, additional extensive interviews with all of the principals, and composer Jimmy Webb playing his song "Time Flies" on piano while photos are shown from Rosemary Clooney's life.

♪ Ruby Braff Trio in Concert
(1995, 47 minutes, Storyville)

Cornetist Ruby Braff teams up with guitarist Howard Alden and bassist Frank Tate on this performance film from the 1991 Brecon Jazz Festival. The trio plays eight numbers, including "It's Only a Paper Moon," Mary Lou Williams's "Lonely Moments," "I've Grown Accustomed to Your Face" and "Them There Eyes," with Alden and Tate collaborating on a version of Duke Ellington's "Black Beauty." The swing-oriented music is fine although not quite as exciting as one might expect from these players.

♪ A Salute to Buddy Rich
(1999, 105 minutes, Hudson Music)

On October 3, 1998, the Buddy Rich big band had a reunion, featuring Phil Collins in the drum spot. Their concert at the Manhattan Center in New York City is on this tape, along with some comments sandwiched between songs and a few excerpts taken from Buddy Rich performances. After Collins plays his "I Don't Care Anymore" with the orchestra, drummer Steve Smith is featured with a sextet from the big band on "Airegin" and the funky "No Jive." The next two songs (a brief "All Blues" and "Rocky and His Friends") have drummer Dennis Chambers playing with a trio and the orchestra. The remainder of the tape features Collins and the big band performing a variety of older charts plus a couple of the drummer's originals ("Mercy, Mercy, Mercy," "That's All," "Norwegian Wood," "Milestones," "Birdland," "Sussudio"), with Collins finishing the concert by singing "The Way You Look Tonight" for the show's producer Cathy Rich. The music overall is quite nice and swinging with Steve Marcus (on tenor and alto) taking most of the solo space. But the most exciting solo is easily Buddy Rich's on a 1984 version of "Channel One Suite."

♪ Salute to Jelly Roll
(1992, 60 minutes, Leisure Jazz Video)

The 1992 version of the Dukes of Dixieland performs 14 Jelly Roll Morton–associated tunes ("Wolverine Blues,"

"Milenburg Joys," "Buddy Bolden's Blues," "Black Bottom Stomp," "Fingerbuster," "Kansas City Stomps," "King Porter Stomp," "Someday Sweetheart," "The Pearls," "Tijuana," "Sweet Substitute," "New Orleans Joy," "Grandpa's Spells," "Panama") in pleasing if predictable fashion. The music is fine, but the high points of this tape are the two features for singer/banjoist Danny Barker: "Winin' Boy Blues" and "Don't You Leave Me Here."

 ### Sarah Vaughan & Friends: A Jazz Session
(1986, 60 minutes, A*Vision)

This television special, originally made for HBO, teams Sarah Vaughan with what must be the weirdest trumpet section of all time: Dizzy Gillespie, Maynard Ferguson, Don Cherry, Chuck Mangione and Al Hirt! Even stranger is that Hirt generally takes solo honors. The all-star group has Herbie Hancock, Ron Carter and Billy Higgins as their rhythm section. On Sassy's solo features, she is joined by her regular trio (pianist George Gaffney, bassist Andy Simpkins and drummer Harold Jones). There is almost too much talent for the hour ("Watermelon Man," "I Can't Give You Anything but Love," "Just Friends," "Send in the Clowns," "Bemsha Swing," "I Can't Get Started," "'Round Midnight," "Bags' Groove," "Take the 'A' Train"), but each of the musicians has a chance to shine, with Sassy cutting just about everyone. It does seem strange to see Hirt, Cherry and Mangione in the same picture.

 ### Sarah Vaughan: The Divine One
(1991, 60 minutes, BMG Video)

Of all the tapes released by BMG Video in their **Masters of American Music** series, this is the most successful. Made a year after the death of Sarah Vaughan, the project expertly blends together performances (most of which are meaningful excerpts) and interviews (including one of Sassy on the **Dick Cavett Show**) to tell the Sarah Vaughan story. One hears from Ada Vaughan (Sarah's mother), Paris Vaughan (her daughter), singers Billy Eckstine and Joe Williams, pianist George Gaffney (whose stories are particularly insightful), drummer Roy Haynes and arranger Marty Paich. The narrative (written by Dan Morgenstern) is excellent and the performances are uniformly excellent and occasionally wondrous. Among the songs are "A Foggy Day" (one of several numbers from late in Vaughan's career featuring her teamed with an orchestra conducted by Michael Tilson Thomas), a slow chorus on "The Shadow of Your Smile," "Day In, Day Out," "Someone to Watch Over Me," "I've Got a Crush on You," a medley of "Misty" and "Tenderly" plus "Send in the Clowns." Best is a complete performance of "Once in a While" on which Vaughan backs herself on piano. What a voice she had!

 ### Satchmo *(2003, 87 minutes, Columbia Legacy)*

Written by Gary Giddins (in conjunction with his book of the same name) and filmed in 1989 as part of the **American Masters** series, this documentary serves as a solid introduction to the life of Louis Armstrong. Unfortunately, very few clips are shown complete, and most of the performance excerpts are quite brief. Along the way there are comments from Wynton Marsalis, Tony Bennett, George Avakian, Joe Muranyi, Doc Cheatham, Bud Freeman, Zilner Randolph, Milt Hinton, Milt Gabler, Dexter Gordon, Marty Napoleon, Lester Bowie, Barrett Deems, Arvell Shaw, Dave Brubeck and Iola Brubeck, plus some from Satch himself. There are brief glimpses of home movies, some excerpts taken from film and a few television appearances. But one wishes that a lot more music was included.

 ### Sippie *(1986, 23 minutes, Rhapsody Films)*

Filmed in 1982 when Sippie Wallace was 83 (she passed away in 1986), this short documentary features the last of the surviving classic blues singers of the 1920s briefly in concert (where she is effective despite no longer having much of a voice) and talks a bit about her past. The footage is invaluable, but one wishes there was much more of it.

♪ *The Small Black Groups*
(2001, 59 minutes, Storyville)

A variety of high-quality performances from 1942–48 are on this continually intriguing videotape. The Nat King Cole Trio (consisting of Cole, guitarist Oscar Moore and bassist Johnny Miller) is featured on four Soundies (**Is You Is or Is You Ain't My Baby**, **I'm a Shy Guy**, **Who's Been Eating My Porridge**, **Frim Fram Sauce**), two of which also have singing from Ida James. The Cole Trio is also shown performing their numbers from the films **Killer Diller** ("Oh, Kickeroony," "Now He Tells Me," "Breezy and the Bass") and **Breakfast in Hollywood** ("Solid Potato Salad," "It's Better to Be by Yourself"). The John Kirby Sextet (bassist Kirby, trumpeter Charlie Shavers, clarinetist Buster Bailey, altoist Charlie Holmes, pianist Billy Kyle and drummer Big Sid Catlett) is featured on two numbers from the film **Sepia Cinderella** ("Broadjump" and "Can't Find a Word to Say"), which is probably the group's only appearance on film. There are three songs taken from the film **Boy! What a Girl**. Sid Catlett heads a septet (trumpeter Dick Vance, trombonist Benny Morton, altoist Don Stovall, a young Eddie "Lockjaw" Davis on tenor, pianist Ram Ramirez and bassist John Simmons) that is joined by Gene Krupa on "Just a Riff" (which has drum solos by both Catlett and Krupa along with an amusing joke) and backs singer Betti Mays on "Crazy Riffin'." Also from the film, the Slam Stewart Trio (bassist Stewart, pianist Beryl Booker and guitarist John Collins) swings nicely on "Oh Me, Oh My, Oh Gosh." A pair of Louis Jordan Soundies (**Old Man Mose** and **Jordan Jive**) are included that were not released on other collections. Also on this tape is the 16-minute short **O'Voutee O'Rooney**, which features guitarist/pianist/singer Slim Galliard, bassist Bam Brown and drummer Scat Man Crothers live at Billy Berg's in 1946. They perform Galliard's unique brand of talking jive and swing for six numbers ("O'Rooney's Overture," "Dynamite's O'Rooney," "Spanish Melody and Swing," "Chile and Beans O'Voutee," "Dunkin' Bagel," "Laguna").

♪ *The Snader Telescriptions: The Big Bands, Vol. 1*
(1988, 64 minutes, Storyville)

This video has seven selections by Duke Ellington's 1952 orchestra and ten from Lionel Hampton's 1950–51 bands, all originally made as Snader Telescriptions for television. Everyone in Duke's big band (trumpeters Cat Anderson, Clark Terry and Willie Cook, Ray Nance on cornet and violin, trombonists Quentin Jackson, Britt Woodman and Juan Tizol, Russell Procope on clarinet and alto, clarinetist Jimmy Hamilton, altoist Willie Smith, Paul Gonsalves on tenor, Harry Carney on baritone and bass clarinet, bassist Wendell Marshall and drummer Louie Bellson in addition to the leader on piano) except Terry and Marshall have opportunities to solo along the way. The numbers are "Sophisticated Lady," "Caravan," a classic rendition of "The Mooche," "VIP's Boogie" (which has short statements from a lot of different players), "Solitude" (with singer Jimmy Grissom), "Mood Indigo" and a drum feature on "The Hawk Talks." The Lionel Hampton performances primarily showcase the leader on vibes, drums, occasional vocals and (on "T.V. Special") playing speedy two-fingered piano. There are some spots for the passionate tenor of Johnny Board, trombonist Al Grey, pianist Milt Buckner and various trumpeters, but Hampton is always in the spotlight, often showboating a bit. The music is quite excitable, particularly during "Beulah's Boogie" (during which Hampton jumps on his drums at the end), "Air Mail Special" (which has Board and Gil Bernal in a tenor battle while backed by screaming brass) and "Cobb's Idea"; the latter has singer Betty Carter scatting for a half-chorus. Other soloists heard from are guitarist Billy Mackel and flutist Jerome Richardson, but the band is mostly used as a prop behind Hampton. Together they perform "Midnight Sun," "Beulah's Boogie," "Love You Like Mad, Love You Like Crazy," "Ding Dong Baby," "Cobb's Idea," "Vibe Boogie," "T.V. Special," "Bongo Interlude," "Air Mail Special" and "Slide Hamp Slide."

♪ 5   *The Snader Telescriptions: The Big Bands, Vol. 2*
(1988, 47 minutes, Storyville)

Performances from four of the surviving swing bands of 1950–52 are featured on this videotape. Of greatest interest are five selections by Charlie Barnet's 1950 orchestra although unfortunately this was a year after Barnet had broken up his more innovative bebop big band. Most of the sidemen are obscure except for Bill Holman (who plays tenor in the ensembles). Barnet is the key soloist, playing tenor, alto and his haunting-sounding soprano on "Skyliner," "My Old Flame," "Andy's Boogie," "Caravan" and "Cherokee." Les Brown's orchestra is featured in 1951 on four dance band numbers, with the lineup including trombonist Ray Sims, Dave Pell on tenor, guitarist Tony Rizzi and drummer Jack Sperling. Of lesser interest are four tunes from Ralph Flanagan's unit in 1952 and three from Tony Pastor's band the previous year (including "Your Red Wagon" and "Come on-a My House").

♪ 8   *The Snader Telescriptions: Nat King Cole*
(1988, 50 minutes, Storyville)

Filmed during 1950–52, these 17 performances showcase Nat King Cole during a transitional period when he evolved from a jazz pianist who sang a bit to a pop crooner who occasionally played some piano. Nine of the selections feature Cole with guitarist Irving Ashby, bassist Joe Comfort and usually Jack Costanzo on bongos in what was the last real version of his trio/quartet. Cole is in excellent form on such numbers as "Route 66," "Sweet Lorraine," "Little Girl," "The Trouble with Me Is You" and "For Sentimental Reasons." On "Calypso Blues" he sings while backed just by Costanzo's bongos. The other seven performances have the group sweetened by an unseen string section; these include "Home," "Mona Lisa" and "Nature Boy." This set is a must for Nat King Cole fans and collectors.

♪ 8   *The Snader Telescriptions: Dixieland Jazz Vol. 1*
(1988, 58 minutes, Storyville)

Dixieland fans should definitely love this tape for it features two high-quality bands jamming a variety of standards.

The Bobcats, the hot group that came originally out of the Bob Crosby Orchestra in the 1930s, is featured during a 1951 reunion performing eight numbers: "Muskrat Ramble," "Big Noise from Winnetka," "March of the Bobcats," "Savoy Blues," "Who's Sorry Now," "Complainin'," "Lazy Mood" and "Panama." The all-star band consists of trumpeter Billy Butterfield, trombonist Warren Smith, clarinetist Matty Matlock, tenor saxophonist Eddie Miller, pianist Jess Stacy, guitarist Nappy Lamare, bassist Bob Haggart and drummer Ray Bauduc. All of the players are heard in prime form. The second half of the video features Jack Teagarden in 1951 shortly after he left Louis Armstrong's All-Stars and put together his own Dixieland group. His band features trumpeter Charlie Teagarden, altoist Heinie Beau, tenor saxophonist Pud Brown, clarinetist Don Bonner, stride pianist Don Ewell, bassist Ray Leatherwood and drummer Ray Bauduc. Their ten songs are "Lover" (always a fine showcase for the trombonist's impressive technique), "Basin Street Blues," "Wolverine Blues," "Rockin' Chair," "That's a Plenty," "Nobody Knows the Trouble I've Seen," "Jack Armstrong Blues," "Stars Fell on Alabama," "Dark Eyes" and "Georgia on My Mind." The performances are a joy to watch.

♪ 7   *The Snader Telescriptions: Dixieland Jazz Vol. 2*
(1988, 53 minutes, Storyville)

Three top-notch Dixieland bands are featured on their Snader Telescriptions from 1950–51. Cornetist Pete Daily's group (trombonist Burt Johnson, Pud Brown on clarinet and tenor, pianist Skippy Anderson, banjoist Len Esterdahl, Bud Hatch on tuba and drummer Hugh Allison) jam "Over the Waves," "Daily Double," "Goat Blues," "O Tannenbaum" and "Please Don't Talk about Me When I'm Gone." The Firehouse Five Plus Two mix together spirited Dixieland with their own brand of humor on "Hook and Ladder Blues," "Brass Bell," "Everybody Loves My Baby," "Red Hot River Valley," "South" and "Firehouse Stomp." The band consists of trombonist Ward Kimball, cornetist Danny Alguire, clarinetist Clark Mallory, pianist

Frank Thomas, banjoist Harper Goff, Ed Penner on tuba and drummer Monte Mountjoy. Finally, cornetist Red Nichols and his Five Pennies (trombonist King Jackson, clarinetist Rosie McHargue, bass saxophonist Joe Rushton, pianist Bobby Hammack and drummer Rollie Culver) perform some of the most intriguing music of the tape with their chamber jazz versions of "Three Blind Mice," "American Patrol," "Battle Hymn of the Republic," "Entrance of the Gladiators" and "Back Room Blues." As with **Vol. 1**, trad jazz collectors will definitely want this opportunity to see three of the best Dixieland groups of the era.

♪ 9 *The Snader Telescriptions: The Small Jazz Groups*
(1988, 49 minutes, Storyville)

Three superior jazz combos from 1950–51, two of which were short-lived, are featured on this enjoyable tape. In 1949, Count Basie reluctantly had to cut back to a combo from his big band although his new orchestra in 1952 would be quite successful. Basie's septet is an all-star unit featuring Clark Terry, clarinetist Buddy DeFranco, tenor saxophonist Wardell Gray, Freddie Green, bassist Jimmy Lewis and drummer Gus Johnson. "Basie Boogie" shows how well Basie could play (Gray and DeFranco also have solos), "If I Could Be with You" is a superior showcase for singer Helen Humes, "Basie's Conversation" mostly puts the spotlight on Lewis (who has short trade-offs with Basie and the horns including a humorous Terry), "I Cried for You" has a warm statement from Gray before Humes's vocal, and "One O'Clock Jump" includes short solos all around and some infectious riffing. Although it would have been nice to have Terry featured more, this miniset is a rare chance to see Wardell Gray.

Always world famous, Cab Calloway by 1947 was forced to break up his big band and, after touring with a sextet, he cut back to a quartet that consisted of Jonah Jones, pianist Dave Rivera, Milt Hinton and drummer Panama Francis. Calloway is as much of a showman and entertainer as usual on "Minnie the Moocher," "One for

My Baby" (a fine showcase for his voice) and a classic rendition of "St. James Infirmary." "I Can't Give You Anything but Love" features Jones's singing and trumpet playing, but Calloway's dancing and mugging are rather distracting. "Calloway Boogie" works better, with Cab singing and dancing while Jones takes a spectacular solo.

This tape concludes with five numbers ("Move," "I'll Be Around," "Conception," "I'll Never Smile Again," "Swedish Pastry") from the 1951 George Shearing Quintet (with vibraphonist Joe Roland, guitarist Chuck Wayne, bassist John Levy and drummer Denzil Best), a group that differs from the original Shearing Quintet only by having Roland on vibes rather than the retired Marjorie Hyams. Shearing at times sounds like both Bud Powell and Milt Buckner (the latter when he plays speedy block chords) and shows how he made bebop sound accessible without compromising his music.

♪ 8 *The Snader Telescriptions: The Vocalists*
(1988, 61 minutes, Storyville)

Four of the top vocalists of 1950–51 are featured on this set of Snader Telescriptions. Peggy Lee is backed by husband Dave Barbour's quartet (with pianist Hall Schaefer), performing "Why Don't You Do Right," a wistful "I Cover the Waterfront," "I May Be Wrong," "I Only Have Eyes for You," "What More Can a Woman Do" and her "I Don't Know Enough about You." Sarah Vaughan is outstanding on "You're Mine You," "The Nearness of You," "You're Not the Kind," "These Things I Offer" and "Perdido." June Christy is heard early in her solo career with backing from pianist Claude Williams and Ernie Felice's quartet, performing a coolly emotional version of "He's Funny that Way," "Taking a Chance on Love," a heartfelt "Imagination" and "All God's Children Got Rhythm." Finishing off the tape is a very young-looking Mel Tormé with pianist Al Pellegrini's group, swinging on "Blue Room," "April Showers," "You're Driving Me Crazy" and "You Oughta Be in Pictures."

Solo Flight: The Genius of Charlie Christian
(1996, 31 minutes, View Video)

Putting together this film must have been a real challenge for producer Gary Rhodes. Charlie Christian only lived to be 26, died back in 1942 and never appeared on film. Rhodes tracked down many of Christian's childhood friends from Oklahoma who shed light on the pioneering electric guitarist's early days. Jay McShann, Herb Ellis and Lionel Hampton also make a few comments and many rare photos are shown, so this half-hour portrait is as complete as possible considering its handicaps and impossible limitations.

 Song of the Spirit: The Story of Lester Young
(1988, 110 minutes, Song of the Spirit)

Bruce Fredericksen's Lester Young documentary is quite definitive. Frederickson utilizes still photos and includes a lot of interviews (since there is very little footage of Young), including storytelling from Norman Granz, John Hammond, Dizzy Gillespie, Count Basie, Harry "Sweets" Edison, Red Callender, Roy Eldridge, Jon Hendricks, Andy Kirk, Connie Kay and Jo Jones, telling the great tenor's story coherently and with accuracy. A special bonus is the inclusion at the end of this tape of the complete 1944 short **Jammin' the Blues** and three songs (a slow blues, "On the Sunny Side of the Street" with singer Marie Bryant, and a heated blues) colorfully photographed that feature Young and Edison, pianist Marlowe Morris, guitarist Barney Kessel, bassist Red Callender and Jo Jones and Big Sid Catlett on drums, with a guest appearance from the screaming tenor of Illinois Jacquet on the final number.

 Sonny Criss and the L.A. All Stars Plus Les McCann Trio
(1997, 56 minutes, Rhapsody Films)

Both of these 28-minute programs were originally part of the **Jazz on Stage** television series. **L.A. All Stars** is primitively recorded but valuable. It features pianist Hampton Hawes, bassist Leroy Vinnegar, drummer Bobby Thompson, Harry "Sweets" Edison, altoist Sonny Criss and Teddy Edwards on instrumental versions of "Memory Lane Blues" and "Teddy's Blues." They also back Big Joe Turner on "Feeling Happy" and "Shake, Rattle & Roll." The show was filmed at Memory Lane in Los Angeles and is one of the very rare examples of Hawes and Criss on film. The second half of this DVD features pianist Les McCann and his trio, around the time that he triumphed at the 1968 Montreux Jazz Festival. Performing at Shelly's Manne Hole in Los Angeles, McCann, bassist Jimmy Rowser and drummer Donald Dean perform "Right On," "Sunny," "With These Hands" and McCann's hit "Compared to What." The versions are excellent and feature the funky pianist before his singing began to dominate his music.

Sonny Rollins Live
(1986, 36 minutes, Rhapsody Films)

Sonny Rollins is seen and heard in 1973 (shortly after he ended another long retirement) performing at a concert with pianist Walter Davis, Jr., guitarist Masuo, electric bassist Bob Cranshaw and drummer David Lee. While the rhythm section is fine, the emphasis throughout is on the great tenor, who digs into "There Is No Greater Love," "Don't Stop the Carnival," "Alfie" and "St. Thomas," never seeming to run out of ideas.

Sonny Rollins: Saxophone Colossus
(1995, 101 minutes, Rhapsody Films)

This lengthy film from 1986 has several particularly memorable moments, including a very unusual incident. Performing at a concert in upstate New York, Rollins and his quintet (trombonist Clifton Anderson, pianist Mark Soskin, bassist Bob Cranshaw and drummer Marvin "Smitty" Smith) play "G-Man" and "The Bridge" before he launches into an unaccompanied tenor solo. During the latter Rollins decided to jump offstage. The jump was not smooth and he broke his heel. But not one to stop the show, Rollins laid on his back and continued playing his solo for the amazed audience! Also in this film, along with some brief interviews, is Rollins performing the

"Concerto for Tenor Saxophone and Orchestra" in Japan with a symphony orchestra along with "Don't Stop the Carnival." No matter what the setting, Sonny Rollins is heard throughout the documentary at his prime.

 Sound?? *(1988, 27 minutes, Rhapsody Films)*

This film from 1967 is largely a waste. Although it stars the remarkable multi-reedist Rahsaan Roland Kirk and classical composer John Cage, the two never actually meet. The action jumps back and forth between the two, with Kirk shown in a few amusing situations, including playing duets in the zoo with a variety of animals and interacting with members of his audience at a club after he had handed out whistles. In contrast, Cage is mostly seen wandering around asking unanswerable (and often nonsensical) questions and looking overly serious. If this half-hour film had concentrated solely on Rahsaan and allowed him to stretch out, it might have been significant.

 The Sound of Jazz
(2003, 56 minutes, Music Video Distributors)

The Sound of Jazz is, in this writer's estimation, the greatest of all jazz films. Part of the *Seven Lively Arts* television series, this one-hour special was broadcast on CBS on December 8, 1957, a Sunday afternoon. The roster of musicians was organized by Nat Hentoff and Whitney Balliet, the bit of talking and narration was relevant, and the performances were spontaneous, with the music allowed to speak for itself. This DVD is so full of excitement, suspense, and spontaneity that it rewards repeated viewings.

First up, Count Basie leads an all-star band on "Open All Night," "Dickie's Dream" and "I Left My Baby." The lineup of musicians gives one an idea as to the richness of this show: Roy Eldridge, Joe Newman, Joe Wilder, Doc Cheatham and Emmett Berry on trumpets, trombonists Vic Dickenson, Dickie Wells and Benny Morton, altoist Earle Warren, both Ben Webster and Coleman Hawkins on tenors, Gerry Mulligan, Freddie Green, bassist Eddie

Jones (Walter Page had been scheduled but became seriously ill) and Jo Jones with Jimmy Rushing singing on "I Left My Baby." Other than Cheatham and Warren, all of the horns get to solo. "Wild Man Blues" and "Rosetta" feature the Red Allen All-Stars. In addition to Allen (who sings a chorus on "Rosetta"), the band includes Pee Wee Russell (whose squeak on "Wild Man Blues" becomes a logical part of his very speechlike solo), Rex Stewart (who satirizes Russell and challenges Allen with a high note), Coleman Hawkins, Vic Dickenson, pianist Nat Pierce, guitarist Danny Barker, Milt Hinton and Jo Jones. The breaks on "Wild Man Blues" are full of drama, and "Rosetta" is a joyous romp.

The Thelonious Monk Trio (with bassist Ahmed Abdul Malik and drummer Osie Johnson) plays "Blue Monk." The reactions of Hawkins (pride at having hired the pianist for his group back in 1944), Basie (happy surprise) and Rushing (looking up to the heavens as if Monk was nuts) are fascinating and humorous. The Jimmy Giuffre Three (with Giuffre on clarinet, tenor and baritone, guitarist Jim Hall and bassist Jim Atlas) plays folk jazz on "The Train and the River" and Giuffre meets up with Pee Wee Russell on "Incomplete Blues for Two Clarinets." However, the emotional high point of the hour is Billie Holiday's touching rendition of "Fine and Mellow." Lady Day's voice had become erratic by 1957, but she sounds in her prime singing her blues with Eldridge, Cheatham, Dickenson, Hawkins, Webster, Mulligan, pianist Mal Waldron, guitarist Danny Barker, Hinton and Osie Johnson. Lester Young, who was weak and unable to perform on the other numbers, rises to the occasion with a remarkable one-chorus solo that steals the show.

This DVD is truly essential.

 Space Is the Place
(1993, 63 minutes, Rhapsody Films)

In 1974, Sun Ra made this rather bizarre movie. The plot is occasionally coherent, but overall little of it makes a great deal of sense except as a platform for Ra's esoteric philosophizing. Ra cast himself as the world savior for Blacks, supposedly disappearing during a 1969 tour of Europe so as to colonize a new planet that could serve as an escape for Blacks. There is one amusing scene cast in 1943 Chicago (although it looks like the 1960s) where Ra performs boogie-woogie piano and then begins playing thunderous free-form explorations that virtually destroy a club. Otherwise he spends much of the time in an odd card game with a head pimp, leading to adventures on earth including speaking at a Black youth center, running an outer space employment agency, planning a concert, being kidnapped, and leaving Earth with a few volunteers before the planet blows up. The special effects are remarkably cheesy; they could have been from a B movie in the 1950s. Unfortunately, Sun Ra's Arkestra only appears briefly a few times (John Gilmore and Marshall Allen are seen in short stretches) and, although June Tyson gets a few vocals, the music is mostly a prop and none of the songs are close to complete. It is a pity that a full concert by Ra was not filmed instead of this laughably bad movie.

Stan Getz: A Musical Odyssey
(1993, 60 minutes, The National Center for Jewish Film)

This obscure documentary from 1978 features highlights from Stan Getz's three-week visit to Israel in 1977. He is seen performing in concert and, most interestingly, playing with a Kurdish drummer, a Hassidic wedding band and a dance troupe. Getz clearly enjoyed himself, placing his tenor and his jazz skills in a wide variety of unusual settings, playing beautifully in all of them.

Stan Kenton *(1992, 60 minutes, Vintage Jazz Classics)*

The 1962 Stan Kenton orchestra is featured during this hour special. The key players in the big band at the time were pianist Kenton, altoist Gabe Baltazar, trumpeter Jack Sheldon, trombonist Dee Barton and tenor saxophonist Buddy Arnold, all of whom get solo space. Considered Kenton's last significant orchestra, the 22-piece big band includes a four-piece mellophonium section (with Carl

Saunders and Gene Roland) and 14 brass in all. Sue Raney takes vocals on "Let There Be Love" and "I Got It Bad," the Sportsmen sing "The Green Leaves of Summer" and, in addition to the theme "Artistry in Rhythm," the Stan Kenton Orchestra performs nine instrumentals ("Tico-Tico," "All the Things You Are," "The Blues Story," "Maria," "The Peanut Vendor," "Intermission Riff," "My Old Flame," "Limehouse Blues," "Malaguena") with power, some bombastic moments and plenty of drama. Although this particular version of the Kenton big band was not as hard-swinging as the one from a few years earlier, it contains its share of talent.

Stanley Jordan: Live in Montreal
(2003, 59 minutes, Image Entertainment)

The remarkable guitarist Stanley Jordan is featured at his July 1, 1990, concert at the Montreal Jazz Festival on unaccompanied solos and in a trio with bassist Charnett Moffett and drummer Tommy Campbell. Jordan's tapping technique is still astounding at times, and on some tunes (most notably "Autumn Leaves"), he plays two guitars at once. Most of the repertoire on this set ("Flying Home," "Cousin Mary," "Autumn Leaves," "All the Children," "One Less Bell to Answer," "Eleanor Rigby," "Willow Weep for Me," "What's Going On," "Lady in My Life," "Stairway to Heaven") is comprised of rock and pop standards ("Flying Home" is not the Lionel Hampton tune but a Jordan original) although the improvising is certainly jazz. Still, one wishes the songs were stronger. The bonus material is comprised of an additional selection (the 18-minute "Return Expedition," which starts out with a long bass solo) and a 12-minute interview with Jordan in which he discusses his beginnings, his newest release at the time (*Standards*) and the usual topics.

Stanley Turrentine: In Concert
(1990, 60 minutes, Kultur)

For this performance film, the soulful tenor Stanley Turrentine and a competent if somewhat anonymous backup group (keyboardist Bob Fox, guitarist Dave Stryker, bassist Scott Ambush and drummer Scott Peeker) perform eight selections ("Sugar," "Oop Bop Sh'Bam," "La Place Street," "Indian Summer," "My Romance," "Salt Song," "Gibraltar," "Impressions"). Turrentine is in superior form and the mostly straightahead material is more challenging than usual, inspiring him to stretch himself and show why he was consistently both a commercial and an artistic success throughout his career.

Stephane Grappelli: A Life in the Jazz Century
(2002, 120 minutes, Music on Earth)

The bulk of this two-DVD set is a definitive biography of Stephane Grappelli. After Grappelli plays a bit of "Night and Day" with a quartet, his story is told in great detail. The violinist was interviewed in 1996 when he was 88 and, although his voice was weak, his mind was still very sharp. The narration and editing are excellent throughout the lengthy portrait, which covers his childhood, the beginning of his professional career in 1923, his musical partnership with Django Reinhardt (starting 28 minutes into the film) and his many decades of accomplishments after he and Reinhardt went their separate ways in 1939. In addition to Grappelli, promoter Lew Grade, bassist Coleridge Goode, British talk show host Michael Parkinson, Yehudi Menuhin, Diz Disley, violinist Nigel Kennedy and guitarist Martin Taylor are among those interviewed. Plenty of photos are shown along with a generous amount of film clips, some of

A long-lost film short of Django Reinhardt, Stephane Grappelli and the Quintet of the Hot Club of France is included in *Stephane Grappelli: A Life in the Jazz Century.*

which are complete. Grappelli plays "Minor Swing" in 1956, "Tangerine" with Teddy Wilson in the late 1960s, "Jalousie" with Menuhin and "Let's Fall in Love," "Shine," "Nuages," "How High the Moon" plus a medley of "Someone to Watch Over Me" and "I Got Rhythm" with his own groups.

But that is not all. The second disc has an additional hour of extras, including interview segments that were left out of the film and the complete versions of three remarkable films. A 1928 short has Grappelli playing as part of the violin section with Gregor et ses Gregorians, a 16-piece band led by a clowning leader; Grappelli looks a little embarrassed in spots. The 14-minute, five-song short **Stephane Grappelli and His Quintet** from 1946 has the violinist performing "Piccadilly Stomp," "Wendy," "Sweet Georgia Brown," "Evelyne" and "Stephane's Blues" with a group including pianist George Shearing, guitarist Dave Goldberg, bassist Coledridge Godley and drummer/singer Ray Ellington. But most remarkable of all is 1937's **Jazz Hot**. All of the other existing footage of Django Reinhardt (a couple of short silent segments taken from newsreels and a brief appearance in a movie in which he plays on a train) is included on this release's first DVD. **Jazz Hot**, which is six minutes long, starts with a band illustrating the difference between classical and jazz music. Then Reinhardt and Grappelli play a beautiful, unidentified melody while the other members of the Quintet of the Hot Club of France look on while playing cards. Finally the full group performs the number. It is amazing, looking at Reinhardt's fingering, that he could play chords while only using two fingers on his crippled left hand.

The latter film is priceless, and **A Life in the Jazz Century** (which is available from www.musiconearth.co.uk) is a gem.

 ### Stephane Grappelli: Live in New Orleans
(2001, 59 minutes, Image Entertainment)

Originally out on a videotape released by Leisure Video, this DVD features violinist Stephane Grappelli in superior form at a 1989 club date. Eighty-one at the time, Grappelli

plays with a quartet also including electric guitarist Martin Taylor (who has plenty of solos), rhythm acoustic guitarist Marc Fosset and bassist Patrice Caratini. There are individual features for Taylor ("Ol' Man River"), Fosset (who sings along with his guitar in odd harmonies on "After You've Gone") and Caratini ("Armando's Rhumba"), but it is the quartet pieces ("Cheek to Cheek," "Love for Sale," "Shine," "Are You in the Mood," "Medley: Someone to Watch Over Me, I Got Rhythm," "I Get a Kick Out of You," "You Are the Sunshine of My Life," "Sweet Georgia Brown," "Honeysuckle Rose," "Daphne") that are the most fun. As usual, Grappelli makes it all look so easy.

 ### Stephane Grappelli: Live in San Francisco
(1990, 60 minutes, Rhapsody Films)

Violinist Stephane Grappelli may have been 77 when he performed at the two 1985 concerts that are on this video, but he still had plenty of energy and creativity left. Joined by guitarist Diz Disley and bassist Jack Sewing, Grappelli is featured at the Paul Masson Vineyards in Northern California and at San Francisco's Great American Music Hall, swinging on such numbers as "I Got Rhythm," "Fascinating Rhythm," "Let's Fall in Love," "Swing '42," "You Are the Sunshine of My Life," "Minor Swing," "Here, There and Everywhere," "St. Louis Blues," "Tea for Two," "Them There Eyes" and "After You've Gone." For the explosive versions of "Sweet Georgia Brown" and "Honeysuckle Rose," Grappelli's group is joined by violinist Mike Marshall and both David Grisman and Mike Marshall on mandolins. This is a very enjoyable tape that does Stephane Grappelli justice.

 ### Steps Ahead: Copenhagen Live
(1994, 60 minutes, Storyville)

On April 1, 1983, Steps Ahead (vibraphonist/leader Mike Mainieri, tenor saxophonist Michael Brecker, pianist Eliane Elias, bassist Eddie Gomez and drummer Peter Erskine) filmed an hour's performance at a museum in Copenhagen. Other than at the tape's beginning when the musicians are shown walking in the museum, this is a straight performance film with Steps Ahead playing Don Grolnick's "Pools" and group originals ("Islands," "Skyward Bound," "Northern Cross," "Loxodrome," "Sara's Touch," "Duo in Two Parts," "Both Sides of the Coin"). The musicianship is excellent with Brecker's fiery flights consistently taking solo honors, and it is interesting to see Elias at the age of 18. However, the songs are a bit dull and only fans of this eclectic group will find the music to be very memorable.

The Steve Huffsteter Big Band
(2004, 62 minutes, AIX Records)

Trumpeter Steve Huffsteter heads a 20-piece Los Angeles big band (trumpeters Buddy Childers, Mike McGuffey, Lee Thornburg and Larry McGuire, trombonists Jock Ellis, Les Benedict, Jack Redmond and Morris Repass, altoist Kim Richmond, tenors Jerry Pinter and Doug Webb, baritonist Jim Cowger, Bill Perkins on tenor and soprano, guitarist Jamie Findley, pianist Mark Massey, bassist Kevin Axt, drummer Dave Tull and percussionist Dee Huffsteter) on this DVD. Filmed on April 17, 2003, at the Zipper Concert Hall in the Coburn School for Performing Arts, Huffsteter's band performs eight of the leader's songs ("Moacir," "Circles," "Nightwalk," "The Quest," "3½," "Autumn Returns," "Fool's Silver," "A Waltz & Battery"). There is no audience other than the film crew and no talking, but the music communicates well by itself. None of the selections are explosive (one wishes that an uptempo romp had been included), but the music is reasonably unpredictable within the modern mainstream. Huffsteter solos on half of the selections and plays piano on "Fool's Silver," the closest that the music comes to sounding like a dance band number. There are spots for Richmond, both the tenors and guitarist Findley, among others. Bill Perkins, who passed away less than four months after this set, has several solos and sounds quite modern. The most interesting pieces are "Circles" (which is a little reminiscent of "Giant Steps"), "The Quest" (which has a Middle Eastern feel) and "Autumn Returns." In addition as bonus material, Huffsteter is featured on 33 minutes of interview excerpts covering the band, Perkins, the other

sidemen, the individual songs and his background. There is also a three-minute excerpt of an unidentified number performed by the big band at a local club, Fitzgerald's.

Steve Lacy: Lift the Bandstand
(1986, 50 minutes, Rhapsody Films)

Soprano saxophonist Steve Lacy has had a rather diverse career and he talks about each period of his life during this excellent documentary. Lacy thoughtfully discusses his experiences playing Dixieland and Thelonious Monk's music, as well as playing with Cecil Taylor and with his longtime sextet. He also performs "Gay Paree Bop" and the adventurous "Prospectus" with his sextet which includes altoist Steve Potts and singer Irene Aebi. This film is both educational and entertaining, serving as a perfect introduction to Steve Lacy's music.

The Story of Jazz *(1993, 98 minutes, BMG Video)*

This attempt at telling the history of jazz in under 100 minutes is particularly intriguing for its parallels to Ken Burns's **Jazz**, which would be filmed a half-decade later. As with the latter film, **The Story of Jazz** emphasizes the 1920s and '30s, not reaching the bebop era until the documentary is at the two-thirds mark. Mixing together familiar film clips (all of which are excerpts) and comments from veteran musicians (plus Wynton Marsalis), the early years of jazz are depicted fairly accurately except for some unfortunate errors. It is said about 1924, "At that time there was no greater arranger than Fletcher Henderson," even though Don Redman wrote nearly all of the charts for Henderson's band and Henderson did not really start arranging until the early 1930s. Also, the omission of nearly every White musician (other than Bix Beiderbecke) is inexcusable. One would think from this documentary that the swing era had been launched by Count Basie; Benny Goodman and the other White bandleaders are dismissed very quickly. After covering classic bebop, such genres as cool jazz (other than a moment on Miles Davis), hard bop, soul jazz, revival Dixieland and bossa nova are not even mentioned. There is a bit on late 1950s Miles Davis and John Coltrane and a couple of minutes on Ornette Coleman's quartet, but nothing much on the rest of the avant-garde, which is quickly dismissed. After a brief mention of Davis's work in fusion, the 1970s, '80s and '90s are completely skipped although the film ends optimistically. One wonders if Ken Burns saw **The Story of Jazz** before working on his documentary, for it contains many of the same faults. Best are the interview segments (some of which were also used in other documentaries), including comments from Harry "Sweets" Edison, Bud Freeman, Doc Cheatham, Lester Bowie, Milt Hinton, Zilner Randolph, Randy Weston, Billy Taylor, Jay McShann, Buddy Tate, Claude Williams, Heywood Henry, Grover Mitchell, Tony Bennett, Carmen McRae, Buck Clayton, Annie Ross, Jimmy Heath, Billy Eckstine, Dizzy Gillespie, Ben Riley, Roy Haynes, Joe Williams, Rashied Ali and Wayne Shorter. But overall, this documentary misses its mark by sticking almost entirely to pre-1965 jazz, and by serving as a predecessor for Ken Burns.

♪ Storyville—The Naked Dance
(2000, 60 minutes, Shanachie)

Storyville was the red light district in New Orleans from 1898–1917, 16 square blocks that were populated by up to 2,000 prostitutes. Due to the permissive nature of the district, early jazz music also prospered in the area. Pianists were hired to play background music in whorehouses, and brass bands played parades, dances and large functions. This intriguing documentary utilizes jazz in the background, but is primarily about the lives of the prostitutes. There are many photos (particularly the shots of E.J. Bellocq), and rare short films (which were nickelodeon "peep shows") that give one the flavor of the era.

♪ The String Trio of New York: Built by Hand
(1988, 30 minutes, Rhapsody Films)

This brief video contains a lot of music and information about the String Trio of New York. The avant-garde trio was comprised in 1988 of violinist Charles Burnham,

guitarist James Emery and bassist John Lindberg. The film has each of the musicians talking about their hopes and goals for the group. They perform six originals, starting out with the fairly accessible "Wise Old Owl Blues," "Epherema-Trilogy" and "Texas Koto Blues," gradually evolving into "Multiple Reasons," Hendrix's "Manic Depression" and the intense "Seven Vice." This tape serves as an excellent introduction to the group.

♪ Supershow *(1969, 93 minutes, Eagle Entertainment)*

Primitively filmed, this British DVD documents a very interesting two-day festival. A variety of pop and rock stars (including Jack Bruce, Eric Clapton, Buddy Miles, Stephen Stills and even Glen Campbell) plus bluesman Buddy Guy are featured. But there is also the Modern Jazz Quartet performing "Under the Jasmine Tree" and "Visitor from Venus," and some rare footage of Rahsaan Roland Kirk, who romps on "Primitive Ohio" and "I Say a Little Prayer" in addition to sitting in with Buddy Guy and Eric Clapton.

♪ Swing: The Best of the Big Bands, Vol. 1
(1987, 50 minutes, MCA Home Video)

The four videotapes in this series feature the highlights of a variety of musical shorts filmed by Universal Pictures. Despite its title, the music was recorded after the swing era died in 1946, and mostly dates from 1947–52. Each of the performances is complete in itself and there are many great moments along the way. **Vol. 1** has numbers from Tommy Dorsey's 1951 band (nostalgic re-creations of "Opus One" and "Boogie Woogie"), the Hi-Lo's ("Rockin' Chair"), Ray Anthony ("Skip to My Lou"), Benny Carter's part-time orchestra ("Harlequin Bounce" and "Congeroo," the latter featuring the King Cole Quartet with percussionist Jack Costanzo), the vocal duo of Tony Pastor and Rosemary Clooney ("Movie Tonight"), Harry James ("Charmaine" and "Trumpet Blues"), Billie Holiday (a priceless clip from 1951 with the Count Basie Septet, performing "God Bless the Child" and "Now or Never"),

Charlie Barnet (remakes of "Redskin Rumba" and "Pompton Turnpike"), Duke Ellington ("On a Turquoise Cloud" with singer Kay Davis and "Frankie and Johnny" with trombonist Tyree Glenn), from **Symphony in Swing**, the Blackburn Twins and Marian Colby ("I'm in a Dancing Mood") and Gene Krupa's 1947 big band (boppish renditions of "Lover" and "Leave Us Leap"). Each of the videotapes in this series has memorable performances, but the collection on **Vol. 1** is particularly valuable.

🎵 *Swing: The Best of the Big Bands, Vol. 2*
(1987, 50 minutes, MCA Home Video)

Vol. 2 in this four-video series is nearly the equal of the first. Shown in complete performances are the big bands of Charlie Barnet ("Skyliner" and "Jeepers Creepers"), Lionel Hampton ("Baby Don't Love Me No More" and "International Blues"), trumpeter Ralph Materie ("A Trumpeter's Lullaby" and "After Midnight"), Gene Krupa ("Boogie Blues"), the Dorsey Brothers ("Yes Indeed" and "Well, Git It"), Tex Beneke (at the head of the Glenn Miller ghost band for "Chattanooga Choo Choo" and "Hey Baba-Re-Bop"), Stan Kenton ("Eager Beaver" and "Reed Rapture") and Woody Herman's Second Herd of 1948 (memorable if brief versions of "Caldonia" and "Northwest Passage"). In addition, Sugar Chile Robinson plays boogie-woogie piano on "Number's Boogie," the Nat King Cole Trio is featured on "Ooh Kickeroonie" and "Route 66," and Sarah Vaughan sings "Don't Blame Me" and "I Cried for You."

🎵 *Swing: The Best of the Big Bands, Vol. 3*
(1987, 50 minutes, MCA Home Video)

Vol. 3 in this valuable series features Jimmy Dorsey playing some Dixieland ("Sweet Georgia Brown" and "South Rampart Street Parade"), singer Billy Daniels ("Them There Eyes" and "That Old Black Magic"), the big bands of Les Brown ("Turkey Hop"), Freddie Martin ("La Tempesta" and "Do Do Do"), Duke Ellington in 1950 ("History of Jazz in Three Minutes" and "Violet Blue"), Harry James

("Brave Bulls" and "I've Got a Crush on You"), Count Basie ("Red Bank Boogie") and Charlie Barnet ("Smooth Sailing" and "Murder at Peyton Hall"), the Gene Krupa Trio ("Stompin' at the Savoy" and "Melody in F"), Teresa Brewer ("Old Man Mose") and the Ink Spots ("If I Didn't Care" and "Shanty in Old Shanty Town"). The Dorsey and Krupa selections take honors.

🎵 *Swing: The Best of the Big Bands, Vol. 4*
(1987, 50 minutes, MCA Home Video)

The final video in this four-tape series is the weakest overall but has a few notable tracks. The Count Basie Orchestra performs a medium-tempo blues inaccurately titled "One O'Clock Jump" plus "Swingin' the Blues." Jimmy Dorsey plays "Am I Blue" (a feature for singer Dottie O'Brien) and a straight dance band version of "Lover." Tex Beneke leads the Glenn Miller ghost band in 1946 through "I've Got a Gal in Kalamazoo" and "Little Brown Jug." The Mills Brothers (just three of them) perform "Paper Doll" and "Opus One" before a live audience. Ray Anthony plays versions of "All Anthony and No Cleopatra" and "Mr. Anthony's Boogie" that find him emulating Harry James as usual. The Skylarks sing an overly dramatic "Swing Low, Sweet Chariot" and a corny rendition of "Darktown Strutters Ball." Things improve as the Stan Kenton Orchestra performs a full-length version of "Artistry in Rhythm" plus "Taboo." Louis Prima sings "That Old Black Magic" with his big band and features Buddy Rich on a very rapid version of "Sing, Sing, Sing." Finally, Buddy Rich's combo showcases vibraphonist Terry Gibbs on "Burn" and Rich solos with his big band on "Not So Quiet Please."

🎵 *Swing into Christmas*
(1995, 60 minutes, Sony)

Wynton Marsalis, Marcus Roberts, Terence Blanchard, Grover Washington, Jr., and tenor saxophonist David Sanchez are among the jazz stars celebrating Christmas on this obscure video, which is similar to the CD of the

same name. Among the songs featured are "Have Yourself a Merry Little Christmas," "Carol of the Bells" and "Let It Snow! Let It Snow! Let It Snow!"

🎵 *Swing, Volume One* (1990, 54 minutes, Storyville)

Five complete shorts and an excerpt from a film are on this interesting videotape. The Benny Goodman Orchestra is featured on 1937's **Auld Lang Syne**, a fund-raiser for the Will Rogers Memorial. Filmed at the same time as **Hollywood Hotel**, this short has the Benny Goodman Orchestra (with Harry James and Gene Krupa) playing brief versions of "I've Got a Heartful of Music," "Avalon" (with Lionel Hampton) and "House Hop." **Class in Swing Time** (1938) was meant as an introduction to swing, for it has a narrator explaining swing and unfortunately often talking over the music, giving a play-by-play of the Artie Shaw Orchestra's performances of "Nightmare," "Table D'Hote," "I Have Eyes" (with Helen Forrest) and "Shoot the Likker to Me John Boy" (with Buddy Rich). Next, Artie Shaw and a 1940 studio orchestra that includes Billy Butterfield perform "Concerto for Clarinet" from the Fred Astaire movie **Second Chorus**.

The short **Jimmy Dorsey and His Orchestra** is a well-constructed film from 1940. Dorsey shows off his technique on alto during the tricky "Beebe," Helen O'Connell sings a juvenile novelty ("Rubber Dolly"), Bob Eberly croons a ballad ("Only a Rose") and the band has fun on the instrumental "Long John Silver." **Hoagy Carmichael** (1939) has the Jack Teagarden big band performing a variety of Carmichael tunes, including concise versions of "Two Sleepy People," "That's Right, I'm Wrong," "Washboard Blues," "Lazy Bones," "Small Fry," "Rockin' Chair" and "Star Dust." Meredith Blake takes a couple of vocals, Carmichael sings a little, and Teagarden (who helps out vocally on "Small Fry") takes a few short trombone solos. The best film included on this tape is 1947's **Let's Make Rhythm**, an amusing romance story with a lot of spots for the Stan Kenton Orchestra which at the time included (among others) trumpeters Ray Wetzel, Chico Alvarez

and Buddy Childers, trombonists Kai Winding and Milt Bernhart, altoist Boots Mussulli, tenors Vido Musso and Bob Cooper, bassist Eddie Safranski and drummer Shelly Manne along with June Christy and the Pastels. The music ("Artistry in Rhythm," "Down in Chi-Hua-Hua," "Just a Sittin' and a Rockin'," "Concert to End All Concertos," "Tampico") fits very well into the happy plot and is an excellent showcase for the Kenton band.

🎵 *Talmage Farlow* (1986, 58 minutes, Rhapsody Films)

This film by director Lorenzo De Stefano is everything that a documentary should be. Guitarist Tal Farlow had a fascinating story as one of the top bop guitarists of the 1950s who actually preferred being semi-retired in New England, choosing to work as a sign painter after dropping out of the jazz scene in the late '50s. His day-to-day life is depicted colorfully, his early career is expertly summarized, and he is seen preparing for a rare New York engagement. Unlike too many jazz documentaries, this one also has a complete performance (without voiceover): an exciting trio version of "Fascinatin' Rhythm" with pianist Tommy Flanagan and bassist Red Mitchell. One comes away from this film both admiring and understanding Tal Farlow, and sporting a smile as big as his.

🎵 *The Swingin' Singin' Years*
(1991, 51 minutes, Vintage Jazz Classics)

This videotape is an hour special that was telecast on March 8, 1960, featuring some of the survivors of the swing era with Ronald Reagan as the host. Along the way the Woody Herman Orchestra (with Bob Cooper and Bill Perkins on tenors) performs "Your Father's Mustache," Ella Mae Morse and Freddie Slack revive "Cow Cow Boogie," Freddy Martin's orchestra with pianist Jack Fina plays "Tonight We Love" and "Bumble Boogie," and Jo Stafford performs "The Gentleman Is a Dope" and her humorous "Tim-Tay-Shun" (a hillbilly version of "Temptation" with Red Ingle's Natural Seven). In addition, Eddy

Howard sings "To Each His Own," Dinah Washington does a medley of "What a Difference a Day Makes" and "Makin' Whoopee," Louis Jordan brings back "Choo Choo Ch'Boogie" Charlie Barnet plays soprano on "Wanderin' Blues," Vaughan Monroe warbles "Racing with the Moon" and "There, I've Said It Again," and, for the finale, Stan Kenton's big band digs into "Malaguena." There are enough strong moments along the way to make this nostalgia show worth picking up.

Tenor Legends: Coleman Hawkins & Dexter Gordon
(1994, 57 minutes, Shanachie)

Two unrelated films are on this video. The superior one features Coleman Hawkins in Brussels in 1962 with pianist Georges Arvanitas, guitarist Mickey Baker, bassist Jimmy Woode and drummer Kansas Fields. Hawkins plays a remarkable unaccompanied "Blowing for Adolphe Sax" and then with the group performs a heated version of "Disorder at the Border," "South of France Blues" and "Hawk Hunt." The second half of the tape is more conventional but still of interest. Dexter Gordon is featured at the Club Montmartre in 1969 with pianist Kenny Drew, bassist Niels Pedersen and drummer Makaya Ntshoko. The camerawork starts off overly hyper but eventually settles down. Gordon is in particularly fine form on "Those Were the Days" and "Fried Bananas."

Tenor Titans *(1992, 60 minutes, Video Arts International)*

Branford Marsalis hosts and is featured on this collection of filmed performances from the major tenor saxophonists. Seen along the way are Coleman Hawkins, Bud Freeman, Georgie Auld, Don Byas, Ben Webster, Lester Young, Wardell Gray, Warne Marsh, Zoot Sims, Stan Getz, Paul Gonsalves, Eric Dixon, Sal Nistico, Frank Foster, Eddie "Lockjaw" Davis, Sam "The Man" Taylor, Illinois Jacquet, Dexter Gordon, Charles Rouse, John Coltrane, Wayne Shorter, Archie Shepp, Sonny Rollins and David Murray.

Texas Tenor: The Illinois Jacquet Story
(1993, 81 minutes, Rhapsody Films)

One problem with this documentary is that it does not focus that much on the life story of Illinois Jacquet. Instead it constantly skips around and mostly shows some of his activities of 1988–91. Filmed in black and white (which was a mistake) and often emphasizing close-ups, the film shows Jacquet in a variety of settings, including backstage at the Blue Note, at the 1988 Floating Jazz Festival, on a bus, at a saxophone repair shop and buying a hat in Paris. Jacquet briefly talks about his early years and there are laudatory comments from the likes of Lionel Hampton, Sonny Rollins, Dizzy Gillespie, Buddy Tate, Arnett Cobb, Wild Bill Davis, Dorothy Donegan, Jonah Jones, Al Hibbler, Milt Hinton, Harry "Sweets" Edison, Les Paul, Dan Morgenstern, Javon Jackson, Walter Blandings, Jr., Clark Terry, Cecil Payne, Milt Hinton and others, most of which are fairly brief. Jacquet is seen performing with his big band, but none of the selections are complete; he also plays a capella on a few occasions. Among the songs are a blues, "Stompin' at the Savoy," "Ghost of a Chance," "On the Sunny Side of the Street," "Sophisticated Lady" and "Flying Home." But although this film has its moments, it never really coherently concentrates on its star.

That Old Black Magic
(2001, 60 minutes, Music Video Distributors)

This intriguing DVD has ten performances from the 1950s and '60s that originally appeared on Canadian television and have rarely if ever been seen since. With the exception of Duke Ellington, who is featured with a quintet that includes Johnny Hodges and Harry Carney on a medley of his hits in 1958 and at the end of the tape playing "Sophisticated Lady" with a trio, all of the headliners are singers. Cab Calloway (1958) performs an energetic version of "Minnie the Moocher," Ella Fitzgerald (1955) sings "A-Tisket, A-Tasket," "Imagination" and "Lady Be Good," Billy Eckstine (1955) is fine on "September Song,"

Sarah Vaughan (1959) performs a typically wondrous version of "Misty" and duets with the host (Wally Koster) on "How about You," Dinah Washington (1959) swings an uptempo "Lover Where Can You Be" and "Send Me to the 'Lectric Chair," Marian Anderson (1959) is featured on a beautiful "Ave Maria," Sammy Davis, Jr., (1959) sings and dances on "Gypsy in My Soul" and "Perdido," playing a few notes on trombone, vibes and drums during the latter, and Della Reese (1960) on "Someday You'll Want Me to Want You" humorously uses an arrangement with a half dozen false endings. Most memorable of all is Nat King Cole (1961) on "Stay with Love," performing a routine at a party (which includes several good jokes) and playing a bit of piano. This DVD is well worth picking up.

 ### Thelonious in Europe, in America, in Japan
(2003, 97 minutes, Anonymous Film Archive #26)

This bootleg videotape is too valuable to ignore since it features Thelonious Monk in six different settings, some of them rare. Monk, tenor saxophonist Charlie Rouse, bassist Larry Gales and drummer Ben Riley are featured in London in 1965 performing "Straight No Chaser," "Hackensack," "Rhythm-a-Ning" and "Epistrophy" (the latter has an interesting false ending before resuming). Although the walking bass solos are not too exciting, both Monk and Rouse are in excellent form, and the film, though a bit grainy, has fine camerawork. The most unique performance on this tape is a 19-minute solo set (filmed in color) from Berlin in 1969 that has Monk playing Duke Ellington songs ("Sophisticated Lady," "Caravan," "Solitude") that he only recorded once, back in 1955. Perhaps this concert was to celebrate Ellington's 70th birthday. "Caravan" is given a fast and hypnotic stride. The next two clips are much more familiar. Monk, bassist Ahmed Abdul Malik and Osie Johnson perform "Blue Monk" from the 1957 television broadcast **The Sound of Jazz**, and Monk's 1964 quartet (with Rouse, Gales and Riley) plays "'Round Midnight" and "Crepuscule with Nellie," performances that are made available on **Monk in**

Oslo. After a solo version of "Comin' on the Hudson" from 1970, the remainder of the tape is from a Japanese television appearance in 1963 with Rouse, bassist Butch Warren and drummer Frank Dunlop. While part of this version of "Evidence" was used in the film **Straight No Chaser**, "Blue Monk," "Just a Gigolo," "Ba-lue Bolivar Ba-lues-are" and "Epistrophy" were previously unknown. Thelonious Monk fans should search for this valuable if unauthorized videotape.

 ### Thelonious Monk: American Composer
(1993, 60 minutes, BMG Video)

This one-hour documentary does a good job of introducing viewers to the music of Thelonious Monk. Randy Weston and Orrin Keepnews are particularly prominent in discussing Monk's legacy and style, and there are also interesting comments from Barry Harris, Billy Taylor, Ben Riley, T.S. Monk and Thelonious's sister Marion White. There are many clips (most fairly familiar) that are utilized, but they are all excerpts. However, one does get a good idea of how Monk's music sounded and of its unique qualities. And to its credit, this film focuses much more on his music than on Monk's personal life, covering the basics and whetting one's appetite for more.

 ### Thelonious Monk: Monk Round the World/ Monk in London
(28 minutes, 2004, Hyena Records)

Monk Round the World is a seven-song CD featuring the Thelonious Monk quartet on previously unreleased performances from 1961-64. Also included in this release is the DVD **Monk in London** which features the pianist, tenor-saxophonist Charlie Rouse, bassist Larry Gales and drummer Ben Riley on three numbers ("Rhythm A Ning," "Nutty" and "Criss Cross") performed at a London concert on March 14, 1965. There is a sameness in the framework to the performances, with each song having a melody statement followed by tenor, piano, and routine bass and drums solos before the melody ends the piece.

Rouse is in particularly good form and Monk is at his best on "Rhythm A Ning."

Thelonious Monk: Straight No Chaser
(90 minutes, 1988, Warner Home Video)

In 1968, Michael and Christian Blackwood shot a lot of footage of pianist/composer Thelonious Monk, both onstage and in his private life. Those reels serve as the basis for this full-length film by Bruce Ricker and result in one of the great jazz documentaries. The Thelonious Monk story is told quite colorfully through interviews with many associates, including Tommy Flanagan, Barry Harris, Baroness Nica de Koenigswarter, Charlie Rouse and T.S. Monk. One gets to see Monk touring Europe with an under-rehearsed octet (which includes Johnny Griffin and Phil Woods), in many personal scenes (including lying in bed at a hotel while ordering room service) and performing a large assortment of songs, many of which are shown complete ("Evidence," "Rhythm-a-Ning," "'Round Midnight," "Well You Needn't," "Bright Mississippi," "Blue Monk," "Trinkle Tinkle," "Ugly Beauty," "Ask Me Now," "Just a Gigolo," "Crepuscule with Nellie," "I Should Care," "We See," "Oska T.," "Evidence," "Epistrophy," "Don't Blame Me," "Ruby My Dear," "I Mean You," "Lulu's Back in Town," "Off Minor," "Pannonica," "Boo Boo's Birthday," "Misterioso," "Monk's Mood," "Sweetheart of All My Dreams"). The film also does not shy away from Monk's decline in the early '70s and gives as good an explanation as to the reasons behind it as possible. **Straight No Chaser** sets the standard for jazz documentaries.

Things to Come
(1993, 55 minutes, Vintage Jazz Classics)

The two most significant big bands of the bebop era (other than Woody Herman's First and Second Herds) are featured on this videotape. The first half has Billy Eckstine and his orchestra from 1946 featured in the short film **Rhythm in a Riff**. The plot (such as it is) is dispensed with early on. The band, featuring tenors Gene Ammons and Frank Wess, baritonist Leo Parker (who unfortunately has no solos), trumpeters Hobart Dotson and King Kolax, pianist Jimmy Golden and drummer Art Blakey (who is quite explosive) was still very advanced in 1946 even though it was two years after Dizzy Gillespie and Charlie Parker had departed. Eckstine, who also plays some valve trombone, sings the swinging "Rhythm in a Riff," "You Call It Madness," "Lonesome Lover Blues," "I Want to Talk about You" and "Prisoner of Love" while Ann Baker vocalizes on "I Cried for You." The orchestra gets to romp on the instrumentals "Second Balcony Jump," "Taps Miller" and "Our Delight."

The latter half of the tape features the Dizzy Gillespie Orchestra during their eight onscreen numbers from 1947's **Jivin' in Be-Bop**, leaving out all of the specialty numbers that showcased other acts. Helen Humes sings "Be-Baba-Leba" and "Crazy 'Bout a Man," Kenny Hagood does what he can with "I Waited for You" and Gillespie vocalizes on "He Beeped When He Should Have Bopped." Best are "Salt Peanuts," "Oop-Bop Sh'Bam," "One Bass Hit" (featuring Ray Brown) and "Things to Come." In addition to Gillespie, altoist Scoops Carey, Milt Jackson, John Lewis, Ray Brown and drummer Joe Harris are featured. The band also includes trumpeter Dave Burns and James Moody although they do not solo.

Three Piano Portraits
(1997, 63 minutes, Rhapsody Films)

A trio of shorts featuring top jazz pianists are reissued in full on this videotape. **Anything for Jazz**, a 25-minute film from 1979, focuses on Jaki Byard, a very versatile pianist capable of playing anything from stride to free. Byard is seen playing solo piano on a portion of "Meditations on Integration," leading his big band (the Apollo Stompers) on excerpts from a couple of songs (including "Once in a While") and performing a suite dedicated to his family. Unfortunately the picture is often very dark, the editing is erratic, and none of the performances are complete. There are brief comments from Ron Carter and Bill

Evans (shortly before his death), but these say little except how underrated Byard has always been. The 15-minute **Nutman's Got the Blues** has Cyrus Chestnut in 1997 at 2:00 A.M. (after performing in the same club where this was filmed) talking a bit about his music and playing okay versions of "The Nutman's Blues," a thoughtful "Sweet Hour of Prayer" and a boppish "Revelation." Finally there is Barry Harris's **Passing It On** (1984, 23 minutes). Harris, who says, "I consider bebop to be the beginning and end of music," is portrayed as a teacher who had just founded the Jazz Cultural Theatre. He jams briefly with a quartet, emphasizes the importance of creating a young audience for jazz during a television interview with Joe Franklin, takes a piano lesson from a classical teacher (impishly playing a stride version of "Liza" when she temporarily leaves to answer the door), plays a little bit of "Epistrophy" and "Ruby My Dear" with a trio, and is seen backstage talking with baritonist Pepper Adams, trumpeter Red Rodney and tenor saxophonist Clifford Jordan.

In each of these films, it is a pity that there is not more music, even in the shorts. If Harris had jammed a complete song with Adams and Rodney, it would have given today's viewers an opportunity to see three classic bop greats playing together. As it is, the three shorts have their moments of interest, but each falls short of its potential.

 Toots Thielemans in New Orleans
(2001, 59 minutes, Image Entertainment)

Toots Thielemans has been the top jazz chromatic harmonica player since the mid-'50s, and nearly the only one. Though the instrument looks easy to play, Toots's mastery of inhaling and exhaling to fit rapid melody lines and his ideas is unprecedented. This live DVD from 1988 (formerly out as a video from Leisure Jazz) teams Thielemans with pianist Fred Hersch (who is in superior form), bassist Harvie Swartz and drummer Adam Nussbaum. Their repertoire ("The Days of Wine and Roses," "Medley: 'Round

Midnight, Little Rootie Tootie," "The Meaning of the Blues," "On Green Dolphin Street," "Three and One," "If You Go Away," "Only Trust Your Heart," "Bluesette") holds together well as a complete set with "Little Rootie Tootie" and Thad Jones's "Three and One" as high points and Toots whistling along with his guitar on his hit "Bluesette." There are also three interview segments that have Toots talking about his beginnings in Brussels, how he started on his instruments and his inspirations. Recommended.

 Toshiko Akiyoshi Jazz Orchestra—Strive for Jive
(1993, 48 minutes, View Video)

Filmed in Chicago around 1992, this video features the Toshiko Akiyoshi Big Band. Other than some brief interview clips of Akiyoshi and Lew Tabackin between songs and a little bit of talking over the first number, the emphasis is entirely on the music. Akiyoshi's five compositions are the boppish "Yellow Is Mellow," "Strive for Jive" (based on "I Got Rhythm"), the modern jazz waltz "Quadrille, Anyone," the complex yet moving "Autumn Sea" and "Warning, Success May Be Hazardous to Your Health," which has a Brazilian samba beat. The main soloists are Tabackin on tenor and (during "Autumn Sea") flute, altoist Frank Wess, trombonist Hart Smith, trumpeter Brian Lynch, Walt Weiskopf on soprano, tenor saxophonist Ed Xiques and altoist Jim Snidero, with Akiyoshi heard on piano.

 Tribute to John Coltrane:
Select Line Under the Sky '87
(1999, 56 minutes, Image Entertainment)

On July 26, 1987, in Japan, soprano saxophonists Wayne Shorter and Dave Liebman joined with pianist Richie Beirach, bassist Eddie Gomez and drummer Jack DeJohnette to pay tribute to John Coltrane. Shorter talks briefly about meeting 'Trane and then the group digs into a blistering version of "Mr. P.C." Liebman and Beirach play a long duet on "After the Rain," "Naima," and finally the full band jams for over a half hour on a medley of "India" and "Impressions." Although Liebman gets solo honors, Shorter is very close behind and the rhythm section is powerful. This is a memorable set.

Trumpet Kings
(1985, 72 minutes, Video Artists International)

Wynton Marsalis is the host on this project, presenting a series of clips featuring major trumpeters. Some of the selections are more familiar than others and quite a few are excerpts that only feature the trumpet solo. Louis Armstrong is seen in the famous 1933 film of "Dinah" and "I Cover the Waterfront," Henry "Red" Allen performs "St. James Infirmary" in 1964, Bunny Berigan's only film appearance is here ("Until Today" from 1936), Red Nichols plays "Everybody Loves My Baby" in 1934, and Freddie Jenkins is featured on "Cotton Club Stomp" with Duke Ellington in 1929. Also seen are Cootie Williams (1964's "Concerto for Cootie" with Ellington), Muggsy Spanier ("Someday Sweetheart"), Cat Anderson ("Rockin' in Rhythm"), Harry James on a classical piece, Rex Stewart ("Wild Man Blues"), Charlie Shavers and Buck Clayton on a memorable trumpet battle ("This Can't Be Love" from 1958), Roy Eldridge ("Sunday"), Dizzy Gillespie ("One Bass Hit" and a fast blues), Lee Morgan (a minor blues), Miles Davis ("So What"), Art Farmer ("Bernie's Tune"), Shorty Rogers on an unknown piece, Clark Terry ("In a Mellotone"), Nat Adderley ("Work Song"), Freddie Hubbard ("I Can't Get Started" in 1982), Lester Bowie with the Art Ensemble of Chicago jamming over rhythm changes and Gillespie and Armstrong collaborating on "Umbrella Man." Marsalis wraps it all up by jamming an uptempo blues. As is typical of any project that Wynton is involved with, there is no avant-garde jazz to be heard (Bowie comes the closest), so do not look for Don Cherry or Leo Smith. However, there are some memorable moments along the way.

TV's First Music Videos
(2001, 51 minutes, Storyville)

This 1986 documentary serves as an introduction to Lou Snader and the Snader Telescriptions, the series of three-minute, one-song films that he put together for television during 1950–52. Gene Norman is the narrator and there are comments from producer Duke Goldstone. Although an interesting story is told, all of the performances shown are just excerpts, tantalizing glimpses of the telescriptions, most of which are available in more complete form elsewhere. Along the way there are brief moments from the likes of Duke Ellington, Charlie Barnet, Lionel Hampton, Mel Tormé, Peggy Lee, Teresa Brewer, Sarah Vaughan, Cab Calloway, the Ink Spots, Jack Teagarden, George Shearing, Count Basie and Nat King Cole (in fairly complete versions of "Mona Lisa" and "Route 66").

The Universal Mind of Bill Evans
(1991, 45 minutes, Rhapsody Films)

A longer version of **Bill Evans: On the Creative Process** (which is just 20 minutes), this 1966 film features the pianist being interviewed by his older brother Harry Evans, an educator who was also a frustrated pianist. The rivalry between the brothers (Harry was obviously jealous of Bill's great success and talent) is felt just beneath the surface. For the extended version, Steve Allen, who is just heard making a brief introduction in the 20-minute version, is featured more extensively talking about Bill Evans. The interview section is also a bit longer with a little more music. Evans plays the "Spartacus Love Theme" and "How about You," examines the structure of "Star Eyes" and, at Harry's request, just plays the straight melodies of three of his songs: "Very Early," "Time Remembered" and "My Bells." The interaction between Harry and Bill Evans is quite intriguing.

Variety at the Apollo Theatre
(1989, 58 minutes, Storyville)

A wide variety of performers, most of them of interest to jazz, are featured on this set. Although the program (which originally was compiled for television in 1955) makes it appear that all of the music took place on the stage of the Apollo Theatre before a large enthusiastic audience, the selections by the Nat King Cole Trio ("For Sentimental Reasons," "You Call It Madness," "Mona Lisa"), Lionel Hampton ("Midnight Sun," "Cobb's Idea") and Cab Calloway ("Minnie the Moocher") are actually Snader Telescriptions from 1950–51 and are available on other videotapes. Of the actual Apollo Theatre performances, Dinah Washington steals the show on a swinging "Such a Night" (she also sings the emotional ballad "Only a Moment Ago" and "I Don't Hurt Anymore") with the Delta Rhythm Boys faring well on "Dry Bones" and "Take the 'A' Train." Also featured are some colorful tap dance numbers from Bill Bailey, the team of Coles and Atkins, Little Buck and the Businessmen of Rhythm and some pre–rock 'n' roll doo-wop from the Clovers ("Lovey Dovey," "Little Momma"). Willie Bryant is the genial emcee on this entertaining if not essential program.

♪ Vintage Collection Vol. 2: 1960–61
(1992, 45 minutes, A*Vision)

Despite its generic name and the fact that the dates are inaccurate (all of the music is from 1959), the contents of this tape are timeless. **Vintage Collection Vol. 1** was essentially **The Sound of Jazz** with all of the titles stripped off; better to get the Vintage Jazz Artists release. **Vol. 2** starts off with the music performed on the television special **Jazz from Studio 61**. The classic Ahmad Jamal Trio with bassist Israel Crosby and drummer Vernel Fournier sounds typically distinctive on "Darn that Dream" and "Ahmad's Blues." Ben Webster, with pianist Hank Jones, bassist George Duvivier and Jo Jones, caresses the ballad "Chelsea Bridge" and with Buck Clayton and trombonist Vic Dickenson helping out, roars through "Duke's Place."

The second half of this tape has Miles Davis's half-hour special from 1959, originally called **Theater for a Story**. Other than a newsreel from 1957, this is the earliest appearance of the innovative trumpeter on film. He performs "So What" with his quintet (John Coltrane, pianist Wynton Kelly, bassist Paul Chambers and drummer Jimmy

Cobb) and is showcased on "The Duke," "Blues for Pablo" and "New Rhumba" with Gil Evans's orchestra. Evans (who conducts the music) and trombonist Frank Rehak are prominent onscreen, while Davis (who would not appear on film again until the mid-'60s) plays beautifully.

♪ Vintage Getz, Volume 1 *(1990, 56 minutes, A*Vision)*

The performances on this disc along with its second volume were not all that vintage when it was released, being from 1983. The great tenor Stan Getz is seen at a concert in California's Napa Valley, leading a quartet also including pianist Jim McNeely, bassist Marc Johnson and drummer Victor Lewis. The group plays three of McNeely's harmonically advanced originals ("Over the Edge," "From the Heart" and "Answer Without Question") plus a warm rendition of "Spring Can Really Hang You Up the Most" and boppish versions of Miles Davis's "Sippin' at Bells" and Bud Powell's "Tempus Fugit." Getz plays as beautifully as always and seems challenged by the McNeely pieces.

♪ Vintage Getz, Volume 2 *(1990, 52 minutes, A*Vision)*

This tape features the same quartet (Stan Getz, Jim McNeely, Marc Johnson and Victor Lewis) at the same concert as **Volume 1**. It is particularly intriguing hearing Getz play concise versions of his bossa nova hits "Desafinado" and "The Girl from Ipanema" (which he rarely ever played in concert), and then looking embarrassed afterwards as if he had done something bad! This volume gets the edge over the first set due to the superior material, which also includes "Lush Life," "Alone Together," "It's You or No One," "In Your Own Sweet Way" and "Blood Count."

♪ Voices of Concord Jazz: Live at Montreux
(2004, 105 minutes, Concord Video)

At the Montreux Jazz Festival in July 2003, the Concord label took over one night, featuring seven singers on this DVD who record for their company. Singer/pianist Peter Cincotti and his quartet (with bassist Barak Mori, drummer Mark McLean and sometimes Scott Kreitzer on tenor) sound fine on "I Changed the Rules," "Sway" (one of the better songs that Cincotti regularly performs) and "Ain't Misbehavin'." Karrin Allyson with her regular guitarist Danny Embrey plus pianist Frank Chastenier, bassist John Goldsby and drummer Gregg Field, is bluesy on "Moanin'," which she also expertly scats. In addition, she sings in both Portuguese and English on "Little Boat." Monica Mancini displays her beautiful voice on her father Henry's "Charade," a slow and expressive "A Day in the Life of a Fool" and "Springsville," taking the latter as a vocal duet with Curtis Stigers. Her backup group (Chastenier, Goldsby, Field and guitarist Paul Stigihara) is joined in spots by tenor saxophonist Tom Scott and vibraphonist Dave Samuels.

The other four singers are accompanied by the WDR Big Band, an 18-piece orchestra conducted by Tom Scott. Diane Schuur belts out "Deedle's Blues," shares the spotlight with Karrin Allyson on the amusing "Stay Away from Bill" and is excellent on "Meet Me at Midnight." Curtis Stigers sings and plays tenor on "Swingin' Down at 10th and Main" and "How Could a Man Take Such a Fall," while Nnenna Freelon shows off her versatility on "Better Than Anything," "The Lady Sings the Blues" and "Out of this World." But the one who steals the show is Patti Austin, who is exciting on her Ella-inspired versions of "Mr. Paganini" and "How High the Moon" plus the beautiful Gershwin piece from **An American in Paris**, "Home Blues." This varied concert, which is so consistent that, other than Austin, it has few memorable high or low points, concludes with all seven singers coming back to share an anticlimactic version of "How High the Moon."

Wes Montgomery: 1965
(1998, 25 minutes, Vestapol)

Considering how popular Wes Montgomery was in the 1960s, it is surprising that more film of him has not been made available in recent times. This black-and-white video has the great guitarist appearing on a television show in Belgium, playing "Impressions," "Twisted Blues,"

"Here's that Rainy Day," "Jingles" and "The Boy Next Door" with pianist Harold Mabern, bassist Arthur Harper and drummer Jimmy Lovelace. Although his studio recordings were beginning to become commercial, Montgomery's live performances still found him stretching himself, and he is in excellent form throughout this well-received set.

Wilbur DeParis in Europe
(2000, 60 minutes, 30N-80W Records)

Trombonist Wilbur DeParis's New New Orleans Jazz Band was one of the most spirited and infectious of the trad bands active in the 1950s. Their appearances at a French jazz festival on June 9, 10 and 12, 1960, were fortunately filmed by a French crew. Although the picture on this video is a bit blurry (particularly during the first few numbers), the sound quality is fine and the playing is excellent. Clarinetist Omer Simeon, a fixture with the group, had died in 1959, but otherwise the band is intact from its prime period. In addition to Wilbur DeParis, the lineup includes both Sidney DeParis and Doc Cheatham on trumpets, clarinetist Garvin Bushell, pianist Sonny White, banjoist John Smith, bassist Hayes Alvis, and Wilbert Kirk on drums and harmonica. Both of the DeParis brothers, Cheatham, Bushell and Alvis were active in the 1920s and were still playing quite well. There are a few times when the film veers away from the playing to show sheet music and photos of Jelly Roll Morton, and this can be a bit distracting. The final number, "Battle Hymn of the Republic," cuts off before the end and a three-minute interview with the siblings (which is mostly in French) does not result in any great revelations. However, the music is quite enjoyable. The band performs an uptempo "High Society," a version of "Royal Garden Blues" that has an odd half-time arrangement, "Minorca," "Beale Street Blues," a brief "Charleston," "The Pearls," "Wolverine Blues," "I've Found a New Baby" (with clarinetist Claude Luter, trumpeter Pierre Derveaux and trombonist Jean-Louis Durand temporarily giving the band seven horns), "That's a Plenty" and "Battle Hymn of the Republic." While Sidney DeParis (who uses various mutes colorfully) generally takes solo honors, each of the horn players has their moments and the results are often exciting. This historic video has been made available through the Jazz Crusade label.

Willie "The Lion" Smith
(2001, 57 minutes, NJN Public Television)

Willie "The Lion" Smith was one of the big three stride pianists of the 1920s, along with his pals James P. Johnson and Fats Waller. Unlike the other two, Smith survived into the age of television, not passing away until 1973. On the evidence of this documentary, a great deal of film exists of Smith. Unfortunately, none of the many clips included on this video are shown complete without voice-over, but one does get a strong flavor of Smith's music and talents. There are tantalizing glimpses of Smith on the David Frost show in 1970 with Duke Ellington, playing a true piano trio with Ellington and Billy Taylor, plus many TV appearances from the 1950s and '60s, but these are just brief excerpts. Otherwise this is a very effective biography. The film, put together by Marc Fields, uses Smith's voice and that of his associates (including Dick Hyman, Jean Bach and Mike Lipskin) in covering the legacy of stride piano, Harlem rent parties, the music scene before Smith's arrival and his entire career.

The Wonderful World of Louis Armstrong
(2001, 65 minutes, Winstar Video)

This British documentary on Louis Armstrong is a major disappointment. Although it has a few good moments, every worthwhile performance clip is talked over and much of the artsy photography is completely irrelevant. Humphrey Lyttelton, George Melly, writer Tad Jones, Dan Morgenstern, Wynton Marsalis, Lil Hardin Armstrong, Gary Giddins, George Avakian, Max Roach, Milt Gabler, Arvell Shaw, Dave Brubeck and Wynton Marsalis all get to comment. But as an example, after Giddins raves about

Louis Armstrong's recorded solo of "When You're Smiling" from 1957, the recording is played, and talked over!

Woody Herman & the Famous Alumni
(1988, 60 minutes, Rendezvous Productions)

This privately organized tape features Woody Herman and an all-star band full of alumni from his past orchestras celebrating his 50th anniversary as a bandleader in 1986 with selections from two concerts in San Diego and a version of "Blowin' Up a Storm" from a slightly later Carnegie Hall concert. Among the musicians seen along the way are tenor saxophonists Bob Cooper, Dick Hafer and Bob Efford, altoist Med Flory, trumpeters Conte Candoli, Pete Candoli, Don Rader, Bill Berry and Mark Lewis, trombonists Buster Cooper, Carl Fontana and pianist Nat Pierce. The 13 songs include the usual hits such as "Woodchopper's Ball," "Four Brothers," "Early Autumn" and "Blowin' Up a Storm" plus a vocal by Herman on "Sonny Boy." Overall, this was a labor of love and one should overlook the technical flaws (both in the loose playing and the camerawork) and enjoy its historic value.

Woody Herman & the Ultimate Herd 1986
(1988, 60 minutes, Rendezvous Productions)

As with the Famous Alumni video, this one was privately filmed and is a low-budget affair, but it documents some worthwhile music. Woody Herman and his final big band are seen aboard the *S.S. Norway* during October 12–18, 1986, performing 11 songs, including "Four Brothers," "Woodchopper's Ball," "Caldonia," "I've Got News for You" (with guest singer Joe Williams) and "Early Autumn." The band also backs Cab Calloway on "Minnie the Moocher," and tenor saxophonist Al Cohn sits in on "Body & Soul." The Herman big band at the time included trombonist John Fedchock, tenor saxophonist Frank Tiberi (who would take over the orchestra after Herman's death a year later), baritonist Mike Brignola and bassist Dave Carpenter. Woody Herman fans will want to search for this valuable if not flawless tape.

Woody Herman Remembered
(1991, 60 minutes, Leisure Video)

This tribute to Woody Herman's life mostly has performances of his late '70s and 1980s big band, including "Woodchoppers Ball," "Four Brothers," "Reunion at Newport," "April in Paris," "Blues in the Night" and "Fanfare for the Common Man." There is also a brief biographical sketch although nothing all that unusual occurs on this DVD.

 The World According to John Coltrane
(1991, 59 minutes, BMG Video)

An interesting documentary on the life of John Coltrane, this tape takes most of the footage of the great saxophonist from his two television appearances (released in full on **The Coltrane Legacy**). Most interesting is that there is also an excerpt of a concert version of "My Favorite Things" (probably from 1965) and some silent color footage from 1966. Coltrane's life is pieced together through interviews including comments from Alice Coltrane, Tommy Flanagan, Jimmy Heath, Wayne Shorter, Rashied Ali and Roscoe Mitchell plus storytelling from friends and relatives.

 World of Rhythm *(2002, 90 minutes, TDK Mediactive)*

Despite its title, which makes the DVD sound as if it showcases percussionists, this is an acoustic trio date featuring Herbie Hancock, Ron Carter and Billy Cobham. Filmed during a 1983 European concert, the date is primarily comprised of Hancock originals ("Toys," "First Trip," "Speak Like a Child," "Little Waltz," "Willow Weep for Me," "Dolphin Dance," "Ili's Treasure," "Princess," "Eye of the Hurricane," "Walkin'") with a couple of exceptions. The challenging post-bop songs inspire the musicians to play at their most creative, and the music is often passionate and intense even when quiet. "Speak Like a Child" travels through many moods, "Willow Weep for Me" and "Ili's Treasure" are unaccompanied solos for, respectively, Carter and Cobham, and the high points are "Dolphin Dance" and a very explorative "Eye of the Hurricane."

 Wynton Marsalis: Blues and Swing
(1988, 79 minutes, Sony Video)

Wynton Marsalis was not yet 27 when he became the subject of this extended edition of **Great Performances**. Marsalis is seen lecturing music students at Harvard and the Duke Ellington School of the Arts (he is at his most charming and witty) and performing with his quartet of the time (pianist Marcus Roberts, bassist Bob Hurst and drummer Jeff "Tain" Watts). Marsalis was just beginning to become much more individual in his playing (emerging from the shadow of Miles Davis) and is in excellent form on a fiery original, "Caravan," "Delfeayo's Dilemma," "Do You Know What It Means to Miss New Orleans," "Cherokee," "J Mood" and (with tenor saxophonist Todd Williams added) "Crepuscule with Nellie."

 Zardis—The Spirit of New Orleans
(1994, 88 minutes, Rhapsody Films)

This documentary from 1989 is supposedly about Chester Zardis, a pioneering bassist who was one of the last early New Orleans jazz musicians still active in the late '80s, but it wanders around, often quite aimlessly. In fact, the first ten minutes of the film contain scenes of New Orleans, glimpses of an unidentified jazz group, a church service and a brass band at a parade. Eventually Zardis does appear, but his life story is only hinted at and the logic of the film's continuity is difficult to figure out. Best is a stretch where Milt Hinton talks about the role of the bass and demonstrates the older style, and a closing monologue by Alan Lomax (which seems to be completely apart from the film) in which he discusses the importance of New Orleans and Chester Zardis's role in jazz history. Otherwise, there are comments from writer Bill Russell and guitarist/banjoist Danny Barker, a few reminiscences from Zardis and his wife Bertha Zardis, more footage of a parade and a spirited church congregation, and a little bit of music. Zardis is seen on excerpts of a few trad songs and most of "Some of these Days," "Eh

Les Bas" and "Bourbon Street Parade" (the latter two are duets with Barker). Other musicians seen and heard along the way include trumpeter Wendell Brunious, trombonist Louis Nelson (who is erratic) and clarinetist Dr. Michael White (who is sometimes out of tune). There probably was a definitive film here somewhere, but odd editing and the meandering nature of the results make this a disappointment.

 ### *Zoot Sims Quartet/Shelly Manne Quartet*
(1997, 56 minutes, Rhapsody Films)

A pair of shows from the late '60s **Jazz on Stage** television series are combined on this DVD. The technical quality of the Zoot Sims set, performed at Donte's in Los Angeles, is not the best, but the swinging tenor is in generally fine form. Backed by pianist Roger Kellaway, bassist Chuck Berghofer and drummer Larry Bunker, Sims swings his way through "Zoot's Piece," "My Old Flame," "On the Trail" and "Motoring Along," giving viewers a relatively rare opportunity to see Zoot stretch out on film. The second film features tenor saxophonist Bob Cooper, pianist Hampton Hawes, Ray Brown and Shelly Manne at the legendary Shelly's Manne-Hole club. The quartet of West Coast Jazz all-stars perform "Blues in the Basement," "Stella by Starlight" and "Milestones" sometime in the late '60s. The musicians all play quite well.

Review Section Two:

Hollywood Movies

🎬5 ♪5 Ah! Quelle Equipe
(1956, 96 minutes)

Sidney Bechet has one of the leading roles in this French comedy, which features many European show business performers of the era. Bechet plays with Andre Reweliotty's orchestra.

🎬5 ♪3 Alabama's Ghost
(1972, 96 minutes)

This is a crazy, horror cult film involving magic, Nazis, vampires, a ghost and a witch doctor. Early on, there is a brief appearance by Turk Murphy and his band.

🎬5 ♪4 Ali Baba Goes to Town
(1937, 81 minutes)

This amusing Eddie Cantor movie is both a little reminiscent of Mark Twain's *A Connecticut Yankee in King Arthur's Court* and a satire of FDR's New Deal. Cantor, working at odd jobs in Hollywood, falls asleep and dreams about being in the *Arabian Nights*, getting into some humorous adventures. The Raymond Scott Quintette performs their hit "Twilight in Turkey" dressed in Arab outfits while playing odd ancient instruments that do not correspond to the music.

🎬7 ♪5 L'Alibi *(1937, 84 minutes)*

Erich Von Stroheim plays a possible murderer who pressures a dance hostess into providing his alibi in this French film. Bobby Martin's orchestra (with tenor saxophonist Johnny Russell, pianist Ram Ramirez and drummer Kaiser Marshall) and trumpeter/singer Valaida Snow appear at the dance hall.

🎬6 ♪7 All Night Long
(1961, 95 minutes)

The Othello story is altered in this British film, which teams a White singer with a Black bandleader. Patrick McGoohan (whose drumming is ghosted by Alan Ganley) wants to break up the marriage of Paul Harris and Marti Stevens while also taking over the jazz group. Charles Mingus ("Peggy's Blue Skylight") and Dave Brubeck play onstage briefly as do tenor saxophonist Tubby Hayes, trumpeter Harry Beckett, John Dankworth and some other British musicians.

🎬3 ♪3 All the Fine Young Cannibals
(1960, 122 minutes)

A Robert Wagner/Natalie Wood melodrama, **Cannibals** is full of clichés about Southern life, young love and complex triangles. Wagner, playing a role that might very well have gone to Chet Baker if Baker had not become a busted drug addict, portrays a trumpeter who idolizes an alcoholic singer (Pearl Bailey) and cannot seem to connect with Wood. Musically, Wagner is mostly seen playing overly sentimental ballads. Bailey, who consistently steals the show, sings "Happiness Is a Thing Called Joe" and "God Bless the Child," but it is not enough to save the picture.

🎬5 ♪2 Almost Married
(1942, 65 minutes)

Wealthy Charles Lamont gets unemployed singer Jane Frazee to marry him so he can escape from his fiancée. Slim Galliard makes a brief appearance.

♪ An American in Paris
(1951, 114 minutes)

This famous film features the singing and dancing of Gene Kelly, who is matched with Leslie Caron, performing many Gershwin songs. Benny Carter appears in a night-club scene with a band that includes trumpeter Gerald Wilson and drummer Lee Young. However, he is only seen for a few seconds and is mostly inaudible while playing a medley that includes "But Not for Me," "Our Love Is Here to Stay" and "Someone to Watch Over Me"; otherwise there is no jazz.

♪ American Hot Wax
(1978, 91 minutes)

Pioneering rock 'n' roll disc jockey Alan Freed is depicted in a story centered around a 1959 concert. Many stars

DUKE ELLINGTON
Duke with Jimmy Stewart circa 'Anatomy of a Murder', 1959

COLUMBIA   LEGACY

Duke Ellington wrote the soundtrack for *Anatomy of a Murder* and appeared in this one scene playing piano with Jimmy Stewart.

from rock 'n' roll perform including Screaming Jay Hawkins, Chuck Berry and Jerry Lee Lewis. Organist Bill Doggett plays his hit "Honky Tonk Part II," and there is a background big band led by guitarist Ira Newborn that includes trumpeter Al Aarons and tenors Buddy Collette and Don Menza.

♪ Anatomy of a Murder
(1959, 160 minutes)

Jimmy Stewart and Lee Remick star in this superior courtroom drama. Duke Ellington wrote the score (his first) which, although it stands alone well on the sound-track album, is often a bit intrusive in the movie itself. Ellington (as "Pie Eye") briefly plays a piano duet with Jimmy Stewart in one scene and has two lines. Otherwise no musician appears on-screen. The main theme of "Anatomy of a Murder" was later outfitted with words by Peggy Lee and turned into "I'm Gonna Go Fishin'."

♪ Andy *(1965, 86 minutes)*

This is a sensitive drama about the everyday life of a mentally retarded, middle-aged man struggling in New York City. Drummer Zutty Singleton appears briefly, as a clarinetist.

♪ Appointment with Crime
(1946, 91 minutes)

In this British drama, a man double-crossed by his gang and sent to prison for jewel theft devises an elaborate scheme to get even after he is released. In dance hall scenes, Lew Stone's orchestra and the Buddy Feather-stonhaugh Sextet provide atmosphere.

♪ Artists and Models
(1937, 97 minutes)

This is a rather forgettable comedy for Paramount featuring Jack Benny and Ida Lupino. Singer Connie Boswell sings "Whispers in the Dark," and there is a lengthy and fairly pointless production number, "Public Melody

Number One," with singer Martha Raye in blackface and Louis Armstrong (who is mostly used as a prop).

5 ♪ *Atlantic City* (1944, 87 minutes)

Set during 1910–30, this is a fictional story (starring Brad Taylor and Constance Moore) about a man who builds an empire of theatres and hotels but neglects his wife. Both Louis Armstrong and Paul Whiteman's orchestra are largely wasted, with Armstrong heard singing "Ain't Misbehavin'" before his trumpet solo is buried beneath dialog. Paul Whiteman has little to do, and specialty numbers from Buck and Bubbles and Dorothy Dandridge are forgettable.

5 ♪ *Auf Wiedersehn*
(1961, 79 minutes)

Louis Armstrong makes a small contribution to this West German spy film. Armstrong and his All-Stars (Trummy Young, clarinetist Peanuts Hucko, Billy Kyle, bassist Mort Herbert and drummer Danny Barcelona) perform brief versions of "Back O'Town Blues," "Pretty Little Missy," "Dippermouth Blues" and "The Faithful Hussar."

1 ♪ *The Bad and the Beautiful*
(1951, 123 minutes)

This classic film about the rise and fall of an amoral but talented producer stars Kirk Douglas, Lana Turner, Dick Powell and Walter Pidgeon. In one scene, pianist Hadda Brooks sings "Temptation."

7 ♪ *Ball of Fire* (1941, 112 minutes)

Gary Cooper (as an English professor) and Barbara Stanwyck star in a humorous film later remade as **A Song Is Born**. One scene has Gene Krupa's band playing "Drum Boogie" with brief solos for trumpeter Roy Eldridge, clarinetist Sam Musiker and tenor saxophonist Walter Bates. Stanwyck's vocal is ghosted by Martha Tilton, and Krupa has a drum solo that ends up with him playing matchsticks.

6 ♪ *The Baltimore Bullet*
(1980, 103 minutes)

James Coburn, a veteran pool hustler, befriends and teaches the younger Bruce Boxleitner, whom he inevitably meets in an important match. The Olympia Brass Band of New Orleans is featured briefly.

6 ♪ *Band of Thieves*
(1962, 69 minutes)

The plot of this British comedy perfectly fits the title. A group of ex-cons travel with their Dixieland band, using it as a cover for robberies. Clarinetist Acker Bilk is the star and his band members include trumpeter Colin Smith, trombonist Jonathan Mortimer and pianist Stan Grieg. Among the songs they perform are "All I Want to Do Is Sing" and "Kissin'."

5 ♪ *Bargain with Bullets*
(1937, unknown length)

Also known as **Gangsters on the Loose**, this Black crime film stars Ralph Cooper as a gangster in a love triangle who is trying to beat a murder rap. Background music is provided by Les Hite's Cotton Club Orchestra and clarinetist Eddie Barefield's trio with pianist Eddie Beal and bassist Al Morgan.

3 ♪ *The Beat Generation*
(1959, 93 minutes)

This low-quality murder mystery has a murderer pretending to be a beatnik. Starring Steve Cochran and Mamie Van Doren (with a small role for Ray Anthony), much of this movie takes place in what purports to be the beatnik scene with a variety of all-so-cool hipsters essentially loafing. Louis Armstrong and the All-Stars (with Trummy Young, Peanuts Hucko, Billy Kyle, Mort Herbert and Danny Barcelona) perform briefly at a beatnik's hangout (which makes little sense), playing "Someday You'll Be Sorry," mostly in the background. Armstrong also sings the title number during the opening credits.

🎞️ 🎵 Beat the Band *(1947, 67 minutes)*

A forgettable Francis Langford/Ralph Edwards film, **Beat the Band** has a couple of very good spots for the Gene Krupa Orchestra. Krupa is excellent on "Shadow Rhapsody" (which is mostly a drum solo), and his band romps a bit on "Calling Dr. Gillespie." The orchestra includes trumpeter Red Rodney, Gerry Mulligan (on alto) and both Buddy Wise and Charlie Kennedy on tenors.

🎞️ 🎵 Bell, Book and Candle *(1958, 102 minutes)*

This frivolous but fun movie about urban witchcraft stars Jimmy Stewart, Kim Novak and Jack Lemmon. Lemmon plays bongos in a jazz group that features brothers Conte and Pete Candoli on trumpets. The Brothers Candoli appear briefly in three scenes, at one point playing a demented medium-tempo "Stormy Weather," but do not have any lines and are primarily in the background.

🎞️ 🎵 Belle of the Nineties *(1934, 75 minutes)*

For this Mae West comedy, Duke Ellington and his orchestra pop up on a few occasions, with Sonny Greer prominent in spots. The band backs West on "When a St. Louis Woman Goes Down to New Orleans," "Memphis Blues" and "My Old Flame" (which was introduced in this film).

🎞️ 🎵 Bells Are Ringing *(1960, 125 minutes)*

In this Judy Holliday/Dean Martin musical comedy, the song "Just in Time" was introduced. There is no real jazz, but Gerry Mulligan (who was going with the actress at the time) is featured in a humorous if over-the-top scene as Holliday's rather clumsy suitor.

🎞️ 🎵 The Benny Goodman Story *(1955, 116 minutes)*

The plot of this clichéd biography (which ends with the famous 1938 Carnegie Hall concert) is so fictional that it cannot be taken too seriously, but the music is constant and rewarding. Steve Allen plays the King of Swing, Donna Reed is his love interest (never mind that Benny Goodman did not become serious about his future wife until 1939), and there are appearances by trombonist Kid Ory, drummer Ben Pollack, Gene Krupa, Teddy Wilson and Lionel Hampton, all of whom have lines. In addition, Sammy Davis, Sr., plays Fletcher Henderson, and such musicians as Harry James, Ziggy Elman (who was ailing, so his solo on "And the Angels Sing" was ghosted by Manny Klein), singer Martha Tilton, Buck Clayton, Stan Getz, trumpeters Chris Griffin, Manny Klein and Alvin Alcorn (with Ory), guitarist Allan Reuss and bassist George Duvivier make appearances. Benny Goodman himself ghosts the clarinet solos for Allen. Although BG was a pioneer in integrating jazz, no mention is made of that, or of Buck Clayton suddenly popping up in his trumpet section. The music is excellent even if the orchestra often sounds more like Goodman's 1950s group than his original big band. Among the many songs performed are "Let's Dance," "Slipped Disc," "Goody-Goody," "Stompin' at the Savoy," "Memories of You," "One O'Clock Jump," "Avalon," "Bugle Call Rag," "Don't Be that Way," "And the Angels Sing," "Moon Glow" and "Sing, Sing, Sing."

🎞️ 🎵 Bernardine *(1957, 94 minutes)*

Notable for being Pat Boone's first film and a return to movies for Janet Gaynor after a couple of decades, this high school musical comedy is rather weak and uneventful. Bongo player Jack Costanzo is seen leading a big band but has little to do.

🎞️ 🎵 Best Foot Forward *(1943, 94 minutes)*

This MGM musical stars June Allyson. Harry James and his big band (with tenor saxophonist Corky Corcoran) make a couple of strong appearances, stretching out quite winningly on memorable versions of "Two O'Clock Jump" and "Flight of the Bumble Bee."

Beware
(1946, 60 minutes)

One of several Louis Jordan movies from the second half of the 1940s, this film has a basic throwaway story that serves as an excuse for one fine number after another by Jordan's Tympany Five. Among the selections are "Long Legged Lizzie," "Good Morning Heartache" (a rare example of Jordan singing a standard ballad), "Don't You Worry about that Mule," "Salt Pork, West Virginia" and "Beware." All of the music from this film along with that of two other Jordan movies is available on the videotape **Louis Jordan and His Tympany Band**.

The Big Beat *(1957, 82 minutes)*

This tale about a record company is a good excuse to feature a variety of music groups. Despite its title, the emphasis is not totally on rock 'n' roll though Fats Domino does sing "I'm Walking." There are spots (mostly brief) for Charlie Barnet, Harry James's orchestra (backing singer Gogi Grant on "Lazy Love") the George Shearing Quintet, the Mills Brothers, Cal Tjader's group and Jeri Southern, not to mention Freddie Martin and Russ Morgan.

The Big Broadcast
(1932, 80 minutes)

Bing Crosby's first full-length film has a lightweight but fun plot about a radio station, serving as an excuse for some very special performances. Crosby sings "Please" and a version of "Dinah" that has some prominent Eddie Lang guitar. The Mills Brothers are wonderful on "Tiger Rag," Vincent Lopez and his orchestra are entertaining on "I'm the Drummer" and Cab Calloway sings "Kickin' the Gong Around" with help from his big band. Most memorable is the finest performance on film by the Boswell Sisters who are quite exciting on a swinging "Crazy People."

The Big Broadcast of 1936
(1935, 97 minutes)

The most obscure of the four **Big Broadcast** films has Jack Oakie stealing an early version of television (called a "radio eye") and attempting to find a customer for his so-called invention. George Burns and Gracie Allen have prominent roles in this musical comedy as does Bing Crosby who sings "I Wished on the Moon." Among the many musical acts are Bill "Bojangles" Robinson, the Nicholas Brothers, the Dandridge Sisters (with a 13-year-old Dorothy and a very young Etta Jones), Ina Ray Hutton's orchestra (playing an unidentified instrumental) and Ray Noble's band (with Bud Freeman, trumpeters Pee Wee Erwin and Charlie Spivak, trombonists Will Bradley and Glenn Miller, clarinetist Johnny Mince and guitarist George Van Eps). Unfortunately, Noble's band has little to do other than play "Goodnight Sweetheart."

Martha, Connie and Vet Boswell, who are wonderful singing "Crazy People" in *The Big Broadcast*, formed the immortal Boswell Sisters.

5 6 *The Big Broadcast of 1937*
(1936, 99 minutes)

This movie features Jack Benny, Burns and Allen, Martha Raye and a parade of musical acts, including Larry Alder on harmonica and Leopold Stokowski with his symphony orchestra. Most significant is that it has the first appearance on film by Benny Goodman's orchestra, which at the time included trumpeters Pee Wee Erwin and Chris Griffin, tenor saxophonist Arthur Rollini, Jess Stacy and Gene Krupa. Although the band and Goodman pop up briefly in a few situations (including backing Martha

Raye on "Here Comes the Bride"), the high point is its version of "Bugle Call Rag."

7 3 *Big City* *(1948, 103 minutes)*

This heartwarming if sometimes sappy Margaret O'Brien/Danny Thomas film has the Page Cavanaugh Trio (with guitarist Al Viola and bassist Dean Pratt) appearing twice, backing Betty Garrett's singing on "You're Going to See an Awful Lot of Me" (which is sandwiched by very brief renditions of "Shoo Shoo Baby") and playing eight bars of "Don't Blame Me" and a novelty number. The trio

Forest Whitaker as Charlie "BIRD" Parker

BIRD

Columbia
8803

Forest Whitaker did an excellent job of portraying Charlie Parker in *Bird,* fingering his saxophone solos perfectly.

(which is sometimes joined by an unseen orchestra) is mostly used as a prop.

6 9 *Bird* (1988, 161 minutes)

Clint Eastwood's Hollywood depiction of the life and times of Charlie Parker has both good and bad points. On the minus side, the screenplay emphasizes Bird's decline excessively (much of the first 20 minutes after the opening number is difficult to sit through), never really explains to the average listener why Parker was considered such an innovator, and it is often just semi-fictional; one looks in vain for Jay McShann, Miles Davis or Max Roach. Bird was a much more intriguing and complex personality than is depicted. On the other hand, Forest Whitaker's acting as Parker is excellent, his fingering during his solos is impeccable, and both Chan Parker and trumpeter Red Rodney come across as genuine characters. There are some excellent moments along the way, including some of the musical sequences and an all-too-brief view of 52nd Street. Arranger Lennie Niehaus took Parker's actual solos (which were isolated from their original contexts) and mixed them in with contributions from current bop musicians (including Rodney playing his own solos and Jon Faddis substituting for Dizzy Gillespie); the results are often magical. In fact, the best moments in this film (which is available from Warner Home Video) make one regret that all of it is not on the same level, for this movie should have been a classic.

7 9 *Birth of the Blues* (1941, 86 minutes)

This movie, a humorous and fictional look at the beginnings of jazz, is a great deal of fun. Set in New Orleans in the 1890s and mostly featuring a White cast, the plot deals with a clarinetist (Bing Crosby) and a trumpeter (Brian Donlevy) struggling to get their jazz band to catch on while also fighting over the affections of Mary Martin and avoiding gangsters. A special treat is the participation of Jack Teagarden as a trombonist, singer and actor.

Teagarden's trumpeter of the period, Pokey Carriere, ghosts some exciting solos for Donlevy, Danny Polo ghosts for Crosby's clarinet playing, and pianist Harry Barris (formerly one of the Rhythm Boys with Bing) is cast as the band's bassist. Two numbers, "Wait Till the Sun Shines Nellie" and Johnny Mercer's "The Waiter and the Porter and the Upstairs Maid," are quite memorable and there are also hot versions of "At a Georgia Camp Meeting," "Memphis Blues," "Tiger Rag," "Melancholy Baby," "St. Louis Blues" and "Shine," with Rose Murphy (who plays a maid) performing one number.

2 4 *Bix—An Interpretation of a Legend* (1990, 100 minutes)

There was plenty of potential for this film on 1920s cornetist Bix Beiderbecke. The sets look beautiful and authentic, the casting is excellent, and the music provided by Bob

Jack Teagarden had his best screen role in the Bing Crosby film *Birth of the Blues,* a fictional history of jazz.

Wilber (featuring cornetist Tom Pletcher, clarinetist Kenny Davern, pianist Keith Nichols and bassist Vince Giordano) sounds very much like the 1920s. Even one of the fictional subplots, about a mysterious girlfriend whom cornetist Bix Beiderbecke mentioned in his letters to his parents, is intriguing. But the screenplay is a complete mess, the editing is very confusing (jumping around constantly between periods without making it obvious what year it is supposed to be), many of the tales have been fictionalized and trivialized, and the results are a major disappointment. It is a pity because the acting is excellent and some of the historic characters (who include Beiderbecke, violinist Joe Venuti, bandleader Paul Whiteman, pianist Hoagy Carmichael and C-melody saxophonist Frankie Trumbauer) act a bit like the real thing. But only experts on Bix Beiderbecke's life will have the slightest idea what is going on much of the time, and they will be outraged at how the movie's semifictional plot is so incoherent.

♪ Blazing Saddles
(1974, 123 minutes)

Mel Brooks's spoof on Westerns is one of his most famous films. There is a funny cameo by Count Basie and his orchestra (in their one scene the band is actually comprised mostly of studio musicians) unexpectedly turning up in the desert playing "April in Paris." If one looks closely, on the bandstand with Basie can be seen such musicians as altoist Marshall Royal, Teddy Edwards on tenor, trumpeters Al Aarons and Cat Anderson, guitarist John Collins, bassist Red Callender and drummer Harold Jones.

♪ Block Busters
(1944, 60 minutes)

The East Side Kids (a low-budget version of the Dead End Kids) are the stars of this routine juvenile delinquent film from Monogram. However, clarinetist Jimmie Noone pops up in one scene, playing "Apex Blues" and "Boogie Woogie" with his group.

♪ The Blue Gardenia
(1953, 90 minutes)

This Ann Baxter crime mystery has Nat King Cole, who is billed but does not have any lines, seen at a piano singing "The Blue Gardenia." Although seen on-screen with violin, guitar and bass in a quartet, he is actually backed by a full string orchestra, singing with plenty of warmth as usual.

♪ The Blue Lamp
(1949, 84 minutes)

This British crime drama starring Dirk Bogarde has a brief club scene in which one can see a bop-based group led by drummer Jack Parnell.

♪ Blue Note
(1989, 95 minutes)

Peter MacNicol leads a cast of unknowns in this tale set in 1961, which deals with a young jazz quintet's adventures and struggles to stay together. Despite a few good moments (such as when the band desperately hires a nonmusical fan to play bass on an important gig after a two-minute lesson), the screenplay is quite weak with no real beginning or end, and much of the time one waits in vain for something to happen. The music is just okay, with originals by Larry Schanker who plays piano on the soundtrack; other participating musicians (none seen on-screen) are saxophonists Ron Blake and John Adair, trumpeter Steve Rashid, bassist Miles Hahn and drummer Kevin Connelley. The basic plot had potential, but the poor writing sinks this effort.

♪ The Blues Brothers
(1980, 133 minutes)

This John Belushi/Dan Aykroyd movie is rightfully famous and often hilarious in the tale of Jake and Elwood Blues putting together a blues-oriented comeback show to raise money for an orphanage. There are some remarkable car chases and many very funny moments. James Brown, Aretha Franklin and Ray Charles are showcased on a spectacular number apiece with dancers, and John Lee Hooker also performs. Cab Calloway plays a small role and is featured on an excellent version of "Minnie the Moocher," nearly 50 years after he debuted the song. The Blues Brothers band both on-screen and on the soundtrack includes trumpeter Alan Rubin, trombonist Tom Malone and tenor saxophonist Lou Marini.

🎞6 🎵5 *Blues for a Junkman*
(1962, 75 minutes)

This film was originally an episode in the television series **Cain's Husband** and later expanded and released in England into a movie called **The Murder Men**. Dorothy Dandridge stars in a story about a junkie singer and her attempts at a comeback despite the interference of the mob. Dandridge sings "The Man I Love," "I'll Get By" and "Taking a Chance on Love" while backed by a jazz combo; the trumpet parts are ghosted by Conte Candoli.

🎞5 🎵5 *Blues in the Night*
(1941, 88 minutes)

A rather fanciful drama about the struggles of a jazz combo, this film is reasonably entertaining. In one scene the Jimmie Lunceford Orchestra plays "Blues in the Night," (trombonist Trummy Young has a solo) with some assistance from actor Jack Carson, whose trumpet solos throughout the movie are ghosted by Snooky Young. Stan Wrightsman ghosts on piano for actor Richard Whorf. Also heard in the film is "This Time the Dream's on Me."

🎞3 🎵7 *Boarding House Blues*
(1948, 85 minutes)

The first half of this all-Black film is dreadful, with inane dialog, stupid humor and a potentially interesting plot ruined by overacting, mugging and ridiculous stereotypes. However, once the melodrama about paying the rent for a boarding house is dispensed with, a show is performed. Though some of the acts are forgettable, there is a remarkable one-legged one-armed dancer (Crip

Heard), singer/pianist Una Mae Carlisle is in fine form on "Throw It Out of Your Mind" and "It Ain't Like That," and there are sketches for Dusty Fletcher and Moms Mabley. Lucky Millinder's orchestra is featured on the final five numbers, performing a medium-tempo blues with plenty of solos, backing Paul Breckenridge's straight vocal on the ballad "Sweet Slumber," rocking a bit with singer Anasteen Allen on "Let It Roll," accompanying Bull Moose Jackson on a definitive version of his hit "I Love You, Yes I Do," and riffing hard on "The Hucklebuck."

🎞6 🎵5 *Borsalino* *(1970, 123 minutes)*

This popular French/Italian gangster yarn, set in the 1930s, has a brief appearance by the Art Ensemble of Chicago, altoist Anthony Braxton and violinist Leroy Jenkins performing at a hotel bar.

🎞5 🎵3 *Borsalino & Co.* *(1974, 110 minutes)*

The sequel to **Borsalino** is, like its predecessor, a rather violent gangster movie set in the early '30s. Also as in **Borsalino**, Claude Bolling wrote the film score and, in this case, he makes a brief appearance on piano in one scene.

🎞5 🎵5 *La Botta e Risposta*
(1950, 80 minutes)

This obscure Italian film is a comedy and mystery about a lost dress and a radio quiz contest. A few different entertainers (mostly Italians) get to perform. A seven-minute stretch features the Louis Armstrong All-Stars (Jack Teagarden, Barney Bigard, Earl Hines, bassist Arvell Shaw, Cozy Cole and singer Velma Middleton) who perform a brief "Struttin' with Some Barbecue," "That's My Desire" (a comedy feature for Armstrong and Middleton) and Hines's showcase on "Boogie Woogie on the St. Louis Blues."

🎞7 🎵4 *Boulevard du Rhum*
(1971, 125 minutes)

Brigitte Bardot plays a silent screen star in the 1920s who is involved in humorous fashion with Lino Ventura, a smuggler of rum. Joe Turner (the stride pianist, not Big Joe Turner) is cast as a bartender who plays piano and sings.

⑤ ♪ *Boy! What a Girl*
(1946, 70 minutes)

This weak all-Black comedy, which partly deals with a man stuck being dressed like a woman for much of the film, has a few memorable musical moments. On "Just a Riff," drummer Big Sid Catlett and his band (which includes trumpeter Dick Vance, trombonist Benny Morton, altoist Don Stovall, tenor saxophonist Eddie "Lockjaw" Davis, pianist Ram Ramirez and bassist Johnny Simmons) are joined by surprise guest Gene Krupa. The group also backs singer Betti Mays on "Crazy Riffin'." In addition, the Slam Stewart Trio with guitarist John Collins and pianist Beryl Booker (not Mary Lou Williams as is often listed) performs "Oh Me, Oh My, Oh Gosh," which has bassist Stewart taking a vocal. Those three numbers are available on the videotape **The Small Black Groups**. There are also appearances by the Harlem Maniacs and such numbers as "I Just Refuse to Sing the Blues," "Just in Case You Change Your Mind," "Satchel Mouth Baby" and "Slamboree."

⑤ ♪ *Breakfast in Hollywood*
(1946, 91 minutes)

Also known as **The Mad Hatter**, this film is about a radio show, serving as a good excuse to feature a variety of acts. The Nat King Cole Trio (with Oscar Moore and Johnny Miller) performs a brief version of "Solid Potato Salad" and "It's Better to Be Yourself." The two numbers are also available on the Storyville videotape **The Small Black Groups**.

⑧ ♪ *Broadway Gondolier*
(1935, 100 minutes)

This humorous Warner Bros. musical comedy stars Dick Powell and Joan Blondell. In addition to crooning a few numbers, Powell joins the Mills Brothers on a memorable version of "Lulu's Back in Town."

⑤ ♪ *Broadway Rhythm*
(1944, 114 minutes)

George Murphy, Ginny Simms (who sings "All the Things You Are") and Charles Winniger star in this so-so musical comedy. As is often the case, there is not much plot, but there is good humor and a fair amount of music. Tommy Dorsey's band mostly backs other acts (including Nancy Walker on "Milkman, Keep Those Bottles Quiet") although TD has an amusing bit with Winniger on "I Love Corny Music." Lena Horne is featured on "Brazilian Boogie" and "Somebody Loves Me," but pianist Hazel Scott completely steals the show during a two-minute stretch where she turns a classical theme into heated stride.

⑨ ♪ *Buena Vista Social Club*
(1999, 105 minutes)

In 1996, American guitarist Ry Cooder first visited Cuba and recorded some of the survivors of the music scene of the 1940s and '50s for his **Buena Vista Social Club** album. In 1998, he returned with a film crew. During the first half of this heartwarming movie, Cooder meets up with some aging but talented Cuban singers and musicians who had been neglected for decades, and their stories are briefly told. The second part of the movie is somewhat miraculous as Cooder takes the veterans (most of whom had never been outside of Cuba) on a very successful tour to Europe and New York. While most of the performers are Cuban folk singers and musicians rather than jazz players, the music of pianist Ruben Gonzalez is closely related to jazz. In any case, this is a wonderful film.

⑤ ♪ *"C" Man*
(1949, 75 minutes)

Dean Jagger and John Carradine star in a crime drama about a customs investigator tracking down a smuggled necklace and a murder. Drummer Bobby Rosengarden (25 at the time) is featured in a nightclub scene.

8 9 ♪ *Cabin in the Sky* (1942, 99 minutes)

One of the all-time great Black musicals, this is a fable where representatives of heaven and hell battle over Little Joe Jackson (Eddie "Rochester" Anderson). He is married to Ethel Waters but tempted by Lena Horne and gambling. There is a lot of fine music along the way, particularly from Waters (who introduces "Taking a Chance on Love," "Happiness Is Just a Thing Called Joe" and "Cabin in the Sky"). Lena Horne sings "Honey in the Honeycomb," Duke Ellington's orchestra plays concise versions of "Things Ain't What They Used to Be" and "Goin' Up," and there is a very brief appearance by Louis Armstrong whose one number ("Ain't It the Truth") was cut out from the movie. The team of Buck and Bubbles (pianist Buck Washington and singer/dancer John Sublett) and the Hall Johnson Choir also appear. Forget the stereotypes that pop up and enjoy the music, the fine acting and the sly humor.

5 4 ♪ *Cairo* (1942, 101 minutes)

This World War II spy drama stars Jeannette McDonald and casts Ethel Waters as her maid and assistant. As part of a medley, Waters sings a chorus of "Waiting for the

Ethel Waters stole the show from Lena Horne in *Cabin in the Sky*.

Robert E. Lee" and she also has one feature, a colorful jive song that is part of a humorous scene.

♪ Calling All Stars
(1937, 75 minutes)

A thin story about a record label is a good excuse for this British film to have performances by singers Evelyn Dall ("Organ Grinders' Swing" and "I Don't Wanna Get Hot"), Turner Layton ("East of the Sun") and Elizabeth Welch ("Nightfall"), the team of Buck and Bubbles ("The Rhythm's OK in Harlem"), the Nicholas Brothers ("Za Zu Za Zu"), harmonica wizard Larry Adler ("Stardust" and "St. Louis Blues") and Ambrose's orchestra ("Serenade in the Night," "Peanuts," "Body and Soul," "Eleven More Months and Ten More Days" and "When Day Is Done").

♪ Campus Sleuth
(1948, 57 minutes)

A group of college students try to solve a murder, and bandleader/trumpeter Bobby Sherwood is a prime suspect. Sherwood's orchestra is featured on "Sherwood's Forest," "What Happened," "Baby, You Can Count on Me," "Neither Could I" and "Jungle Rhumba."

♪ Captain Henry's Showboat
(1933, unknown length)

This long-forgotten movie was billed as "the picturization of one of the favorite radio programs." Most of the other acts and actors are obscure, with Lanny Ross and Don Voorhees's orchestra appearing, but this production is chiefly significant for having the only film appearance known to exist of the wonderful singer Annette Hanshaw. The 22-year-old Hanshaw is introduced from the audience, walks on stage and sings "We Just Couldn't Say Goodbye" (one verse and one chorus). Her backup band (the Don Voorhees Orchestra) is not seen, but one can briefly hear Benny Goodman and a trumpeter who is probably Manny Klein.

♪ Carmen Jones *(1954, 103 minutes)*

Bizet's Carmen is transformed in this all-Black version, with Oscar Hammerstein providing the lyrics. Although it stars Dorothy Dandridge, Harry Belafonte and Diahann Carroll, their singing is ghosted by opera singers. Drummer Max Roach, pianist Richie Powell and bassist Curtis Counce are on-screen very briefly.

♪ Carnegie Hall *(1947, 133 minutes)*

In this tribute to the temple of classical music, an employee of Carnegie Hall raises her son in the hall in hopes that he will become a musician. Many classical musicians perform along the way and Harry James makes a cameo, being featured on "Brown Danube."

♪ Casablanca *(1942, 102 minutes)*

This classic Humphrey Bogart movie would not have been the same without the vocals of Dooley Wilson, particularly his versions of "As Time Goes By" and "The Very Thought of You." Since Wilson was not a pianist, his piano playing was ghosted by Elliott Carpenter.

♪ Cat Ballou *(1965, 96 minutes)*

This fun Western parody stars Jane Fonda and Lee Marvin. Nat King Cole and Stubby Kaye are shown allegedly playing banjos (although Kaye never bothers changing his fingering) and acting as singing narrators between acts. They sing enthusiastically, Cole is featured on a ballad, and they pop up briefly in two scenes with Cole seen (but not heard) playing piano. This was Nat King Cole's last work before his death a few months later from lung cancer.

♪ C'est la Vie Parisienne
(1953, 100 minutes)

Two love stories, one in the 1890s and the other in the 1950s, are interrelated with the characters in the latter as the grandchildren of the main actors in the former. The 1950s portion finds actor Phillipe Lemaire playing a trumpeter and has an appearance by clarinetist Claude Luter.

Chatterbox *(1943, 76 minutes)*

The greatly underrated comic actor Joe E. Brown plays a bragging radio cowboy who suddenly has to prove his stuff in person. Spade Cooley's band plays some Western swing, and the Mills Brothers sing "Sweet Lucy Brown."

Check and Double Check *(1930, 75 minutes)*

The one movie to star Amos 'N' Andy (White radio stars in blackface) is a rather weak story only of interest for its historic value and for the music. The Duke Ellington orchestra performs an exciting version of "Old Man Blues" (which is also available on **Duke Ellington 1929–1943**) that has solos from Harry Carney, Johnny Hodges on soprano and trumpeter Freddie Jenkins. The band also backs the Rhythm Boys (Bing Crosby, Harry Barris and Al Rinker) on a brief "Three Little Words" (although on-screen the vocal trio is actually Ellington's trumpet section) and plays "The Mystery Song" as background music. The Ellington orchestra at the time consisted of Jenkins, Cootie Williams, Arthur Whetsol, Tricky Sam Nanton, Juan Tizol, Barney Bigard, Hodges, Harry Carney, Fred Guy, Wellman Braud, Sonny Greer and Ellington.

China Gate *(1957, 90 minutes)*

Nat King Cole is billed third and has one of his best acting roles in this Angie Dickinson/Gene Barry action adventure set in 1954 Vietnam. Cole sings the title cut twice, but there is no jazz.

Chotard et Cie *(1933, 113 minutes)*

This lesser-known Jean Renoir French film has an appearance by pianist Freddy Johnson, an American living in Paris at the time.

The Cincinnati Kid *(1965, 102 minutes)*

Steve McQueen, Edward G. Robinson, Ann-Margret and Karl Malden are among the stars in this yarn about a poker match in New Orleans. Cab Calloway has a very small (and rather insignificant) acting role and, during a brief scene, the Preservation Hall Jazz Band (with pianist/singer Sweet Emma Barrett, clarinetist George Lewis, trombonist Jim Robinson and trumpeter Punch Miller) plays a few choruses of a blues. The opening credits are a real delight, featuring the Eureka Jazz Band at a funeral jamming on "Oh, Didn't He Ramble" although some cuts of the film having them playing "The Saints."

Cinderfella *(1960, 88 minutes)*

Jerry Lewis's take on Cinderella finds him winning Princess Charming with the help of his fairy godfather (Ed Wynn). There are a couple of appearances of Count Basie's big band with Joe Williams. The songs include "Somebody," "Princess Waltz" and "Let Me Be a People."

Cinerama Holiday *(1955, 119 minutes)*

This plotless film's main purpose was to showcase its three-camera process and a great deal of beautiful scenery from around the world. Included is a version of "Tiger Rag" filmed a couple of years earlier and featuring trumpeter Oscar Celestin with his Original Tuxedo Jazz Band.

The Connection *(1961, 105 minutes)*

The groundbreaking Jack Gelber play deals with drug addiction and is centered around a group of men, some of whom are jazz musicians, waiting in an apartment for their heroin connection to arrive. The little-known film version made for Living Theatre captures the essence of the production. Although the plot is a bit depressing, pianist Freddie Redd wrote the score, and there is fine hard bop music performed by Redd, altoist Jackie McLean, bassist Michael Attos and drummer Larry Ritchie, who also appear as actors. This film was released on video by Mystic Fire.

Confessions of a Co-ed
(1931, 74 minutes)

This little-known melodrama has the third and final film appearance by the Rhythm Boys (Bing Crosby, Harry Barris and Al Rinker). Early in the film at a school dance, Crosby sings "Out of Nowhere" and joins in with the Rhythm Boys on "Ya Got Love."

The Cotton Club *(1984, 128 minutes)*

The Cotton Club should have been an ideal centerpiece for a motion picture, but this film suffers from a confusing, overloaded and ultimately nonsensical screenplay. A gangsters and jazz movie, the production is at its best during its occasional musical moments, such as when actor Richard Gere plays his own cornet solos (hinting at Bix Beiderbecke) or whenever tap dancer Gregory Hines is on-screen; Maurice Hines is also an asset. Cab Calloway and Duke Ellington are portrayed very briefly, and the music (mostly Ellington pieces arranged by Bob Wilbur), though sounding authentic, is overshadowed by the mundane plot and the gangsters.

Cowboy Canteen *(1944, 72 minutes)*

When Charles Starrett gets drafted, he turns his ranch into an entertainment venue for servicemen. In addition to many Western bands, the Mills Brothers perform "Up the Lazy River."

Crazy House/Funzapoppin'
(1943, 80 minutes)

A so-so Olsen and Johnson comedy, this B movie has an appearance by Count Basie's orchestra performing brief versions of "Rigoletto Quartet" and "Pocket Full of Dreams" as part of a couple of huge production numbers.

The Crimson Canary
(1945, 64 minutes)

In this murder mystery, a singer is killed and two of the musicians are suspected of her murder. Folk/blues singer/guitarist Josh White performs "Joshua Fit the Battle of Jericho" and "One Meat Ball," but the main reason to view the film is for a three-minute version of "Hollywood Stampede" (based on "Sweet Georgia Brown") which features Coleman Hawkins's quintet with trumpeter Howard McGhee, pianist Sir Charles Thompson, bassist Oscar Pettiford and drummer Denzil Best.

Daddy Long Legs *(1955, 127 minutes)*

This is an excellent later Fred Astaire movie in which he plays the anonymous benefactor of Leslie Caron. Although the music is fine, the amount of jazz in this film is minimal. Astaire plays drums effectively, but only for a brief time in one scene. Trumpeter Ray Anthony plays a blues with a small group for a few moments, but is in the background as his singers and orchestra perform the corny "Sluefoot."

Dance Hall *(1950, 80 minutes)*

Dance Hall is a British film about four working-class women (including Petula Clark) who go out dancing at night looking for adventure. Ted Heath's big band ("Lovely Weekend," " Saturday Night Drag," "Post Horn Boogie," "Quickie") and Geraldo's orchestra are the bands onstage during much of the movie.

Dance Team *(1931, 83 minutes)*

James Dunn and Sally Eilers star in an adaptation of a Sarah Addington novel. Pianist Claude Hopkins and his big band make a brief appearance.

Dancing Co-ed
(1939, 84 minutes)

For this moderately interesting Lana Turner film, the actress plays a showgirl planted on a college campus so she can win a phony amateur dance contest. Turner met Artie Shaw while making this movie, and their resulting marriage did not last much longer than the film. Shaw and his very popular orchestra perform "Nightmare," "Non-Stop Flight," "I'm Coming Virginia" and "Jungle Drums" along the way, although most of the songs are just heard as excerpts or partly behind dialog. The best feature for the Shaw big band (which includes tenor saxophonist Georgie Auld and Buddy Rich) is "Traffic Jam."

The Dark Corner
(1946, 99 minutes)

This film noir features Mark Stevens as a detective who seems to be getting framed a second time. Lucille Ball, Clifton Webb and William Bendix are all excellent in their parts. Eddie Heywood's band appears once, playing "Heywood Blues."

A Date with a Dream
(1948, 56 minutes)

Four wartime performers have a reunion and decide to team up again in postwar England. Bandleader Victor Lewis has a small acting role, and his orchestra performs "Here Comes the Show," "You Made Me Mad," "Whose Turn Now" and "How about Me for You?"

A Day at the Races
(1937, 109 minutes)

A typically hilarious Marx Brothers movie, this film has a sequence where Harpo Marx leads a mostly Black aggregation through "Who's that Man." That immediately segues into a large production number version of "All God's Chillun Got Rhythm" with Duke Ellington's Ivie Anderson singing quite prominently.

Delovely *(2004, 125 minutes)*

Kevin Kline does an excellent job of portraying Cole Porter in this entertaining and generally true (if at times fanciful) biographical film, which is a major improvement on 1946's nonsensical **Night and Day**. Porter is shown at the end of his life looking back at the highlights of his life as if it were a movie musical. His bisexuality is treated honestly as is his marriage, although he was actually married to an older (not younger) woman. There is plenty of music in the film, mostly performed decently by contemporary pop singers. The lone jazz performer, Diana Krall, has most of her version of "Just One of Those Things" buried beneath dialog; maybe that is why she does not smile once. Elvis Costello fares best on "Let's Misbehave."

Dementia
(1953, 55 minutes)

Dementia is a bizarre horror film that has no dialog from the actors. It stars Adrienne Barrett as a woman who may have committed a couple of murders, or might have dreamt the whole thing. At one point she wanders into a jazz club where Shorty Rogers and his Giants (trumpeter Rogers, tenor saxophonist Jimmy Giuffre, John Graas on French horn, trombonist Milt Bernhart and a rhythm section) play "Wig Alley." The film was also released in edited form (but with the jazz scene intact) a couple of years later as **Daughter of Horror**.

Le Desordre et la Nuit
(1958, 92 minutes)

This French detective story (which is also known as **Night Affair**) stars Jean Gabin as an inspector searching for the murderer of a nightclub owner. Hazel Scott has a small role as Valentine Horse.

Die Nacht vor der Premiere
(1959, 96 minutes)

Marika Rokk stars in this West German film, which has several different performers at various times performing "Kisses in Der Nacht." Louis Armstrong's All-Stars (with Trummy Young, Peanuts Hucko, Billy Kyle, Mort Herbert and Danny Barcelona) are seen briefly, and Satch sings the lyrics of "Kisses in Der Nacht" in German.

🎞️5 🎵4 *Ding Dong Williams*
(1946, 75 minutes)

Glenn Vernon plays a Dixieland/swing clarinetist who is hired to write a modern symphony for the climax of a Hollywood movie, before it is discovered that he cannot read or write music. Marcus McGuire plays his love interest in this light and somewhat amusing comedy. Vernon is heard playing a long Dixieland blues (partly behind dialog), an original ballad and a few short bluesy pieces. Although it has not been confirmed, his playing sounds suspiciously like Barney Bigard.

🎞️5 🎵3 *Dingo* *(1990, 90 minutes)*

In 1990, Miles Davis had his only opportunity to appear in a movie. Actor Colin Friels (whose trumpet playing is ghosted by Chuck Findley) plays an Australian trumpeter working a day job and unsure about his life's direction. His idol is the trumpeter who Miles Davis portrays; he befriends his hero and learns some valuable lessons along the way. Michel Legrand arranged and composed the music, which is mostly quite forgettable while the story is a bit confusing and often trivial. Davis essentially plays a variation of himself and, although this film (available from Greycat Home Video) is a rare opportunity to hear him in a modified straight-ahead setting this late in life, he is overshadowed musically by Findley.

🎞️5 🎵8 *Disc Jockey* *(1951, 77 minutes)*

Ginny Simms is an unknown singer selected for stardom by disc jockey Michael O'Shea. The plot is lightweight, but there are many interesting performances along the way from the likes of the George Shearing Quintet ("Brain Wave"), Sarah Vaughan, Herb Jeffries, banjoist/singer Nick Lucas, Tommy Dorsey's orchestra and a hot all-star group ("Jam Session Blues") that includes cornetist Red Nichols, Joe Venuti, Red Norvo, tenor saxophonist Vido Musso, trombonist Russ Morgan and drummer Ben Pollack.

🎞️3 🎵3 *Do You Love Me* *(1946, 91 minutes)*

Harry James has one of his biggest roles in this musical, co-starring with Maureen O'Hara and singer Dick Haymes. Unfortunately, the screenplay for the jazz vs. classical story is not too inspired, and the musical numbers that James plays with his big band and behind Haymes ("As If I Didn't Have Enough on My Mind," "I Didn't Mean a Word I Said," "Moonlight Propaganda," " Do You Love Me?") are instantly forgettable except for the annoying title song.

🎞️3 🎵3 *La Donna di Notte* *(1962, 95 minutes)*

This Italian travelogue, designed to mostly show women dancing in various nightclubs around the world, has an appearance by Louis Prima and Sam Butera.

🎞️5 🎵4 *Dr. Terror's House of Horrors*
(1965, 98 minutes)

Five travelers on a train have Peter Cushing read their tarot cards and predict how they will die. Roy Castle plays a trumpeter (his parts are ghosted by Jimmy Deuchar) who makes the mistake of publicly playing music that he heard at a voodoo ceremony. He is seen performing with the Tubby Hayes Quintet.

🎞️5 🎵7 *Dragnet* *(1954, 88 minutes)*

This famous crime drama, with the same matter-of-fact narrative as the later television series, casts Jack Webb as cop Joe Friday. A year before he ghosted for Webb's trumpet playing in **Pete Kelly's Blues**, trumpeter Dick Cathcart is featured in an excellent scene playing three hot ensemble choruses on a blues with a Dixieland septet that includes pianist Ray Sherman. Cathcart also discusses details of the case with Webb and another cop.

🎞️5 🎵5 *The Dreamer* *(1947, unknown length)*

Mabel Lee and Mantan Moreland star in this all-Black musical comedy. The film is most notable for June Richmond's "All You Want to Do Is Eat," "You'll Never

Get Nothin' without Trying" and "My Man Is Workin' Again."

♪ Drums of Africa
3 | 1
(1963, 92 minutes)

Frankie Avalon battles slave traders in 1897 East Africa in this adventure film. There is a brief appearance by tenor saxophonist Clifford Scott.

♪ Du Barry Was a Lady
6 | 8
(1943, 101 minutes)

Red Skelton, Gene Kelly and Lucille Ball star in an amusing if somewhat silly musical comedy that is highlighted by a long sequence in which Skelton dreams he is back in the 1700s. The Tommy Dorsey Orchestra appears early in the film, performing a brief version of "I'm Getting Sentimental Over You" and a classic rendition of "Well, Git It." The latter features clarinetist Heinie Beau, tenor saxophonist Don Lodice, Buddy Rich, a famous trumpet tradeoff by Ziggy Elman and Chuck Peterson, and two pianists (Milt Raskin and an unidentified keyboardist who looks a bit like Joe Bushkin). In addition, the band (wearing powdered wigs and 18th-century costumes) plays "Katie Went to Haiti" (Elman gets off a hot trumpet solo), the second half of which features the Pied Pipers with Jo Stafford and Dick Haymes.

Harry James did his best to save the dull film *Do You Love Me,* but he had better moments in *Best Foot Forward.*

6 8 *Earl Carroll Vanities*
(1945, 90 minutes)

Constance Moore plays a European princess who prefers jazz to Mozart. She is in the United States trying to get a loan for her kingdom and is discovered by Earl Carroll who wants to have her star in his show. Woody Herman's First Herd (which includes Herman on clarinet, trumpeters Neal Hefti, Ray Wetzel and Pete Candoli, trombonist Bill Harris, tenor saxophonist Flip Phillips, pianist Ralph Burns, vibraphonist Marjorie Hyams, guitarist Billy Bauer, bassist Chubby Jackson and drummer Dave Tough) plays a brief but priceless version of "Apple Honey."

5 2 *Earl Carroll's Sketchbook* (1946, 90 minutes)

Constance Moore is a singer and William Marshall is her boyfriend, a songwriter who (over her objections) has decided to write radio jingles rather than worthwhile songs. Buddy Rich has a brief appearance playing with a string orchestra.

9 5 *East Side of Heaven* (1939, 90 minutes)

The screenplay for this lesser-known Bing Crosby film has many hilarious lines. Crosby, who works as a singing cabdriver, wants to marry Joan Blondell but various incidents, including getting mixed up in a child custody case, keep on interfering. Actor Mischa Auer, Bing's roommate and sidekick, has never been funnier. Although none of the songs from this movie became famous, they are all enjoyable. On the likable "Hide Your Heart on a Hickory Limb," Bing is joined by violinist Matty Malneck's quintet with trumpeter Manny Klein.

5 6 *Einbrecher* (1930, 85 minutes)

In this German movie featuring pop stars of the era, Sidney Bechet and a seven-piece band accompany dancers on an uptempo song based on "Tiger Rag." This was Bechet's first appearance on film. Einbrecher means "burglar" in English, and this film was subtitled "A Musical Marriage Comedy."

5 3 *Every Day's a Holiday*
(1938, 79 minutes)

This typical Mae West comedy features Louis Armstrong at one point in a parade singing and playing trumpet on "Jubilee." Seen briefly in this production number are many musicians (some carrying instruments that they do not normally play), including clarinetist Eddie Barefield (pretending he is playing trombone), tenor saxophonist Jack McVea, drummer Lee Young, bassist Red Callender, altoist Marshall Royal and trumpeter Teddy Buckner.

5 4 *The Exterminator* (1980, 102 minutes)

Robert Ginty becomes a one-man vigilante against muggers and street criminals in this thriller. Stan Getz and his group appear briefly playing Chuck Loeb's "Kali Au."

7 5 *The Fabulous Baker Boys*
(1989, 116 minutes)

Jeff and Beau Bridges play the Fabulous Baker Boys, a duo piano team that performs at lounges in New York City. When jobs become scarce, the brothers hire Michelle Pfeiffer as their singer and suddenly business booms. While Beau is quite happy playing tunes such as "Feelings," Jeff would prefer to be working in jazz clubs. When the latter becomes involved with Pfeiffer, the story heats up. Dave Grusin (who wrote the score) ghosts for Jeff while John Hammond plays the piano for Beau. Michelle Pfeiffer sings her own part and does a surprisingly effective job on "More than You Know," "Ten Cents a Dance" and "Makin' Whoopee."

3 7 *The Fabulous Dorseys*
(1947, 87 minutes)

In one of the first semifictional Hollywood jazz biographies, Tommy and Jimmy Dorsey play themselves. Unfortunately, the screenplay about the battling Dorseys is weak and sometimes absurd, and the music (mostly a trotting-out of their hits) is generally uninspired or nostalgic at best. Paul Whiteman has an acting role (he is treated throughout as a hero), and along the way one gets to see cornetist Henry Busse, banjoist Mike Pingitore, clarinetist Abe Most and singers Bob Eberly, Helen O'Connell and Stuart Foster. Among the songs played by a mixture of the two Dorsey orchestras are "Marie," "Green Eyes," "Running Wild," "The Object of My Affection" and a rather pompous "Dorsey Concerto." However, there is an essential five-minute section that has Art Tatum playing solo briefly in a club (partly under dialog) and then leading a blues (first at a slow tempo and then cooking) in a jam session with Jimmy Dorsey (on clarinet), Tommy Dorsey, Ziggy Elman, Charlie Barnet (on alto) and drummer Ray Bauduc along with an unidentified bassist and guitarist. It is for that clip (one of the very few appearances of Tatum on film) that this movie is worth seeing.

52nd Street
(1937, 80 minutes)

52nd Street was Swing Street during 1935–47, a remarkable area in New York that had a dozen jazz clubs within a couple of blocks. There is a great story to be told, both about the area's gradual birth and about life on the Street. Unfortunately, this movie (which includes a fictional story about the aristocracy being pushed out by show business) misses the point completely, having nothing to do with 52nd Street other than continually using its name. Although there is a lot of period music utilized that covers the years 1912–37, nearly every performer who appears in this film (and every song) is long forgotten. Ella Logan has the best numbers (including "Let Your Hair Down and Swing"), there are a couple of very brief cameos from Jerry Colonna, and for a couple of seconds one can see (but not hear) violinist Stuff Smith. It is remarkable that none of the jazz combos that were actually playing on 52nd Street (and making it famous) appear in this mess.

The Five Pennies
(1959, 117 minutes)

The fictionalized story of cornetist Red Nichols's life stars Danny Kaye. Kaye plays Nichols as a free spirit fighting for the music he loves in the 1920s, one who chucks it all when his neglected daughter contracts polio in the late 1930s before making a comeback at the end of the film. Although the real cornetist was actually quite straitlaced and most of these events did not happen as portrayed, the movie is very entertaining. Kaye and Barbara Bel Geddes make for an appealing couple, Louis Armstrong has one of his best roles, the arrangements by Leith Stevens, Benny Carter and Heinie Beau are excellent, and there is lots of good music. One of the great moments is when Kaye

Danny Kaye portrays cornetist Red Nichols and interacts with Louis Armstrong during the highly enjoyable if fictional 1959 film *The Five Pennies*.

comes out of the audience to battle his hero Louis Armstrong on the "Battle Hymn of the Republic." Sylvia Fine (Kaye's wife) contributed three originals ("The Five Pennies," "Lullaby in Ragtime" and "Goodnight, Sleep Tight") that conveniently all have the same chord changes so they could be sung together by Kaye, Armstrong and Susan Gordon, who plays Nichols's daughter as a child. Among the other major songs are "Bill Bailey," "Indiana," "Follow the Leader" and "The Wail of the Winds" (Nichols's later theme song). Kaye's solos are ghosted by Red Nichols himself, Eileen Wilson sings for Bel Geddes, Bob Crosby plays a cornball bandleader named Will Paradise, Ray Anthony has a small role as Jimmy Dorsey, Shelly Manne appears as drummer Dave Tough, Bobby Troup fills in for pianist Arthur Schutt, and Louis Armstrong's All-Stars (with Trummy Young, Peanuts Hucko, Billy Kyle, Mort Herbert and Danny Barcelona) appear on some of his numbers. Go out of your way to see this one!

The Flamingo Affair (1948, 58 minutes)

A British crime film (also known as **Blonde for Danger**) about an attempted robbery, this movie has an appearance by Stephane Grappelli and his quintet playing a ballad in a club.

The Fleet's In (1942, 94 minutes)

If it were not for the participation of the Jimmy Dorsey Orchestra, this mundane musical comedy would be completely forgotten. In addition to backing Dorothy Lamour and Betty Hutton, the Dorsey band introduces "I Remember You," plays a brief version of JD's theme song "Contrasts," and performs a classic rendition of "Tangerine" featuring singers Helen O'Connell and Bob Eberly.

Follow the Band (1943, 61 minutes)

Eddie Quillan plays a farmboy who wants to become a musician, despite doubts by his girlfriend. Skinnay Ennis helps him realize his dream. Along the way there are numbers played by Ennis's Groove Boys, Alvino Rey, the King Sisters and Ray Eberly including "My Melancholy Baby," "My Devotion," "Ain't Misbehavin'," "Swingin' the Blues," "Spellbound" and "Rosie the Riveter."

Follow the Boys (1944, 122 minutes)

George Murphy stars in an all-star salute to the USO. There are spots for the orchestras of Freddie Slack, Charlie Spivak (a forgettable ballad) and Ted Lewis, the Delta Rhythm Boys and Louis Jordan. Jordan's segment is noteworthy, as he and his Tympany Five perform a memorable version of "Is You Is or Is You Ain't My Baby" and back George Murphy's soft-shoe dancing in the rain on "Sweet Georgia Brown."

Follow the Fleet (1936, 110 minutes)

This typically enjoyable Fred Astaire/Ginger Rogers musical comedy has a rare instance of Astaire playing solo piano. His instrumental performance of "I'm Building Up to an Awful Lowdown" (a song he co-wrote with Johnny Mercer) features him playing some rather impressive stride piano live.

Fools for Scandal (1938, 81 minutes)

In this Carole Lombard comedy reminiscent of **My Man Godfrey**, a famous actress becomes involved with a penniless but charming Frenchman. Rodgers and Hart wrote the score (most of which was cut out) and Les Hite's orchestra appears in one brief scene, backing a female singer for a verse and half a chorus before disappearing.

For Singles Only (1968, 91 minutes)

This is a juvenile romantic comedy starring John Saxon and Mary Ann Mobley. Along with several pop and rock bands, Cal Tjader's group makes an appearance.

For the Boys
(1991, 145 minutes)

An underrated saga of the up-and-down relationship of a fictional showbiz couple, Dixie Leonard (Bette Midler) and Eddie Sparks (James Caan), this film spans 50 years (World War II, the Korean War and the Vietnam War). The Sparks character has a resemblance at times to Bob Hope, while Bette Midler is slightly reminiscent of Martha Raye in spots. Midler performs a previously unrecorded Hoagy Carmichael song ("Billy-A-Dick"), a touching version of "Come Rain or Come Shine," "Stuff Like That There," "P.S. I Love You," the Beatles' "In My Life" and "Every Road Leads Back to You" while Caan's theme song is "I Remember You." Jack Sheldon has a bit part (with a few lines and brief spots on trumpet) as bandleader Wally Fields; the nucleus of the orchestra he leads on-screen became his regularly working big band.

Four for Texas
(1963, 124 minutes)

Frank Sinatra and Dean Martin play rival con men who alternate between being enemies and friends in this Western set in 1870 Texas. Near the end of the film, a riverboat scene features some Dixieland from trumpeter Teddy Buckner's band (with trombonist Willie Woodman and clarinetist Caughey Roberts) including "The Saints."

Four Jills in a Jeep
(1944, 90 minutes)

A World War II movie about four women (including Kay Francis and Martha Raye) performing overseas for American troops and having romances, this film has a number for crooner Dick Haymes ("You Send Me") and a small role for Jimmy Dorsey. Dorsey's orchestra backs a few specialties and is featured on one hot instrumental, a Sonny Burke arrangement of "The Champ." The trumpeter, who takes a half-chorus and sounds both mildly bopish and influenced by Harry James, is a young Red Rodney.

Freddie Steps Out
(1946, 75 minutes)

Freddie Stewart plays both a band singer and a college student. When the singer disappears, rumors are started by friends that the student is actually the swing star. Charlie Barnet and his big band appear and the songs include "Patience and Fortitude," "Let's Drop the Subject" and "Don't Blame Me."

French Quarter
(1978, 101 minutes)

An impoverished young woman goes to New Orleans in the late '70s, is only successful getting work as a topless dancer, and is magically transported to 1910 Storyville by a voodoo queen. This low-budget yarn has a weak screenplay full of clichés and historic errors, although a few bawdy scenes of life in a decadent Storyville bordello ring true. Dick Hyman wrote the score and is on the soundtrack along with pianist Butch Thompson. Louis Armstrong is portrayed as a boy and the role of Jelly Roll Morton is sympathetically played by Vernel Bagneris. Musically the best moment is when Bagneris and another actor perform a hot version of "King Porter Stomp."

The Fugitive Kind
(1959, 121 minutes)

The Tennessee Williams play *Orpheus Descending* was adapted to become this very downbeat movie starring Marlon Brando and Anna Magnani. Saxophonist Jerome Richardson is prominent during a brief jazz scene.

The Gang's All Here
(1943, 103 minutes)

This 20th Century Fox musical stars Alice Faye, Carmen Miranda and James Ellison. Although Benny Goodman and his orchestra (which at the time included trumpeter Lee Castle, trombonist Miff Mole, altoist Hymie Schertzer, Jess Stacy and Louie Bellson) appear, the music is much less interesting than usual. Goodman sings "Minnie's in the Money" and "Paducah" (the latter with Miranda) and otherwise is mostly just heard in the background.

Garden of the Moon
(1938, 94 minutes)

Nightclub owner Pat O'Brien and bandleader John Payne fight over everything, including Margaret Lindsay, in this Busby Berkeley musical. Joe Venuti (leading his Swing Cats, which includes Jerry Colonna on trombone) makes an appearance, joining in on "Girlfriend of the Whirling Dervish."

Un Homme Qui Me Plait
(1969, 95 minutes)

This French film is about a love affair between an actress and a movie composer, both of whom are married. In one scene at Al Hirt's club in New Orleans, singer Sweet Emma Barrett and trumpeter Alvin Alcorn's band perform.

The Gene Krupa Story
(1959, 101 minutes)

Although Sal Mineo does a fine job of portraying Gene Krupa, the screenplay of this biography is full of clichés and misinformation. Krupa's rise and fall (centering on his marijuana bust of 1943) and eventual comeback is made very melodramatic. One scene that has made jazz historians chuckle for decades has Krupa in the late '30s introducing Bix Beiderbecke (who had died in 1931) to some friends at a party. Despite all of this, much of the music is worthwhile. Krupa ghosted the drumming for Mineo, cornetist Red Nichols guests on "Royal Garden Blues" and "Indiana," Anita O'Day sings "Memories of You" and the other numbers include "I Love My Baby" (with a vocal from Ruby Lane), "Cherokee," "Way Down Yonder in New Orleans" and "Song of India." Shelly Manne gets to play drummer Dave Tough again (as he did in **The Five Pennies**) and Bobby Troup has a minor role. Surprisingly, "Drum Boogie" and "Let Me Off Uptown" are not included and there is no sign of Roy Eldridge. The less one knows about Krupa (and marijuana), the more they will enjoy this film.

George in Civvy Street
(1946, 88 minutes)

Veteran British actor George Formby plays a returning serviceman involved in a beer war between two rival pubs. Trumpeter Johnny Claes's band, an octet that includes Ronnie Scott on tenor, plays "Mop Mop" and backs Formby on six songs including "I Won't Need a License for That."

George White's Scandals
(1945, 95 minutes)

This backstage story is a tribute to George White's *Scandals*, an annual production. Gene Krupa is seen several times throughout the film, having a few lines, backing some of the acts and being featured with his "strings that swing" orchestra. The band (with tenor saxophonist Charlie Ventura and trumpeter Don Fagerquist) is featured on a good version of "Leave Us Leap." Krupa also takes part in a weird and giant production number ("Bolero in the Jungle"), organist Ethel Smith plays "Liza" and Rose Murphy (who plays a maid) has a brief number.

Get Yourself a College Girl
(1964, 85 minutes)

Although this is a remarkably dumb teenage comedy, jazz viewers will definitely want to see it due to one number. Tenor saxophonist Stan Getz and his group (with vibraphonist Gary Burton) join Astrud Gilberto in a classic version of "The Girl from Ipanema" that stands apart from the rest of the film. Otherwise, organist Jimmy Smith romps on a couple of tunes (including "When Johnny Comes Marching Home"), and there are a variety of dated songs from pop/rock groups.

Ghost Catchers *(1944, 68 minutes)*

Ole Olsen and Chic Johnson "rescue" their neighbor and his two daughters from a haunted house in this corny if crazy comedy. Some of the film (which includes an exorcism by swing) is bizarre, but there are some musical moments. Ella Mae Morse sings with backing from the Morton Downey Orchestra (with Mel Tormé on drums). The songs include "Blue Candlelight," "These Foolish Things," "I'm Old Enough to Dream" and "Swanee River."

🎞5 🎵3 *The Ghost Goes Gear* (1966, 79 minutes)

This movie was filmed as a device for the Spencer Davis rock group (who recall the Monkees a bit in their humor) and to show off the British music scene of the mid-'60s. It is mostly of interest to jazz listeners for the appearance of clarinetist Acker Bilk's Paramount Jazz Band, which performs "Henry the 9th."

🎞7 🎵6 *Giant Steps* (1992, 94 minutes)

Billy Dee Williams plays a veteran jazz pianist who is not dissimilar to Thelonious Monk. Singer Ranee Lee (an effective actress) is Williams's past and possibly present love who wants him to cut back on the late night avant-garde jam sessions and play standards with her in clubs. Michael Mahoren is a young trumpeter who idolizes and befriends Williams, learning some important lessons. A few eccentric characters (including a punkish drummer who is dedicated to playing free jazz, a rock caricature who keeps on trying to hire him, a groupie, Mahoren's drunken father and a girlfriend trying desperately to cheat in her geometry class) keep the story interesting and many of the jazz scenes seem realistic. Eric Leeds wrote the original music, Doc Cheatham has a bit part (but only holds rather than plays his trumpet), and some of the on-screen bands include keyboardist Bill King (of *The Jazz Report* magazine) and drummer Graeme Kirkland. This underrated movie is worth a viewing.

🎞5 🎵5 *Gift of Gab* (1934, 71 minutes)

This musical comedy has a throwaway story about a radio announcer who is fired after giving a false interview and

fights to redeem himself. It is more significant for the performances by entertainment personalities. None of the songs made it ("Talking to Myself" came the closest), but there are features for Ruth Etting (who is billed third), Ethel Waters, Gene Austin, Candy and Coco, the Gus Arnheim orchestra and the Beale Street Boys.

🎞8 🎵7 *The Gig* (1985, 91 minutes)

One of the best Hollywood movies made about jazz, **The Gig** tells the story of what happens when five part-time, middle-aged Dixieland players get their first gig, an engagement in the Catskills. Their difficulties in adjusting their music to please the audience and the management, their different aspirations, and how the job alters their lives are shown in both humorous and serious episodes. Warren Vache is one of the actors and plays his own cornet solos. The soundtrack also features cornetist Bob Bernard, clarinetist Kenny Davern, trombonist George Masso, pianists Dick Wellstood and John Bunch, bassists Milt Hinton and Reggie Johnson and drummer Herb Harris.

🎞6 🎵4 *The Girl Can't Help It* (1956, 97 minutes)

This is an amusing movie about a gangster (Edmond O'Brien) hiring a theatrical agent (Tom Ewell) in an attempt to make his untalented girlfriend (Jayne Mansfield) a hit in show business. Most of the music is by current rock 'n' roll groups, but Julie London sings her hit "Cry Me a River," Abbey Lincoln makes her screen debut with the pseudo-gospel piece "Spread the World," and Ray Anthony leads the big band backing Mansfield during her attempts to sing/squeal.

🎞8 🎵4 *Girl Crazy* (1943, 99 minutes)

This famous Judy Garland/Mickey Rooney film has many Gershwin songs, which mostly feature the stars. Tommy Dorsey's orchestra (with trumpeters Ziggy Elman and Chuck Peterson, clarinetist Heinie Beau, tenor saxophonist

Don Lodice, and pianist Milt Raskin) pops up in three scenes including being used as a prop in the closing production number (a lengthy "I Got Rhythm") and playing an arrangement of "Fascinating Rhythm" (with Mickey Rooney doing a good job of pretending to play piano) that owes a great deal to "Rhapsody in Blue." Dorsey has a few lines and looks happy to be on-screen, drawing an easy paycheck.

Le Glaive et la Balance (1962, 140 minutes)

This French-Italian mystery, whose title translates into English as **Two Are Guilty**, looks at three possible suspects in a child's murder along with problems with the French legal system. During the opening credits, one can see a group consisting of organist Lou Bennett (who wrote the film's score), altoist Sonny Criss, trumpeter Sonny Grey, drummer Kenny Clarke and singer Mae Mercer.

Glamour Girl (1948, 68 minutes)

A young woman from Tennessee is discovered by a talent scout, comes to the big city and struggles to become a hit. There are no big names in the cast other than Gene Krupa, who performs "Gene's Boogie," "Anywhere" and "Melody in F" with his orchestra.

The Glass Wall (1953, 82 minutes)

A European sneaks illegally into the United States in this thriller and is assisted by two people, one of whom is a jazz musician. In an odd but successful coupling, a nightclub scene has Jack Teagarden performing with Shorty Rogers's Giants (which includes Jimmy Giuffre and Shelly Manne). Rogers and clarinetist Bob Keene ghost for a couple of the actors.

The Glenn Miller Story (1953, 116 minutes)

This is a very sentimental but enjoyable depiction of the life of Glenn Miller, starring Jimmy Stewart and June Allyson. The screenplay is well written if often fictional. Due to problems with the Miller estate, there is no mention along the way of Ray Eberle, Marion Hutton or Tex Beneke. One scene has Glenn Miller (Stewart), Gene Krupa and tenor saxophonist Babe Russin sitting in with Louis Armstrong's All-Stars (which include Trummy Young, Barney Bigard, Marty Napoleon, Arvell Shaw and Cozy Cole) for a version of "Basin Street Blues" that is mostly a drum feature for Krupa and Cole. Otherwise the music is primarily from the Glenn Miller repertoire. Trombonists Joe Yukl and Murray McEachern ghost for Stewart throughout the movie, Ben Pollack has a small role, and most of the Miller hits are heard, including "Moonlight Serenade," "A String of Pearls," "Pennsylvania 6-5000," "Tuxedo Junction," "In the Mood," "American Patrol," "Little Brown Jug" and "St. Louis Blues March."

Jimmy Stewart, pictured with his co-star June Allyson, always said that he enjoyed playing the lead in *The Glenn Miller Story*.

⑤ ⑥ *Glory Alley* (1952, 79 minutes)

This rambling drama deals with the conflict between a boxer accused of cowardice and his prospective father-in-law. Because the plot is set in New Orleans, it serves as a good excuse to have Louis Armstrong as one of the supporting characters. Satch sings several numbers and is featured with Jack Teagarden in a band including clarinetist Gus Bivona, pianist Milt Raskin, guitarist Jack Marshall, bassist Artie Shapiro and drummer Frankie Carlson. The songs include "St. Louis Blues," "Glory Alley" and "That's What the Man Said."

⑥ ② *Go Man Go* (1954, 83 minutes)

The dramatized story of the Harlem Globetrotters is told, along with their struggle to survive in a racist society. Slim Galliard has a small role.

⑥ ⑥ *Going Places* (1938, 84 minutes)

This amusing Dick Powell comedy deals with horse racing and a wild racehorse named Jeepers Creepers who is only pacified when it hears the song "Jeepers Creepers" sung by Louis Armstrong. Satch, whose character's name is Gabe, introduced the Johnny Mercer song in this movie and also appears in a production number with Maxine Sullivan, performing "Mutiny in the Nursery."

③ ④ *The Golden Disc* (1958, 78 minutes)

This British film takes place in the "Lucky Charm Coffee Bar," with a thin plot as an excuse to feature a large assortment of British groups, ranging from rock and skiffle to vocalists and just a bit of jazz. Drummer Phil Seamen's sextet, a unit including Don Rendell on tenor and baritonist Ronnie Ross, performs "Lower Deck."

⑤ ① *Good Neighbor Sam* (1964, 130 minutes)

Jack Lemmon is a family man forced to pretend to be his neighbor's husband in this complicated and rather unlikely comedy. Turk Murphy's band (with clarinetist Bob Helm) appears for a total of 40 seconds at Earthquake McGoon's, playing one chorus before the dialog interferes. The Hi-Los also appear very briefly, singing part of a Hertz commercial three times.

⑤ ③ *The Good Sport* (1931, 67 minutes)

This romantic drama with John Boles and Greta Nissen has spots for Eubie Blake's orchestra and singer Evelyn Preer.

② ⑥ *The Great Morgan* (1946, 56 minutes)

Actor Frank Morgan, playing himself, talks the studio boss into letting him produce a film. The results (to the boss's dismay) are a complete mess, a series of unrelated short subjects and nonsensical outtakes; this film could have been a lot funnier. However, the last part of the movie has a delightful number featuring singer/actress Virginia O'Brien (famous for her deadpan expression) and Tommy Dorsey's orchestra on "I Fell in Love with the Leader of the Band." The clip has spots for Ziggy Elman and Buddy Rich.

⑦ ② *The Great White Hope* (1970, 103 minutes)

This is a semifictional, but entertaining and dramatic version of heavyweight champion Jack Johnson's life. At one point, a band appears briefly that includes clarinetist Joe Darensbourg and trumpeter Andy Blakeney.

③ ② *Grounds for Marriage* (1950, 90 minutes)

Van Johnson and Kathryn Grayson do what they can with the weak material in this romantic comedy. One scene has the two principals going to a club where the Firehouse Five Plus Two are playing a heated and humorous version of "Tiger Rag." Unfortunately, the music is marred by Johnson's mugging which makes fun of the group and the song, largely ruining the scene.

🎞️🎵 *Hallelujah* (1929, 109 minutes)

The first big budget, all-Black film, this movie depicts the life of a laborer who, after succumbing to gambling and women, discovers religion and then encounters other difficulties. Despite overacting, some outrageous mugging and stereotypes, it does have its moments, especially musically. Blues singer Victoria Spivey plays the "good girl" and primarily has a nonmusical dramatic role. Nina Mae McKinney clearly has fun playing the "bad girl" and gets to sing and dance on "Swanee Shuffle." Drummer Curtis Mosby's Blue Blowers, a top Los Angeles band that includes trombonist Lawrence Brown, performs briefly on "Tiger Rag" (which includes a drum solo) and is featured prominently on "Swanee Shuffle" and "Blue Blowers' Blues"; the latter is partly in the background. Irving Berlin wrote "Waiting at the End of the Road" for the film.

🎞️🎵 *The Hanged Man* (1964, 110 minutes)

This is a television remake of the Western drama **Ride the Pink Horse**, with Robert Culp seeking revenge for the death of a friend and getting involved in a love triangle in New Orleans. Stan Getz, in a nightclub scene

Nina Mae McKinney (far right) was the perfect "bad girl" in 1929's *Hallelujah*.

with vibraphonist Gary Burton and singer Astrud Gilberto, performs Benny Carter's "Only Trust Your Heart."

Happy Landing
(1938, 102 minutes)

Sonja Henje, Don Ameche, Cesar Romero (who plays bandleader and occasional pilot Duke Sargent) and Ethel Merman get involved in amusing romantic complications. This musical (which includes three ice skating features for Henje) has the Raymond Scott Quintette performing a memorable version of "War Dance for Wooden Indians"; the second half of that number features some impressive tap dancing from the Condos Brothers dressed up as American Indians. In addition, Scott's unique group backs Ethel Merman on "You Appeal to Me."

Hard Times
(1975, 93 minutes)

Charles Bronson is cast as a street fighter in 1933 New Orleans who makes his living by winning bets for his manager James Coburn. The movie holds one's interest although the jazz content is minimal. A scene in a New Orleans bar has trumpeter Thomas Jefferson and clarinetist Louis Cottrell in a group that plays "Way Down Yonder in New Orleans" and a medium-tempo blues, mostly behind dialog and dancers. The jazzmen are on-screen twice, for a total of eight seconds.

Harlem Is Heaven
(1932, 60 minutes)

Dancer Bill "Bojangles" Robinson plays the lead in this all-Black film, his only full-length movie made for a small independent company. Bojangles is cast as the star and director of a Harlem theatre, dancing while backed by Eubie Blake's orchestra, singing "Is You Is You Ain't" and playing a reluctant matchmaker. Singer Putney Dandridge has a role as a stage manager.

The Heat's On
(1943, 79 minutes)

The last movie of Mae West's prime years is a disappointment on all levels, with West rarely even on-screen. The low-budget film is about a scheming producer, a morals foundation and a wisecracking star. Xavier Cugat's band has a few numbers, but more importantly Hazel Scott sings and plays hot piano on "When the Black Keys Meet the White Keys" (performing on two pianos at once) and a production version of "The Caissons Go Marching Along" that becomes surprisingly wistful at its conclusion.

Hell's Horizon
(1955, 78 minutes)

This is an oddball story about a bombing mission during the Korean War, with Chet Baker cast as a trumpet-playing pilot. Baker plays his trumpet briefly on a couple of occasions, hitting a few notes unaccompanied. This role could have led to greater things, but Baker's drug problems (along with his limited acting ability) soon short-circuited any chance that he had for a Hollywood career.

Hello, Dolly!
(1969, 148 minutes)

This overlong Barbara Streisand movie only has one minute of jazz, but it is a great 60 seconds as Streisand and Louis Armstrong share a wonderful chorus of the title cut. While Satch steals the show, Streisand's scatting shows that she could have been a top jazz singer if she had desired though, alas, she never made the attempt again. Otherwise, Armstrong's only line is "One more time!"

Hellzapoppin'
(1941, 83 minutes)

The most famous movie by the dated comedy team of Olsen and Johnson has an instrumental featuring Slim and Slam (Slim Gaillard on piano and guitar and bassist Slam Stewart) who are joined by Rex Stewart, drummer

Cee Pee Johnson and a combo for a heated jam. The second half of the number features some wild lindy hopping from the Harlem Congaroo Dancers. Otherwise, the film is forgettable.

Here Comes Elmer
(1943, 74 minutes)

This obscure musical comedy, starring Al Pearce and Dale Evans, is about the search for a sponsor for a radio show. In addition to numbers for Evans, Pinky Tomlin and Jan Garber's orchestra, the King Cole Trio (comprised of Nat King Cole, guitarist Oscar Moore and bassist Wesley Prince) perform their early hit "Straighten Up and Fly Right."

Here Comes the Band
(1935, 87 minutes)

Ted Lewis stars in this musical, supported by Virginia Bruce and Ted Healy, playing a songwriter who is ripped off by a crooked music publisher and needs to prove that a hit song is really his. Along the way Lewis and his orchestra (which includes cornetist Muggsy Spanier) perform "Heading Home," "Roll Along Prairie Moon," "Tender Is the Night," "You're My Thrill" and "I'm Bound for Heaven."

Here Comes the Groom
(1951, 114 minutes)

This Bing Crosby musical with Jane Wyman, which introduced Hoagy Carmichael's "In the Cool, Cool, Cool of the Evening," has a cameo appearance by Louis Armstrong during a plane ride. A variety of other celebrities (including Dorothy Lamour and Phil Harris) perform "Misto Christofo Columbo."

Hey Boy! Hey Girl!
(1959, 81 minutes)

This movie is a delight from start to finish. Louis Prima, Keely Smith, Sam Butera and the Witnesses not only perform one fun number after another but prove to be good actors too. Prima romances Smith and works with the musicians in helping to establish a youth center. "Hey, Boy! Hey Girl!" and "Oh Marie" are the standout numbers, but there are a variety of other songs ("A Banana Split for My Baby," "You Are My Love," "Fever," "Lazy River," "Nitey-Nite," "When the Saints Go Marching In," "Autumn Leaves") in this good-natured, charming and often-humorous film.

Hi-De-Ho *(1947, 61 minutes)*

Cab Calloway is the star of this all-Black, low-budget film. The first half of the movie has a lightweight plot in which Calloway has both women and gangster problems, but they are soon resolved and the latter half is purely music. Calloway's big band (which would soon break up) is seen prominently in spots, including Jonah Jones, trombonist

Louis Prima and Keely Smith make a delightful team in the highly enjoyable 1959 film *Hey Boy! Hey Girl!*.

Quentin Jackson, tenor saxophonist Sam "The Man" Taylor, pianist Dave Rivera, Milt Hinton and drummer Panama Francis although none of the sidemen get a single line. Along with a few instrumentals and specialty numbers featuring the Peters Sisters and the Miller Dancers, Calloway performs a definitive version of "St. James Infirmary" and is in fine form on "At Dawn Time," "Hey Now," "The Hi-De-Ho Man" and an a capella "Minnie's a Hepcat Now."

Hi, Good Lookin' (1944, 62 minutes)

Harriet Hillard plays the lead in this obscure comedy, cast as a singer who makes it big in Hollywood. There are jazz-oriented numbers for her husband Ozzie Nelson's orchestra, the Delta Rhythm Boys and Jack Teagarden's big band ("Aunt Hagar's Blues").

High Society (1956, 107 minutes)

This famous Bing Crosby/Frank Sinatra/Grace Kelly musical comedy (a remake of **The Philadelphia Story**) has a few special musical moments even if Cole Porter's score was partly cut out. Crosby sings "True Love" and "I Love You Samantha" while Sinatra is featured on "Who Wants to Be a Millionaire" (with Celeste Holm) and "Mind If I Make Love to You." The one Crosby/Sinatra collaboration, "Well, Did You Evah," is a bit of a disappointment. Louis Armstrong with his All-Stars (Trummy Young, Edmond Hall, Billy Kyle, Arvell Shaw and Barrett Deems) performs "High Society Calypso," and Armstrong's trumpet is heard on a few occasions backing Crosby. The best number, "Now You Has Jazz," features Crosby interacting with Satch and his band in memorable fashion.

His Captive Woman
(1929, 92 minutes)

A cop falls in love with a cabaret dancer suspected of murder whom he is supposed to arrest. Speed Webb's band makes a brief appearance.

Hit Parade of 1937 (1936, 78 minutes)

Frances Langford is wanted by the police and also involved in a search for a singer to perform on an important radio show. Several acts are featured, including the Eddy Duchin Orchestra. Duke Ellington's big band with Ivie Anderson performs a fine version of "I've Got to Be a Rugcutter" (which is available on the video **Duke Ellington 1929–1943**) and excerpts of "It Don't Mean a Thing," "Sophisticated Lady" and "Love Is Good for Anything that Ails You," mostly under dialog. Rex Stewart, Barney Bigard, guitarist Fred Guy, bassists Hayes Alvis and Billy Taylor, and Sonny Greer are among those seen briefly.

Hit Parade of 1943
(1943, 86 minutes)

John Carroll plays a washed-up songwriter and Susan Hayward is his ghostwriter. There is a lot of music in this film, including from Freddie Martin's orchestra, the Golden Gate Quartet, the short-lived Ray McKinley big band, and most notably Count Basie's orchestra (which at the time included trumpeters Buck Clayton and Harry Edison, trombonist Dickie Wells, tenors Buddy Tate and Don Byas, rhythm guitarist Freddie Green and drummer Jo Jones). This film is also known as **Change of Heart**. Among the songs performed are "Who Took Me Home Last Night," "Harlem Sandman," "Yankee Doodle Tank," "Nobody's Sweetheart" and "A Change of Heart."

Hit Parade of 1947
(1947, 90 minutes)

Eddie Albert and Constance Moore are part of a nightclub act that breaks up when Moore signs a movie contract. This film is most valuable for the opportunity to see Woody Herman's First Herd (including trumpeter Shorty Rogers, trombonist Bill Harris, tenor saxophonist Flip Phillips, pianist Jimmy Rowles, Red Norvo, bassist Joe Mondragon and drummer Don Lamond) play two songs.

5 4 *Hit Parade of 1951*
(1950, 85 minutes)

John Carroll plays two roles (a gambler and a singer for the "Hit Parade"), switching places to escape various problems. The Firehouse Five Plus Two gets a feature number, but otherwise the 1951 music scene is unrepresented in this film.

5 3 *Hi'ya Sailor* *(1943, 63 minutes)*

In this B movie, four sailors try to get one of their songs published. Among the musical acts that are featured are singer Ray Eberle, the Delta Rhythm Boys and trumpeter Wingy Manone, who plays an instrumental with an unidentified band that is partly in the background behind dialog.

5 2 *Holiday Rhythm*
(1950, 61 minutes)

In hopes of putting together a big show, three people go around the world viewing acts from different countries. Thirty-three different performances (including 15 songs) are featured in one hour, among them a number by Nappy Lamare's Dixieland group.

7 5 *Hollywood Canteen*
(1944, 125 minutes)

This tribute to the Hollywood Canteen, where wartime servicemen were entertained, has an improbable love story between a movie star and a soldier. A giant all-star cast of MGM stars make appearances. The Jimmy Dorsey Orchestra plays an instrumental based on "King Porter Stomp" and backs some specialty acts, while the Golden Gate Quartet is featured singing "The General Jumped at Dawn."

5 8 *Hollywood Hotel*
(1937, 109 minutes)

This film is quite a hodgepodge with acting roles for Dick Powell, Rosemary Lane, Lola Lane, Ted Healy, Johnny "Scat" Davis, Frances Langford and Ronald Reagan,

among others. "Hooray for Hollywood" is introduced, and there are two significant appearances by Benny Goodman. He performs a shortened but powerful version of "Sing, Sing, Sing" with his orchestra (which includes trumpeters Harry James, Ziggy Elman, Chris Griffin, tenors Vido Musso and Arthur Rollini, Jess Stacy, guitarist Allan Reuss, bassist Harry Goodman and Gene Krupa). Even better is an exciting and very hyper rendition of "I've Got a Heartful of Rhythm" by the Benny Goodman Quartet (with Krupa, Lionel Hampton and Teddy Wilson).

5 7 *Hooray for Love* *(1935, 72 minutes)*

In general this is a forgettable movie starring Gene Raymond about putting together a stage show. However, there is a nine-minute sequence that features the singing and dancing of Bill "Bojangles" Robinson and Jeni Legon plus Fats Waller performing "Living in a Great Big Way." If the rest of the movie were on the same level as this interlude, the film would have been a gem.

7 2 *Hotel* *(1967, 124 minutes)*

Rod Taylor leads a large cast through a drama about the last days of a posh hotel in New Orleans. The interrelated stories (dealing with attempts to sell the hotel, find a thief and track down a drunk driver) hold one's interest. Unfortunately, the jazz is very minor. Carmen McRae (who is billed ninth) plays and sings with a quintet in the hotel's club, but although she has a couple of lines and appears four times, she is never on-screen for more than eight bars and her music is very much in the background. Twice one sees some New Orleans musicians for a couple of seconds, and these include trumpeter Andrew Blakeney and bassist Ed Garland, but their talents are wasted.

3 5 *How Dooo You Do?*
(1945, 81 minutes)

Two radio comedians (Bert Gordon and Harry von Zell) in a hotel get mixed up with a dead body in this mildly amusing murder mystery. Ella Mae Morse performs two numbers including "Boogie Woogie Cindy."

5 6 How's About It?
(1943, 61 minutes)

The Andrews Sisters are working as elevator operators in a music publisher's building, but their dream is to sing with the Buddy Rich Orchestra. Near the end of the film they finally get their chance. Rich is featured on "Take It and Git."

5 2 Hush Hush Sweet Charlotte
(1964, 134 minutes)

Bette Davis plays a spinster who had been accused of a grisly murder many years earlier. Olivia de Havilland co-stars in this overly dramatic horror movie. There is an appearance by trumpeter Teddy Buckner's Dixieland group.

5 1 Hussy *(1979, 94 minutes)*

In this British film, an American becomes involved with a prostitute and criminals in London. Altoist Peter King is in the nightclub band.

9 4 The Hustler
(1961, 133 minutes)

The most famous of all movies about pool players stars Paul Newman, Jackie Gleason, George C. Scott and Piper Laurie. A dramatic party scene near the end has some hot Dixieland and allows one to briefly see and easily hear clarinetist Kenny Davern, trombonist Roswell Rudd and trumpeter Dan Terry.

5 6 I Dood It *(1943, 102 minutes)*

Red Skelton and Eleanor Powell star in a musical comedy dealing with a tailor wooing a stage star. The film starts with an exciting version of "One O'Clock Jump" (partly played over the opening credits) by Jimmy Dorsey and his orchestra; tenor saxophonist Babe Russin and pianist

Johnny Guarnieri are among the soloists. Everything else in the film is anticlimactic although Dorsey returns with singers Helen O'Connell and Bob Eberle to introduce "Star Eyes" and pianist Hazel Scott shows off her technique on "Takin' a Chance on Love." Scott is also part of a ridiculous production number with Lena Horne ("Jericho") and there is a humorous cameo by Tommy Dorsey.

9 6 I Want to Live
(1958, 120 minutes)

Susan Hayward plays a party girl (the real life Barbara Graham) who is convicted of murder and eventually executed. The acting and the screenplay are quite stirring and a bit scary. Johnny Mandel arranged and composed the jazz soundtrack. In the opening scene, a septet comprised of Gerry Mulligan, trumpeter Art Farmer, altoist Bud Shank, trombonist Frank Rosolino, pianist Pete Jolly, bassist Red Mitchell and Shelly Manne are on-screen in a nightclub, playing an uptempo original for a beatnik-oriented audience.

3 1 Ich—Ein Groupie
(1970, 103 minutes)

This West German drama features a woman who wanders around Europe living the life of a groupie. There is a brief appearance in a disco by altoist Pony Poindexter.

6 6 Idea Girl
(1946, 60 minutes)

A song contest suggested by Julie Bishop causes headaches for her boss (a music publisher) in this worthwhile comedy. Charlie Barnet's orchestra performs "Xango," "I Don't Care" and "I Can't Get You Off My Mind."

5 3 If I'm Lucky
(1946, 80 minutes)

This average Carmen Miranda musical has a small part for Harry James and his orchestra, mostly playing the forgettable title cut.

🎞️6 🎵7 I'll Get By (1950, 82 minutes)

June Haver and Gloria DeHaven are cast as singers with Harry James's orchestra who try to help song pluggers William Lundigan and Dan Dailey. In addition to some interesting cameos, this film has plenty of spots for Harry James ("There Will Never Be Another You," "I'll Get By," "Taking a Chance on Love," "Once in Awhile," "I've Got the World on a String," "You Make Me Feel So Young") and his orchestra, which at the time included trombonists Ziggy Elmer and Juan Tizol, altoist Willie Smith and tenor saxophonist Corky Corcoran.

🎞️7 🎵1 I'll See You in My Dreams (1951, 109 minutes)

Danny Thomas plays lyricist Gus Kahn while Doris Day is cast as a fictional version of his wife. There are a lot of vintage numbers from the 1920s but no real jazz. In one scene, Thomas is joined by a group that includes drummer Ray Bauduc and trumpeter George Thow although they are not on the soundtrack.

🎞️9 🎵1 Imitation of Life (1959, 124 minutes)

This remake of an intriguing tale of race relations and finding one's identity stars Lana Turner and holds its own with the 1934 version. The funeral sequence near the end of the film has Mahalia Jackson singing "Trouble of the World" and a brass band (which unfortunately is not heard on the soundtrack) is seen briefly. Bassist Ed Garland is on snare drum, and the large band also includes clarinetist Joe Darensbourg and trumpeters Andrew Blakeney and Teddy Buckner, but they are all inaudible.

🎞️7 🎵5 In a Lonely Place (1950, 93 minutes)

An excellent if somewhat downbeat Humphrey Bogart murder mystery, **In a Lonely Place** is one of his better movies of the 1950s. In one scene, Bogie and Gloria Grahame are in a nightclub listening to singer/pianist Hadda Brooks perform "I Hadn't Anyone 'Til You."

🎞️5 🎵5 L'Inspecteur Connait la Musique (1955, 90 minutes)

This French murder mystery film is about a blues singer and has major roles for Sidney Bechet (who is billed third) and Claude Luter. In fact, Luter kills Bechet with a clarinet.

🎞️5 🎵6 International House (1933, 72 minutes)

This is a bizarre and erratic film about a scientist in China who invents television, starring the improbable team of W.C. Fields and Bela Lugosi. Unfortunately, it only has occasional funny moments. Cab Calloway and his orchestra perform a hot version of "Reefer Man."

🎞️6 🎵6 It's a Wonderful World (1956, 89 minutes)

Terence Morgan and George Cole play a pair of struggling songwriters who reverse one of their songs and say that it came from a famous foreign composer. Naturally the tune becomes a hit and the critics rave. Ted Heath's orchestra performs a few numbers, most notably "The Hawaiian War Chant."

🎞️5 🎵4 It's All Over Town (1963, 55 minutes)

A stage worker daydreams about the bands he would rather be seeing. His taste is primarily current British rock groups, but Acker Bilk's Paramount Jazz Band gets to perform a colorful version of "Song of the Volga Boatmen."

🎞️6 🎵8 It's Trad, Dad (1962, 73 minutes)

Also known as **Ring-A-Ding Rhythm**, this exuberant British comedy is similar to many other rock 'n' roll movies in that it pits conservative grown-ups against their more enlightened children (resulting in a festival), but there is a twist. In addition to some rock/pop stars (Chubby Checker, Gary "U.S." Bonds and Gene Vincent among them), there is a lot of trad jazz performed since the Dixieland movement was at the height of its popularity in pre-Beatles England. One can enjoy the likes of Kenny Ball ("1919 March" and "Beale Street Blues"), Chris Barber and Ottilie Patterson ("Yellow Dog Blues," "Down by the Riverside" and "The Saints"), Acker Bilk ("In a Persian Market," "High Society" and "Frankie and Johnny"), Terry Lightfoot ("Tavern in the Town" and "Maryland My Maryland"), the Temperance Seven ("Everybody Loves My Baby" and "Dream Away Romance"), Bob Wallis's Storyville Jazzmen ("Bellisima" and "Aunt Flo") and from the U.S., the Dukes of Dixieland ("By and By").

Jam Session
(1944, 77 minutes)

Ann Miller plays a dance contest winner who tries to get a movie career going in Hollywood. Along the way there are many musical performances, including Louis Armstrong ("I Can't Give You Anything but Love"), Glen Gray's Casa Loma Orchestra ("No Name Jive"), Alvino Ray ("St. Louis Blues"), Charlie Barnet ("Cherokee"), Jan Garber (who was playing swing that year), Teddy Powell, Nan Wynn and the Pied Pipers.

Jamboree
(1957, 86 minutes)

An involved couple are both singers rising to the top of the music world but are constantly kept apart. In addition to all of the rock 'n' roll acts (Fats Domino, Frankie Avalon, Carl Perkins, Connie Francis and Jerry Lee Lewis among them), the Count Basie Orchestra is seen playing "One O'Clock Jump" and accompanying Joe Williams on "I Don't Like You No More."

Jazz Boat
(1959, 96 minutes)

Anthony Newley brags that he is a cat burglar so he is pressed into service by some rookie crooks in this British juvenile crime story. Ted Heath (who wrote the score)

and his big band are featured throughout the musical numbers.

The Jazz Singer
(1953, 105 minutes)

The second of three versions of **The Jazz Singer** (which was also filmed in 1927 with Al Jolson and in 1980 with—of all people—Neil Diamond in the lead) is mostly pretty forgettable. This time around, Danny Thomas is the cantor's son who has to choose between Broadway and following in his father's footsteps. Peggy Lee, who plays Thomas's girlfriend, largely saves the picture with her singing of such songs as "Lover," "Just One of those Things," "This Is a Very Special Day," and "The Birth of the Blues."

Je N'Aime que Toi
(1949, 93 minutes)

This French musical comedy, which translates into **I Like Only You,** has clarinetist Hubert Rostaing and his quintet appearing in one scene.

Juke Box Jenny
(1942, 61 minutes)

Harriet Hilliard is a young singer who becomes a jukebox star with the help of Ken Murray. Charlie Barnet's Orchestra (backing the Wilde Twins on "Fifty Million Nickles"), Wingy Manone, the Milt Herth Trio and the Charlie Beal Trio all perform. Among the numbers are "Swing It Mother Goose," "Give Out," "Macumba," "Sweet Genevieve" and "Then You'll Remember Me."

Junction 88
(1940, 49 minutes)

The plot of this all-Black film has potential. Singer/pianist Bob Howard, cast as a song publisher, is searching for a talented songwriter and the only clue is that he lives in an area known as "Junction 88." This film also has a funny opening line: "Music is like sugar. Too much and it makes you sick!" But not much is done with the story, and the emphasis shifts to the music, part of which is played at a climactic show. Howard is featured on "Yes Indeed I Do," "Somewhere Happy with You," "Walking with Caroline," "Down in Savannah" and "Where Does the Wind Go?" Noble Sissle leads an unidentified but swinging sextet behind a female singer on "Junction 88," and the band has a few opportunities to solo although Sissle (who has a couple of lines) does not sing.

Junior Prom (1946, 69 minutes)

This high school comedy, an obscurity from Monogram, starts out with strong potential by featuring pianist/singer Harry "The Hipster" Gibson in a classroom scene. But it soon bogs down in a mundane plot about the election for student body president and its second half is quite forgettable. In one scene a student puts a nickel in a jukebox and one gets to see Eddie Heywood's septet (which has two trombonists who are probably Britt Woodman and Henry Coker) playing "Loch Lomond" in an arrangement similar to Heywood's earlier hit version of "Begin the Beguine."

Just Like a Woman (1966, 89 minutes)

This is a British film about the colorful marital difficulties of a singer and her husband, a television director. Mark Murphy makes a brief appearance, singing in a nightclub while backed by a group that includes tenor saxophonist Tony Coe.

Kaerlighedens Melodi (1959, 87 minutes)

Nina and Frederik star in this Danish film. Louis Armstrong and his All-Stars (with Trummy Young, Peanuts Hucko, Billy Kyle, Mort Herbert, Danny Barcelona and Velma Middleton) romp on "Struttin' with Some Barbecue," and Satch backs the singing of Nina and Frederik on "The Formula for Love." In addition, Danish trumpeter Jorgen Ryg's quartet plays a brief blues.

Kansas City (1996, 115 minutes)

In 1996, this film received a great deal of publicity before its release. Director Robert Altman was supposedly featuring a large group of young, modern all-stars in a jazz and crime melodrama set in 1934 Kansas City. However, the final results are nearly unwatchable. All of the characters in the kidnapping drama are unsympathetic, and no one but Harry Belafonte is the slightest bit interesting. As for the music, there is a nonstop jam session occurring at the Hey-Hey Club that is used as a prop in 10–20 second segments, never longer than a couple of choruses lest it lose the viewer's attention. None of the musicians are given a single line; all they do is play as if they were a continuous jukebox, and little of it is on-screen. Better to acquire the Rhapsody video **Robert Altman's Jazz** instead. That has the complete musical performances, music apparently too good to include in this turkey.

Killer Diller (1948, 80 minutes)

A lightweight plot about a magician is dispensed with in time to feature a musical variety show that pays tribute to the extinct field of Black vaudeville. There are appearances from Andy Kirk's orchestra, Beverly White and Dusty Fletcher (among others) but most significant are three numbers ("Oh Kickeroony," "Now He Tells Me" and "Breezy and the Bass") from the Nat King Cole Trio (with guitarist Oscar Moore and bassist Johnny Miller). The Cole numbers have been reissued on the videotape **The Small Black Groups**.

King Creole (1958, 116 minutes)

One of the better Elvis Presley movies, this film is set in New Orleans where Presley struggles to avoid getting mixed up with crime while developing his singing career. It is listed in this book because trumpeter Teddy Buckner makes a brief appearance in a backup band.

⑤♪ A King in New York
(1957, 105 minutes)

Charlie Chaplin's last movie is not up to the level of his earlier gems though it has its moments. In one night club scene, he is annoyed by an overly loud British jazz band that includes tenor saxophonist Tubby Hayes.

⑤♪ King of Burlesque
(1935, 90 minutes)

Warner Baxter and Alice Faye star in this "burlesque to Broadway and back" melodrama. A love triangle results when Baxter becomes involved in artistic shows that flop rather than the revues that made him famous, before Faye eventually saves him. Fats Waller steals the show with his version of "I've Got My Fingers Crossed"; trumpeter Teddy Buckner is in his band. Waller also performs "I Love to Ride the Horses" and other songs in this movie include "I'm Shooting High" and "Spreading Rhythm Around."

②♪ The King of Jazz
(1930, 88 minutes)

This could and should have been one of the greatest jazz films of all time. In 1929, the Paul Whiteman Orchestra ventured to Hollywood in anticipation of being filmed for a major picture. Unfortunately, no script had been written and, after killing a few months, the orchestra (which at the time included cornetist Bix Beiderbecke) went back to the East Coast. By the time they returned in 1930, Bix was home in Davenport, Iowa, trying to kick his alcoholism. The resulting movie is weird, to say the least, celebrating Whiteman as an American icon without letting his band do very much most of the time. Overproduced dance numbers, weak comedy, semi-operatic singers and a fouled-up version of "Rhapsody in Blue" dominate the film. A remarkably tedious closing "Melting Pot of Music" production has samples of all types of European folk music (which allegedly formed jazz) but no examples of Black music or blues. Despite it all, there are a few special moments. Early on, Whiteman introduces various members of his band and they perform brief numbers. After Harry Goldfield does a humorous version of "Hot Lips," the team of violinist Joe Venuti and guitarist Eddie Lang (in their only joint film appearance) jam for a precious 60 seconds. Clarinetist Izzy Friedman, pianist Roy Bargy, trombonist Wilbur Hall and banjoist Mike Pingitore also have their spots, although C-melody saxophonist Frankie Trumbauer does not. He is only seen briefly during the "Happy Feet" number, and there is no sign of cornetist Andy Secrest. The Rhythm Boys (Bing Crosby, Harry Barris and Al Rinker) are featured on a medley of "Mississippi Mud" and "The Blackbirds and the Bluebirds Get Together" with Barris totally stealing the show. The Rhythm Boys also surface briefly during the lengthy "Bench in a Park" number and the first part of "Happy Feet" before the latter tune degenerates completely. Also of interest is an amusing bit by Wilbur Hall that climaxes with him playing "Pop Goes the Whistle" on a bicycle pump. But this pioneering color film could have been so much more.

⑥♪ King of the Gypsies
(1978, 112 minutes)

Sterling Hayden and Shelley Winters are among the stars in this tale of gypsy life, with Eric Roberts reluctantly battling his father to become "king of the gypsies." A gypsy-style band (called the Smith Street Society Band) pops up on-screen a few times. It includes (in various combinations) violinists Stephane Grappelli and Matt Glasser, David Grisman and Andy Statman on mandolins, guitarists Diz Disley and John Carlini, bassist Buell Neidlinger and percussionist Dom Um Romao; Grisman wrote the score.

⑤♪ Kings Go Forth
(1958, 109 minutes)

Frank Sinatra, Tony Curtis and Natalie Wood star in a World War II story about a love triangle, Wood being half

Black and the fight against the Nazis. At one point, Tony Curtis picks up a trumpet and sits in with Red Norvo's quintet (guitarist Jimmy Wyble, tenor saxophonist Richie Kamuca, bassist Red Wooten and drummer Boone Stines). Pete Candoli ghosts for Curtis while Mel Lewis actually plays the drum part.

Kiss of Death
(1947, 90 minutes)

This classic gangster movie was quite a debut for Richard Widmark as the sadistic cackling killer who enjoyed his work while plotting revenge against Victor Mature. A nightclub scene has a group led by drummer Jo Jones in the background but the two songs ("Beautiful Moods" and "Congo Conga") are actually played on the soundtrack by a band headed by drummer J.C. Heard.

Kiss the Boys Goodbye
(1941, 85 minutes)

Mary Martin, Don Ameche and Oscar Levant star in a musical about the search for an actress to play a leading role on Broadway. It is a bit of a satire on the frenzy that took place two years earlier for a suitable Scarlett O'Hara to star in **Gone with the Wind**. Connie Boswell sings "Sand in My Shoes," and Harry Barris has a tiny role.

Kobenhavn, Kalundborg
(1934, 70 minutes)

Filmed in Denmark, this movie focuses on top radio performers, including Roy Fox (known as "The Whispering Cornetist"), Erik Tuxen's Orchestra, Teddy Brown (on xylophone, tenor and drums), Roy Fox's band, Lili Gyenes's all-female orchestra and, most importantly, Louis Armstrong. Satch (from October 28, 1933) is seen fronting a nonet for nine minutes, performing exciting versions of "I Cover the Waterfront," "Dinah" and "Tiger Rag." The 32-year-old trumpeter/vocalist is both brilliant and delightful. Check out how he sets the tempo (getting the band to speed up a little after a slow start), his scatting and classic solo on

"Dinah," and his crowd-pleasing antics on "Tiger Rag." These clips (the earliest example of Armstrong performing in public) have often been used in documentaries and are available on **Jazz Band Ball**.

The Ladies' Man
(1961, 106 minutes)

Jerry Lewis wants to be a woman hater but finds it impossible in this comedy. Harry James has a cameo, performing "Bang Tail."

Lady Sings the Blues
(1972, 144 minutes)

From literally the first second of the film (when it shows Billie Holiday being busted in 1936 rather than 1947), everything is wrong with the screenplay of this alleged retelling of the Billie Holiday story. On the good side, Diana Ross is mostly believable as Lady Day, although she never ages. Her singing is pretty close at times, particularly in her phrasing ("All of Me" is excellent), so the soundtrack is worth picking up. But rather than tell the real story, the film is entirely fictional and full of clichés, even having the Ku Klux Klan attack the band bus when Holiday is touring with a White orchestra. Billy Dee Williams plays Louis McKay (who was in real life an abusive husband) as a heroic figure, Richard Pryor is Holiday's best friend (a nonexistent character named Piano Man), and Michel Legrand's music score (also worked on by Gil Askey, Oliver Nelson and Benny Golson) cannot decide what year it is, the 1920s, 1950s or 1970s. Although such players as tenor saxophonist Red Holloway, trombonist Grover Mitchell and drummer Panama Francis can be seen in a couple of performance spots, no figures from Holiday's history ever make appearances in the screenplay. There is no Lester Young, Count Basie, Artie Shaw, Teddy Wilson or John Hammond in the film. Nor is there any evolution to the character Diana Ross plays, perhaps because she too cannot figure out what decade she is in. **Lady Sings the Blues** is such a mess that it is nearly unbearable for anyone familiar with the real story of Billie Holiday.

5 5 *Las Vegas Nights*
(1941, 87 minutes)

This musical comedy is set in Las Vegas and stars Constance Moore, Bert Wheeler and Phil Regan. Tommy Dorsey's orchestra (with Ziggy Elman, clarinetist Johnny Mince, tenor saxophonist Don Lodice, pianist Joe Bushkin and Buddy Rich) performs "Song of India" and the novelty "The Trombone Man Is the Best Man in the Band" which features a Rich solo. In addition, the orchestra backs the Pied Pipers and Frank Sinatra on "I'll Never Smile Again."

6 4 *Last Tango in Paris*
(1972, 130 minutes)

A famous and controversial Marlon Brando X-rated movie deals with an anonymous yet emotional affair. Gato Barbieri's tenor playing throughout the haunting soundtrack (he wrote the songs while Oliver Nelson provided the arrangements) adds to the steamy atmosphere. Barbieri makes a brief appearance on-screen.

5 2 *The Learning Tree*
(1969, 106 minutes)

A Black teenager grows up in 1920s Kansas and learns valuable lessons about life. Jimmy Rushing proves to be an effective actor as the owner of a honky tonk/brothel; he also sings one song.

7 5 *The Legend of 1900*
(1999, 126 minutes)

1900 is the name given a fictional character (played by Tim Roth) who was abandoned as an infant on a cruise ship where he chooses to spend his entire life, never setting foot on dry land. 1900 unaccountably becomes a genius pianist (ghosted by Gilda Butta), one who has remarkable technique and plays with the ship's orchestra.

The intriguing story is told by a trumpeter friend to a pawnshop owner, including the tale of a piano duel that 1900 wins over Jelly Roll Morton (played by Clarence Williams, III). Most of the music is original although the Morton character (portrayed as an angry braggart) plays "Big Foot Ham," "Jungle Blues," "The Crave" and "Finger Buster."

7 1 *Lenny* *(1974, 112 minutes)*

Dustin Hoffman and Valerie Perrine star in this mostly true-to-life depiction of the life of the controversial and innovative comedian Lenny Bruce. Bruce often performed in jazz clubs, and Ralph Burns's score utilizes plenty of jazz standards from the 1950s. In one club, drummer Jimmy Crawford can be seen.

7 2 *Lepke* *(1974, 110 minutes)*

Tony Curtis plays Louis "Lepke" Buchalter, the founder of Murder Inc. and an important gangster for decades. A jazz group in a speakeasy includes altoist Marshall Royal.

8 3 *Let No Man Write My Epitaph*
(1960, 106 minutes)

This is a powerful drama about struggling in Chicago's skid row in the 1950s and heroin addiction. Shelly Winters, Burl Ives (in one of his best roles) and Bobby Darin star. Ella Fitzgerald, who is billed sixth, is featured in a couple of dramatic scenes and has an unusual role as a junkie singer. She briefly sings parts of "I Can't Give You Anything but Love" and "Angel Eyes" while supposedly accompanying herself on piano; her piano playing is ghosted by Cliff Smalls.

5 4 *Let's Go Steady*
(1945, 61 minutes)

Two young songwriters, after being ripped off by a song publisher, promote themselves by getting a bandleader and a radio station to help out. Skinnay Ennis (who performs with his big band) and Mel Tormé (who is joined by the Mel-Tones) both have small parts, with the latter performing "Baby Boogie."

Let's Make Music
(1940, 85 minutes)

Bob Crosby received his first starring role in this film, but it should have been obvious from the start that his acting career would not be going anywhere. The plot deals with an older music teacher whose corny composition surprisingly becomes a novelty hit. Most of the songs given Crosby's orchestra in this film are quite forgettable. Their version of "Big Noise from Winnetka" becomes a vocal piece with only a hint of the classic Bob Haggart/Ray Bauduc bass/drums duet.

Les Liaisons Dangereuses
(1959, 106 minutes)

This French film, which deals tragically with a promiscuous couple, is famous in the jazz world for its soundtrack, which features Duke Jordan songs played by Art Blakey's Jazz Messengers, plus some songs from Thelonious Monk's quartet. In one party scene, trumpeter Kenny Dorham, tenor saxophonist Barney Wilen, pianist Duke Jordan, bassist Paul Rovere and drummer Kenny Clarke are seen, although it is the Jazz Messengers (with trumpeter Lee Morgan) who are actually heard.

The Lisbon Story *(1945, 101 minutes)*

A British World War II spy movie, this film has an appearance by violinist Stephane Grappelli, who plays one number in a café with pianist Fella Sowande, guitarist Allan Hodgkiss and drummer Jerry da Costa.

Live and Let Die
(1973, 121 minutes)

Roger Moore's debut as James Bond has an outlandish plot, a few remarkable chase scenes, dazzling stuntwork, sly humor and beautiful women. There are two appearances by the Olympia Brass Band playing a funeral parade ("Just a Closer Walk with Thee" and "Joe Avery's Blues"). Trumpeter Alvin Alcorn has a tiny role as an assassin. When the funeral parade passes and Alcorn is asked by an agent who the funeral is for, he replies with his one line— "Yours"— before stabbing him.

Live It Up *(1963, 78 minutes)*

This British rock 'n' roll story is about a lad whose father gives him a month to make it in music or return to working in the post office. Kenny Ball's popular trad band makes an appearance playing "Hand Me Down My Walkin' Shoes."

Look Out Sister
(1948, 67 minutes)

One of the best of the Louis Jordan movies, this all-Black film features the singer/altoist/entertainer mostly playing at a dude ranch out West and wearing a cowboy hat. As usual, the plot is both amusing and fairly minimal. Jordan's Tympany Five at the time included tenor saxophonist Paul Quinichette, trumpeter Aaron Izenhall and pianist Bill Doggett. Among the more memorable numbers are "Caldonia," "Jack You're Dead," "Don't Burn the Candles at Both Ends" and "Boogie in the Barnyard." As with two other Jordan films of the period, all of the music is also available on the Storyville videotape **Louis Jordan and the Tympany Band**.

Lost in a Harem
(1944, 89 minutes)

Even children will have difficulty sitting through this weak Abbott and Costello movie. The plot has something to do with a pair of vaudevillian magicians and Marilyn Maxwell helping someone regain the throne of a desert nation. Jimmy Dorsey's orchestra appears, looking somewhat ridiculous wearing Arab costumes while playing in a parade. However, 45 minutes into the film there is an excellent version of "Long John Silver" featuring some hot Dorsey (on both clarinet and alto) and drummer Buddy Schutz.

🎞️2 🎵4 *Louis Armstrong—Chicago Style*
(1975, 74 minutes)

This made-for-television movie supposedly covers Louis Armstrong's career in the early '30s, but is about as factual as **Lady Sings the Blues**. Ben Vereen's portrait of Armstrong makes one wonder if he was familiar at all with Satch, constantly laughing in an irritating way and moving around excessively onstage. Whether it is seeing Vereen perform "When the Saints Go Marching In" (a song that Armstrong did not play until much later in the 1930s), mixed race audiences in every club scene, or a nonsensical episode in which Armstrong checks himself into jail for one night so he can escape from gangsters, the screenplay is full of malarkey. It seems remarkable that Leonard Feather (who knew Armstrong) was a technical advisor for this film. On the plus side, there is one good scene apiece with actors portraying Jack Teagarden and Lil Harden Armstrong. Benny Carter wrote the arrangements, and it was a wise decision to have Teddy Buckner ghost the trumpet solos (for such songs as "The Saints," "Ain't Misbehavin'," "When You're Smiling," "Sleepy Time Down South" and "Wrap Your Troubles in Dreams"). But the screenplay (which deals with a crooked manager and gangsters) is a real mess and the film ends inconclusively. Surely someone could make a worthwhile movie about Louis Armstrong.

🎞️5 🎵4 *Love and Hisses* *(1937, 84 minutes)*

Walter Winchell and Ben Bernie (both of whom play themselves) feud over Simone Simon in this average musical comedy. Charlie Barnet has a very small acting part (and no lines), while the Raymond Scott Quintette gets a chance to perform their famous "Powerhouse."

🎞️7 🎵2 *Love that Brute* *(1950, 85 minutes)*

Softhearted Chicago gangster Paul Douglas, who is childless, is so interested in Jean Peters that he hires her as a governess, and then has to go out and find a son. Various comical twists result, Peters gets to sing "You Took Advantage of Me" and a band in a party scene includes drummer Zutty Singleton.

🎞️6 🎵3 *Lullaby of Broadway*
(1951, 93 minutes)

Doris Day sings many Warren and Dubin songs in this musical romantic comedy, discovering in time that her mother (Gladys George) is not what she seems. The Page Cavanaugh Trio has one feature.

🎞️8 🎵7 *Lush Life* *(1993, 99 minutes)*

This made-for-television movie broadcast by Showtime is rather unusual for a fictional jazz film in that the musicians act like normal, fun-loving human beings, a refreshing change of pace. Jeff Goldblum (normally a pianist) plays a tenor saxophonist (his solos are ghosted by Bob Cooper), Forest Whitaker (the star of **Bird**) is a trumpeter this time (Chuck Findley plays his parts), and Kathy Baker plays Goldblum's wife, an occasional singer (Sue Raney takes her vocals). Goldblum and Whitaker are best friends who enjoy their lifestyle of being professional New York sidemen who play jazz dates, studio sessions, shows, weddings and parties. Along the way the plot deals with Whitaker developing an incurable brain tumor (although the ambiguous ending makes one wonder if he was ever ill), the marital problems of Goldblum and Baker, a search for a trumpet formerly owned by Clifford Brown, and a giant party thrown by Whitaker before his expected demise. Ernie Andrews sings part of "All the Things You Are," Jack Sheldon has a small bit as a conductor for a Broadway show, Everett Harp plays a saxophonist, and various Los Angeles-based musicians are seen briefly. Lennie Niehaus wrote the arrangements and among the songs performed are "Misterioso," "Walkin'," "I'm Old Fashioned," "Cherokee" and "In Walked Spring" but not "Lush Life"; the film's title is never explained. Although ultimately a bit lightweight, this movie leaves one with a happy feeling.

🎬 🎵 Mad at the World
(1955, 63 minutes)

Four rather cruel juvenile delinquents in Chicago are tracked down by an undercover cop in this low-budget obscurity. During a club scene, Howard Rumsey's Lighthouse All-Stars with trumpeter Conte Candoli, tenor saxophonist Bob Cooper (who is heard prominently), altoist Bud Shank, pianist Claude Williamson, drummer Stan Levey and Rumsey on bass play a dramatic version of "Witch Doctor," partly under dialog. However, the music heard is clearly from an augmented version of this group, one that includes an unseen trombonist (probably Frank Rosolino) and several more horns.

🎬 🎵 Made in Paris *(1966, 103 minutes)*

This lightweight Ann-Margret film features a two-minute sequence near its beginning that has the Count Basie Octet (with Eddie "Lockjaw" Davis, altoist Marshall Royal and Freddie Green) performing a blues including a one-chorus solo from Lockjaw before the musicians permanently disappear. In addition, Mongo Santamaria's band (which includes Hubert Laws) plays in a club behind dialog and some dancing from Ann-Margret.

🎬 🎵 Make Believe Ballroom
(1949, 78 minutes)

The plot of this movie is not much, dealing with a radio show and a music trivia contest, but it serves as a good excuse for a variety of bands from 1949 to appear. Featured are Jimmy Dorsey's orchestra ("Hello Goodbye"), Pee Wee Hunt, Charlie Barnet's orchestra, Ray McKinley (a drum feature on "Comin' Out"), Gene Krupa ("Bop Boogie," "Sabre Dance" and "Disc Jockey Jump"), the King Cole Trio ("The Trouble with Me Is You"), Kay Starr ("The Lonesomest Gal in Town") and Frankie Laine ("On the Sunny Side of the Street"). There is also a jam session version of "Jericho" with Charlie Teagarden, Hunt, Dorsey, Barnet and Jan Garber on violin.

🎬 🎵 The Mambo Kings
(1992, 101 minutes)

This entertaining film is about two singing brothers in the 1950s (portrayed by Armand Assante and Antonio Banderas) who leave their native Cuba to try to make it big in New York. They get a major break when they are discovered by Desi Arnaz, who is logically played by Desi Arnaz, Jr. There is a generous amount of Afro-Cuban jazz and Cuban ballads on the soundtrack, Tito Puente makes a couple of appearances, and Celia Cruz has an acting role.

🎬 🎵 A Man Called Adam
(1966, 103 minutes)

This oddity is an interesting failure about racial problems suffered by a couple of jazz trumpeters: Sammy Davis, Jr. (ghosted by Nat Adderley) and Frank Sinatra, Jr. (whose parts are played by Bill Berry). The movie is over-dramatic but not without interest. Louis Armstrong and his All-Stars (Tyree Glenn, Buster Bailey, Billy Kyle, and for some odd reason bassist John Brown and drummer Jo Jones though their parts are ghosted by Buddy Catlett and Danny Barcelona) perform "Back O' Town Blues" and an excerpt from "Someday Sweetheart"; Satch also has a surprisingly serious acting role. Benny Carter arranged some of the music and contributed a few songs including "All That Jazz" which is sung by Mel Tormé. A party scene has cameo appearances by Joe Williams, multi-reedist Yusef Lateef and writer Dan Morgenstern. There are also brief appearances from saxophonist Frank Wess and singer Babs Gonzales.

🎬 🎵 The Man I Love *(1946, 96 minutes)*

Ida Lupino plays a nightclub singer (ghosted by Peg LaCentra) in this well-conceived melodrama. Quite a few swing standards are heard along the way. Guitarist Tony Romano sings "If I Could Be with You" while backed by a band including trumpeter Frankie Zinzer, clarinetist

Archie Rosate, pianist Stan Wrightsman and drummer Nick Fatool.

The Man with the Golden Arm
(1955, 118 minutes)

In one of his better roles, Frank Sinatra plays a drummer trying to get rid of his heroin habit. One scene has him unsuccessfully auditioning for an important job. During that all-too-brief segment, Sinatra is seen with such musicians as trumpeter/leader Shorty Rogers (who has a few lines), trumpeter Pete Candoli, trombonists Milt Bernhart and Frank Rosolino, altoist Bud Shank, Bob Cooper on tenor, bassist Ralph Pena and Shelly Manne, whom Sinatra briefly replaces on drums.

Manhattan Merry-Go-Round
(1937, 78 minutes)

The plot of this light comedy had potential as a gangster takes over a record company and needs to add talent in a hurry. But the screenplay is so lackluster and mundane that it sinks the movie completely. The music is erratic as Louis Prima is completely wasted backing a schlocky vocal by star Phil Regan, and Ted Lewis sounds as corny as usual on "I'm a Musical Magical Man." The only good number is when Cab Calloway and his orchestra, after playing the ending of "Minnie the Moocher," jam on a spirited "Mama I Wanna Make Rhythm" for three minutes.

Many Happy Returns
(1934, 66 minutes)

This obscure Burns and Allen comedy mostly features Guy Lombardo and His Royal Canadians on a few brief numbers. However, Larry Adler, the top harmonica player of the era, refused to use Lombardo's band as his backup, insisting on Duke Ellington, who was in Hollywood filming **Murder at the Vanities**. So a contingent from Ellington's band (two brass, the reed section and Duke with the rhythm section) backs Adler on "Sophisticated Lady" for a little less than two minutes.

Meet Me After the Show
(1951, 87 minutes)

Betty Grable pretends to lose her memory so she can regain her husband. In one song she is backed on-screen by a band that includes trumpeter Jackie Coon, trombonist Brad Gowans and clarinetist Bernie Billings although they are not actually the ones heard on the soundtrack. Pete Candoli also appears on-screen at one point.

Meet Miss Bobby Socks
(1944, 68 minutes)

Bob Crosby is an ex-GI who discovers that his female pen pal is only 15 years old. Crosby, as a nightclub performer, sings several numbers including "Fellow on a Furlough." Louis Jordan and his Tympany Five have a cameo and perform "Deacon Jones." This film is also known as **Meet Miss Bobby Sox**.

Merry-Go-Round
(1977, 150 minutes)

This French film is an ambitious, lengthy and leisurely thriller about a missing woman, her boyfriend and her sister. Bass clarinetist John Surman and bassist Barre Phillips take several free improvisations on camera, adding to the avant-garde atmosphere.

Mister Big *(1943, 64 minutes)*

Donald O'Connor plays a theatre student who writes a swing-oriented musical comedy for the class play in spite of the school owner's disapproval. The kids stage the hep show anyway despite many obstacles. There is one number featuring former Glenn Miller vocalist Ray Eberle with tenorman Eddie Miller's Bob Cats. This film was also known as **School for Jive**.

Mr. Music
(1950, 114 minutes)

Bing Crosby stars as a lazy songwriter while Nancy Olson is the secretary hired to make him work. The movie is good-natured, but it is a pity that most of the resulting songs, from Jimmy Heusen and Johnny Burke, are not too memorable. The closest number to catching on is "Life Is So Peculiar" which is performed three times: by Bing with Peggy Lee, the Merry Macs and the unlikely duo of Crosby and Groucho Marx.

5 ♪ *Mister Rock and Roll* (1957, 74 minutes)

This film glorifies both Alan Freed and rock 'n' roll in general, seeking to show that the new music was not primarily for juvenile delinquents. Lionel Hampton and his band play briefly in one segment illustrating rock's roots.

7 ♪ *Mo' Better Blues*
(1990, 127 minutes)

Denzel Washington plays trumpeter Bleek Gilliam, a self-centered jazz player having relationships with two different women. The jazz club scenes, onstage and backstage, mostly ring quite true, making this one of the more accurate depictions of the jazz life. Director Spike Lee has a small but important part, playing a leech who indirectly leads Washington to tragedy. Terence Blanchard wrote the score and ghosts Washington's trumpet solos while Branford Marsalis ghosts the tenor solos of Wesley Snipes. Also

Louis Jordan, seen in 1944's *Meet Miss Bobby Socks*, appeared in many films during the '40s and was never overshadowed.

heard are pianist Kenny Kirkland, bassist Bob Hurst, drummer Jeff "Tain" Watts and actress Cynda Williams (one of the lead's love interests) on vocals.

Moon Over Harlem *(1939, 67 minutes)*

This all-Black, low-budget film has a confused script, stereotypes galore and a melodramatic plot full of clichés, allegedly dealing with life in Harlem. Sidney Bechet appears during the first ten minutes of the movie, playing clarinet with a quartet for a wedding and having a few insignificant lines, but he is only seen briefly and his music can barely be heard. Drummer Christopher Columbus leads an unidentified orchestra at a club, appearing twice with the only good number featuring a singer and dancers on "Take a Tip from Me."

Moulin Rouge *(1934, 69 minutes)*

No less than six movies (all unrelated) have been made that have the title **Moulin Rouge**. In this version, Constance Bennett disguises herself as another woman to test her husband Franchot Tone's loyalty. Crooner Russ Columbo has a cameo and the Boswell Sisters sing "Coffee in the Morning and Kisses in the Night." Other Warren and Dubin songs written for this film are "Song of Surrender" and the hit "Boulevard of Broken Dreams."

Mulholland Drive *(2001, 147 minutes)*

This rather bizarre David Lynch mystery thriller will take several viewings to figure out, and even then it might not make much sense. For no real reason, trumpeter Conte Candoli appears briefly in one scene, playing a few notes but not having any lines or adding anything to the story.

Murder at the Vanities *(1934, 98 minutes)*

Kitty Carlisle, Eric Lander and Victor McLaglen star in an obscure mystery that takes place mostly while a revue is being presented onstage. Duke Ellington's orchestra is featured during "Ebony Rhapsody" (partly behind the singing of Barbara Van Brunt) in a classical vs. jazz segment. Otherwise the movie is most notable for introducing "Cocktails for Two."

Murder on Lenox Avenue *(1941, 65 minutes)*

An overly complex plot about workers standing up for their own rights, an out-of-wedlock pregnancy and other melodramatic aspects to life in Harlem are featured in this low-budget, all-Black film. Although a band is seen in a nightclub backing an unidentified singer, and a combo is used for some comedy at a rehearsal, the only significant music in the movie is provided by the pioneering classic blues singer Mamie Smith. Smith, who has a small part, sings an excellent version of "I'll Get Even with You" while backed by a pianist.

Murder with Music *(1946, 57 minutes)*

A reporter tries to crack a case involving a gangster in this postwar Black film. The movie's plot is quite complex and well worth ignoring in favor of the generous amount of music. Bob Howard stars as a newspaper editor and he sings "It's Too Late Baby," while trumpeter Bill Dillard has an acting role. Noble Sissle leads his band through a few instrumentals and sings "Hello Happiness." Skippy Williams, who played tenor briefly with Duke Ellington during the period between Ben Webster and Al Sears, leads a bopish combo on "Can't Help It" and a riff-filled piece similar to "Lady Be Good." In summary, the film has good musicians and terrible actors.

The Music Goes 'Round *(1936, 88 minutes)*

Harry Richman plays a Broadway star who runs away from New York, performs with a riverboat troupe and then brings the amateurs to Broadway in a new show. Mike Riley and Eddie Farley perform their hit "The Music

Goes Round and Round"; Les Hite's orchestra is briefly in the background of a couple of scenes.

5 ♪ *Music in Manhattan* (1944, 80 minutes)

Anne Shirley and Dennis Day try to break into showbiz although mistaken identity and romantic complications arise in this musical comedy. Charlie Barnet and his orchestra have a brief appearance.

5 ♪ *Music Man* (1948, 66 minutes)

The moderately amusing plot deals with a couple of songwriters fighting for the attention of a woman. Jimmy Dorsey and his orchestra are largely wasted, backing Freddie Stewart on "Shy Ann," an Italian pop singer (Phil Brito) on another number and playing a background instrumental blues and a catchy but very brief "Hello, Goodbye."

4 ♪ *Musik, Musik und Nur Musik* (1955, 89 minutes)

This West German film about a composer and his wife has a title that sums up Lionel Hampton's philosophy well. Hamp and his band make an appearance.

6 ♪ *My Gal Loves Music* (1944, 60 minutes)

Grace McDonald, the assistant of a medicine show operator, is persuaded to pretend to be 14 and enter a singing contest. Bandleader Bob Crosby (who gets first billing) falls for her, but is torn by the fact that she is allegedly so young. Crosby sings "Somebody's Rockin' My Rainbow."

5 ♪ *Mystery in Swing* (1940, 66 minutes)

This low-budget, all-Black film is a murder mystery with a better-than-usual story. Who put snake venom on trumpeter Prince Ellis's mouthpiece? Mamie Smith has a small role, while Cee Pee Johnson's orchestra is the house band for the movie, accompanying various acts.

5 ♪ *Negresco* (1968, 93 minutes)

This West German spy film deals with adultery; its title in English is **My Bed Is Not for Sleeping**. Erroll Garner makes a brief appearance.

6 ♪ *New Orleans* (1947, 90 minutes)

New Orleans, which features Louis Armstrong and Billie Holiday (in her only movie), should have been a classic, but instead is heavily compromised in favor of the White nonmusical leads (Dorothy Patrick and Arturo De Cordova). Although there is a bit of a mishmash about the origins of jazz and its fight for respectability in a world dominated by classical music, there is also plenty of music throughout the film along with some memorable moments. (The full soundtrack, which contains the complete selections and more music that was not used, is far superior.) Among the songs that Louis Armstrong (who is joined at times by Kid Ory, Barney Bigard, pianist Charlie Beal, bassist Red Callender, banjoist Bud Scott, drummer Zutty Singleton, trumpeter Mutt Carey, tenorman Lucky Thompson and later in the film by his big band of the period) performs are "West End Blues," "Maryland My Maryland," "Mahogany Hall Stomp, " "Tiger Rag," "Where the Blues Were Born in New Orleans," "Back O'Town Blues," "Basin Street Blues," "The Blues Are Brewing" and "Endie." Billie Holiday performs "Do You Know What It Means to Miss New Orleans" and the haunting "Farewell to Storyville," Meade Lux Lewis (as a painter who just happens to be a brilliant boogie-woogie pianist) plays "Honky Tonk Train Blues," and Arthur Schutt ghosts some of the piano playing of actor and classical pianist Richard Hageman. For no particular reason, Woody Herman's First Herd makes a brief appearance but is largely buried by a symphony orchestra; however, Herman is featured in one humorous scene. Despite falling way short of its potential, and almost in spite of itself, this is a jazz film well worth seeing and enjoying.

New York, New York
(1977, 153 minutes)

Liza Minnelli plays a singer and Robert DeNiro is cast as her obnoxious but oddly charming boyfriend/husband, a tenor saxophonist. The film, set during 1945–55, is overlong and erratic (DeNiro's character is hard to take in spots), but it has some intriguing, touching and humorous moments, such as the proposal scene. The tales of going on a road with a big band ring true. Ralph Burns arranged the authentic music (swing with touches of bop). Georgie Auld is very effective playing bandleader Frankie Harte (he ghosted the tenor solos for DeNiro while his own spots on clarinet were played by Abe Most). Also seen on-screen although without lines are pianist Nat Pierce, bassist Wilfred Middlebrooks and drummer Dick Berk, and bandleader/trombonist Bill Tole does a good job of playing Tommy Dorsey in one long scene. Other than introducing "New York, New York" and a couple of later numbers featuring Minnelli, most of the

To enjoy 1947's *New Orleans,* starring Louis Armstrong and Billie Holiday, one has to appreciate what was filmed as opposed to what could have been.

music is swing-oriented, including the Dorsey/Tole band featured on "Song of India" and "Opus #1." Minnelli sings "You Brought a New Kind of Love to Me," "You Are My Lucky Star," "The Man I Love," "Just You, Just Me" and a couple of newly written show tunes without getting over-the-top until near the end. Although far from perfect, this film is worth seeing once or twice.

Night of the Quarter Moon
(1959, 96 minutes)

This strange movie has John Drew Barrymore marrying Julie London and then finding out that she is one-quarter Black. Nat King Cole sings "To Whom It May Concern" and has a small role, Bing Crosby's niece Cathy Crosby sings "Blue Moon," and Ray Anthony plays a hotel manager.

Nightmare *(1956, 88 minutes)*

This excellent Edward G. Robinson mystery movie is about a New Orleans clarinetist (Kevin McCarthy) who dreams that he committed a murder. He plays with an orchestra led by Billy May (who has a small part), and his clarinet playing is ghosted by Skeets Herfurt, who can be seen playing alto with May. Dick Cathcart ghosts for May's trumpet solos, and pianist Meade Lux Lewis plays briefly in one scene.

Notes for an African Oresteia
(1970, 65 minutes)

Here is an oddity: an Italian film about the work and research that went into a film that was never made. Director Pier Paolo Pasolini had hoped to transfer some Greek mythology to an African setting. Tenor saxophonist Gato Barbieri provided the soundtrack music and is also seen briefly at a recording session.

Number One
(1969, 104 minutes)

Charlton Heston plays an aging quarterback for the New Orleans Saints in this football drama. Bobby Troup has a small acting role, and in a nightclub scene Al Hirt and his band romp on "Down by the Riverside."

On Our Merry Way
(1948, 107 minutes)

This strange movie (also known as **A Miracle Can Happen**) has Burgess Meredith asking a variety of characters (including quite a few major stars) how a child has changed their lives. One of the many segments features Jimmy Stewart and Henry Fonda as musicians, with Harry James making a cameo appearance.

On with the Show
(1929, 108 minutes)

This forgotten but highly enjoyable movie has the entire plot taking place during one day in the life of a show. Arthur Lake, Betty Compson and Joe E. Brown are among the stars in this complicated but logical melodrama. Ethel Waters appears twice in the stage production, sounding wonderful as she introduces "Am I Blue" and "Birmingham Bertha." In a very unusual situation for a Black singer in 1929, she is treated with great respect by the performers even if she was given no lines.

Operator 13
(1934, 86 minutes)

The plot of this Gary Cooper/Marion Davies movie, about Southern spies and Northern soldiers during the Civil War, is almost as absurd as having the Mills Brothers pop up to perform in a medicine show. Odds are that this famous vocal group (who sing "Roll Jordan Roll," "Sleepy Head" and "Jungle Fever") would not be able to pick up too many good gigs in the deep South in 1863!

The Opposite Sex
(1956, 116 minutes)

This musical remake of **The Women** is a disappointment, and it's not all-female like the earlier classic. A World War II flashback scene has Harry James and his big band accompanying star June Allyson's singing on "The Man with a Horn."

7 8 *Orchestra Wives*
(1942, 98 minutes)

One of two films featuring Glenn Miller and his orchestra, **Orchestra Wives** has a better plot than **Sun Valley Serenade**. Cat fighting among the wives of big band members leads to the orchestra falling apart, at least temporarily. This entertaining film has Jackie Gleason as a happily married bassist (his part is ghosted by Doc Goldberg), Cesar Romero as a pianist (Chummy McGregor plays for him) and George Montgomery as a trumpet soloist whose part seems to have been mostly played by Johnny Best although Bobby Hackett and Billy May helped out too. Among the songs on the rich soundtrack are a brief reprise of "Chattanooga Choo Choo" (the hit from **Sun Valley Serenade**), "People Like You and Me" (featuring Marion Hutton and the Modernaires), "At Last" (Pat Friday ghosts the vocal for Lynn Bari), "Bugle Call Rag" (with drummer Maurice Purtill), "Serenade in Blue" and a spectacular version of "I've Got a Gal in Kalamazoo" featuring Tex Beneke, Marion Hutton and the Modernaires. In its second half there is some very exciting dancing from the Nicholas Brothers.

7 4 *Out of the Blue*
(1947, 87 minutes)

This amusing screwball comedy features George Brent who mistakenly thinks that Ann Dvorak (with whom he is fooling around in his wife's absence) has died. Pianist Hadda Brooks appears in one scene, singing "Out of the Blue."

5 4 *The Outfit*
(1973, 101 minutes)

Robert Duvall, Robert Ryan and Karen Black star in a bloody tale of revenge and crime. Anita O'Day sings "I Concentrate on You" in a club.

4 3 *La Paloma*
(1959, 84 minutes)

A West German revue of entertainers has a guest spot for Louis Armstrong near its conclusion, performing "Uncle Satchmo's Lullaby" with singer Gabriele and the Johannes Fehring Orchestra.

3 4 *Panama Hattie*
(1942, 79 minutes)

This musical comedy stars Red Skelton and Ann Sothern but just meanders along and never really catches fire. Cole Porter wrote the score, but there is surprisingly little music of interest. Best is Lena Horne singing a 90-second version of "Just One of those Things" backed by an unseen string orchestra. She is also featured on an odd novelty, "The Sphinx," that has a brief cameo by Leo Watson who is seen looking like a madman on drums.

6 7 *Paradise in Harlem*
(1940, 83 minutes)

One of the best of the low-budget, all-Black films of the 1930s/40s, this movie has a good story (about a Harlem actor who wants to play Othello but is menaced by gangsters after witnessing a murder), better-than-usual acting performances and some excellent music. Mamie Smith, famed for being the first blues singer on records (with "Crazy Blues" in 1920), did not make any recordings after 1931 but appeared in several early '40s films. She is wonderful on "Lawd, Lawd" (which has been reissued on the videotape **The Blues**) and "Harlem Blues." She also has a strong acting role as the owner of a boarding house. Lucky Millinder's orchestra is frequently featured throughout the film (they back Smith on "Lawd, Lawd") with the leader singing a bit like Cab Calloway on "I Gotta Put You Down" and the band sounding strong on the instrumentals. The personnel is unidentified but probably includes tenor saxophonist Stafford Simon and baritonist Ernest Purce, and possibly pianist Bill Doggett and drummer Panama Francis.

🎞️4 🎵4 *Pardon My Rhythm*
(1944, 61 minutes)

Young singer Gloria Jean is the star of this film, which has Mel Tormé as her love interest and Bob Crosby as a bandleader who wants to hire Tormé. Crosby sings "I'll See You in My Dreams," Tormé performs with his Mel-Tones and among the other songs in this film are "Do You Believe in Dreams," "Spell of the Moon," "Shame on Me," "Drummer Boy" and "You've Got to Hand It to the Band."

🎞️7 🎵6 *Paris Blues* *(1961, 98 minutes)*

This intriguing film casts Paul Newman as a trombonist (with his solos ghosted by Murray McEachern), Sidney Poitier as a tenor saxophonist (Paul Gonsalves plays for him), Joanne Woodward and Diahann Carroll. The two musicians live happily in Paris until they begin relationships with Woodward and Carroll, which forces them to make decisions about their lives. Louis Armstrong is cast as visiting jazz great Wild Man Moore, and Duke Ellington provided the score. An augmented version of Duke Ellington's orchestra is heard on the soundtrack (including Ellington who plays "The Clothed Woman" and "Paris Blues" as piano solos) along with trombonist Billy Byers, but none appear in the film. Among the other songs performed are "Take the 'A' Train," "Mood Indigo" and a wild (and rather unlikely) jam session version of "Battle Royal" that supposedly has Armstrong and Newman battling it out.

🎞️8 🎵7 *Pennies from Heaven*
(1936, 80 minutes)

This fun Bing Crosby musical introduced "Pennies from Heaven." Louis Armstrong, featured in his first Hollywood film, has a few scenes in which he plays Bing's genial sidekick. In a nightclub, Armstrong and his band (with Lionel Hampton on drums) plays and sings a hot version of "Skeleton in the Closet" before Satch eventually jumps out the window.

🎞️7 🎵8 *Pete Kelly's Blues*
(1955, 95 minutes)

Jack Webb (best known for **Dragnet**) always loved jazz and this movie gave him a chance to play a trumpeter in 1920s Kansas City. Webb and his sidekick Lee Marvin (who is seen playing clarinet) perform in speakeasies and overcome problems with gangsters. Janet Leigh plays Webb's love interest, Peggy Lee is excellent as an alcoholic moll (singing "I'm There" and "Sugar"), and Ella Fitzgerald (accompanied by pianist Don Abney, bassist Joe Mondragon and drummer Larry Bunker) is wonderful on "Pete Kelly's Blues" and a memorable version of "Hard Hearted Hannah." In addition, guitarist Herb Ellis (who receives a screen credit) is seen on banjo backing Janet Leigh, whose vocal is obviously ghosted. Dick Cathcart ghosts Webb's trumpet solos and the other musicians on the soundtrack (who would soon work in clubs as Pete Kelly's Seven) include clarinetist/arranger Matty Matlock, trombonist Moe Schneider, tenor saxophonist Eddie Miller, pianist Ray Sherman, guitarist George Van Eps, bassist Jud De Naut and drummer Nick Fatool; Miller and Van Eps are seen on-screen. Trumpeter Teddy Buckner is in the film's beginning (set in 1915 New Orleans), playing "Just a Closer Walk with Thee." The other songs heard throughout the film include "Smiles," "I'm Gonna Meet My Sweetie Now" and "Somebody Loves Me." A 1959 television series, **Pete Kelly's Blues**, was based on this movie, ran 13 shows and featured Connee Boswell, Helen Humes and Dick Cathcart's ghosting for actor William Reynolds.

🎞️5 🎵5 *Piedalu Depute* *(1953, 95 minutes)*

This French domestic comedy has brief appearances by Sidney Bechet, Claude Luter and Andre Reweliotty's orchestra.

🎞️7 🎵6 *Pieges* *(1939, 89 minutes)*

Also known as **Personal Column**, this French murder mystery stars Maurice Chevalier and Erich Von Stroheim.

Trumpeter Valaida Snow and pianist Freddy Johnson pop up briefly in nightclub scenes.

🎞 ♪ *Pillow to Post*
(1945, 92 minutes)

Ida Lupino stars in a comedy about a traveling saleslady and an Army lieutenant. Louis Armstrong and his big band back singer Dorothy Dandridge during a minute-and-a-half version of "Whatcha Say" before totally disappearing.

🎞 ♪ *Play Misty for Me*
(1971, 96 minutes)

Clint Eastwood stars as a disc jockey who gets phone calls from a mysterious and disturbing woman who regularly requests "Misty." At one point he visits the Monterey Jazz Festival where for a brief segment one gets to see the Cannonball Adderley Quintet (with cornetist Nat Adderley, keyboardist Joe Zawinul, bassist Walter Booker and drummer Roy McCurdy) playing "Country Preacher"; Johnny Otis's band also appears.

🎞 ♪ *Playgirls International*
(1963, 71 minutes)

An eccentric travelogue, this rarely seen film features dancers (some of whom are nudists) from a variety of locales along with some entertainment. At one point Louis Prima, Sam Butera and the Witnesses perform a twist song in Las Vegas.

🎞 ♪ *The Powers Girl*
(1942, 93 minutes)

George Murphy, Anne Shirley and Carole Landis star in a musical about a model's rise to fame. The Benny Goodman Orchestra (with trumpeter Jimmy Maxwell, trombonist Lou McGarity, Al Klink on tenor, pianist Jimmy Rowles and guitarist Dave Barbour) performs "Let's Dance," "Roll 'Em," "One O'Clock Jump" and "The Lady Who Didn't Believe in Love" (vocal by Peggy Lee) while

Goodman and his quintet (with Rowles) play "I Know that You Know."

🎞 ♪ *Presenting Lily Mars*
(1943, 104 minutes)

Judy Garland and Van Heflin star in a likable film about a member of a large, small-town family who wants to be an actress. One of Garland's younger sisters is played by Annabelle Logan, who later in life would change her name to Annie Ross. While the plot is fine, the big bands of Bob Crosby and Tommy Dorsey are both completely wasted. Crosby's ensemble accompanies some singers on "Think of Me" (Bob Haggart and Ray Bauduc can easily be seen), and Dorsey's band is used as a prop in the final production number, "Broadway Rhythm."

🎞 ♪ *Pretty Baby* *(1977, 110 minutes)*

Life in 1917 Storyville is accurately and lovingly depicted in this memorable if leisurely film. The famed photographer E.J. Bellocq is portrayed by Keith Carradine, while Brooke Shields plays a child prostitute. Early New Orleans jazz music is heard throughout (the soundtrack album has 19 songs), including "Tiger Rag," "Creole Belles," "After the Ball" and many Scott Joplin and Jelly Roll Morton songs. Bob Greene's piano is prominent in the score, Antonio Fargas plays a minor character who is similar to Jelly Roll Morton, and there is a brief appearance early in the film by the Eureka Brass Band with tenor saxophonist Emanuel Paul.

🎞 ♪ *Printemps à Paris* *(1956, 85 minutes)*

A country girl visits Paris in this French film, which features many musical performances. Among the artists is American swing trumpeter Bill Coleman.

🎞 ♪ *Private Buckaroo* *(1942, 69 minutes)*

This patriotic musical comedy has its amusing moments, featuring the Andrews Sisters and Harry James in major roles. Helen Forrest sings "You Made Me Love You" (the hit version for James was actually an instrumental), while James and his orchestra perform "Concerto for Trumpet," "Don't Sit Under the Apple Tree" (with the Andrews Sisters) and the heated "James Session" (on which they back dancers).

Quicksand *(1951, 79 minutes)*

Mickey Rooney works as a mechanic, gets involved with a "bad girl," borrows $20 from his boss's cash register and gradually gets into deeper and deeper trouble. While the film is good, the jazz is negligible. Red Nichols and his Five Pennies are seen for literally two seconds at a club and play an unidentifiable song briefly in the background.

Radio Parade of 1935 *(1934, 96 minutes)*

The staff of a radio station saves the day by putting on a giant show in this British film. A thin plot and too many mediocre production numbers by British performers make this a difficult one to sit through. Alberta Hunter, who was living in England at the time, appears in a color sequence, but sings the dull "Black Shadows" rather than a jazz or blues song.

Rafferty and the Gold Dust Twins *(1975, 91 minutes)*

An erratic Alan Arkin comedy (he is a driving instructor kidnapped by Sally Kellerman and Mackenzie Phillips) mostly misses its mark. At one point the stars are in Las Vegas where Louis Prima, Sam Butera and the Witnesses play part of "I've Got You Under My Skin."

The Rat Race *(1960, 105 minutes)*

Tony Curtis is cast as a saxophonist who arrives in New York with great optimism but has to struggle to make it, with the help of Debbie Reynolds. Joe Bushkin (who was also in the play) and Gerry Mulligan have acting roles.

Reaching for the Moon *(1930, 90 minutes)*

During this lightweight comedy featuring Douglas Fairbanks, Sr., an unbilled Bing Crosby pops on-screen from out of nowhere and sings a hot chorus on "When the Folks High Up Do the Mean Low Down," the only number left in the film from what was originally an Irving Berlin score.

Reet, Petite and Gone *(1947, 75 minutes)*

This is an entertaining all-Black film that is most notable for the many songs performed by Louis Jordan and his Tympany Five; June Richmond also has a few features. The many Jordan songs from the movie (which include "Let the Good Times Roll," "Texas & Pacific" and "Ain't That Just Like a Woman") are also available (without the plot and dialog) on the Storyville videotape **Louis Jordan and His Tympany Band**.

Rendez-Vous de Julliet *(1949, 68 minutes)*

A French drama follows a group of jazz-loving young people in Paris and a scheme by a filmmaker to have his friends join him on a film shoot in Africa. Cornetist Rex Stewart and clarinetist Claude Luter are briefly featured.

Reveille with Beverly *(1942, 78 minutes)*

In this film, every time Ann Miller (who plays a disc jockey) puts on a record, viewers see a live performance by a band. While the wartime plot is lightweight, some of the music is quite good. Appearing along the way are the Mills Brothers ("Cielito Lindo" and "Sweet Lucy Brown"), the Count Basie Orchestra (a classic rendition of "One O'Clock Jump" with Buck Clayton, tenors Buddy Tate and Don Byas, and Dickie Wells), the Bob Crosby Orchestra (a vocal version of "Big Noise from Winnetka" with just a brief moment from Bob Haggart and drummer Ray

Bauduc), Duke Ellington's orchestra ("Take the 'A' Train" with singer Betty Roche and Ben Webster), Ella Mae Morse with Freddy Slack's big band ("Cow Cow Boogie") and Frank Sinatra ("Night and Day").

9 4 *Rhapsody in Blue* (1945, 139 minutes)

The film biography of George Gershwin is quite well done and does not stray too far from the truth, with Robert Alda well cast as Gershwin. There is a lot of music along the way, including a role for Paul Whiteman, who conducts his orchestra (with his reliable banjoist Mike Pingitore) on "Rhapsody in Blue" and manages to look the same in 1945 as he did in 1925. There is actually very little jazz in the film, but singer/pianist Hazel Scott performs a medley of "Fascinating Rhythm" and "I Got Rhythm" (which has a touch of heated stride piano) in a nightclub scene in Paris.

6 7 *Rhythm Inn* (1951, 70 minutes)

The plot is about a Dixieland band, a songwriter and a female vocalist. Trumpeter Wingy Manone's band (with cornetist Pete Daily, trombonist Joe Yukl, clarinetist Matty Matlock, pianist Walter Gross, bassist Budd Hatch and drummer Barrett Deems) performs "Blues" and "When You and I Were Young, Maggie." Most memorable is a "drum exhibition" that shows why Deems was accurately being billed at the time as "the world's fastest drummer."

7 2 *Rhythm on the Range* (1936, 88 minutes)

Bing Crosby plays a singing cowboy in this unusual film, finding romance with Frances Farmer and welcoming a hyper Martha Raye to her debut on-screen. Louis Prima has a cameo appearance. Among the Crosby songs are "I'm a Old Cowhand."

6 5 *Rhythm on the River* (1940, 92 minutes)

Bing Crosby and Mary Martin star in a musical comedy about songwriters who ghost for other much less talented

celebrities. Wingy Manone is an eccentric pal of Crosby's and gets to play "Tiger Rag." He also backs Bing on "Rhythm on the River" and Martin in the movie's hit, "Ain't It a Shame about Mame."

3 7 *Ride 'Em Cowboy* (1941, 85 minutes)

An early but typically juvenile Abbott and Costello film, this movie is chiefly notable for having the first film appearance of Ella Fitzgerald. Fitzgerald performs "Rock 'n' Reelin'" with the Merry Macs and a classic rendition of "A-Tisket, A-Tasket" that she sings on a bus.

6 4 *Riding High* (1950, 112 minutes)

This good-natured Frank Capra horseracing story stars Bing Crosby. Joe Venuti appears with a small group backing Crosby on "The Horse Told Me."

5 3 *Riley the Cop* (1928, 76 minutes)

A cop from New York is assigned to find a man accused of theft who has fled to Europe. Both of the main characters meet women and get involved in romance while enjoying 1928 Berlin. Speed Webb's orchestra makes a brief appearance in a nightclub scene.

4 1 *The Road to Ruin* (1928, 60 minutes)

This moralistic silent film is about the complete downfall of a teenaged girl. Cornetist Mutt Carey's Liberty Syncopators (with Joe Darensbourg on clarinet) is seen (but not heard) playing for dancers.

4 5 *Rock Around the World* (1957, 82 minutes)

Known in England as **The Tommy Steele Story**, this is a decent but not particularly memorable biography of an early rock 'n' roller who had a hit with "Singin' the Blues."

British trad trumpeter Humphrey Lyttelton's band is featured on "Bermondsey Bounce." Steele plays himself.

🎞 🎵 *Rockabilly Baby* (1957, 82 minutes)

Virginia Field is cast as a former fan dancer who settles in a small town and gains respectability, at least until her past is revealed. This movie has plenty of rock 'n' roll, along with an appearance by Les Brown and his big band.

🎞 🎵 *Romance on the High Seas* (1948, 99 minutes)

Doris Day's first feature film is one of her best. Her character is much livelier than it would become a decade later and she introduces "It's Magic." The Page Cavanaugh Trio (pianist Cavanaugh, guitarist Al Viola and bassist Lloyd Pratt) shares a charming chorus with Day on "It's You or No One" and assists her on "Put 'Em in a Box, Tie 'Em with a Ribbon."

🎞 🎵 *Rome Adventure* (1962, 118 minutes)

This average romance film is most notable for a funny five-minute sequence in which trumpeter Al Hirt has a few lines, plays part of a song and gets in a barroom fight, throwing a good punch.

🎞 🎵 *Rookies on Parade* (1941, 70 minutes)

Bob Crosby stars in an Army comedy about a pair of privates (the other one is Eddie Foy, Jr.) who put on a show for the troops. None of the songs (other than the standard "My Kinda Love") are memorable, and Bob Crosby shows once again that he is no match for brother Bing.

🎞 🎵 *Rose of Washington Square* (1939, 86 minutes)

This nostalgic showbiz story stars Alice Faye, Tyrone Power and Al Jolson. Quite a few vintage standards are performed, but jazzwise there is only one scene of interest.

Louis Prima plays trumpet behind Alice Faye on "I'm Just Wild about Harry" and, though he mugs a little, he does not have a single line and is wasted. However, the film is quite enjoyable and musical.

🎞 🎵 *Round Midnight* (1986, 132 minutes)

Tenor saxophonist Dexter Gordon gained an Academy Award nomination for best actor for his performance in **Round Midnight**. Although it is a fictional look at expatriate Americans in Paris in the late '50s and early '60s, some of the incidents are reminiscent of episodes in the lives of Bud Powell and Lester Young. Gordon plays Dale Turner, a burnt-out American tenor player who is treated as a hero when he moves to Paris, particularly by a photographer (based on Francis Paudras) who takes care of him. Many of the scenes (some of which are ad-libbed) ring true, and all of the music is performed live, which is very rare for a Hollywood film. Among the other musicians who are seen along the way are Herbie Hancock and vibraphonist Bobby Hutcherson (both of whom play small parts), trumpeters Freddie Hubbard and Palle Mikkelborg, Wayne Shorter on tenor, pianist Cedar Walton, guitarist John McLaughlin, bassists Ron Carter and Pierre Michelot, and drummers Billy Higgins and Tony Williams. A lot of music is heard, including "'Round Midnight" (sung by Bobby McFerrin over the opening credits), "As Time Goes By," "Society Red," "Fairweather," "Body and Soul," "Now's the Time," "The Peacocks," "Tivoli," "Rhythm-A-Ning" and "Chan's Song." In addition, Lonette McKee sings "How Long Has This Been Going On," and Sandra Reaves-Phillips is featured on "Put It Right There." But it is for Dexter Gordon's sincere and effective performance that this film should be seen by all jazz fans.

🎞 🎵 *La Route du Bonheur* (1953, 92 minutes)

This French-Italian film is about the organization of a benefit performance for a radio station. Among the many acts that perform are Sidney Bechet with Claude Luter's

Dixieland band (playing "Buddy Bolden's Blues"), Aime Barelli's orchestra and a quintet with clarinetist Hubert Rostaing that is called the Django Reinhardt Group although the guitarist is unfortunately not present. The Louis Armstrong All-Stars with Trummy Young, clarinetist Bob McCracken, pianist Marty Napoleon, Arvell Shaw, Cozy Cole and Velma Middleton (who is seen but does not sing) cavort a bit on "Struttin' with Some Barbecue."

🎞️5 🎵6 *St. Louis Blues*
(1939, 92 minutes)

Dorothy Lamour drops out of Broadway to sing on a showboat owned by Lloyd Nolan. Lamour sings five songs (including "St. Louis Blues"), but it is for Maxine Sullivan (who plays Ida and is billed eighth) that this second **St. Louis Blues** (following Bessie Smith's 1929 short) is of strongest jazz interest. She sings her hit "Loch Lomond," "Kinda Lonesome" and "Otchichornya." The Hall Johnson Choir and violinist Matty Malneck's orchestra also help out.

🎞️2 🎵5 *St. Louis Blues*
(1958, 93 minutes)

The real W.C. Handy wrote down some of the blues lyrics that he heard street musicians perform, added ideas of his own, and achieved fame by publishing the resulting classic songs. He also led a band in which he played primitive cornet (never really learning to swing), only singing a bit in his later years. This movie, which casts Nat King Cole as Handy, has a remarkably poor screenplay and completely fictionalizes the story, making Handy a singer with jazz and religion conflicts that seem to have been borrowed from **The Jazz Singer**. There is some good music with Handy's tunes performed by Cole (and as a boy by Billy Preston), Cab Calloway, Ella Fitzgerald, Pearl Bailey, Eartha Kitt and Mahalia Jackson, with such players as Teddy Buckner, Barney Bigard, Red Callender and drummer Lee Young in the accompanying bands. Nelson Riddle did the arrangements, which make the music

sound much more like 1958 than 1918. But the story is difficult to sit through.

🎞️3 🎵1 *Sanctuary*
(1961, 90 minutes)

Lee Remick and Odetta star in this strange and very unlikely movie based on two William Faulkner books: *Sanctuary* and *Requiem for a Nun*. Wilton Felder (of the Jazz Crusaders) has a very small role as a musician.

🎞️4 🎵8 *Sarge Goes to College*
(1947, 66 minutes)

Other than the music, this is a forgettable college comedy. Tenor saxophonist Jack McVea introduces, sings and plays his novelty hit "Open the Door, Richard." In addition, there is an exciting jam session of blues featuring trumpeter Wingy Manone, clarinetist Jerry Wald, Joe Venuti, Les Paul (who looks very amused by everything), Jess Stacy, bassist Candy Candido, drummer Abe Lyman (who reads a newspaper while playing) and a crazed dancer who almost fouls up the works.

🎞️6 🎵3 *The Scarlet Hour*
(1956, 94 minutes)

Carol Ohmart uses Tom Tryon to foil a jewel robbery planned by her husband in this melodrama. In a club, Nat King Cole is featured singing (and introducing) "Never Let Me Go."

🎞️3 🎵2 *Schlagerparade*
(1953, 100 minutes)

This West German production has very little plot (the struggles of a young songwriter to get his songs heard, even after one accidentally becomes a hit) but includes 16 tunes, mostly by German pop groups and singers plus Maurice Chevalier. The Stan Kenton Orchestra (which at the time included trumpeters Buddy Childers and Conte Candoli, trombonist Frank Rosolino, altoist Lee Konitz, tenors Bill Holman and Zoot Sims, guitarist

Barry Galbraith and drummer Stan Levey) performs one unidentified number for two minutes.

🎬 🎵 *The Score* (2001, 123 minutes)

Robert DeNiro plays a jewel thief who also owns a jazz club. He is persuaded by Marlon Brando to get involved in one final robbery before he retires. In the club, Cassandra Wilson sings "You're About to Give In" while backed by her trio, but that segment is less than a minute long. Even more ridiculous, Mose Allison and a bassist perform "City Home" for 20 seconds.

🎬 🎵 *Scott Joplin* (1976, 96 minutes)

This made-for-TV movie is a dramatization of the life of the King of Ragtime, filmed a couple of years after **The Sting** made Scott Joplin's "The Entertainer" a surprise pop hit. The screenplay is reasonably accurate and generally entertaining if a bit downbeat. Billy Dee Williams plays Joplin and Art Carney portrays John Stark, Joplin's publisher and ally. Eubie Blake (who was 93 at the time and one of the few survivors who knew the composer) makes an appearance, many of Joplin's top rags are heard, and Dick Hyman and Hank Jones play the piano parts for Williams.

🎬 🎵 *Screaming Mimi* (1957, 71 minutes)

After Anita Ekberg is almost killed by a lunatic, she spends time in a mental institution, becomes involved with her possessive doctor, has a career as an exotic dancer and is engulfed in a rather ridiculous murder mystery. The Red Norvo Quartet with guitarist Jimmy Wyble is seen on several occasions providing atmosphere, accompanying Ekberg's odd dancing and backing Gypsy Rose Lee on one number, but never has a feature of its own. Norvo gets a few lines.

🎬 🎵 *Second Chorus* (1940, 85 minutes)

This is an erratic but sometimes quite funny comedy with Fred Astaire, Burgess Meredith and Paulette Goddard.

Astaire and Meredith play trumpeters (ghosted by Bobby Hackett and Billy Butterfield) wanting to get into Artie Shaw's band; their audition for Shaw is hilarious. Shaw has quite a few lines, is showcased on "Concerto for Clarinet" and also performs a couple of brief numbers. His original "Love of My Life" is sung by Astaire. Billy Butterfield is seen on-screen and heard with the studio band, including on "Concerto for Clarinet."

🎬 🎵 *The Secret Fury* (1950, 86 minutes)

This mystery thriller stars Claudette Colbert who may or may not be married and is on trial for murder. One scene effectively uses jazz. Colbert and her fiancé Robert Ryan visit her alleged husband, guitarist Dave Barbour (who in real life was married to Peggy Lee). Barbour and an informal band consisting of tenor saxophonist Vido Musso, trumpeter Ernie Royal, pianist Hal Schaefer, bassist Walt Yoder and drummer Alvin Stoller play "Jazz Me Blues" in the background and then a long themeless slow blues; Barbour and Musso solo on the latter. The guitarist has a few lines before getting bumped off.

🎬 🎵 *See My Lawyer* (1945, 69 minutes)

Ole Olsen and Chic Johnson play a couple of nightclub entertainers who will do anything to break their contract with club owner Franklin Pangborn, including humiliating their customers. The Nat King Cole Trio (dressed as cooks) performs "Man on the Little White Keys."

🎬 🎵 *Senior Prom* (1958, 82 minutes)

Too low-budget to be considered a B movie, this juvenile romantic comedy has a barely coherent plot about college life and putting on an all-star show. Whether it is Bob Crosby singing a dull chorus of "Do You Care," Connie Boswell's three choruses of "The Saints" or the Les Elgart Orchestra backing a singer briefly on "Let's Fall in Love," everything about this film is a waste, except for one number. For three magical minutes, Louis Prima, Keely Smith, and Sam Butera and The Witnesses perform a memorable version of "That Old Black Magic."

⎡5̆⎤ 🎵 *Sensations* (1944, 87 minutes)

This movie had all the ingredients of a classic: the brilliant tap dancer Eleanor Powell, both the Woody Herman and Cab Calloway orchestras, and even such performers as Sophie Tucker and (in his last film) W.C. Fields. Unfortunately, the plot is erratic and the film ends up being both intriguing and rambling. Herman is largely wasted backing a variety of other acts, having a brief instrumental in which he emulates Artie Shaw and Benny Goodman (dueting with the drummer who might be Cliff Leeman) and singing "No Never" with an unidentified woman. The second half of the latter becomes background music for dialog. Sophie Tucker's version of "Mammy O' Mine" is enjoyable but brief. Cab Calloway fares better, singing "We the Cats Shall Hep Ya" with his orchestra and a jive talk number in which he interacts with an animated cat. His segment becomes part of the plot because his performance is shown on a giant screen over a busy intersection, stopping traffic as a crowd jitterbugs in humorous fashion. The high point of the film has Calloway conducting his orchestra as Dorothy Donegan turns a classical piece into some remarkable stride piano, showing why Art Tatum admired her technique. After her solo, she trades off with pianist Gene Rodgers and they tear the place apart.

⎡4̆⎤ 🎵 *Sepia Cinderella* (1947, 75 minutes)

This all-Black musical comedy has a mundane plot along with some comedy and a fair amount of music. It is most significant for what might be the only filmed appearance of the John Kirby Sextet, which at the time was comprised of Charlie Shavers, Buster Bailey, altoist Charlie Holmes (in Russell Procope's old spot), pianist Billy Kyle, bassist Kirby and drummer Big Sid Catlett (in place of the late O'Neill Spencer). Kirby's group plays excellent versions of "Broadjump" (partly over the opening credits) and "Can't Find a Word to Say," showing why they were considered a unique band with a sound of its own. These two numbers are fortunately also available on the videotape **The Small Black Groups**.

⎡5̆⎤ 🎵 *Serie Noire* (1955, 88 minutes)

Erich Von Stroheim stars in a lesser-known French gangster film. In a five-minute section, soprano saxophonist Sidney Bechet performs three brief numbers including "Blues Dans le Blues."

⎡6̆⎤ 🎵 *The Servant* (1963, 115 minutes)

In this British psychological drama about a servant and an aristocrat switching roles, John Dankworth is seen playing a brief blues with a quartet.

⎡6̆⎤ 🎵 *Seven Days' Leave* (1942, 87 minutes)

Army private Victor Mature will get a $100,000 inheritance if he can convince wealthy heiress Lucille Ball (who is engaged to someone else) to marry him within a week. Ginny Sims sings "Can't Get Out of this Mood" and there are spots for Les Brown's band (with trumpeter Billy Butterfield, clarinetist Abe Most and drummer Shelly Manne) and Freddie Martin's orchestra. Among the songs are "A Touch of Texas," "Please Won't You Leave My Girl Alone?" "Baby, You Speak My Language," "Puerto Rico" and "Soft Hearted."

⎡7̆⎤ 🎵 *Sex and the Single Girl* (1964, 110 minutes)

This is a rather funny comedy featuring an all-star cast that includes Natalie Wood, Tony Curtis, Henry Fonda and Lauren Bacall; it is highlighted by an endless car chase. Count Basie and his orchestra pop up a couple of times, playing "The Anniversary Song," "What Is This Thing Called Love" and the movie's main theme.

♪ Shake, Rattle and Rock?
(1956, 75 minutes)

Mike Connors wants to open up a music club for under-privileged youths but is met by opposition from anti–rock 'n' roll parents. Big Joe Turner (whose blues singing fit into practically any style) romps on "Feelin' Happy" and "Lipstick, Powder and Paint."

♪ Ship Ahoy
(1942, 95 minutes)

This entertaining Red Skelton musical has a few good spots for Tommy Dorsey's orchestra, which includes Ziggy Elman, tenor saxophonist Don Lodice, clarinetist Heinie Beau and Buddy Rich. The orchestra plays an exciting version of "Hawaiian War Chant" with a tenor solo from Lodice and a duet spot for Elman and Rich. On "I'll Take Tallulah," Rich's drumming co-stars with Eleanor Powell's tap dancing.

♪ Sing as You Swing
(1937, 82 minutes)

A struggling British radio station hosts a large variety show. Featured are many contemporary acts, including the Mills Brothers ("Solitude" and "Nagasaki") and trumpeter Nat Gonella and his Georgians ("Georgia on My Mind").

♪ Sing Sing Thanksgiving
(1973, 82 minutes)

Joan Baez, Mimi Farina and a variety of folk and rock performers are featured at a concert at Ossining Correction Facility in November 1971. Joe Williams and B.B. King also make appearances.

♪ Sing Sinner Sing *(1933, 74 minutes)*

Leila Hyams plays a singer who is accused of her husband's murder. The Les Hite Orchestra (with Lionel Hampton on drums and altoist Marshall Royal) pops up in a few scenes.

♪ Sing Your Worries Away
(1942, 71 minutes)

This mediocre musical comedy, which has theatrical people involved with gangsters, stars June Havoc and Bert Lahr. It is most notable for its opening scene, which features steel guitarist Alvino Rey and his orchestra plus the King Sisters (for one memorable chorus) performing a hot version of "Tiger Rag."

♪ The Singing Kid
(1936, 85 minutes)

Al Jolson, who starred in the groundbreaking partial talkie **The Jazz Singer** in 1927, was not really a jazz singer although some of the songs he sang became jazz standards. His films are generally not listed in this book. However, this Jolson vehicle is included because Cab Calloway (who was influenced by Jolson) has a fairly prominent part and his orchestra performs "Keep that Hi-De-Ho in Your Soul."

♪ Sins of the Fathers
(1928, 87 minutes)

Emil Jannings stars as a restaurant owner who becomes a bootlegger with tragic results. Speed Webb's orchestra makes a brief appearance in this film which is mostly silent.

♪ Sis Hopkins
(1941, 98 minutes)

Judy Canova (Sis Hopkins) stars in a country vs. city rivalry comedy with the up-and-coming Susan Hayward. Bob Crosby plays Hayward's boyfriend, a singer involved with a show. He sings "Look at You, Look at Me" with Hayward (someone ghosts her singing voice) and "I Went and Fell for You" with Canova. The Bob Crosby Band (which at the time included cornetist Muggsy Spanier, tenor saxophonist Eddie Miller, clarinetist Matty Matlock, guitarist Nappy Lamare, bassist Bob Haggart and drummer Ray Bauduc) backs Canova on "It Ain't Hay, It's the USA," but is not given much to do.

4 4

6.5 Special

(1958, 85 minutes)

Two teenagers in England go to London and try out for the *6.5 Special* television show. Many British pop stars of 1958 appear, and there is one song after another. Along with all of the rock 'n' rollers are Lonnie Donegan, the Johnny Dankworth Orchestra with tenor saxophonist Danny Moss and drummer Kenny Clare ("Train Gang") and Cleo Laine accompanied by Dankworth's big band ("What Am I Going to Tell Them Tonight").

7 4

The Small Back Room

(1948, 106 minutes)

This troubling British wartime story about a crippled scientist has a nightclub scene featuring the Ted Heath/Kenny Baker Swing Group.

6 1

The Small World of Sammy Lee

(1962, 190 minutes)

Anthony Newley has to raise money in a hurry to keep his bookie at bay in this British drama, which is partly set in strip clubs. Baritonist Joe Temperley and bassist Coleridge Goode have brief appearances in the background.

4 6

Smart Politics

(1948, 65 minutes)

A group of teenagers fight to turn an abandoned warehouse into a youth center over the opposition of the mayor. Naturally they put on a show. Gene Krupa's orchestra makes an appearance and plays "Young Man with the Beat."

6 4

The Snows of Kilimanjaro

(1952, 114 minutes)

Ernest Hemingway's short story was expanded and embellished for this full-length movie, which has Gregory Peck as a disillusioned and aimless writer and co-stars Ava Gardner and Susan Hayward. In one scene, Benny Carter and a quartet play the ballad "Love Is Cynthia."

6 4

So's Your Uncle

(1943, 64 minutes)

Donald Woods impersonates his elderly uncle to avoid creditors and gets mixed up with Billie Burke (whom he persuades to back his so-called nephew's play) and her daughter. This musical comedy features Jan Garber's orchestra playing "You're Driving Me Crazy" and vocals from the Delta Rhythm Boys ("St. Louis Blues" and "Don't Get Around Much Anymore"), the Tailor Maids ("Liza") and Mary O'Brien ("That's the Way It Goes" and "Dark Eyes"). The latter tune has O'Brien backed by Jack Teagarden and his big band.

5 6

Soldaterkammerater

(1958, 84 minutes)

This little-known Swedish Army comedy is notable for including numbers from Papa Bue's Viking Jazz Band and Stan Getz's combo with Oscar Pettiford.

2 2

Some Call It Loving

(1973, 103 minutes)

This is a very strange movie about the sexual fantasies of a jazz musician with plenty of bizarre and ludicrous scenes that blur the line between reality and fantasy. The main actor, Zalman King, plays baritone (ghosted by Ronnie Lang) and bassist Leroy Vinnegar appears onscreen briefly during a rehearsal.

5 7

Some Like It Hot

(1939, 65 minutes)

Bob Hope takes advantage of Shirley Ross in order to raise money for a show. Gene Krupa gets fourth billing and his big band (which includes tenor saxophonist Sam Donahue and pianist Milt Raskin) is well featured on "Wire Brush Stomp," "Blue Rhythm Fantasy" and "Some

Like It Hot." This movie introduced "The Lady's in Love with You" and was later renamed **Rhythm Romance** so as not to be confused with the better-known **Some Like It Hot** from the 1950s.

4 6 Something to Shout About
(1943, 90 minutes)

A divorcée who has won a big alimony payment decides to back a vaudeville show and perform despite her lack of talent. Don Ameche and Janet Blair star in this average film, most notable for the music, which includes "Jitterbug Stomp" and six Cole Porter songs. "You'd Be So Nice to Come Home To" won an Academy Award, and the other numbers include "Something to Shout About," "Hasta Luego," "Lotus Bloom," "I Always Knew" and "Through Thick and Thin." Pianist Hazel Scott and Teddy Wilson's combo perform.

8 8 A Song Is Born
(1948, 113 minutes)

This Danny Kaye/Virginia Mayo movie, a musical remake of **Ball of Fire**, is entertaining and often very amusing. Seven professors (one of whom is Benny Goodman in an acting role) sponsored by a foundation have been living as hermits as they compile a complete history of music. When they get around to exploring jazz, it is decided that Danny Kaye will go out in the world to do research. He invites a bunch of top jazz musicians to the professors' home plus Virginia Mayo (her singing is ghosted by Jeri Sullivan), who is mixed up with gangsters. Quite a few top-notch jazz musicians (mostly from the swing era) are featured at least briefly including Mel Powell, Tommy Dorsey, Charlie Barnet, the Page Cavanaugh Trio (with Al Viola), Louis Armstrong, Lionel Hampton and the Golden Gate Quartet. Also seen are Buck and Bubbles, guitarist Al Hendrickson, bassist Harry Babasin and Louie Bellson. The best music is heard on "A Song Is Born," "Flying Home" and particularly "Stealing Apples." The latter has Goodman, as a befuddled classical clar-

inetist, instantly learning to play jazz and keep time thanks to Hampton.

5 6 South of Dixie
(1944, 61 minutes)

David Bruce, a writer of Southern pop tunes, decides to visit the South for the first time to gain some credibility, traveling with screenwriter Anne Gwynne who plays Dixie. Ella Mae Morse gets fourth billing, has a romance with Bruce, and sings "Shoo Shoo Baby" and "Never Again."

6 8 Springtime in the Rockies
(1942, 91 minutes)

This all-star musical stars Betty Grable, John Payne and Carmen Miranda. Harry James has a fair number of lines although he is not paired romantically with his future wife Grable. His orchestra with singer Helen Forrest introduces "I Had the Craziest Dream" and also performs "You Made Me Love You," "Two O'Clock Jump," "Ciribiribin" and "Sleepy Lagoon."

6 7 Stage Door Canteen
(1943, 132 minutes)

Tribute is paid to the Stage Door Canteen, a place for servicemen to relax and be entertained during World War II. The plot is thin and a few dozen celebrities are seen in this film, including the big bands of Kay Kyser, Guy Lombardo, Xavier Cugat and Freddie Martin. From the jazz standpoint, one gets to see Ethel Waters singing "Quicksand" while accompanied by the Count Basie big band, Benny Goodman's orchestra (which at the time included trombonist Jack Jenney, Jess Stacy and Louie Bellson) romping behind dancers on "Bugle Call Rag," and Peggy Lee (backed by Goodman) performing her first hit, "Why Don't You Do Right."

5 6 Les Stances à Sophie
(1970, 97 minutes)

A free-spirited woman gradually rebels against her stuffy husband in this French comedy. The Art Ensemble of

Chicago (trumpeter Lester Bowie, Roscoe Mitchell and Joseph Jarman on reeds, bassist Malachi Favors and drummer Don Moye with singer Fontella Bass) provides the soundtrack and is on-screen for one number.

🎞7 🎵2 *Stardust Memories*
(1980, 88 minutes)

Most Woody Allen movies have swing-oriented jazz on the soundtrack and this somewhat erratic but intriguing comedy contains plenty. In one brief fantasy scene, Allen presents "The Jazz Heaven Orchestra," a band of angels that includes trumpeter Joe Wilder, pianist Hank Jones and bassist Arvell Shaw.

🎞4 🎵8 *Stars on Parade* *(1946, 45 minutes)*

This all-Black film has a brief plot about the problems of keeping a radio station afloat, resulting in a big show performed for possible sponsors. Singer/pianist Bob Howard is billed fourth and serves as comedy relief. Happily, nearly half of this movie (19 minutes) is taken up by nine straight numbers. Although the camera often cuts away to show the sponsors and the audience, the music is performed complete. Violinist Eddie South (who was rarely filmed) plays a pair of duets with an unidentified pianist (a classical melody that is swung and "Eddie's Blues"), Bob Howard sings and strides on "Oh My Sweetie's in Love with Me," an imitation of a player piano and "Talk to Me," pianist/singer Una Mae Carlisle is excellent on "Tain't Yours, Leave It Alone" and "Teasing Me," and the Phil Moore Four (a quartet with Johnny Letman probably on trumpet) swings on "I've Got the Blues So Bad" and "Rock Ourselves Away"; Moore sings and plays piano.

🎞2 🎵2 *Start Cheering*
(1938, 79 minutes)

A movie star quits Hollywood to go to college. Since he played a football hero in the films, naturally it is assumed that he will be the star of the college football team. Jimmy Durante, the Three Stooges and other comedians do their

best to interfere. Unfortunately, the screenplay is terrible and bereft of inspired humor. Johnny Green's orchestra makes a few undistinguished appearances, and an unbilled Louis Prima plays trumpet behind Durante on one number and briefly at a party.

🎞5 🎵3 *Stille Dage in Clichy*
(1969, 90 minutes)

This Danish film (**Quiet Days in Clichy**), shot in English, follows a pair of male hedonists through their erotic adventures in Paris. A brief scene in a nightclub has Ben Webster leading the house band.

🎞6 🎵1 *Stolen Hours* *(1962, 97 minutes)*

It is ironic that the most prestigious film that Chet Baker appeared in, a remake of **Dark Victory** starring Susan Hayward, is an extremely brief cameo. Baker is in one of the first scenes and, if one blinks, he is missed altogether.

🎞8 🎵9 *Stormy Weather* *(1943, 78 minutes)*

Although not a perfect film (wasn't Bill "Bojangles" Robinson a little too old for Lena Horne?) and not completely free of racial stereotypes, this all-Black film has many memorable moments, both in the plot and particularly the music. It traces the fictional life of a tap dancer/singer (Bojangles) and his relationship with Horne over a 25-year period. Early on, Jim Europe's military and civilian bands are depicted, with Ernest "Bubbles" Whitman (who would become known as the voice of the Jubilee radio series) playing Europe. Horne sings "There's No Two Ways about Love," "Diga Diga Doo," "I Can't Give You Anything but Love" and "Stormy Weather." Leo Watson is featured on "Yeah Man" (he is the one holding the trumpet), scatting wildly with a group similar to the Spirits of Rhythm. Bill Robinson has several opportunities to dance. Fats Waller is only on-screen for less than ten minutes but has his most memorable screen role, performing "That Ain't Right" with singer Ada Brown and rollicking on "Ain't Misbehavin'," playing some hot stride piano and getting off some of his famous verbal lines. Drummer Zutty Singleton has a solo on "Ain't Misbehavin'," and the rest of the band consists of Benny Carter (on trumpet), trombonist Alton Moore, Gene Porter on clarinet and tenor, guitarist Irving Ashby and bassist Slam Stewart. Near the end of the film when things seem to be flagging a bit, Cab Calloway wakes things up both in his interplay with Bojangles and his singing of "Geechie Joe,""My, My Ain't That Something" and "Jumpin' Jive." After Cab's vocal, "Jumpin' Jive" has some incredible dancing by the Nicholas Brothers (complete with splits) that is one of the great performances on film and serves as the climax of **Stormy Weather**.

Strictly Dynamite
(1934, 74 minutes)

Jimmy Durante stars as a radio personality who is running out of good material and needs to hire a writer in this complicated and typically hyper comedy with Lupe Velez. The Mills Brothers sing "Goodbye Blues."

Strike Up the Band
(1940, 119 minutes)

One of the more famous Mickey Rooney/Judy Garland movies, this musical features Paul Whiteman in an acting role and leading his orchestra behind the stars. Rooney is shown playing drums although his part is ghosted by

Bill "Bojangles" Robinson, Lena Horne and Cab Calloway were the headliners of 1943's *Stormy Weather*, but Fats Waller and the Nicholas Brothers provided the greatest moments.

Lee Young. In addition to the Garland and Rooney specialties, there is a brief version of "When Day Is Done" featuring Harry Goldfield (Henry Busse's successor); banjoist Mike Pingitore and trumpeter Charlie Teagarden can also be seen.

The Strip (1951, 86 minutes)

Mickey Rooney plays an aspiring jazz drummer (his part is ghosted by Cozy Cole) who has constant difficulties with the law. Much of the film is set in a nightclub run by William Demarest who often plays second piano (Eddie Beal plays his part). Louis Armstrong's All-Stars with Jack Teagarden, Barney Bigard and Earl Hines are featured quite winningly on a few occasions although bassist Arvell Shaw actually ghosts for Lloyd Pratt and Cozy Cole does not appear on-screen. The numbers performed include "Shadrack," "The Saints," "Basin Street Blues" (a feature for Teagarden's singing and trombone), "A Kiss to Build a Dream On" and "Ole Miss." In addition, the All-Stars back dancers on a couple of numbers and Vic Damone sings "Don't Blame Me."

The Subterraneans (1960, 89 minutes)

Jack Kerouac's *New Bohemians* is substantially altered for this movie. Novelist George Peppard and free-spirited Leslie Caron meet in San Francisco's North Beach during the height of the beatnik era. Gerry Mulligan has an acting role as a friendly clergyman who also plays baritone sax. André Previn wrote the jazz-oriented film score, which consists primarily of his originals. Carmen McRae sings "Coffee Time," and such musicians as Mulligan, trumpeter Art Farmer, valve trombonist Bob Enevoldsen, altoist Art Pepper, Bill Perkins on tenor, pianists Previn and Russ Freeman, bassist Red Mitchell and drummers Dave Bailey, Shelly Manne and Chico Hamilton get brief chances to play. This is a historical curiosity that has a good sampling of West Coast cool jazz.

Summer Love (1958, 85 minutes)

John Saxon stars in a comedy about a band playing their first job at a summer camp. Although essentially a teenage rock 'n' roll movie, there are appearances by tenor saxophonists Plas Johnson and Dave Pell, pianist Ray Sherman, bassist Bob Bain and drummer Alvin Stoller.

Sun Valley Serenade (1941, 86 minutes)

One of two Hollywood films that feature Glenn Miller's orchestra, this film stars skating star Sonja Henie, John Payne (his piano playing is ghosted by Chummy McGregor) and Lynn Bari, whose singing on "I Know Why (and So Do You)" is actually by Pat Friday. The plot of the romantic comedy is lightweight, but much of the music is memorable. Among the songs performed by the Miller band (which includes trumpeters Ray Anthony, Johnny Best and Billy May, clarinetist Willie Schwartz and baritonist Ernie Caceres) are "It Happened in Sun Valley," "Moonlight Serenade," "I Don't Know Why (and So Do You)" and "In the Mood." However, the high point is an extended and definitive version of "Chattanooga Choo Choo" featuring Tex Beneke and the Modernaires, and some remarkable dancing by the Nicholas Brothers and Dorothy Dandridge.

Sunday Sinners (1941, 66 minutes)

The gist of this all-Black film is the conflict between a preacher, his congregation and the owners of Club Harlem over whether the establishment (which features a fine but unidentified orchestra and a chorus line) should be open on Sunday nights. In addition, there is an unfaithful wife and some trouble with gangsters. Although Mamie Smith gets top billing, her role is actually fairly small. She runs a restaurant that has a pianist so she can sing when she likes.

Smith performs "I'd Do Anything for Love, Love, Love" and, at the end of the film, a brief "This Is the Night for Me."

🎞 6 ♪ 8 *Sweet and Low-Down* (1944, 75 minutes)

This Linda Darnell movie matches her with James Caldwell, who is cast as a trombonist (ghosted by Bill Harris) who plays with Benny Goodman. There is a tremendous uptempo version of "The World Is Waiting for the Sunrise" featuring Benny Goodman in a quartet with Jess Stacy, bassist Sid Weiss and drummer Morey Feld. Lorraine Elliott ghosts some vocals for Lynn Bari, and the Goodman big band at the time includes Bill Harris, a young Zoot Sims and Al Klink on tenors and guitarist

Allan Reuss. Among the other numbers are "I've Found a New Baby," "I'm Making Believe," "Jersey Bounce," "Let's Dance" and "Rachel's Dream."

🎞 7 ♪ 7 *Sweet and Lowdown* (1999, 95 minutes)

No relation to the 1944 film of the same name, this Woody Allen movie portrays a fictional guitarist from the 1930s (Emmet Ray) who thinks of himself as the second greatest guitarist in the world, only topped by his idol Django Reinhardt. Sean Penn does an excellent acting job as the lead (even fingering his guitar correctly), and his character is both humorous and a bit tragic. Dick Hyman arranged the period music quite expertly and the

The Glenn Miller Orchestra, seen in *Sun Valley Serenade*, also starred in *Orchestra Wives*.

soundtrack features Howard Alden ghosting for Penn, rhythm guitarist Bucky Pizzarelli, Hyman on piano, drummer Ted Sommer, clarinetist Ken Peplowski and trumpeter Byron Stripling. On-screen, bassist Vince Giordano and banjoist Eddy Davis are seen, there is a brief party scene with pianist James Williams and the reeds of Jerome Richardson and Frank Wess, and clarinetist Orange Kellin can be spotted in a jam session. Swing standards are heard throughout the film, including "When Day Is Done," "I'm Forever Blowing Bubbles," "Shine" and "There'll Be Some Changes Made."

6 4 *Sweet Love, Bitter*
(1966, 92 minutes)

This film can be viewed as a predecessor to **Bird** since there are several similarities. Dick Gregory stars in a story inspired by the life of Charlie Parker although it is quite fictional. Gregory, who plays saxophonist Richie "Eagle" Coles, shows that he was a fine actor, making the self-destructive genius who is always leeching money for drugs and alcohol quite believable. Altoist Charles McPherson, who filled in a bit on the soundtrack of **Bird**, plays all of Gregory's solos and can be seen briefly in a nightclub scene. The band on-screen sometimes includes trumpeter Dave Burns, Chick Corea, bassist Steve Swallow and drummer Al Dreares. Mal Waldron wrote the score to this intriguing but imperfect film, which is available through Rhapsody Films.

7 5 *The Sweet Smell of Success*
(1957, 93 minutes)

A very cynical screenplay casts Burt Lancaster as a powerful and arrogant newspaper columnist (inspired by Walter Winchell) and Tony Curtis as his eager assistant. A young Martin Milner plays guitar (ghosted by Jim Hall) and leads what is really the Chico Hamilton Quintet (Hamilton on drums, Paul Horn on flute and piccolo, cellist Fred Katz and bassist Carson Smith). The band is only featured on part of three numbers,

providing atmosphere and an important character in Milner; some of the musicians (particularly Hamilton) have a few casual lines. Also, for a couple of seconds, trombonist Frank Rosolino and his combo are on-screen. Elmer Bernstein's score for the film is jazz-oriented.

4 6 *Sweetheart of the Campus*
(1941, 67 minutes)

Ruby Keeler (in her final starring role) teams up with Ozzie Nelson and Harriet Hilliard in this comedy about starting a nightclub on a college campus in order to raise money for the struggling university. Nelson's underrated orchestra plays seven numbers along the way, including "When the Glee Club Swings the Alma Mater," "Where," "Tap Happy," "Here We Go Again" and "Zig Me Baby with a Gentle Zag." There is also a feature for the Spirits of Rhythm starring Leo Watson ("Tom Tom the Elevator Boy").

4 6 *Swing*
(1938, 68 minutes)

Most of the films produced by Black studios in the 1930s and '40s feature amateurish acting, poor editing, stereotypes and a very low budget. **Swing**, by pioneer Black film producer Oscar Micheaux, is no exception, but unlike most of these movies, it has some jazz. The throwaway plot is about a two-timing woman and the preparation for a stage show. However, Leon Gross's orchestra is featured throughout (having a medium-tempo "Dear Old Southland" as its showcase), actress Cora Green sings a few numbers, and blues singer Trixie Smith has a small role (although disappointingly no vocals). Most interesting of all is that the completely unknown trumpeter Doli Armena (who apparently never recorded) is featured on three-chorus versions of "I May Be Wrong" and "Chinatown, My Chinatown" playing hot solos. Whatever happened to her?

🎞️ 🎵 Swing Fever
(1944, 81 minutes)

One of several underrated Kay Kyser films, this one is a bit silly, involving Kyser (as a reluctant hypnotist) with boxers and gangsters. In one funny scene, Kyser's attempt to get his band to play his new modern symphony is interrupted when Tommy Dorsey and Harry James jam a blues for a couple of choruses. Their verbal interplay and put-downs of Kyser are quite funny. Lena Horne pops up for a forgettable number ("You're Indifferent") later in the movie.

🎞️ 🎵 Swing Hostess
(1944, 76 minutes)

Martha Tilton, who sang with Benny Goodman's orchestra during 1937–39, stars in this average film about an out-of-work band singer who works as a switchboard operator for a jukebox company and falls for a bandleader. Among the many songs are "I'll Eat My Hat," "Let's Capture This Moment," "Say It with Love," "Music to My Ears," "Highway Polka" and "Got an Invitation."

🎞️ 🎵 Swing in the Saddle
(1944, 69 minutes)

This low-budget Western musical, which features the Hoosier Hotshots, is about a couple of actresses (one of whom is a mail-order bride) who are mistaken for cooks on a ranch. Near the end of the story, the King Cole Trio (Nat King Cole, Oscar Moore and Wesley Prince), who are otherwise not in the film, plays a heated version of "By the River St. Marie" for three minutes.

🎞️ 🎵 Swing Kids
(1993, 113 minutes)

This is definitely a strange film. A group of German teenagers who love swing music, both as collectors and dancers, are coming of age during the early years of Nazi Germany. Ignoring the peril of their situation, they defy the Nazis not because of any real political differences, but because the Nazis forbid them from listening to swing. There are some spectacular dance scenes in ballrooms and a few happily esoteric moments such as when a couple kids debate over whether Pee Wee Erwin or Bunny Berigan is on a certain Benny Goodman record. But in general, one wonders why the youths are so blind, as the Nazis eventually crack down on them completely. The soundtrack music (which has a liberal dose of Goodman) and the dancing are this movie's only saving graces.

🎞️ 🎵 Swing Parade of 1946
(1946, 75 minutes)

Singer Phil Regan opens a nightclub next door to his straitlaced father's business, while Gale Storm cannot decide whether to serve Regan a foreclosure notice or try out for his show. The Three Stooges and Edward Brophy add to the confusion. Bandleader Will Osborne has a surprisingly major part, but the most interesting music is provided by Louis Jordan and his Tympany Five ("Caldonia" and most of "Don't Worry about the Mule") and Connee Boswell (a lightly swinging "Just a Little Fond Affection" and an overly dramatic "Stormy Weather"). Otherwise, the songs are largely forgettable (though Storm does a good job on "On the Sunny Side of the Street"), and the plot completely runs out long before the movie ends.

🎞️ 🎵 Synanon *(1965, 106 minutes)*

This melodrama is a fictional and somewhat whitewashed account of Synanon, an organization that helped some drug addicts re-enter society. A new resident goes through the treatment, meets up with some colorful characters and has personal difficulties. Eartha Kitt has a major part, while pianist Arnold Ross and bassist Charlie Haden (who were actual residents of Synanon at the time) are among the residents.

🎞️ 🎵 *Syncopation*
(1942, 88 minutes)

Syncopation is a fictional history of jazz movie with some authenticity and lots of good intentions. Jackie Cooper plays a trumpeter who at times seems a little like Bix Beiderbecke and Bunny Berigan (although without the alcohol problems), Bonita Granville (his love interest) is a pianist who can play boogie-woogie and the blues, and Todd Duncan is a trumpeter slightly reminiscent of Louis Armstrong. The story takes place in 1906 New Orleans, 1916 Chicago and throughout the 1920s, with much of the music fitting the period. There is a silly "jazz on trial" scene, Cooper at one point is stuck in a symphonic orchestra (à la Paul Whiteman) and the film ends optimistically. Connee Boswell guests near the end to sing "Fallen Star"(Stan Wrightsman ghosted Granville's piano solos) and Cooper's trumpet playing was performed by either Bunny Berigan (whose decline from alcoholism prevented him having a more active role) or Manny Klein. At the film's conclusion, seven bandleaders who were voted to the Saturday Evening Post All-American Jazz Band jam a blues together: Benny Goodman, Harry James, trombonist Jack Jenney, Charlie Barnet, Joe Venuti, steel guitarist Alvino Rey and Gene Krupa, plus an unseen Howard Smith on piano and Bob Haggart.

🎞️ 🎵 *Talk about a Lady*
(1946, 72 minutes)

Jinx Falkenburg plays a small-town girl who wants to be a singer and inherits both a fortune and a nightclub. The Stan Kenton Orchestra plays "Avocado" (sung by June Christy and Gene Howard), "The Mist Is over the Moon," "I Never Had a Dream Come True" and "You Gotta Do Whatcha Gotta Do." The Kenton band at the time included trumpeters Buddy Childers and Ray Wetzel, tenors Vido Musso and Bob Cooper, and bassist Eddie Safranski.

🎞️ 🎵 *Taxi*
(1932, 68 minutes)

This Jimmy Cagney/Loretta Young melodrama is about rival taxicab companies who battle it out with the assistance of organized crime. In a nightclub scene, the Les Hite Orchestra is seen for a couple of seconds backing two singers on an uptempo "Georgia on My Mind" and are heard in the background on "I Need Lovin'."

🎞️ 🎵 *Tea for Two*
(1950, 97 minutes)

In this film, Doris Day loses her money in the 1929 Wall Street crash, but does not know it and her lawyer does not have the heart to tell her. She offers to finance a revival of "No No Nanette" and then is involved in a plot similar to the show in order to win the money she needs. Day sings such vintage tunes as "I Know that You Know," "Tea for Two," "I Want to Be Happy" and "Oh Me, Oh My" and is sometimes backed by the Ernie Felice Quartet with Felice on accordion, clarinetist Dick Anderson, guitarist Dick Fisher and bassist Rolly Bundock.

🎞️ 🎵 *The Terminal*
(2004, 128 minutes)

Tom Hanks plays an Eastern European who arrives in New York just as his country ceases to exist. Falling through the bureaucratic cracks, he is stuck as a man without a country at an airport terminal for a year, surviving on his wits and making friends among the airport employees. Near the end of this fanciful if partly true film, it is revealed that the reason Hanks came to New York was to fulfill a promise given to his late father that he would get an autograph from Benny Golson, the only musician in the famous "Great Day in Harlem" photograph that his father is missing from his collection. He finally meets up with Golson in one scene, the saxophonist has a few lines and plays three choruses of "Killer Joe" with pianist Mike LeDonne, bassist Buster

Williams and drummer Carl Allen. This is certainly the only Steven Spielberg movie in which the name Max Kaminsky is mentioned!

Texas Carnival
(1951, 75 minutes)

This MGM musical with Red Skelton, Esther Williams, Ann Miller and Howard Keel has its amusing moments although it is a lesser vehicle for the stars. Vibraphonist Red Norvo and guitarist Tal Farlow with an expanded group back Miller on one dance number, but are wasted. Despite reports to the contrary, there is no sign of Charles Mingus (who was a member of Norvo's trio in 1950) in this film.

Thanks a Million
(1935, 85 minutes)

A disappointing musical comedy about politics that features Dick Powell, Fred Allen and Ann Dvorak, this film has Paul Whiteman's Orchestra in the background of some scenes and accompanying Powell's vocals. In the band at the time but not given much of anything to do are Jack Teagarden, Charlie Teagarden, Frankie Trumbauer and pianist Ramona.

That Girl from Paris
(1936, 105 minutes)

This is a frequently funny Lily Pons movie in which the opera star chases Van Johnson, Jack Oakie and their jazz band to New York. Although no jazz musicians appear on-screen, the storyline deals with the struggle of a swing combo to make it, and there is plenty of music heard along the way.

That's My Baby
(1945, 67 minutes)

An interesting plot for a film: the head of a comic magazine constantly suffers from depression. Pianist Gene Rodgers makes an appearance.

Theatre Royal
(1943, 101 minutes)

To save the Theatre Royal from bankruptcy, a prop man organizes the theatre's staff into a successful show. This British comedy has such notables as pianist George Shearing (his earliest appearance on film), trombonist Ted Heath and Victor Feldman, who at the time was a nine-year-old drummer.

They Live by Night
(1948, 96 minutes)

This underrated crime drama starring Farley Granger and Cathy O'Donnell is about a couple trying against all odds to escape the criminal world. Marie Bryant (best remembered for her appearance in **Jamming the Blues**) sings "Your Red Wagon" in one scene.

They Shoot Horses, Don't They?
(1969, 120 minutes)

This is an intriguing if very downbeat Jane Fonda movie about a dance marathon in 1932. Many standards from the period are heard on the soundtrack. The ten-piece band seen on-screen includes Bobby Hutcherson (just appearing as the bandleader), trumpeter Teddy Buckner, trombonist Thurman Green, tenors Harold Land and Teddy Edwards, pianist Ronnell Bright, bassist Ike Isaacs and drummer Joe Harris.

This Could Be the Night
(1957, 103 minutes)

Paul Douglas and Anthony Franciosa are good-natured gangsters who run a nightclub, while Jean Simmons is a shy schoolteacher hired to work as the club's secretary. Ray Anthony and his orchestra (the club's house band) are well featured, with the film including such songs as "This Could Be the Night," "Hustlin' News Gal," "I Got It Bad," "I'm Gonna Live Till I Die," "Taking a Chance on Love," "Trumpet Boogie," "Mamba

Combo," "Blue Moon," "Dream Dancing" and "The Tender Trap."

🎞4 🎵5 *This Joint Is Jumpin'*
(1947, unknown length)

This obscure, all-Black musical features Bob Howard, Una Mae Carlisle, Hadda Brooks and the Phil Moore Four.

🎞7 🎵4 *Thousands Cheer*
(1943, 126 minutes)

A soldier (Gene Kelly) falls in love with his commanding officer's daughter (Kathryn Grayson) with plenty of complications, and helps organize a show for the armed forces. In addition to many MGM stars, a few jazz performers have brief appearances. Kay Kyser's band performs "I Dug a Ditch" and "Should I." Bob Crosby's orchestra is wasted behind the unlikely vocal trio of Virginia O'Brien, June Allyson and Gloria DeHaven on "In a Little Spanish Town." Best is "Honeysuckle Rose," which has Benny Carter and his band playing a swinging half-chorus before backing Lena Horne's singing.

🎞7 🎵5 *Thrill of a Romance*
(1945, 104 minutes)

This is an enjoyable Esther Williams/Van Johnson romantic comedy with plenty of music along the way but very little jazz. The Tommy Dorsey Orchestra functions as the movie's house band, but mostly plays behind dialog so one only hears a tiny bit (and sees even less) of "Song of India," "I Should Care," "Opus No. One" and a few other tunes. TD has a minor role and welcomes his young daughter (actually actress Helene Stanley) to a jazz-oriented version of "Hungarian Rhapsody"; she might be playing piano but is certainly not singing. Of greatest interest is a jam on "I Got Rhythm" that has clarinetist Buddy DeFranco, pianist Joe Bushkin and Buddy Rich (who takes an outstanding two-chorus solo), though that departure from the story lasts less than two minutes.

🎞7 🎵5 *Thunderbolt*
(1929, 86 minutes)

George Bancroft was nominated for a best actor Oscar for this role as a gangster involved in a triangle with Fay Wray and honest Richard Arlen. In a nightclub, Teresa Harris sings "Daddy, Won't You Please Come Home," backed by Curtis Mosby's Blue Blowers. "Thinkin' about My Baby" is also performed.

🎞3 🎵4 *Time Flies*
(1944, 88 minutes)

This British comedy is occasionally amusing, but more often quite dumb. A con man, a theatrical couple and an inventor take a time machine back to the 1600s where they encounter Queen Elizabeth, Sir Walter Raleigh, Shakespeare and Pocahontas. Occasionally the leads break out into song, and at one point they are joined by violinist Stephane Grappelli's group on an unidentified number that progresses quickly from classical music to swing. Grappelli gets twelfth billing but does not have a single line.

🎞6 🎵4 *Too Late Blues*
(1961, 103 minutes)

Bobby Darin and Stella Stevens have an on-again, off-again relationship while Darin tries to keep his jazz combo together in this serious and underrated drama. Slim Gaillard is featured in an early scene while the actors are ghosted by such musicians as trumpeter Uan Rasey, altoist Benny Carter, trombonist Milt Bernhart, pianist Jimmy Rowles, bassist Red Mitchell and drummer Shelly Manne.

🎞6 🎵6 *Top Man*
(1943, 83 minutes)

Donald O'Connor becomes the head of his family when his father is drafted during World War II. To help the cause, he organizes a show for a local factory, and among his stars is the Count Basie Orchestra. **Top Man** (also released as **Man of the Family**) has the Basie band performing a fine version of "Basie Boogie" (which showcases the leader) and backing the Bobby Brooks Quartet (a group similar to the Ink Spots) on "Wrap Your Troubles in Dreams."

Transatlantic Merry-Go-Round
(1934, 92 minutes)

This film is a forgettable romantic comedy set on an ocean liner that stars Gene Raymond, Nancy Carroll and Jack Benny. It is chiefly of interest for featuring the Boswell Sisters on one number, "Rock and Roll."

Trocadero
(1944, 73 minutes)

Rosemary Lane and Johnny Downs star in a minor musical based around a nightclub. There are brief spots for the bands of Gus Arnheim and Bob Chester, while trumpeter Wingy Manone with violinist Matty Malneck's group performs an excerpt from "The Music Goes Round and Round."

Tune in Tomorrow
(1990, 108 minutes)

Barbara Hershey, Keanu Reeves and Peter Falk (who steals most of his scenes) star in this odd comedy, set in 1951 New Orleans, about a soap opera writer who is hired to save a failing radio show, and uses real-life scenes and dialog in the radio series. Wynton Marsalis wrote the score (the soundtrack album is excellent) and makes a couple of cameos with his band.

Twenty Million Sweethearts
(1934, 89 minutes)

Dick Powell, working as a singing waiter, is discovered by fast-talking Pat O'Brien in this humorous musical. O'Brien wants to make Powell a radio star and the idol of women everywhere, but Powell's wife (Ginger Rogers) is not quite sold on the idea. "I'll String Along with You" is one of several excellent Warren and Dubin songs sung by Powell. "How'm I Doin'" features the Mills Brothers with assistance from Powell.

Twilight on the Prairie
(1944, 62 minutes)

A New York cowboy radio band on its way to Hollywood gets stranded in Texas and ends up running a ranch. In addition to quite a bit of Western music, Jack Teagarden has a solid role and is featured on three numbers with his big band, including "The Blues."

Twist All Night
(1961, 85 minutes)

It may not be high art, but this film is quite fun. It features Louis Prima (after he had broken up with Keely Smith), Sam Butera and the Witnesses attempting to capitalize on the Twist dance craze. The plot (which involves keeping a club open) is no big deal, but there is quite a bit of music and several big dance numbers. Prima did not have to adjust his music at all to make it danceable. Among the many songs performed are "The Saints Waltz," "Alright, Okay You Win," "Oh Mama Twist," "Everybody Knows," "The Continental Twist," "Coolin'," "When the Saints Go Marching In," "Sam's Boogie," "Tag That Twistin' Doll," a three-song medley ("When You're Smiling," "I Can't Believe That You're in Love with Me," "I Can't Give You Anything but Love"), "Society Waltz," "Trombone Staccato," "Mood Indigo," "Fool Around," "Better Twist Now Baby" and "Twisting the Blues."

Two Girls and a Sailor
(1944, 124 minutes)

June Allyson and Gloria DeHaven are cast as vaudevillians setting up an entertainment canteen for servicemen. Van Johnson, Jimmy Durante and many guest stars make appearances. Lena Horne sings "Paper Doll," and Harry James and his big band (with Corky Corcoran on tenor) perform "Sweet and Lovely," an excellent version of "Charmaine," "Estrellita," "In a Moment of Madness" (with Helen Forrest), "Young Man with the Horn," and "Inka Dinka Doo" with Durante.

Two Guys from Texas
(1948, 84 minutes)

Jack Carson and Dennis Morgan are reminiscent of Bob Hope and Bing Crosby in this musical comedy, playing two broken-down nightclub entertainers who are stranded on a Texas dude ranch. Early in the film, violinist Joe Venuti is seen playing in a group with guitar, bass and three harmonica players, but he can barely be heard on a brief blues and supporting other acts.

Two Tickets to Broadway
(1951, 106 minutes)

This splashy musical stars Janet Leigh, Tony Martin, Ann Miller and Eddie Brackeen as Broadway hopefuls. Near the end of the movie it becomes their goal to be on the Bob Crosby television show. Crosby has a few lines and sings "Let's Make Comparisons" to a dummy of Bing Crosby.

Un Été Sauvage
(1968, 90 minutes)

This French love story, set in a summer resort during the late '60s, features an adventurous soundtrack (played by a quintet including altoist Marion Brown and vibraphonist Gunter Hampel) and a brief appearance on-screen by bassist Barre Phillips.

Unchained *(1955, 74 minutes)*
Unchained is set in Chino prison and deals with prison reform and life behind bars. Dexter Gordon, who was in prison at the time (due to drugs), has a few lines in this film and appears to play tenor on one song although his playing was actually ghosted by a studio musician. He

would have to wait 30 years before he had a major role in **Round Midnight**.

Uncle Joe Shannon
(1978, 108 minutes)

Burt Young plays a trumpeter whose life collapses after his wife and child are killed in a fire, until it is redeemed by a handicapped child in this overly sentimental story. Maynard Ferguson ghosts for Young who apparently never learned to finger the trumpet. A fair number of musicians pop up on-screen including saxophonist Med Flory (who is seen playing keyboards), trumpeter Al Aarons, bassist Henry Franklin and drummer Mat Marucci.

Uneasy Terms
(1948, 91 minutes)

In this British murder mystery starring Michael Rennie, Ted Heath's band is seen in the nightclub scenes.

The Unsuspected
(1947, 90 minutes)

This memorable murder mystery stars Claude Rains and is well worth seeing. However the jazz can easily be missed if one blinks in the wrong spot. In the opening scene in a nightclub, Jo Jones and a quintet are on-screen for four bars (less than ten seconds), playing "I Got Rhythm."

Urlatori alla Sbarra
(1959, unknown length)

A teenager makes her father, a record company executive, mad by hanging out with a couple of bikers in this Italian rock 'n' roll movie. Chet Baker plays a stoned trumpeter who is constantly nodding off and sings "Arrivederci" in the closing scene.

La Vie Conjugale
(1963, 224 minutes)

This two-part French movie (112 minutes apiece) tells about the disintegration of a marriage between two law

in this musical. There is not much jazz, just Lena Horne on "Where or When" and a definitive version of "The Lady Is a Tramp," plus Mel Tormé faring well on "Blue Moon."

♩ WUSA
(1970, 117 minutes)

Paul Newman moves to New Orleans where he becomes involved with a right-wing radio station in this downbeat drama. The Preservation Hall Jazz Band makes a brief appearance.

♩ Yes Sir, Mr. Bones
(1951, 54 minutes)

A boy visits a home for retired minstrel show performers and in a flashback is told a story about the early days. In the large cast are veteran singer Monette Moore, Emmett Miller and Pete Daily's Chicagoans.

♩ You Can't Have Everything
(1937, 99 minutes)

Alice Faye is a struggling playwright, Don Ameche the man who gets her play produced and Gypsy Rose Lee is his girlfriend. This musical comedy features Louis Prima and his group on "Rhythm on the Radio" and "It's a Southern Holiday."

♩ Young Man with a Horn
(1949, 112 minutes)

This greatly underrated jazz movie stars Kirk Douglas playing a trumpeter (ghosted by Harry James) who struggles to find his own place in the jazz world. Although this story is always said to be inspired by that of Bix Beiderbecke, it actually has nothing in common with Bix's life. Parts of the movie are pretty realistic, at least until a neurotic Lauren Bacall shows up and drives Douglas crazy. Doris Day's vocals are excellent, Hoagy Carmichael has one of his best roles, and Douglas is quite believable as a trumpeter who lives only for his music. Many jazz standards are performed including "Chinatown, My Chinatown," "I Got a Right to Sing the Blues," "Moanin' Low," a Dixielandish "Get Happy," "Too Marvelous for Words," "The Blue Room," "With a Song in My Heart," "I May Be Wrong," "Taking a Chance on Love," "Someone to Watch Over Me" and "Limehouse Blues."

♩ You're a Big Boy Now
(1966, 97 minutes)

This is a coming-of-age comedy that is an early effort by director Francis Ford Coppola. Set in New York City, at one point Rufus Harley is seen playing bagpipes in Central Park.

♩ You're a Sweetheart
(1937, 96 minutes)

The plot may be highly unlikely (involving a scheme to make a half-empty Broadway opening night look sold out), but it is fun. Alice Faye and George Murphy star and there is a generous amount of singing and dancing. The pioneering jazz harpist Casper Reardon has a tiny role and is seen playing.

♩ Zachariah
(1970, 93 minutes)

Imagine Elvin Jones as a gunslinger and Country Joe and the Fish as bank robbers who also play rock music in 1870! This silly Western (which is mostly played straight) also has Pat Quinn as Belle Starr backed by the New York Rock Ensemble. Elvin Jones takes a drum solo on "Camino Waltz," showing that he has the fastest sticks in the West.

7 ♪ *Zig Zag*
(1970, 105 minutes)

George Kennedy is an insurance investigator who learns he is dying. He confesses to a murder he did not commit in order to get the reward for his family, and then, after an operation saves his life, he has to figure out who the real murderer is. Anita O'Day has a small part as a nightclub singer and sings part of "On Green Dolphin Street."

Review Section Three:

Shorts, Television Specials and More Documentaries

 Abbey Lincoln: You Gotta Pay the Band
(1991, 60 minutes)

This PBS documentary features singer Abbey Lincoln performing at a couple of clubs and at a recording session. In addition to the music (which includes her originals "Bird Alone," "I Got Thunder," "People in Me," "Wholey Earth" and "You Gotta Pay the Band" plus her lyrics to "Up Jumped Spring"), Lincoln's life story is told through interviews of her brother, Stan Getz, Hank Jones, Charlie Haden, Linda Hopkins, Ruth Brown, Tony Bennett, Max Roach, Dan Morgenstern, Spike Lee and the singer herself. The talking is informative and clips are shown from Lincoln's film appearances (**The Girl Can't Help It**, **Nothing but a Man**, **For Love of Ivy** and **Mo' Better Blues**). It ties together quite nicely in this well-conceived hour.

Accent on Girls *(1936, 9 minutes)*

See: **All Girl Bands** (page 19)

 Afro-American Music: Its Heritage
(1960, 16 minutes)

This short was made for students in hopes of introducing them to some of the styles of jazz. Pianist Calvin Jackson's quartet with Buddy Collette (on tenor, alto and flute), bassist Dave Robinson and drummer Chuck Flores plays brief musical examples.

After Hours *(1961, 27 minutes)*

See: **After Hours/Jazz Dance** (page 18)

 After Seven *(1929, 15 minutes)*

Blackface comedian James Barton (who starred years later in **A Tree Grows in Brooklyn**) and various dancers are featured in this short. This is a brief sequence in a nightclub in which the Chick Webb Orchestra backs a few dancers. The Webb selection is included on **Jazz Band Ball**.

 An All-Colored Vaudeville Show
(1935, 23 minutes)

Not really a vaudeville show, this short consists of lots of dancing and music. The Three Whippets are quite acrobatic (while wearing cook's outfits) on "Nagasaki," Adelaide Hall sings "To Love You Again" and proves to be a fine dancer too, and the dancing Nicholas Brothers romp on two songs. The Five Racketeers (a quintet with four guitars/ukuleles and a percussionist) are reminiscent of the Spirits of Rhythm, accompanying singer Eunice Wilson on "I Don't Know Why I Feel This Way" and closing the show with an uptempo "Hold That Tiger." This film was reissued in 1946 as **Dixieland Jubilee**, adding a bit of narration along with Cab Calloway and his orchestra performing "Some of These Days."

 All Star Bond Rally
(1944, 19 minutes)

Quite a few Hollywood stars make cameo appearances in this morale-boosting short film which has to do with the Seventh War Loan drive for World War II. Among those appearing are Bob Hope, Harpo Marx, Carmen Miranda,

Joe E. Brown and Martha Raye. Bing Crosby performs "Buy, Buy, Buy a Bond," and Harry James and his orchestra back Frank Sinatra on "Saturday Night."

All Star Swing Festival
(1972, 52 minutes)

The more time that passes, the better this one-hour television special looks. It is an updated version of the Timex specials of the late '50s. The lineup of musicians is amazing and, even though a little too much was packed into the show, most of the stars fare quite well. Hosted by Doc Severinsen, the show begins with Ella Fitzgerald singing "Lady Be Good" backed by the Count Basie Orchestra. Duke Ellington's big band, with Cootie Williams, Harry Carney, trombonist Booty Wood, Russell Procope and Harold Ashby, plays "C Jam Blues" and "It Don't Mean a Thing." Fitzgerald returns to sing "Goody Goody" and "Body and Soul" while accompanied by the Tommy Flanagan Trio. The Dave Brubeck Quartet with Paul Desmond performs "Take Five," the Count Basie big band plays "Jumpin' at the Woodside" (with solos from tenorman Eddie "Lockjaw" Davis and trombonist Al Grey) and Joe Williams (with Basie) sings "Alright, Okay, You Win." One of the high points is a mini-set by the original Benny Goodman Quartet (with Gene Krupa, Lionel Hampton and Teddy Wilson plus bassist George Duvivier) which was their last filmed reunion. After "Avalon" and "Moonglow," the group catches fire on "I'm a Ding Dong Daddy from Dumas." A tribute to the recently deceased Louis Armstrong features Doc Severinsen, Bobby Hackett, Dizzy Gillespie, Max Kaminsky and (all too briefly) Earl Hines, Tyree Glenn, Barney Bigard, Arvell Shaw and Barrett Deems on a medley of Satch's songs ("Sleepy Time Down South," "Blueberry Hill," "Basin Street Blues," "Struttin' with Some Barbecue") before Fitzgerald sings "Hello Dolly," in a close imitation of Armstrong's voice. The memorable show ends with both Basie and Ellington on piano for "One O'Clock Jump."

All-Star Swing Revue
(1983, 90 minutes)

A 1983 tour by an all-star sextet resulted in this concert, which was originally televised on PBS. Clark Terry, Zoot Sims, Teddy Wilson, Red Norvo, Milt Hinton and Louie Bellson are heard in prime form. After the group jams "In a Mellotone," Terry is featured on "God Bless the Child," Norvo sounds fine on "We'll Be Together Again" and Teddy Wilson puts plenty of life into "Stompin' at the Savoy." "Undecided" features the full group, Terry is in the spotlight on "On the Trail," Sims is warm on "Over the Rainbow" and Bellson has a drum solo on "Cotton Tail." Among the other highlights are Wilson on a Gershwin medley and the sextet on "All of Me" before the show concludes with "Jumpin' at the Woodside." This is a strong and swinging program by some of the best.

Always for Pleasure *(1978, 58 minutes)*

This Les Blank film celebrates the music and culture of New Orleans, providing tastes of the city's parades, street celebrations and Mardi Gras. Most of the music (by Professor Longhair, the Neville Brothers and the Wild Tchoupitoulas) is R&B rather than jazz, but there are some brief moments from Harold Dejan's Olympia Brass Band (playing at a funeral), trumpeter Kid Thomas Valentine ("Panama") and Doc Paulin's Jazz Band ("'Lil Liza Jane").

Ambitus *(1967, 16 minutes)*

The avant-garde pianist Cecil Taylor recites a poem in this very obscure French short and performs with his quartet (altoist Jimmy Lyons, bassist Alan Silva and drummer Andrew Cyrille). Although valuable as possibly Taylor's earliest appearance on film, his poetry is definitely an acquired taste.

Ambrosetti's Jazz Family *(2000, 58 minutes)*

The Swiss flugelhornist Franco Ambrosetti, his father saxophonist Flavio Ambrosetti and Franco's son Gianluca, who also plays saxophone, are featured. This documentary shows how they balance their jazz careers with their highly successful "day jobs" as defense contractors.

♪ Amsterdamned Jazz: The Willem Breuker Kollektief
(2000, 52 minutes)

The music of the Willem Breuker Kollektief is often quite cinematic, so it is only right that a documentary be made about the remarkable ensemble. Although avant-garde, Breuker's music often utilizes complex arrangements and is overflowing with humor, some of it obvious and some of it rather abstract. This film about Breuker, which mixes together interviews with excerpts from performances, is generally as entertaining as a typical show by the Kollektief.

♪ And All That Jazz *(1979, 47 minutes)*

The popular trad trumpeter Kenny Ball and his band (with clarinetist Andy Cooper and trombonist John Bennett) play such numbers as "Midnight in Moscow," "St. James Infirmary," "I Shall Not Be Moved" and "When the Saints Go Marching In" in this British film. The band is seen in concert and Ball is interviewed about his early days.

♪ Anita Ellis—For the Record
(1980, 28 minutes)

Anita Ellis was a cabaret rather than jazz singer, but this short is included because her accompanist is pianist Ellis Larkins. In addition to talking about her life, Ellis is featured at a record date performing "Prelude to a Kiss," "Spring Will Be a Little Late this Year," "I Hear Music" and "Sometimes I Feel Like a Motherless Child."

Anything for Jazz *(1980, 25 minutes)*

See: **Three Piano Portraits** (page 133)

♪ Artie Shaw: Time Is All You've Got
(1986, 115 minutes)

This superb documentary by Brigitte Berman won the Oscar for best documentary in 1987, but unfortunately, due to litigation problems, has not been available for viewing by the general public in a decade. The definitive profile of Artie Shaw, this lengthy but always compelling film has extensive interviews with the colorful clarinetist, some vintage footage and interviews with Evelyn Keyes (his seventh wife), Mel Tormé, Buddy Rich, trumpeters Johnny Best and Lee Castle, and Helen Forrest among others. Each of Shaw's bands, retirements and marriages are covered.

♪ Artie Shaw and His Orchestra
(1938, 10 minutes)

The earliest film by Artie Shaw's very popular orchestra features the band performing "Nightmare," "Begin the Beguine," "Let's Stop the Clock" (with Helen Forrest), "Non-Stop Flight" and "Prosschai" (which Tony Pastor sings).

Artie Shaw's Class in Swing *(1939, 9 minutes)*

See: **Swing, Volume One** (page 130)

♪ Artie Shaw's Symphony of Swing
(1939, 10 minutes)

The Artie Shaw Orchestra, which at the time included tenor saxophonist Georgie Auld and drummer Buddy Rich, performs "Alone Together," "Jeepers Creepers" (with Tony Pastor's vocal), "Deep Purple" (with Helen Forrest) and "Lady Be Good." Some trick photography in spots lowers the quality a little, but the music is excellent.

♪ Artistry in Rhythm
(1944, 20 minutes)

Stan Kenton's 1944 orchestra is featured on this short. At the time the band included trumpeters Buddy Childers and Karl George, altoist Boots Mussulli and baritonist Bob Gioga in its personnel along with the leader on piano. The already distinctive big band performs its first hit "Eager Beaver," "Tabby the Cat" (with Anita O'Day), "Siboney," "Taboo," "She's Funny that Way" (a ballad vocal by Gene Howard), "I'm Going Mad for a Pad" (singing by O'Day) and "Memphis Lament."

Auld Lang Syne *(1937, 10 minutes)*

See: **Swing, Volume One** (page 130)

 Banquet of Melody *(1946, 15 minutes)*

In addition to Matty Malneck's group, the Delta Rhythm Boys ("Dem Bones") and Rosa Linda, this Universal short features Peggy Lee on "I Don't Know Enough About You" and "Don't Blame Me."

 Barber Shop Blues
(1933, 9 minutes)

The plot of this short is simple and silly. The Claude Hopkins Orchestra plays in a barbershop, the head barber wins the lottery, and he soon opens up a ridiculously fancy shop, complete with tap dancing barbers (the Four Step Brothers). Along the way the band performs fine versions of "St. Louis Blues," "Nagasaki," and "Careless Love," backing singer Orlando Roberson on a semi-operatic version of "Trees." Surprisingly, pianist Hopkins never gets around to soloing, but there are spots for trumpeter Ovie Alston, clarinetist Edmond Hall, trombonist Fernando Arbello and tenor saxophonist Bobby Sands.

 BBC Voice of Britain
(1935, 56 minutes)

One in a series of documentary films made in the mid-'30s in Great Britain, this one focuses on a variety of performers who were featured on BBC radio. The only interesting jazz-related performances are Nina Mae McKinney singing "Dinah" and Henry Hall's BBC Dance Orchestra's version of "Piccadilly Ride."

 Beat Me Daddy, Eight to the Bar
(1940, 17 minutes)

In this short, Wingy Manone's septet (with trombonist King Jackson and pianist Stan Wrightsman) backs the Fashionaires, Cathlyn Miller, Alphonse Berg, Maxine Grey and Larry Blake on several specialty numbers. The band does get to cut loose a bit on "Ostrich Walk," "Sing, Sing, Sing" and a blues.

 Bennett & Basie Together
(1982, 60 minutes)

Half of this PBS television special has Tony Bennett singing his usual brand of middle-of-the-road pop music and hits, with backing by his trio, pianist Dave McKenna and Count Basie's orchestra; the big band is mostly used as a prop. However, the six opening numbers ("Jumpin' at the Woodside," "Shiny Stockings," "Blues," "April in Paris," "Freddie Green Blues," "Wind Machine") are instrumentals featuring Basie's band in excellent if predictable form.

 Ben Pollack and His Orchestra
(1934, 9 minutes)

This is a disappointing short of the Pollack band filmed a year before it became the Bob Crosby Orchestra. The only jazz moments on the four songs (which include "Mimi," "L'amour, Toujours, L'amour" and "The Beat of My Heart") are on "I've Got the Jitters" where one hears just a touch of Yank Lawson's trumpet. Also in the band at the time are trumpeter Charlie Spivak, trombonist Glenn Miller, clarinetist Matty Matlock, tenorman Eddie Miller, guitarist Nappy Lamare and drummer Ray Bauduc. But nearly all of the time is spent focusing on Doris Robbins (Pollack's girlfriend who is actually not too bad a vocalist), Pollack's terrible singing and dancers. One can understand why the band had a mutiny before the year ended!

 Ben Pollack and His Park Central Orchestra
(1929, 9 minutes)

This legendary short features the 1929 Pollack band with Benny Goodman (doubling on baritone), Jack Teagarden and cornetist Jimmy McPartland playing a medley ("California Here I Come," "Memories" and "The Sweetheart of

Sigma Chi"), "My Kinda Love" (vocals by Pollack and Teagarden) and "Song of the Islands."

🎵 Billboard Girl
(1931, 21 minutes)

Bing Crosby is a magazine salesman who writes to a model whom he admires on a billboard. Her brother sees his letters and sends a response, inviting him to visit. Crosby's surprise appearance upsets the woman's boyfriend and humorous complications arise. Crosby sings "Were You Sincere" and "For You."

🎵 Bill Coleman from Boogie to Funk
(1961, 9 minutes)

This rather brief French short features expatriate American trumpeter Bill Coleman along with trombonist Quentin Jackson, tenor saxophonist Budd Johnson and a French rhythm section in a Paris jazz club playing "Bill, Budd and Butter" and an excerpt from "Colemanology."

🎵 Bill Evans *(1968, 17 minutes)*

The highly influential pianist is seen with his 1968 trio (bassist Eddie Gomez and drummer Arnold Wise) performing "Jade Visions," "Stella by Starlight" and "Emily."

🎵 A Bit of Jazz *(1921, 10 minutes)*

This may be the earliest sound film of a jazz-related group. **A Bit of Jazz** features the Van Eps Trio (banjoist Fred Van Eps, alto saxophonist Nathan Glantz and pianist Frank Banta) performing "Love Nest," "Japanese Sandman," "Whispering," "Swanee" and "Listen to the Mockingbird."

Black and Tan *(1929, 19 minutes)*

See: **Duke Ellington 1929–1943** (page 47)

🎵 The Black Network
(1936, 15 minutes)

Although this Black short is copyrighted in 1936, it appears to be from a few years earlier. The plot revolves around a radio program on which the sponsor's wife wants to sing despite her lack of talent. Featured are Nina Mae McKinney ("Half of Me Wants to Be Good"), the Nicholas Brothers (who sing and dance on "Lucky Numbers") and the Washboard Serenaders (a group that probably consists of Harold Randolph on kazoo, pianist Arthur Brooks, an unknown guitarist and Bruce Johnson on washboard). The latter band performs hot versions of "Dark Eyes" and "St. Louis Blues."

🎵 Blue of the Night
(1932, 20 minutes)

On a train, a woman tells reporters that she is engaged to Bing Crosby. Crosby happens to be aboard, plays along with her and eventually has to prove that he is really Bing by singing "Where the Blue of the Night." He

Jazz singer Bing Crosby is seen here in 1932, the same year he filmed *Blue of the Night*.

also croons "My Silent Love," "Auf Wiedersehen My Dear," "Every Time My Heart Beats" and "There'll Be a Hot Time in the Old Time Tonight" during this Mack Sennett short.

Blues for Central Avenue
(1986, 50 minutes)

This interesting documentary focuses on both the life of singer Ernie Andrews (who found success early on before going through a period of neglect) and the Los Angeles Central Avenue scene of the 1940s. Andrews, who sings "'Round Midnight" and excerpts from a couple of blues, discusses his early life and points out where some of the legendary L.A. clubs used to be. Also interviewed along the way are singer Herb Jeffries, multireedist Buddy Collette, pianist Eddie Beal, Harry "Sweets" Edison, Andrews's wife Delores, pianist Nat Pierce, drummer Frank Capp and several former clubowners. Upon its release, the film was valuable in giving some overdue attention to the legacy of Central Avenue, and it resulted in Los Angeles's vintage jazz scene finally being documented more fully.

Bob Crosby and His Orchestra
(1938, 10 minutes)

At the time that they recorded this film short, the Bob Crosby Orchestra was particularly strong, with Billy Butterfield, Yank Lawson and Charlie Spivak as its trumpet section and such fine soloists as trombonist Warren Smith, clarinetist Matty Matlock, tenor saxophonist Eddie Miller and pianist Bob Zurke. The band (and occasionally its leader/vocalist) is featured on concise versions of "How'd Ja Like to Love Me," "Moments Like This," "Romance in the Dark" and most notably "Pagan Love Song."

Bobby Hackett Sextet *(1962, 24 minutes)*

See: **Jazz Festival Vol. 1** and **Jazz Festival Vol. 2** (pages 74–75)

Boogie Woogie Blues
(1948, 10 minutes)

In this short, Hadda Brooks sings and plays piano on "Don't Take Your Love from Me," "Don't You Think I Ought to Know" and "I'm Tired of Everything but You."

Boogie Woogie Dream *(1941, 13 minutes)*

See: **Boogie Woogie** (page 28)

Bound to Be Heard
(1972, 52 minutes)

Also known as **Crusade for Jazz**, this documentary features the Stan Kenton Orchestra during a tour, on the bus and onstage. Kenton (who narrates much of the film) and some of his sidemen talk about the music they love, their joys and their struggles.

The Boy from New Orleans
(1970, 53 minutes)

A variety of footage of performances, interviews and rehearsals is used in this tribute to Louis Armstrong. Taken from Satch's last year (mostly from an October 1970 concert in England), he is featured with Tyree Glenn, clarinetist Danny Moss, bassist Arthur Watts and drummer Eric Delauney, not only singing but playing a little bit of trumpet. Armstrong performs "When It's Sleepy Time Down South," "Boy from New Orleans," "Pretty Little Missy," "Blueberry Hill," "What a Wonderful World," "Mack the Knife" and "Hello Dolly." In addition, Tony Bennett, who is joined by Ruby Braff and pianist John Bunch, sings "They All Laughed" and "I'll Begin Again."

Bright and Breezy
(1956, 16 minutes)

This later Charlie Barnet short features the saxophonist (who was only playing part-time during the era) with a big band (mostly studio musicians) and vocalists. They whiz through eight songs in 16 minutes: "Redskin

Rhumba,""Skyliner,""You Were Meant for Me,""Lullaby of Birdland,""Smooth Sailing,""Shadrack,""Easy Street" and "Open Up Your Heart."

♪ Bubbling Over
(1934, 20 minutes)

This Black short film is largely forgettable except for the contributions of Ethel Waters who is featured on "Harlem Express,""Taking Your Time" and the unfortunate "Darkies Never Cry."

♪ Buddy Rich and His Orchestra
(1948, 15 minutes)

The short-lived Buddy Rich big band of the mid-to-late '40s was open to the influence of bebop. They are seen performing seven songs, including "Burn" (with vibraphonist Terry Gibbs), "Let's Get Away from It All" (featuring the Mello-Larks), "John Had the Number," "But No Nickle" (which has a Rich vocal) and "One O'Clock Boogie." Tenor saxophonist Allan Eager is one of the band's key soloists. In addition, Rich tap dances on "Swingin' the Blues" and takes an explosive drum solo on "Not So Quiet Please." The last song and "Burn" have been released on **Swing: Best of the Big Bands, Vol. 4**.

♪ Buddy Rich and His Orchestra
(1948, 15 minutes)

Buddy Rich's bebop big band plays three numbers in this entry from the *Thrills of Music* series. Rich dances on "Great Head," sings a duet with Betty Bonney on "A Man Can Be a Wonderful Thing" and solos on "Kicks with Sticks."

♪ A Bundle of Blues
(1933, 9 minutes)

The Duke Ellington Orchestra plays brief versions of "Lightnin'" and "Rockin' in Rhythm" (trombonist Tricky Sam Nanton has a solo on the latter), has a full-length feature for Ivie Anderson on "Stormy Weather" (Arthur Whetsol and Lawrence Brown get solos) and backs a couple of dancers on "Bugle Call Rag." In the band at the time were Whetsol, Cootie Williams, Freddie Jenkins, Nanton, Brown, Juan Tizol, Barney Bigard, Otto Hardwicke, Johnny Hodges, Harry Carney, Ellington, Wellman Braud and Sonny Greer, with Benny James substituting for Fred Guy on guitar.

♪ But Then, She's Betty Carter
(1980, 52 minutes)

Filmed in 1980 shortly before she was finally discovered and celebrated, the adventurous vocalist Betty Carter is seen performing at Howard University, talking with Lionel Hampton about the early days of bebop and singing "Most Gentlemen Don't Like Love." She also discusses the struggle of being a highly individual jazz singer.

♪ By Request
(1935, 10 minutes)

This lesser-known short features the 1935 Claude Hopkins big band, an ensemble with such fine players as trumpeter Ovie Alston, trombonist Fred Norman, clarinetist Edmond Hall, altoist Hilton Jefferson, tenor saxophonist Bobby Sands and the leader on stride piano. The band, with singer Orlando Roberson and dancers Tip, Tap and Toe, perform "California, Here I Come,""Chasing My Blues Away,""Chinatown, My Chinatown,""I Would Do Anything for You," a medley of "A Quarter to Nine" and "Shine," and "To Call You My Own."

♪ Cab Calloway's Hi-De-Ho
(1934, 10 minutes)

This amusing short has Cab Calloway fooling around with the wife of a train porter, magically appearing whenever his band plays on the radio. Along the way he performs "Harlem Camp Meeting,""Zaz-Zuh-Zah" and "The Lady with the Fan." This film is not to be confused with the 1937 short **Hi-De-Ho** or Calloway's full-length 1947 movie **Hi-De-Ho**.

Cab Calloway's Jitterbug Party *(1935, 8 minutes)*

See: **Meet the Bandleaders** (Swingtime Video 112) (page 101)

(page 101)

 Cachao! Como Se Ritmo No Hay Dos
(His Rhythm Is Like No Other) (1993, 112 minutes)

This loving film, directed by Andy Garcia, led to the rediscovery and comeback of Cuban bassist Israel "Cachao" Lopez. In addition to summing up his life and vastly underrated accomplishments, the documentary has highlights from an all-star concert featuring altoist Paquito D'Rivera, trumpeter Chocolate Armenteros, flutist Nestor Torres, Gloria Estefan and Cachao himself.

 Caldonia
(1945, 18 minutes)

Louis Jordan and his Tympany Five are featured on this short. The plot is forgettable, but the performances ("Caldonia," "Honey Chile," "Tillie" and "Buzz Me") are enjoyable, showing once again that Jordan was equally talented as a musician/singer and a showman.

 Campus Capers
(1941, 18 minutes)

This obscure Universal music short features Jack Teagarden and his big band in a supportive role. They back vocalist Susan Miller on "Stormy Weather" and "Walk with Me" and accompany a variety of other singers, dancers and comedians.

 Carnegie Hall Salutes the Jazz Masters
(1994, 90 minutes)

Filmed as part of the PBS **Great Performances** series, this show is a tribute to Verve Records. When it first aired, it was criticized for emphasizing Verve's then-current roster of players at the expense of the players who were no longer on their roster, and for not having more jam session numbers. But now with the passing of so many of the greats who are on the show, this concert film grows in value and becomes more historic with each year. Herbie Hancock and singer Vanessa Williams are the hosts, and many stars are featured along the way. An opening version of "Tea for Two" goes through three tempos and has spots for Hancock, trombonist J.J. Johnson, Joe Henderson and guitarist Kenny Burrell. Many of the other songs serve as tributes to earlier Verve artists, most of whom are shown in brief film clips. Pianist Hank Jones is featured on "Willow Weep for Me," Dee Dee Bridgewater (with pianist Renee Rosnes and the Carnegie Hall Jazz Band) performs "Shiny Stockings" and "Just One of Those Things," guitarist John McLaughlin and Hancock duet on "Turn Out the Stars," and Betty Carter (with trumpeter Roy Hargrove) hints at Ella Fitzgerald during "How High the Moon." Antonio Carlos Jobim (in one of his last performances) sings and plays piano on "Desafinado" with the assistance of Henderson, guitarist Pat Metheny, bassist Charlie Haden and drummer Al Foster. Jimmy Smith performs "Walk on the Wild Side." A token fusion number, "It's About That Time," is played by Hancock, McLaughlin, tenor saxophonist Gary Thomas, keyboardists Jeff Lorber and Renee Rosnes and others. "The Eternal Triangle" is a jam for Hargrove, altoist Jackie McLean and Metheny in a sextet. Abbey Lincoln (with J.J. Johnson and Hank Jones) sings "I Must Have That Man." Hargrove, Steve Turre (on conch shells) and percussionist Don Alias are featured on "Manteca," and "Call It '94" has Hancock, altoist Art Porter, Gary Thomas, Hargrove and Lorber getting funky. The long show concludes with a jam session version of "Now's the Time" that has trade-offs by Ray Brown and Christian McBride on basses, Hancock and Hank Jones on pianos, Henderson with Hargrove, Burrell with drummer Omar Hakim, and Betty Carter with J.J. Johnson and McLean.

 Catalina Interlude
(1948, 17 minutes)

Although this short has a plot about a private detective tracking down a runaway female (Virginia Maxey) who wants to become a band singer, it is used largely as an excuse to show some pretty scenery from Catalina Island and to feature Jimmy Dorsey's band. "Muskrat Ramble" is played by a Dixieland combo out of Dorsey's orchestra including the leader on clarinet, trumpeter Charlie Teagarden, trombonist Brad Gowans and drummer Ray Bauduc. Maxey sings "Hit the Road to Dreamland," "Catalina" and "My Ideal," and the full Dorsey orchestra performs "Perfidia."

Celebrating a Jazz Master: Thelonious Sphere Monk
(1986, 75 minutes)

Quite a cast was assembled on October 6, 1986, to pay homage to pianist/composer Thelonious Monk, who passed away four years earlier. Featured in various combinations on this PBS special are Dizzy Gillespie ("Bebop"), David Amram (on pennywhistle), Gerry Mulligan ("'Round Midnight"), Wynton Marsalis ("Raised Fourth"), Jon Hendricks ("Rhythm-A-Ning"), Branford Marsalis ("I Mean You"), altoist Marshall Keys, pianists Billy Taylor, Walter Davis, Jr., Herbie Hancock ("Blue Monk"), Ellis Marsalis, Cyrus Chestnut, Marcus Roberts and Kenny Kirkland, bassists Percy Heath, Ron Carter, Delbert Felix, Bob Hurst and Victor Gaskin, drummers Jeff "Tain" Watts, Lewis Nash and Roy Haynes and singer Urszula Dudziak (on an odd version of "Well You Needn't" with electronics) among others. Although one misses Monk (none of the pianists really capture his sound), this lengthy concert (which has comments from many of the participating musicians) holds one's interest.

Celebrating Bird: The Triumph of Charlie Parker
(1987, 58 minutes)

Filmed as part of the **Masters of American Music** series and released in conjunction with Gary Giddins's excellent book of the same name, **Celebrating Bird** is a definitive portrait of Charlie Parker. Giddins, who wrote and directed this documentary, uses all of the available silent

film of the great altoist effectively, and concludes the work by showing the complete film clip (**Stage Entrance**) of Charlie Parker and Dizzy Gillespie receiving a Downbeat award from a moderately prejudiced and somewhat befuddled Earl Wilson and Leonard Feather in 1952. Bird says a few words and then they launch into a brilliant version of "Hot House" (with pianist Dick Hyman, bassist Sandy Block and drummer Charlie Smith). Among the people interviewed are Jay McShann, Dizzy Gillespie, Leonard Feather, Roy Haynes, Frank Morgan, Roy Porter and two of Bird's wives: Rebecca Parker Davis and Chan Parker. Familiar and little-known stories are combined to cover the entire life and career of Charlie Parker, who despite his personal problems, emerges as a triumphant genius.

Charles Lloyd—Journey Within
(1968, 58 minutes)

In 1968, Charles Lloyd led one of the most popular groups in jazz, a post-bop unit that often performed at rock palaces. This documentary has its interesting moments and features Lloyd on tenor and flute with his group (pianist Keith Jarrett, bassist Ron McClure and drummer Jack DeJohnette) at several different concerts, playing such numbers as "Sombrero Sam," "Voice in the Night," "Pre-Dawn" and their hit "Forest Flower."

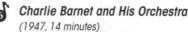 Charlie Barnet and His Band
(1949, 11 minutes)

In 1949, Charlie Barnet's orchestra was quite bop-oriented. This short has the band (with trumpeter Doc Severinsen, pianist Claude Williamson, bassist Ed Safranski and drummer Cliff Leeman) performing "Redskin Rhumba," "Atlantic Jump" and "My Old Flame."

Charlie Barnet and His Orchestra
(1947, 14 minutes)

Charlie Barnet's 1947 swing big band, with singers and dancers, performs "I'll Remember April," "No Can Do,"

"You're a Sweetheart,""Rhumba Fantasy" and "I Believe in Miracles." Best is the closing "Murder at Peyton Hall," which features trumpeter Shorty Rogers and guitarist Barney Kessel.

Charlie Barnet and His Orchestra
(1948, 11 minutes)

The Charlie Barnet big band (with pianist Claude Williamson) plays "Pompton Turnpike" "Stormy Weather" and "Civilization."

Chasing a Snake
(1984, 60 minutes)

This intriguing documentary, made by the BBC and aired on the Arts & Entertainment Network, focuses on Wynton Marsalis, who was just 23 at the time. Marsalis is seen playing baroque music with a symphony orchestra, rehearsing at home and performing in a New York club. Marsalis is typically articulate in expressing his viewpoints, a little arrogant in spots but also largely charming. One of the main topics is the difference between classical music (which he calls the Western art form of the past) and jazz (music of the present). The trumpeter's mother (Dolores Marsalis), father (pianist Ellis Marsalis), classical teacher (Dr. Bert Braud) and Art Blakey comment on aspects of Wynton's life. The hour concludes with a ten-minute original uptempo blues featuring Marsalis playing many ensembles with his brother tenor saxophonist Branford Marsalis, pianist Kenny Kirkland, bassist Charles Fambrough and drummer Jeff "Tain" Watts. This film gives viewers a snapshot of where Wynton Marsalis was, musically and in his state of mind, in 1984.

Chick Corea *(1971, 32 minutes)*

Around the time that they were recording **A.R.C.** for ECM, Chick Corea, bassist Dave Holland and drummer Barry Altschul (who, with Anthony Braxton, were all members of Circle) were captured on film for this West German production. The musicians play together a bit in the studio and talk about their lives in music.

Choo Choo Swing
(1943, 13 minutes)

This short from Universal (which was reissued in 1949 as **Band Parade**) is most notable for featuring the Count Basie Orchestra on "Choo Choo Swing," "Swingin' the Blues" and "The Band Parade." Jimmy Rushing sings "Sent for You Yesterday but Here You Come Today," and there are spots for the Bobby Brooks Quartet, the Delta Rhythm Boys and the Layson Brothers. The Basie band at the time included Buck Clayton, Harry "Sweets" Edison, Snooky Young, Buddy Tate, Don Byas and Dickie Wells.

Chris Barber Jazz Band
(1956, 16 minutes)

Trombonist Chris Barber's trad band (with trumpeter Pat Halcox, clarinetist Monty Sunshine, a pianoless rhythm section and singer Ottilie Patterson) performs "Lead Me On," "Poor Man's Blues" and "Lord You've Sure Been Good to Me."

Claude Thornhill and His Orchestra
(1947, 10 minutes)

The 1947 Claude Thornhill Orchestra (which includes clarinetist Danny Polo and guitarist Barry Galbraith) plays "A Sunday Kind of Love" (a hit for singer Fran Warren), "Oh You Beautiful Doll" (featuring a vocal from Gene Williams) and "Arabian Dance."

Claude Thornhill and His Orchestra
(1950, 15 minutes)

By 1950 pianist Thornhill's big band was past its prime although still quite musical. This short from Universal features the orchestra with vocals by the Snowflakes, Marion Colby and Joaquin Garay in addition to one song from banjoist Nappy Lamare's Straw Hat Strutters (which has valve trombonist Brad Gowans and tenorman Pud

Brown). The selections include "Poor Lil," "Temptation," "Sweet and Lovely" and "Everything Is Latin in the USA."

Clint Eastwood: Piano Blues
(2003, 90 minutes)

The seventh and final part of the PBS project **Martin Scorsese Presents the Blues—A Musical Journey** was directed by Clint Eastwood and is the most jazz-oriented project in the series. Rather than attempt to trace the history of the blues piano chronologically, Eastwood conducted interviews at the piano with a few notable survivors, mostly discussing their original inspirations for playing piano and the blues. His subjects all have an opportunity to play and sing a bit, and there are many vintage film clips of them as well as earlier players. Ray Charles, Dave Brubeck (who plays an emotional minor-toned blues), Dr. John, Marcia Ball, Pinetop Perkins, Henry Gray, Jay McShann and Pete Jolly are all featured. Among those seen in films are Albert Ammons and Pete Johnson, Martha Davis, Dorothy Donegan, Duke Ellington, Charles Brown, Oscar Peterson, Nat King Cole, Professor Longhair (a classic version of "Tipitina"), Fats Domino, Otis Spann (outstanding on "Tain't Nobody's Business" and "Blues Don't Like Nobody"), Phineas Newborn and Count Basie. Some of the clips are just excerpts, but generally they are long enough to give viewers a good idea as to how the pianists sounded. The rarest performance, of Art Tatum playing "Humoresque" sometime in the 1950s, is partly talked over by Ray Charles (it should have been shown complete), and the last ten minutes of this documentary could have been cut due to repetition. But overall this is an admirable and heartfelt effort. It is thus far only available as part of the entire series on a seven-DVD set from www.pbs.org.

Close Farm-ony
(1932, 9 minutes)

The Boswell Sisters (Connie, Martha and Vet) show how jazz can help increase the productivity and improve the spirit of animals at a farm. They perform three hot obscure numbers ("Hittin' the Hay-Hey," "Give, Cow, Give," "The Little Red Barn Is a Red-Hot Barnyard Now") for an elderly farm couple and a variety of happy animals during this memorable short.

Connee Boswell and Les Brown
(1950, 15 minutes)

The Les Brown Orchestra (with clarinetist Abe Most, Dave Pell on tenor, trombonist Ray Sims and drummer Jack Sperling) back the Moon Mists, the Dale Sisters and the team of Teddy and Phyllis Rodriguez. But the obvious high points are Connee Boswell's two numbers: "I Don't Know Why" and a classic rendition of "Martha," which she had recorded more than a decade earlier with Bob Crosby.

Connee Boswell and Ada Leonard
(1952, 14 minutes)

Although singer Connee Boswell gets first billing, this short from Universal is more of a variety show, with Ada Leonard's "all-girl" orchestra featured on "El Cubanchero" and supporting several acts. Pianist Freddie Slack's trio plays "Pig Foot Pete," violinist Anita Aros performs some classical music, and there is some so-so comedy from Bob Hopkins. Boswell is showcased on "Come on and Smile in the Sunshine" and "Basin Street Blues."

Cool and Groovy
(1956, 15 minutes)

This wide-ranging short features several interesting groups. The original Chico Hamilton Quintet (comprised of Buddy Collette on clarinet, guitarist Jim Hall, cellist Fred Katz, bassist Carson Smith and drummer Hamilton) plays "A Nice Day." Clarinetist Buddy DeFranco's quartet (with pianist Pete Jolly, bassist Bob Bertaux and drummer Bob White) performs "I'll Remember April" and backs Anita O'Day on "Honeysuckle Rose," two years before her famous version at the Newport Jazz Festival. In addition, the Hi-Los are featured on "Jeepers Creepers," the Conley Graves Trio plays "Conley's Blues" and the Tune Jesters sing "Jericho" and "Dry Bones."

 ### The Cotton Club Remembered
(1985, 55 minutes)

Part of the **Great Performances** series on PBS, this hour was filmed just in time while there were still some key performers from the Cotton Club of the 1930s around. Billy Taylor is the narrator, some historic clips are shown, and all of the key performers have opportunities to reminisce. In addition, a house band backs tap dancer Chuck Green on a few numbers, and there are features for the Nicholas Brothers (who sing "I've Got a Gal in Kalamazoo" and "Chattanooga Choo Choo"), vocalist Adelaide Hall ("Creole Love Call" and "When a Woman Loves a Man"), trumpeter Doc Cheatham with drummer Max Roach ("Cotton Tail") and Cab Calloway ("Get Happy," "It Ain't Necessarily So" and "Blues in the Night"). Cheatham concludes the program by singing and playing "I Guess I'll Get the Papers and Go Home."

 ### The Cradle Is Rocking
(1968, 12 minutes)

This rare film, made by the U.S. Information Agency, profiles New Orleans trumpeter Kid Sheik Cola. He reminisces and plays briefly with his Storyville Jazz Band.

 ### Crazy Frolic
(1953, 19 minutes)

Les Brown's orchestra (with tenor saxophonist Dave Pell) is featured on "Ramona," "It's Bigger than Both of Us" and "Montana Express," and accompanies singers Eileen Wilson and Robert Monet, the dancing Dupree Trio, and acrobat Wayne Marlin. Lucy Ann Polk (the band's regular singer) is in winning form on "It's a Good Day."

 ### Dance Demons
(1957, 14 minutes)

Along with some other acts, Les Brown's Band of Renown gets to swing, accompanying Butch Stone on "Let's Talk About a Party," Jo Ann Greer on "Moonlight in Vermont" and a famous comedy dance routine by Stumpy Brown and Butch Stone.

Dancing to a Different Drummer
(1994, 80 minutes)

Drummer Chico Hamilton has had a fascinating and very productive career. He was a member of the original Gerry Mulligan Quartet in 1952 and lead a series of chamber jazz quintets during 1955–64 that featured the likes of Buddy Collette, Fred Katz, Jim Hall, Paul Horn, Eric Dolphy, Gabor Szabo and Charles Lloyd. He has stayed contemporary and in the 1990s headed an adventurous modern jazz group called Euphoria. This well-meaning documentary mostly features Hamilton in the present day playing with Euphoria, traveling around Europe and commenting on anything that comes to mind. There are brief appearances from Gerry Mulligan, producer George Avakian, Rolling Stones drummer Charlie Watts, Andrew Hill and director Roman Polanski, and a couple of short excerpts from Hamilton's quintets of 1955 and 1959 (with Eric Dolphy seen briefly on clarinet). Unfortunately, the film never bothers to tell Hamilton's story in any coherent chronological sequence, no selections are shown complete (which is inexcusable considering the rare clips from the 1950s), and such obvious interview choices as Collette, Hall, Lloyd and Arthur Blythe (who is never mentioned) are overlooked. The results are interesting but far short of definitive.

 ### Date with Dizzy
(1956, 10 minutes)

This humorous short finds Dizzy Gillespie and his group (baritonist Sahib Shihab, pianist Wade Legge, bassist

Nelson Boyd and drummer Charlie Persip) trying to create the music for a cartoon commercial that advertises an instant rope ladder.

♪⁶ A Date with Duke
(1947, 7 minutes)

In this worthwhile George Pal puppetoon, Duke Ellington interacts with animated puppets and plays excerpts from his "Perfume Suite," particularly "Balcony Serenade" and "Dancers in Love." Some of his band members (including Oscar Pettiford and Sonny Greer) are on the soundtrack, but Ellington is the only musician on-screen, and he seems to be enjoying himself.

♪⁷ Dave Brubeck: Live at the Vineyards
(1982, 59 minutes)

The 1982 version of the Dave Brubeck Quartet (with tenor saxophonist Jerry Bergonzi, Chris Brubeck on electric bass and bass trombone, and drummer Randy Jones) is featured during a concert at the Paul Masson Winery. Brubeck is typically adventurous, and it is interesting to hear the John Coltrane–inspired tenor of Bergonzi in the group. The repertoire includes "Music Maestro Please," "Peace of Jerusalem," "Tritonis," "Paper Moon," "Black & Blue," "St. Louis Blues" and "I Hear a Rhapsody." In addition, there are a few brief interview segments and an excerpt of "Take Five" by the Brubeck quartet (with Paul Desmond) taken from Ralph Gleason's **Jazz Casual** series.

♪⁷ Dave Brubeck: Moscow Night
(1989, 60 minutes)

Dave Brubeck is featured in 1989 (with clarinetist Bill Smith, Chris Brubeck and Randy Jones) in Moscow performing "St. Louis Blues," "Tritonis," "Koto Song," "Take Five" and "Blue Rondo à la Turk." There are a few brief interview segments between the songs, but otherwise this is a regular performance film, and it is never particularly obvious that the Brubeck quartet is performing in Moscow. The musicians are all in fine form.

♪⁷ Deep Purple
(1949, 15 minutes)

Gene Krupa's orchestra was at its most bopish when it filmed this 1949 short. Frank Rosolino plays trombone and scats on his feature "Lemon Drop," tenor saxophonist Buddy Wise has his spots, and the band is showcased on "Deep Purple," "Bop Boogie" and "Melody in F." The orchestra also backs acrobats on "Acrobatic Boogie."

♪⁶ De L'Autre Cote du Chemin de Fer
(1967, 20 minutes)

This very obscure French short film (which translates as **The Other Side of the Tracks**) features the avant-garde pianist Cecil Taylor talking about his music and rehearsing with altoist Jimmy Lyons, bassist Alan Silva and drummer Andrew Cyrille during a period of time when he rarely recorded.

♪⁶ Deviled Hams
(1937, 10 minutes)

Set in hell before a silly-looking devil and his followers, this short features some novelty vocals (including Satan singing "Rockin' Chair") and dance numbers. It also has a single jump number from the Erskine Hawkins Orchestra with brief spots for the leader, trumpeter Dud Bascomb, tenor saxophonist Paul Bascomb, baritonist Heywood Henry and probably altoist Jimmy Mitchelle (though pianist Avery Parrish is unfortunately not seen). This is one of the few film appearances by the popular Erskine Hawkins band.

♪⁷ Dewey Redman: Dewey Time
(2000, 89 minutes)

The vastly underrated tenor saxophonist Dewey Redman is profiled during this well-conceived documentary. Among those interviewed are Redman, his son Joshua Redman, Joe Lovano and Michael Brecker.

Dexter Gordon Quartet: Jazz at OSU
(1979, 57 minutes)

Three years after making his triumphant return to the United States, veteran tenor saxophonist Dexter Gordon was captured on this hour-long performance filmed for public television. Joined by pianist Albert Dailey, bassist Rufus Reid and drummer Eddie Gladden, Gordon is featured on soprano sax during an unidentified song and then switches to his customary tenor for lengthy versions of a cooking "Secret Love," "Come Rain or Come Shine" and his medium-tempo blues "Long Tall Dexter." Dexter Gordon is heard throughout in good humor and in his playing prime.

 Disneyland After Dark
(1962, 46 minutes)

This entry from **The Wonderful World of Disney** television series features Walt Disney at Disneyland welcoming Annette Funicello, Bobby Rydell, the Osmond Brothers (in their television debut) and other acts. Of greatest interest is a reunion of Louis Armstrong with Kid Ory and banjoist Johnny St. Cyr (all three had been in Satch's Hot Five during 1925–27) plus clarinetist Paul Barnes, pianist Harvey Brooks, drummer Alton Redd, trumpeter Andrew Blakeney and singer Monette Moore. They perform "Kansas City" (which has a Monette Moore vocal), "Up the Lazy River," "Muskrat Ramble" (the only song from the Hot Five days) and "Bourbon Street Parade."

Dixieland Jubilee *(1946, 15 minutes)*

See: **An All-Colored Vaudeville Show** (page 214)

 Dizzy *(2001, 120 minutes)*

This extended biography, which was made for the Arts & Entertainment network, focuses on the life of Dizzy Gillespie. His story is well told through the comments of Benny Carter, Frank Wess, writer Scott Yanow, Lionel Hampton, Jean Bach, James Moody, Wynton Marsalis, photographer William Gottlieb, Jimmy Heath, Jon Faddis, Slide Hampton, drummer Joe Harris, Ray Brown, Claudio Roditi, bassist John Lee, Annie Ross, Lorraine Gordon and Gillespie himself. Quite a few film and performance clips are shown, but all are excerpts. Less talking and more music would have increased the impact of this film although overall it is successful.

 Dizzy Gillespie
(1965, 22 minutes)

Director Les Blank's first work, this short documentary features Dizzy Gillespie performing at the Lighthouse with his quintet (tenor saxophonist James Moody, pianist Kenny Barron, bassist Chris White and drummer Rudy Collins), playing briefly with Stan Kenton's Neophonic Orchestra and talking about his music.

 Dizzy Gillespie: A Night in Havana
(1988, 82 minutes)

Dizzy Gillespie, who with conga player Chano Pozo helped to found Afro-Cuban (or Latin) jazz in 1947, first visited Cuba in 1979. This documentary features him during his return visit in 1985 and afterwards in an interview reflecting on his experience. The great trumpeter is seen playing, dancing and thoroughly enjoying himself in Havana during his happy return; he even meets a friendly Fidel Castro. One gets the impression from watching this film that Cubans are all happy, musical and somewhat joyous, even those living in poverty. Despite its naivety, the film is informative in spots and has some worthwhile music. However, its two most exciting pieces, a version of "A Night in Tunisia" by Gillespie's regular group with guest trumpeter Arturo Sandoval and a big band rendition of "Manteca" with Sandoval and pianist Gonzalo Rubalcaba, are temporarily interrupted by Dizzy's comments; they should have been shown complete. In addition, there is a good version of "Gee Baby Ain't I Good to You." Gillespie's regular sextet of the time included baritonist/clarinetist

Sayyad Abdul Al-Kahbyyr (who hits some ridiculous high notes on baritone) and pianist Walter Davis, Jr. Both Sandoval (who is well featured) and Rubalcaba are impressive. Even Dizzy plays better here than he usually did in the 1980s, and there are enough humorous moments throughout the film to keep one smiling.

Django Reinhardt
(1958, 21 minutes)

Made much too late (five years after the death of the rarely filmed guitarist), this French tribute has some music from such Django Reinhardt alumni and friends as Stephane Grappelli, clarinetist Hubert Rostaing, altoist André Ekyan, bassist Eugene Vees and Django's brother guitarist Joseph Reinhardt.

Don Redman and His Orchestra
(1934, 10 minutes)

The Don Redman Big Band performs a spirited rendition of "Yeah Man," "I'll Wind" (with Harlan Lattimore singing), "Nagasaki" (backing the dancing and singing of Red and Struggles) and "Why Should I Be Tall," the latter a philosophical talking vocal by Redman. Unfortunately, Redman does not play any instruments at all, sticking to conducting the band and singing. The Redman orchestra at the time included trumpeter Sidney DeParis, trombonists Benny Morton and Quentin Jackson, and tenor saxophonist Bob Carroll.

Dorsey Brothers Encore *(1953, 16 minutes)*

Shortly after Jimmy Dorsey broke up his big band and joined forces with his brother Tommy (after 18 years of having separate careers), the new Dorsey Brothers Orchestra made this worthwhile short. The Dorseys jam a Dixieland version of "Muskrat Ramble," back singer Gordon Polk on "Ain't She Sweet," perform "Street Scene Theme," romp with singer Lynn Roberts on "Yes Indeed" and revisit "Well Git It." The latter two songs are available on **Swing: Best of the Big Bands, Vol. 2**.

Dream House *(1931, 19 minutes)*

One of six Mack Sennett shorts that Bing Crosby filmed during 1931–32, this bit of silliness has him playing a singing plumber who has to overcome both his girlfriend's mother and a lion. Along the way he croons "When I Take My Sugar to Tea," "It Must Be True," "Merrily We Roll Along" and "Dream House."

Drummer Man *(1947, 15 minutes)*

The Gene Krupa Orchestra is in swinging and even bopish form during this short. The very popular drummer and his band (which includes altoist Charlie Kennedy, tenor saxophonist Buddy Wise and singer Carolyn Grey) perform "Lover," "Boogie Blues," "Stompin' at the Savoy," "Blanchette" and "Leave Us Leap." "Lover" and "Leave Us Leap" are on **Swing: Best of the Big Bands, Vol. 1**, and "Boogie Blues" appears on **Vol. 2**.

Duke Ellington and His Orchestra *(1943, 9 minutes)*

See: **Duke Ellington 1929–1943** (page 47)

Duke Ellington and His Orchestra *(1962, 24 minutes)*

See: **Jazz Festival Vol. 2** (page 75)

Duke Ellington at the White House
(1969, 28 minutes)

In this film Duke Ellington is honored at the White House at the time of his 70th birthday. The music is all very brief excerpts (which have since been released in full on CD) but more significant than the playing is the opportunity to glimpse such musicians as Ellington, Cab Calloway, Billy Eckstine, Benny Goodman, Dizzy Gillespie, Dave Brubeck, Willie "The Lion" Smith, Billy Taylor, George Wein, Marian McPartland, Earl Hines, Clark Terry, Bill Berry, J.J. Johnson, Paul Desmond, Gerry Mulligan, Hank Jones, Jim Hall, Milt Hinton, Louie Bellson and Joe Williams, not to mention President Richard Nixon and his wife Pat (to whom Ellington dedicates a freely improvised solo piano piece which he called "Pat").

Duke Ellington: Love You Madly
(1965, 95 minutes)

This extraordinary television special (which was nominated for an Emmy after it aired in 1967) was supervised by writer Ralph Gleason and filmed during August and September, 1965. Duke Ellington was followed around by cameras for a couple of months so one gets a good idea what his day-to-day life was like during the era. Ellington's band is seen at San Francisco's Basin Street West, the Monterey Jazz Festival, at a recording date and as Duke prepared for the first of his sacred concerts at Grace Cathedral. The music is mostly just excerpts, although there is a longer version of "Take the 'A' Train." Among the other songs played (sometimes in the background) are "Come Sunday," "David Danced Before the Lord," "The Far East Suite," "In the Beginning, God," "The Lord's Prayer," "Love Came," "Rockin' in Rhythm," "Sugar Hill Penthouse" and "Things Ain't What They Used to Be." Among the soloists are Cootie Williams, Cat Anderson, Lawrence Brown, Buster Cooper, Jimmy Hamilton, Russell Procope, Johnny Hodges, Paul Gonsalves and Louie Bellson. There are also interviews with Dizzy Gillespie and Earl Hines, some tap dancing from Bunny Briggs and singing from Jon Hendricks and Esther Marrow. But more than the music, this film is valuable in giving the viewers glimpses of what it must have been like to be Duke Ellington. **Love You Madly** is long overdue to be released on DVD.

Duke Ellington: Reminiscing in Tempo
(1992, 89 minutes)

This entry in the **American Experience** PBS television series is as much about Duke Ellington's life and personality as his music. Rare home movies and interesting storytelling by Mercer Ellington, Sonny Greer, Gunther Schuller, Irving Mills, Fayard Nicholas, Duke's granddaughter

Mercedes Ellington, Herb Jeffries, Barry Ulanov, Louie Bellson and George Wein (among others) make this a colorful documentary. Vintage interviews with Duke also add to the documentary's value although, as is too often true, every film clip of his band performing is talked over.

A Duke Named Ellington
(1988, 110 minutes)

Although the chronological story of Duke Ellington is told in part, this two-hour entry in the **American Masters** series focuses more on the musical brilliance and innovations of Ellington, and what it was like to be in his band. There are excerpts from a wide variety of film clips and performances (including "Take the 'A' Train," "Old Man Blues," "All Too Soon," "Mood Indigo," "Eighth Veil," "Chelsea Bridge," "Lotus Blossom," "Don't Get Around Much Anymore" and part of "The Far East Suite"), but most valuable are the interviews with Willie "The Lion" Smith, Herb Jeffries, Adelaide Hall, Clark Terry, Cootie Williams, Russell Procope, Jimmy Hamilton, Leonard Feather, Louie Bellson, Ben Webster, Charles Mingus and Herbie Hancock.

Eddie Condon All-Stars *(1962, 24 minutes)*

See: **Jazz Festival Vol. 1** (page 74)

Eddie Condon's *(1951, 10 minutes)*

This film offers a brief visit to Eddie Condon's jazz club in Greenwich Village. Although one sees a little of Condon's band with cornetist Wild Bill Davison, singers Johnny Ray and Dolores Hawkins dominate on "For You, My Love," and "Tell the Lady I Said Goodbye."

Eddie Rosner: Jazzman from the Gulag
(1999, 58 minutes)

This fascinating documentary focuses on the ill-fated career of German trumpeter Eddie Rosner. Rosner, who had the misfortune to come of age in Berlin during the 1930s, fled to the Soviet Union, where he was one of Russia's top jazz musicians (leading a big band) during World War II. After the war ended, Stalin changed his mind about Rosner and sent him to Siberia, where he spent a decade. His last years were spent trying to restart his career in the Soviet Union. The interviews, film clips and evidence that are pieced together about his life are intriguing and ultimately tragic.

♪ Ellis Larkins *(1975, 8 minutes)*

The subtle swing pianist is portrayed during this brief Swiss film, which shows him playing in a New York club.

♪ Eubie Blake Plays *(1923, 7 minutes)*

Among the earliest sound films of jazz, **Eubie Blake Plays** was recorded around the same time as the Blake and Noble Sissle short **Snappy Songs**. An experimental film produced by Lee De Forest four years before **The Jazz Singer**, this primitive but historic short has Eubie Blake on piano playing two versions of "Swanee River."

♪ Featuring Gene Krupa and His Orchestra
(1948, 10 minutes)

The Gene Krupa Big Band performs "Bop Boogie" (with singer Dolores Hawkins) "Sabre Dance" and Gerry Mulligan's "Disc Jockey Jump." The group at the time included trumpeter Don Fagerquist and Buddy Wise on tenor.

♪ Festival Pan Africain D'Alger
(1970, 110 minutes)

This African documentary of a music festival held in Algeria in July, 1969 features Archie Shepp on an extended piece (probably "Brotherhood at Ketchaoha") with cornetist Clifford Thornton, trombonist Grachan Moncur and an Algerian rhythm section.

♪ Fiddler's Dream *(1987, 24 minutes)*

Violinist Claude Williams (who was destined to be the last active survivor from the 1920s jazz scene) is portrayed on

Fiddler's Dream. In addition to brief performance clips of Williams, there are interviews with Andy Kirk, Big Joe Turner, Jay McShann and Stephane Grappelli.

♪ Film Vodvil No. 2
(1943, 10 minutes)

The 1943 Cootie Williams Orchestra (which includes altoist/singer Eddie "Cleanhead" Vinson and tenor saxophonist Sam "The Man" Taylor, but not yet pianist Bud Powell) performs an excerpt from their theme ("Keep on Jumping") and versions of "Wild Fire" and "Things Ain't What They Used to Be." They also accompany the dancing of the Douglas Brothers and the Lindy Hoppers; Laurel Watson sings "Giddap Mule."

♪ Flying Fingers
(1961, 9 minutes)

The fine swing/stride pianist Dill Jones performs "A Nightingale Sang in Berkeley Square" and "Penny Serenade" in this British short.

Follow that Music *(1946, 18 minutes)*

See: **Meet the Bandleaders** (Swingtime Video 104) (page 99)

♪ Freddie Hubbard—Live at the Village Vanguard
(1984, 59 minutes)

Filmed in 1982, this performance has trumpeter Freddie Hubbard, pianist Cedar Walton, bassist Ron Carter and drummer Lennie White stretching out on "Happy Times," "Guernica," "Little Waltz" and "Fantasy in D."

♪ Freddie Rich and His Orchestra
(1936, 11 minutes)

Fred Rich leads a pretty decent (though unidentified) hot dance/swing orchestra in this short. The Three Symphonettes sing "Education" and are joined by Nan Wynn on "Loch Lomond." The band is featured on "Loch

Lomond" and joined by acoustic guitar soloist Joe Sodja on a heated "Chinatown, My Chinatown."

 Frog Dance *(1985, 52 minutes)*

The life, struggles and music of British avant-garde soprano saxophonist Lol Coxhill are covered in this documentary.

 Future One *(1963, 8 minutes)*

This valuable but brief Danish film features the New York Contemporary Five (cornetist Don Cherry, Archie Shepp on tenor, altoist John Tchicai, bassist Don Moore and drummer J.C. Moses) at the Cafe Montmartre performing "Trio."

 Gene Krupa: America's Ace Drummer Man and His Orchestra *(1941, 10 minutes)*

Although it is a pity that this short was not filmed later in 1941 when singer Anita O'Day and trumpeter Roy Eldridge were in Gene Krupa's orchestra, it does give a good overview of the band in early 1941. After a catchy instrumental ("Hamtramck"), Howard Dulaney sings "Perfidia," he shares "The Call of the Canyon" with Irene Daye (a fine vocalist) and the short concludes with a good jam on "Jungle Madness." Trumpeter Shorty Sherock is the main soloist other than the leader.

Glenn Miller: America's Musical Hero *(1991, 60 minutes)*

The Glenn Miller story is competently covered during this PBS television special. Private home movies and clips from Miller's two films help out, but it is the storytelling that makes this a worthwhile documentary. Commenting along the way are actor Jimmy Stewart (who played the lead in **The Glenn Miller Story**), tenor saxophonist Jerry Jerome, Tex Beneke, writer George Simon, trombonist Paul Tanner, trumpeter Zeke Zarchey, drummer Ray McKinley, trumpeter Johnny Best, Henry Mancini, Billy May and pianist Mel Powell.

 Grace Johnston and the Indiana Five *(1929, 9 minutes)*

One of many Vitaphone shorts that are being restored, this formerly lost film features singer Grace Johnston on "Bashful Baby" and "Glad Rag Doll" plus an instrumental rendition of "Clarinet Marmalade" from the Original Indiana Five.

 The Great Rocky Mountain Jazz Party *(1977, 103 minutes)*

This historic film documents the 1976 Colorado Jazz Party. Dick and Maddie Gibson, the party's hosts and organizers, narrate the star-filled documentary. Among the all-time greats who are seen and heard performing are trumpeters/cornetists Ruby Braff, Clark Terry, Jon Faddis, Pee Wee Erwin, Billy Butterfield, Joe Wilder and Joe Newman, trombonists Frank Rosolino, Trummy Young, Al Grey, Carl Fontana and Bill Watrous, the reeds of Zoot Sims, Phil Woods, Bob Wilber, Kenny Davern, Peanuts Hucko, Buddy Tate, Budd Johnson, Al Cohn, Benny Carter, Buddy DeFranco and Flip Phillips, guitarist Bucky Pizzarelli, pianists Eubie Blake, Tommy Flanagan, Roger Kellaway, Dick Hyman, Roland Hanna and Ralph Sutton, bassists Milt Hinton, Major Holley, Ray Brown and George Duvivier, drummers Gus Johnson and Roy Haynes and violinist Joe Venuti. The repertoire is comprised of swing and bop standards, including "Struttin' with Some Barbecue," "Speak Low," "Memories of You," "Hello Dolly," "Stealin' Apples" and "Perdido." Hopefully this priceless performance documentary will be available on DVD someday.

 Great Vibes: Lionel Hampton & Friends *(1982, 60 minutes)*

In 1982, Lionel Hampton was honored at the White House by Ronald Reagan and celebrated at a special concert in Washington, D.C. This television special has some storytelling and reminiscing along with historical background, but mostly features Hampton and some of his friends performing live. Hampton plays vibes, drums and sings on "Sweet Georgia Brown," "Birth of the Blues" and "Hey Ba-Ba-Re-Bop." Pearl Bailey, backed by a quartet with Louie Bellson, performs "Memories of You" and "There'll Be Some Changes Made." Hampton is joined by Dave Brubeck, Ron Carter, drummer Frankie Dunlop, Illinois Jacquet and Clark Terry for "Things Ain't What They Used to Be," Betty Carter stretches out on an adventurous uptempo piece, and Freddie Hubbard jams "I Got Rhythm." The closer, "Jumpin' at the Woodside," is the most exciting number and has spots for Jacquet, Terry, Al Grey, Zoot Sims, altoist Marshall Keys, pianist George Wein, Milt Hinton, Bellson and a delighted Hampton.

 Gus Arnheim and His Ambassadors
(1928, 9 minutes)

Gus Arnheim's dance band filmed several Vitaphone music shorts in the late '20s. This one is the most jazz-oriented, featuring the orchestra performing "I Ain't Got Nobody," "If I Can't Have You," "Mighty Like a Rose," "There's Something About a Rose" and "Tiger Rag."

 The Happiness Remedy
(1931, 8 minutes)

Although Ted Lewis's band at the time includes Jack Teagarden and guest cornetist Red Nichols, they have nothing much to do during this short film but look unhappy (Teagarden particularly has a sour expression on his face) as Lewis sings a pair of corny songs ("Homemade Sunshine" and "Laugh It Down") in his unique fashion.

 Happy New Year USA
(1987, 180 minutes)

On New Year's Eve, 1987, PBS hosted three hours of jazz and classical music. The jazz portion was mostly performed at singer Ethel Ennis's club. Among the stars are Mel Tormé, the Manhattan Rhythm Kings, Diane Schuur (her version of "Bob White" is a highlight), Wynton Marsalis (in top form on "Just Friends") and Ennis herself. McCoy Tyner is excellent on "I Didn't Know What Time It Was" and on versions of "I Can't Give You Anything but Love" and "Willow Weep for Me" he meets up successfully with Stephane Grappelli; an album would result in the near future.

Harlem Jam Session *(1946, 8 minutes)*

See: **All Girl Bands** (page 19)

 Harry James and the Music Makers
(1943, 14 minutes)

This short film features Harry James and his big band with singer Gale Robbins performing "Charmaine," "I've Got a Crush on You," "Moanin' Low," "The Brave Bulls," "I'm in a Jam" and "Trumpet Blues."

 Hello Satchmo *(1965, 25 minutes)*

This obscure documentary features Louis Armstrong and his All-Stars during their very successful visit to Czechoslovakia in 1965. In addition to Armstrong, his group consists of trombonist Tyree Glenn, clarinetist Eddie Shu, pianist Billy Kyle, bassist Arvell Shaw and drummer Danny Barcelona.

 Herman's Herd *(1949, 15 minutes)*

The later version of Woody Herman's Second Herd (after Stan Getz, Zoot Sims, Al Cohn and Gene Ammons had departed) performs "Jamaica Rhumba," "I've Got News for You," "It's a Great Day for the Irish," "Lollypop," "Skip to My Lou" and "Keen and Peachy." In addition to the vocal group the Mello-Larks, this **Universal Band Name** musical has solos from vibraphonist Terry Gibbs, Buddy Savitt on tenor, trumpeters Ernie Royal and Shorty Rogers, trombonists Earl Swope and Bill Harris, and baritonist Serge Chaloff.

Hi-De-Ho (1937, 11 minutes)

One of three Cab Calloway films titled "Hi-De-Ho," this short has a moderately silly story that serves as a good excuse for Calloway to sing "I've Got a Right to Sing the Blues," an excellent version of "The Hi-De-Ho Miracle Man," "Frisco Flo" and a mostly instrumental (other than scatting) rendition of "Some of These Days." The latter song has a rare early flute solo by Walter Thomas and spots for guitarist Morris White, probably Keg Johnson on trombone and clarinetist Garvin Bushell. Also in the band at the time are trumpeter Doc Cheatham, trombonist Claude Jones, Ben Webster, pianist Bennie Payne and Milt Hinton. Cab is in great form throughout.

 His Pastimes (1926, 6 minutes)

This experimental short from 1926 features the talented Roy Smeck showing off his technique and wit on his various axes, including guitar, Hawaiian guitar, ukulele and banjo.

 Hit Tune Jamboree (1942, 16 minutes)

The Mills Brothers perform "Sleepy Time Gal" and "Tiger Rag," bandleader George Olsen sings "I'll See You in My Dreams" while backed by his orchestra, and vocalist Martha Mears is featured on "He's My Guy."

Hoagy Carmichael (1939, 10 minutes)

See: **Swing, Volume One** (page 130)

 Hootie's Blues (1978, 30 minutes)

A decade or so after he started to become rediscovered, this short documentary was made about pianist/singer Jay McShann. He is interviewed about his life and association with Charlie Parker, and performs "Take the 'A' Train," "Tenderly" and "Mack the Knife."

How About that Jive (1946, 8 minutes)

See: **All Girl Bands** (page 19)

 I Ain't Got Nobody
(1932, 8 minutes)

This vintage Paramount cartoon features a bouncing ball in its sing-along segment. The Mills Brothers are seen in their earliest appearance on film, performing "Tiger Rag" and "I Ain't Got Nobody."

 I Heard (1933, 7 minutes)

Don Redman conducts his big band on "Call of the Freaks" and then sings on the soundtrack of this Betty Boop cartoon while his orchestra provides the music. As usual with this series, the animation is remarkable and there are many funny jokes. Coal miners (shown as cartoon animals) relax during their lunch hour at Betty Boop's Tavern. The band performs "How'm I Doing" and "I Heard."

 I'll Be Glad When You're Dead, You Rascal You
(1932, 7 minutes)

For this Betty Boop cartoon, Louis Armstrong appears briefly at its beginning with a ten-piece group including trumpeter Zilner Randolph and trombonist Preston Jackson. Otherwise he is seen and heard in animated form, interacting with Ms. Boop and performing "High Society," "Shine," "I'll Be Glad When You're Dead" and "Chinatown, My Chinatown."

🎵 *In Performance at the White House: Celebrating the 40th Anniversary of the Newport Jazz Festival*
(1993, 56 minutes)

With President Bill Clinton as the host, T.S. Monk as the emcee and producer George Wein in the audience, the Newport Jazz Festival was celebrated at the White House during this star-filled concert. The Wynton Marsalis Septet plays a medium-tempo blues, Michel Camilo is impressive on solo piano during his "Caribe," Rosemary Clooney performs "Our Love Is Here to Stay" and "Sweet Kentucky Ham," and Bobby McFerrin creates an unaccompanied piece. Pianist Dorothy Donegan shows off both her technique and her legs on a medley of "I Can't Get Started," "Flight of the Bumblebee" and other songs. Herbie Hancock and tenor saxophonist Joe Henderson duet on "Lush Life," and Joe Williams is backed by an all-star cast on "I'd Rather Drink Muddy Water." The closing jam on "All Blues" has Clinton himself joining in on tenor. There are also glimpses of other performances not shown, making one wish that this was a two-hour telecast instead. Seen in cameos are Clark Terry, Red Rodney, Illinois Jacquet, Joshua Redman, Jimmy Heath, Grover Washington, Jr., Dick Hyman, John Lewis and Christian McBride, among others.

The International Sweethearts of Rhythm
(1946, 8 minutes)

See: **All Girl Bands** (page 19)

In the Swing *(1983, 60 minutes)*

Much of this PBS television special, which is hosted by Steve Allen, features swing dancers and nostalgic vocals (including by Patty Andrews). However, the backup band is the Nat Pierce-Frank Capp Juggernaut, which at the time included pianist Pierce, drummer Capp, trumpeter Al Aarons, trombonist Buster Cooper, altoist Marshall Royal and tenor saxophonist Red Holloway among the key players. The big band backs Ernie Andrews on "Take the 'A' Train" and gets to romp on Count Basie–oriented versions of "Avenue C" and "Wind Machine."

Ina Ray Hutton and Her Orchestra
(1943, 9 minutes)

Though Ina Ray Hutton gained her fame for leading an all-female orchestra, by 1940 she was singing and dancing in front of a male big band. During this short, she performs "Knock Me a Kiss," "Smiles," "Angry" and "My Silent Love."

L'Invention *(1967, 14 minutes)*

This little-known but valuable French film features pianist Cecil Taylor with his quartet (altoist Jimmy Lyons,

bassist Alan Silva and drummer Andrew Cyrille) during a year when Taylor did not otherwise record.

I Surrender Dear *(1931, 22 minutes)*

This was the first of six Bing Crosby shorts made for Mack Sennett during 1931–32. Crosby plays himself, a radio crooner, who steals a girl from her boyfriend and sings "I Surrender Dear," "Out of Nowhere," "At Your Command" and "A Little Bit of Heaven."

It's on the Record *(1937, 10 minutes)*

The owner of a music store gets nostalgic for the music of his youth. The Original Dixieland Jazz Band (from **The March of Time Vol. 3, Issue 7**) and guitarist Roy Smeck are among the performers that he remembers.

Jack Teagarden in Thailand *(1958, 15 minutes)*

See: **Jack Teagarden: Far East Tour 1958–59** (page 66)

Jailhouse Blues *(1929, 9 minutes)*

This significant short features Mamie Smith singing the title cut (which she initially recorded in 1923), backed by an unidentified orchestra.

Jammin' the Blues *(1944, 10 minutes)*

See: **Song of the Spirit: The Story of Lester Young** (page 122)

Jammin' with Gene Krupa *(1959, 10 minutes)*

This is a promotional short produced to advertise the release of **The Gene Krupa Story**. Krupa and actor Sal Mineo (who plays the lead in the picture) meet and greet each other (it looks fairly spontaneous), and then Krupa gives Sal Mineo an interesting drum lesson. Mineo does not play badly to begin with, his questions are intelligent, and at one point they both jam together in colorful fashion. The bulk of this film has been included in the video **Gene Krupa: Jazz Legend**.

 Jazz at the Half Note
(1964, 28 minutes)

Filmed as part of the odd religious series **Look Up and Live**, this is an invaluable television special featuring pianist Lennie Tristano, altoist Lee Konitz, tenor saxophonist Warne Marsh, bassist Sonny Dallas and drummer Nick Stabulas. The quintet performs "Subconscious-Lee," "317 East 32nd Street" and "Background Music" and seems oblivious of the pseudo-religious introduction given by Dr. William Hamilton.

Jazz Dance *(1954, 22 minutes)*

See: **After Hours/Jazz Dance** (page 18)

Jazz from Studio 61 *(1959, 25 minutes)*

See: **Vintage Collection Vol. 2: 1960–61** (page 136)

 Jazz Goes Home to Newport
(1984, 60 minutes)

There have been many summary films of the Newport Jazz Festival during various years in the 1980s and '90s, but this is one of the most satisfying hours. In addition to being scenic and giving a little background, the special has superior performances. Pianist Michel Petrucciani's trio (with bassist Palle Danielsson and drummer Eliot Zigmund) performs an original, the Dizzy Gillespie Quintet (James Moody, Walter Davis, Ron Carter and Louie Bellson) jams a happy version of "Birks' Works," and Carter is showcased on a blues. The Dave Brubeck Quartet (with altoist Bobby Militello, electric bassist Chris Brubeck and drummer Randy Jones) performs excellent versions of "Blue Rondo à la Turk" and "Take Five" before the Stan Getz Quartet (with pianist John Campbell, bassist George Mraz and drummer Ralph Penland) closes the show with "Blood Count" and "Time After

Time." Each of the bands is in fine form, with Brubeck taking honors.

 Jazz in America
(1981, 58 minutes)

Dizzy Gillespie clearly had a good time during this engagement at Concerts By the Sea in 1981. He performs "Bebop," "Kush," "Birks' Works" and the "Hard of Hearing Mama Blues" with altoist Paquito D'Rivera, trombonist Tom MacIntosh, guitarist Ed Cherry, pianist Valerie Capers (who is outstanding), acoustic bassist Ray Brown, electric bassist Michael Howell and drummer Tom Campbell. Dizzy sings the last song, makes some of his classic jokes to the audience and is in pretty decent form for it being a bit late in his career.

 Jazz Is My Native Language
(1983, 59 minutes)

Filmed at the time of pianist/composer/bandleader Toshiko Akiyoshi's move from Los Angeles to New York (which necessitated breaking up her big band and forming a new one in New York), this documentary portrays her day-to-day life in 1983. Akiyoshi talks about her music, is seen at home with her husband, tenor saxophonist Lew Tabackin, and is shown rehearsing her Los Angeles big band. She talks about her early life, and there is a mid-'50s clip of her singing on the **What's My Line** show (though it is a pity that the whole segment is not shown). Akiyoshi discusses the difficulties and joys of having such a busy life. There are also comments from Leonard Feather, Tabackin, altoist Dick Spencer and bass trombonist Phil Teele. Musically Akiyoshi performs part of a song with a trio and a few numbers with her big band, but unfortunately everything is just an excerpt.

 Jazz Jamboree
(1953, 10 minutes)

This French short has two remarkable performances by soprano saxophonist Sidney Bechet with Claude Luter's orchestra. They perform very exciting versions of "St. Louis Blues" and "Royal Garden Blues" that are filled with heated riffing and explosive solos, particularly from Bechet. Although a photographer gets a bit intrusive in spots, the music is stirring, making this the most rewarding existing footage of Sidney Bechet.

 ### Jazz Summit *(1987, 28 minutes)*

At a time when the Soviet Union was still powerful but just beginning to open its doors a little, the Russian avant-garde Ganelin Trio (pianist Vyacheslav Ganelin, saxophonist Vladimir Chekasin and drummer Vladimir Tarasov) had an opportunity to make their first American tour. This documentary has brief interviews and excerpts from their performances and that of the Rova Saxophone Quartet, their American counterpart.

Jazz, the Intimate Art *(1968, 58 minutes)*

This documentary features four of the most popular jazz artists of the era rehearsing, talking and playing some music. Louis Armstrong and his All-Stars (with Tyree Glenn, clarinetist Joe Muranyi, Marty Napoleon, Buddy Catlett, Danny Barcelona and Jewel Brown) perform "When It's Sleepy Time Down South," "The Saints" and "Hello Dolly;" the Dizzy Gillespie Quintet (with James Moody and pianist Mike Longo) plays "Swing Low Sweet Cadillac" and "Con Alma;" the Dave Brubeck Quartet (Paul Desmond, bassist Eugene Wright and drummer Joe Morello) interprets "I'm in a Dancing Mood;" and the Charles Lloyd Quartet (with pianist Keith Jarrett, bassist Ron McClure and drummer Jack DeJohnette) plays "Forest Flower."

Jerry Livingston and His Talk of the Town Music
(1939, 11 minutes)

This little-known short, which puts the focus on songwriter Jerry Livingston, has a feature for the Adrian Rollini Trio with Rollini on vibes.

 ### Jimmie Lunceford and His Dance Orchestra
(1936, 10 minutes)

One of the very few appearances on film by the Jimmie Lunceford Orchestra, this ten-minute film is valuable. After a silly number by a singer dressed in a devil suit (à la the Erskine Hawkins short **Deviled Ham**), the Lunceford big band takes over. "Jazznocracy" is followed by an uptempo version of "Rhythm Is Our Business" that features altoist Willie Smith taking the vocal and short spots for drummer Jimmy Crawford, tenor saxophonist Joe Thomas, bassist Mose Allen and high-note trumpeter Paul Webster. Myra Johnson sings "You Can't Pull the Wool Over My Eyes" and a tap dancing trio called the Three Brown Jacks perform "It's Rhythm Coming to Life Again." The film concludes with "Nagasaki" with trombonist Trummy Young on the vocal, two of the saxophonists dancing while holding their horns, and spots for Thomas and Webster. Also in the band are trumpeter/arranger Sy Oliver, trombonist Eddie Durham and pianist Ed Wilcox, with Lunceford verbally introducing the numbers and conducting.

 ### Jimmy Dorsey and His Orchestra
(1938, 9 minutes)

The Jimmy Dorsey Orchestra performs "It's the Dreamer in Me," "I Love You in Technicolor" and "Dusk in Upper Sandusky" (the lone instrumental) with singers Bob Eberly and Evelyn Oak, trumpeter Shorty Sherock, pianist Freddie Slack and drummer Ray McKinley.

Jimmy Dorsey and His Orchestra *(1940, 10 minutes)*
See: **Swing, Volume One** (page 130)

 ### Jimmy Dorsey and His Orchestra:
All Star Melody Masters
(1948, 15 minutes)

This short has Jimmy Dorsey and his big band backing singer Dottie O'Brien, Bill Lawrence and the Mello-Larks on "Am I Blue," "Quien Sabe," "We Hate Cowboy

Songs" and "Jamboree Jones." Of greatest interest is a dance band arrangement of "Lover" and a pretty definitive version of JD's theme, "Contrasts." Seen in the trumpet section are Charlie Teagarden and a young Doc Severinsen.

Jimmy Dorsey's Varieties
(1952, 15 minutes)

The Jimmy Dorsey band was in its last year when it filmed this short. JD's orchestra and combo perform concise versions of six songs, most notably "Sweet Georgia Brown" and "South Rampart Street Parade"; both of those selections have been included as part of **Swing: Best of the Big Bands, Vol. 3**. Herb Jeffries takes the vocal on "In the Bayou" and the Red Norvo Trio with guitarist Tal Farlow and bassist Red Mitchell plays "Temptation."

Jingle Jangle Jingle
(1947, 20 minutes)

The plot is lightweight, but this short is valuable for featuring the Page Cavanaugh Trio (with pianist Cavanaugh, guitarist Al Viola and bassist Lloyd Pratt) on "Walkin' My Baby Back Home," "I'm an Old Cowhand" and "Jingle Jangle Jingle."

Jive Busters *(1944, 15 minutes)*

Trumpeter Sonny Dunham's wartime orchestra and singer Carolyn Grey perform "Poinciana" (a feature for the leader on both trumpet and trombone), "I'm Coming Virginia," "All I Do Is Dream of You," "Don't Blame Me" and "I'm in Love with You Honey."

Jivin' Jam Session *(1942, 15 minutes)*

Considering that Sonny Dunham's orchestra is joined by singers Louis De Pron, Harriet Clark, Jimmie Dodd, the Three Comets and Ray Kellogg, this is not much of a jam session. In addition to such tunes as "Don't Go West Young Man," "Nothing" and "From One Love to Another," Dunham re-creates "Memories of You," a high-note trum-

pet display that was a hit a few years earlier when he was with Glen Gray's Casa Loma Orchestra.

Joe Albany...A Jazz Life
(1980, 58 minutes)

This is an excellent documentary on the life of bop pianist Joe Albany who, due to his excessive drug use, had a very erratic life before settling down in the 1970s. Albany talks about his drug problems, his career and his comeback. There are also excerpts from some historic films, but the bulk of this project features Albany, bassist Chris Berg and drummer Lee Abrams performing an excellent set of music ("My Little Suede Shoes," "Over the Rainbow," "Isn't It Romantic," "There Will Never Be Another You," "Billie's Bounce," "Confirmation," "Fine and Mellow," "Lush Life," "Body and Soul," "'Round Midnight").

John Handy at the Blue Horn
(1965, 26 minutes)

During the same year that altoist John Handy was the hit of the Monterey Jazz Festival, he is seen in Canada in this half-hour special with the same group (violinist Michael White, guitarist Jerry Hahn, bassist Don Thompson and drummer Terry Clarke) plus guest pianist Freddie Redd. They perform a couple of originals and discuss their stimulating music.

Johnny Griffin: Live at the Village Vanguard
(1981, 97 minutes)

Tenor saxophonist Johnny Griffin, pianist Ronnie Mathews, bassist Ray Drummond and drummer Kenny Washington perform "Blues for Gonzi," "Blues for Leslie," "56," "Jean Marie," "A Monk's Dream," "Susanita" and "When We Were One."

Jon Hendricks: The Freddie Sessions
(1990, 28 minutes)

In 1990, the great lyricist Jon Hendricks recorded a remake of Miles Davis's "Freddie Freeloader," singing

John Coltrane's solo and utilizing the voices of Bobby McFerrin (as pianist Wynton Kelly), Al Jarreau (as Miles Davis) and George Benson (as Cannonball Adderley). This short film has Hendricks talking about the project, briefly discussing the history of vocalese and includes some excerpts from the performance although not the entire song. Seen backing the singers are pianist Tommy Flanagan, bassist George Mraz and drummer Jimmy Cobb (who was also on the original version).

 Keep It Cool *(1954, 16 minutes)*

This short from Universal International features the Tony Pastor Orchestra ("Universal Stomp" and "Don't Worry About Strangers"), a few indifferent vocalists and the Red Norvo Trio (with guitarist Tal Farlow and probably bassist Red Mitchell) performing "How Am I to Know."

 King Cole and His Trio *(1950, 15 minutes)*

Nat King Cole and his trio (with guitarist Irving Ashby, bassist Joe Comfort and percussionist Jack Costanzo) perform spirited versions of "Route 66" and "Ooh Kick a Rooney" (both of which have been reissued on **Swing: The Best of the Big Bands, Vol. 2**) and are joined by Benny Carter's orchestra on "Congeroo" (which is on **Vol. 1** in the **Swing** series). In addition, there are features for tap dancer Bunny Briggs and singer Dolores Parker.

 Lee Konitz: Live at the Village Vanguard *(1989, 57 minutes)*

Altoist Lee Konitz, pianist Roland Hanna, bassist George Mraz and drummer Mel Lewis are featured. Among the songs that they play are "Dreamstepper" and "A Story Often Told."

 The Legend of Jimmy Blue Eyes *(1964, 22 minutes)*

This Oscar-nominated short film is about a New Orleans trumpeter who is put in jail for an accidental killing, loses his girlfriend and ultimately sells his soul to the devil for

the ability to play brilliant solos. Teddy Buckner ghosts for the trumpeter on such songs as "Bill Bailey" and "The Saints."

 Lennie Hayton and His Orchestra *(1937, 10 minutes)*

Arranger/composer Lennie Hayton leads his short-lived big band on "Goona Goo," "Mary Had a Little Lamb," "Original Theme Song," "Sweet Sue," "Too Marvelous for Words" and "Trust in Me." The plot deals with a violinist wanting to join his band.

 Les Brown and the Band of Renown *(1949, 15 minutes)*

In 1949, Les Brown led his most bebopish big band before reverting back to swing. There are hints of the newer style in this Universal International short. Brown's orchestra features tenor saxophonist Dave Pell, trombonist Ray Sims and drummer Jack Sperling with vocals being taken by the Mello-Larks, Artie Wayne and Butch Stone. The band is in excellent form on "Leap Frog," "I've Got My Love to Keep Me Warm," "When Francis Dances with Me," "I'm the Man with the Dream," "I Want to Be Kissed" and "Bopple Sauce."

 Let's Dance: A Musical Tribute *(1985, 90 minutes)*

The last significant gig of Benny Goodman's long career was making this special for PBS about six months before he died. The King of Swing, 76 at the time, had taken over what had been the Loren Schoenberg Orchestra and revived a lot of the vintage Fletcher Henderson arrangements. He still sounded strong, and his band featured such soloists as Ken Peplowski on tenor, trumpeters Randy Sandke and John Eckert, and trombonist Eddie Bert. For the special, pianist Dick Hyman and Louie Bellson were added to the orchestra. Goodman performs his classic music for an appreciative dancing crowd, there are several speakers who pay tribute to him (including

Frank Sinatra), and a few film clips trace his career. The big band sounds fine on their numbers ("Let's Dance," "Don't Be That Way," "I Would Do Anything for You," "King Porter Stomp," "You Brought a New Kind of Love to Me," "Blue Room," "Down South Camp Meeting," "Stealin' Apples," "Goodbye") and backs Rosemary Clooney ("Somebody Else Is Taking My Place," "You Turned the Tables on Me," "And the Angels Sing," "There's No Business Like Show Business"). Carrie Smith sings "Gimme a Pigfoot" and "Ja Da," Teddy Wilson (who would also pass away soon) performs a medley of "The Man I Love" and "But Not for Me" in a trio with Bob Haggart and Bellson, bassist Slam Stewart is showcased singing "Flat Foot Floogie," vibraphonist Red Norvo is featured on "There'll Never Be Another You," and Goodman plays "Memories of You" with a small group. All in all, this was a fine closing act for BG.

Let's Make Rhythm (1947, 20 minutes)

See: **Swing, Volume One** (page 130)

 ### *Lionel Hampton and His Orchestra*
(1949, 14 minutes)

The Lionel Hampton big band (with trombonists Al Grey and Jimmy Cleveland, altoist Bobby Plater, guitarist Wes Montgomery, trumpeter Moon Mullins and singer Betty Carter) is captured during one of its best periods in this Universal International short. Hampton is in typically exuberant form on "Wee Albert," "Airmail Special," "Robbin's Nest," "Hamp's Gumbo" and "Flying Home."

 ### *The Little Broadcast*
(1933, 8 minutes)

Four acts perform during this brief film. Donald Novis sings "Love, Here Is My Heart," and Arthur Tracy is heard on "Santa Lucia." Of greater interest are the Mills Brothers happily singing "Old Man of the Mountain" and Vincent Lopez's orchestra playing "Bugle Call Rag."

 ### *Live from Lincoln Center with Wynton Marsalis*
(1994, 110 minutes)

Of the many television specials that feature Wynton Marsalis, this lengthy one from 1994 is one of the most rewarding, helped out by a long list of guests. Among the selections are "Happy-Go-Lucky Local," "Whisper Not" (featuring Benny Golson), "Festive Minor" (with Gerry Mulligan and flugelhornist Art Farmer in a pianoless quartet), "Smokehouse Blues," "Black Bottom Stomp," "Maple Leaf Rag" (modernized by pianist Marcus Roberts), "Stopping the Biscuit" (with trumpeter Roy Hargrove), a vocal by Milt Grayson on "Jelly," an excerpt from "Blood on the Fields" ("Back to Basics"), Joe Henderson on "Take the 'A' Train," Wynton, Doc Cheatham and Harry "Sweets" Edison sharing "Gee Baby Ain't I Good to You," altoists Phil Woods and Charles McPherson causing some sparks to fly on "Steeplechase" plus "Call to Prayer/Procession" and "The Second Line." Other key musicians include trombonist Wycliffe Gordon, clarinetist Michael White, pianist Eric Reed, bassists Ron Carter and George Mraz, drummers Billy Higgins and Al Foster, trombonist Britt Woodman, altoists Norris Turney and Jesse Davis, and baritonist Joe Temperley. Although one wishes there was much more heard from Mulligan, Edison and Cheatham, this is a well-conceived show.

 ### *Living Jazz* (1961, 43 minutes)

Altoist Bruce Turner and his British swing/jump band are profiled in this British documentary. In addition to showing what the jazz life was like in Great Britain in the early '60s, the film has Turner's band (trumpeter John Chilton, trombonist John Mumford, pianist Coolin Bates, bassist Jim Bray and drummer Johnny Armitage) playing some of the leader's swinging originals.

 ### *The Long Night of Lady Day*
(1984, 90 minutes)

This documentary on Billie Holiday, which was made as part of the **American Masters** series, is fairly definitive.

The interviews of Leonard Feather, Artie Shaw, Milt Hinton, John Hammond, Barney Josephson, Sylvia Syms, Thelma Carpenter, Milt Gabler, Norman Granz, Ray Ellis and Yolande Bevan add a great deal to the narrative. The usual film clips (including 1957's "Fine and Mellow" and some television performances from 1958–59) and photos are shown, and the story equally balances the musical and personal lives of Billie Holiday.

Louis Armstrong All-Stars *(1962, 24 minutes)*

See: **Jazz Festival Vol. 1** (page 74)

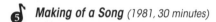 ***Making of a Song*** *(1981, 30 minutes)*

This generally interesting documentary focuses on the Mel Lewis Jazz Orchestra learning and performing Bob Brookmeyer's rather radical arrangement of "My Funny Valentine." The charts make the song seem a bit like modern classical music, but the ensemble handles it quite well.

The March of Time, Volume 3, Issue 7
(1937, 20 minutes)

After stories on the unsuccessful anti-liquor movement of the mid-'30s and of modern Turkey, there is a fascinating piece titled "The Birth of Swing." The swing craze is mentioned and then the narrative centers on the Original Dixieland Jazz Band. Pianist J. Russell Robinson has a couple of lines and the quintet (cornetist Nick LaRocca, trombonist Eddie Edwards, clarinetist Larry Shields, drummer Tony Spargo and Robinson) briefly re-create their 1917 recording of "Livery Stable Blues." The narration makes fun of the then-current swing music, writer Hugues Panassie is shown for a couple of seconds, and there are brief glimpses of Red Norvo, Benny Goodman, Glen Gray, Chick Webb and Stuff Smith's Onyx Club Boys with Jonah Jones (playing an uptempo blues for a chorus). Then the story of the ODJB comeback of 1936 is told and the valuable newsreel concludes with the group playing two choruses of "Tiger

Rag." Although the narration is sometimes a bit fictional, the opportunity to see the ODJB play is priceless.

 ***The March of Time, Volume 10, Issue 5***
(1943, 17 minutes)

The portion of this newsreel titled "Upbeat in Music" discusses the status of American music during World War II. There is a very brief glimpse of Glenn Miller's Army Air Force Band ("St. Louis Blues March"), a discussion with bandleaders (including Benny Goodman, Tommy Dorsey and Paul Whiteman) about a V-Disc program, the Art Tatum Trio (with Tiny Grimes and Slam Stewart) playing for a half-minute, Duke Ellington for twenty seconds, and singer Bea Wain.

The March of Time, Volume 10, Issue 12
(1944, 16 minutes)

A mixture of jazz topics are covered in "Music in America." Benny Goodman is seen briefly lecturing at Julliard and playing an excerpt of "Henderson Stomp" with his big band (which includes Gene Krupa). Also seen is an excerpt from the Original Dixieland Jazz Band story of 1937, George Gershwin briefly playing "I Got Rhythm," a tantalizingly brief spot of Art Tatum (with Tiny Grimes and Slam Stewart) playing at the Three Deuces and a glimpse of Eddie Condon's band.

The March of Time, Volume 12, Issue 8
(1946, 21 minutes)

A segment titled "Nightclub Boom" shows some of New York's many nightclubs. There are quick peeks at (among others) the Jimmy Dorsey Orchestra and Eddie Condon's band (which includes Wild Bill Davison, valve trombonist Brad Gowans and drummer Dave Tough.

The March of Time, Volume 15, Issue 6
(20 minutes)

The "It's in the Groove" section tells the history of recordings, from cylinders to LPs. Part of the Original Dixieland

Jazz Band segment is repeated and there are brief moments from Eddie Condon's band and Paul Whiteman.

March of Time, Volume 16, Issue 1
(1950, 17 minutes)

An otherwise irrelevant mid-century segment has a quick moment from Wild Bill Davison's band.

Martin Block's Musical Merry-Go-Round
(1948, 10 minutes)

This short is hosted by radio deejay Martin Block, who welcomes actress Virginia O'Brien as his guest while he recounts a simplified history of the Les Brown Orchestra. O'Brien sings "Carry Me Back to Old Virginny" in her trademark deadpan style, Eileen Wilson fills in for Doris Day (who left Brown a couple of years earlier) on "Sentimental Journey," and the band performs "Mexican Hat Dance" with the leader heard on clarinet. Although Brown's Band of Renown included tenor saxophonist Dave Pell and trombonist Ray Sims, the group never gets a chance to cut loose.

Mary Lou Williams: Music on My Mind
(1990, 59 minutes)

The life of the remarkable pianist Mary Lou Williams (who died in 1981) is covered in this hour-long documentary. Williams, a major stride pianist in the 1920s, chose to drop out of music for a time in the 1950s when she worked with drug addicts and converted to Catholicism. This film, which effectively covers each of these periods, has interviews with Williams, Dizzy Gillespie, Buddy Tate and Barry Ulanov plus some brief performance clips.

Mayport and All That Jazz
(1982, 60 minutes)

This hour special has highlights from the 1982 Jacksonville Jazz Festival. Dizzy Gillespie is in good form with his band, performing "Manteca," a blues and "Salt Peanuts." Marcus Roberts, a pianist just beginning to become known, confidently leads a group through "Rhythm Changes" and "Totaika." However, the final number is memorable for nonmusical reasons. As Phil Woods and his quartet perform an unidentified ballad, halfway through the song it starts raining heavily. The festival crew covers up the instruments (including both the piano and the pianist) while Woods unhurriedly finishes the song. It is humorous to watch!

Meet the Maestros
(1938, 9 minutes)

A few different bands are seen from earlier film clips, including a number from Isham Jones and Cab Calloway's orchestra performing "Zaz-Zuh-Zah" from 1934's **Hi-De-Ho**.

Mel Tormé: Smooth as Velvet
(1995, 60 minutes)

This Arts & Entertainment biography does a fine job of tracing the long and productive life of singer Mel Tormé. Rare photos and home movies show Tormé as a child, the singer is interviewed throughout the show, and there are also remarks from Steve Allen, Hugh Hefner, Artie Shaw, writer Will Friedwald, singer Vic Damone, Ray Anthony, George Shearing and actor Harry Anderson. As is too often the case in these hour-long documentaries, there is not enough music (everything is excerpts), but one does get the gist of the Mel Tormé story including his unsuccessful film career, his marriages and his battle to sing the type of jazz and swing that he loved.

Melody Masters
(1949, 15 minutes)

The 1949 Charlie Barnet Orchestra, with singers Virginia Maxey and Clark Dennis, performs "Redskin Rhumba," "Jealousie," "Pompton Turnpike," "Jeepers Creepers," "Peg O' My Heart" and "Skyliner."

Melody Parade
(1944, 15 minutes)

This short, not to be confused with the full-length film of the same name from 1943 (which has the orchestras of Anson Weeks and Ted Fio Rita), features Charlie Barnet's orchestra, which at the time included pianist Dodo Marmarosa and singer Kay Starr. Along with other singers and specialty acts, Barnet performs "How Am I to Know," "Redskin Rhumba," "Skyliner" and "Washington Whirligig."

Melody Time *(1946, 18 minutes)*

See: **Meet the Bandleaders** (Swingtime Video 104) (page 100)

 ### Memories of Eubie
(1979, 59 minutes)

This television special for PBS is particularly special for it features veteran pianist/composer Eubie Blake at the age of 96. Still in excellent form, Blake talks about his life and is joined by several guests, although he is the star throughout. Blake performs "Charleston Rag," "Baltimore Buzz," "You're Lucky to Me," "Memories of You," "Classical Rag" and a few of his other songs. Billy Taylor narrates a quick run-through of Blake's life story, interviews Eubie and plays "Melodic Rag" and "Dixie on 7th Avenue." Alberta Hunter, who was 84 herself, reminisces with Blake about performing with him 55 years earlier and sings "All Your Fault" and duets with Blake on "Love Will Find a Way." In addition Gregory and Maurice Hines dance and Lynne Godfrey sings seductively before everyone joins in for the closing "I'm Just Wild About Harry."

Midnight Serenade
(1947, 18 minutes)

Peggy Lee is featured performing three numbers, including "It's a Good Day." She is backed by her husband, guitarist Dave Barbour, and his group.

Mike Bryan Sextet *(1962, 24 minutes)*

See: **Jazz Festival Vol. 2** (page 73)

 ### Miles Ahead—The Music of Miles Davis
(1986, 60 minutes)

This television special, part of the PBS **Great Performances** series, celebrated Miles Davis's 60th birthday. The retrospective has interesting comments from Dizzy Gillespie, Herbie Hancock, George Benson, Gil Evans, Robben Ford, Tony Williams, Wayne Shorter and Keith Jarrett, narration from Oscar Brown, Jr., and a few fascinating interview segments with Miles Davis himself. This is a reasonable one-hour summary of the great trumpeter's life that includes a few familiar performances ("So What," "New Rhumba" and "Blues for Pablo" from 1959) plus a rarer "Footprints" with his 1965 quintet and versions of "Time After Time" and "Human Nature" with his mid-'80s group.

Million Dollar Notes *(1935, 9 minutes)*

See: **Meet the Bandleaders** (Swingtime Video 105) (page 101)

 ### Mills Blue Rhythm Band
(1933, 9 minutes)

The mostly no-name big band, which includes tenor saxophonist Joe Garland, pianist Edgar Hayes, bassist Hayes Alvis, drummer O'Neill Spencer and singer Sally Gooding, performs concise and mostly swinging versions of "The Peanut Vendor," "Tony's Wife," "Love Is the Thing," "Blue Rhythm," "Underneath the Harlem Moon," "I Would Do Anything for You" and "There Goes My Headache."

Milt Hinton: Keeping Time—The Life, Music & Photographs of Milt Hinton
(2002, 61 minutes)

David Berger, Holly Maxson and Kate Hirson produced and wrote this documentary about the beloved bassist/photographer Milt Hinton. The high points of Hinton's lengthy career are touched upon including the Chicago jazz scene of the 1920s, his years with Cab Calloway, his studio work, being part of both the "Great Day in Harlem" photo shoot and **The Sound of Jazz** television special, and his later years. Throughout the film, one sees dozens of Hinton's photographs, including quite a few that are not in his books. Among those seen talking about Hinton are Branford Marsalis, George Wein, Gregory Hines, Doc Cheatham, Clark Terry, Joe Williams, Phil Bodner, Dick Hyman, Joe Wilder, Quincy Jones, Hank Jones, Jon Faddis, writers Dan Morgenstern, Halima Taha, Richard B. Woodward, Nat Hentoff and Amiri Baraka, and bassists Ray Brown, Bill Crow, John Clayton, Rufus Reid, Eddie Gomez, Ron Carter, Christian McBride, Bob Cranshaw, Jay Leonhart and Brian Torff, plus Milt himself. The storytelling is fine, but unfortunately all of the music is talked over including Hinton's feature of his later years, the humorous "Old Man Time." So despite all of the praise, viewers who are not familiar with Milt Hinton's musical legacy will have little chance during this film to hear for themselves why he was such a great bassist.

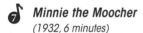

Minnie the Moocher
(1932, 6 minutes)

This Betty Boop cartoon has Cab Calloway seen briefly dancing in front of his orchestra. Betty Boop and her sidekick Bimbo run away from home, encounter a ghostly walrus who sings and dances like Calloway (who is heard throughout the soundtrack with his band) and are finally are chased home by a variety of ghostly monsters while the orchestra plays "Tiger Rag."

Momma Don't Allow
(1955, 22 minutes)

Trombonist Chris Barber's band (with trumpeter Pat Halcox, clarinetist Monty Sunshine, banjoist Lonnie Donegan, bassist Jim Bray, drummer Ron Bowden and singer Ottilie Patterson) is seen playing almost continuously at the Wood Green Jazz Club, a hangout for the young

working class in a British town. Some drama takes place in the audience where one gets to know some of the people, there is almost a confrontation between different classes (the upper-middle-class people soon leave when they are ignored), and various couples dance.

Monterey Jazz
(1970, 81 minutes)

Highlights from the 1970 Monterey Jazz Festival are on this film. The Johnny Otis R&B band backs Big Joe Turner ("Hide and Seek" and "Roll 'Em Pete"), Marge Evans ("I May Be Wrong"), Eddie "Cleanhead" Vinson ("Cleanhead's Blues"), Esther Phillips and Jimmy Rushing ("Every Day" and "Sent for You Yesterday"). The Modern Jazz Quartet performs "Walking Stomp" and Tim Weisberg's quintet plays "A Day at the Fair." In addition, Duke Ellington's orchestra plays two excerpts from the "Afro-Eurasian Eclipse," "I Got It Bad" (with guest altoist Woody Herman), "Don't Get Around Much Anymore" (with Joe Williams plus Herman on alto) and "Every Day" (featuring Williams).

Murder in Swingtime
(1937, 10 minutes)

The Les Hite Orchestra recorded relatively little, most notably 14 selections during 1940–42. However, since the ensemble was based in Los Angeles, they appear in quite a few films. This short features Les Hite's band with singer June Richmond.

Music in Progress *(1978, 44 minutes)*

Pianist/composer Mike Westbrook is profiled in this documentary, discussing his life and performing at a series of concerts with his big band. The adventurous 15-piece orchestra includes singer Phil Minton, Kate Westbrook on tenor horn and vocals, and trombonist Paul Rutherford, interpreting a diverse repertoire ("Tender Love," "The Fields," "Piano-Link," "Wheels Go Round," "Lady Howard's Coach," "Holborne Suite," "Wheel of Fortune,"

"Bartlemy Fair," "Serpent Maigre," "God Bless the Child," "Kanonen Song," "Wheels Go Round," "I See Thy Form," "Hot Jamboree").

 ### Nat Adderley: Live at the Village Vanguard
(1981, 60 minutes)

Cornetist Nat Adderley performs "Book's Back," "Book's Bossa," "Chelsea Bridge," "Jordanian Walk," "Little Boy with Sad Eyes," "The Scene," "Tallahassee Kid" and "Work Song" in a quintet with tenor saxophonist Ricky Ford, pianist

Larry Willis, bassist Walter Booker and drummer Jimmy Cobb. This film is one in a series of **Live at the Village Vanguard** concerts filmed by director Bruce Bushcel.

 ### Nat King Cole: Unforgettable *(1988, 60 minutes)*

This is an effective one-hour biography of the pianist/singer, with comments from Natalie Cole, Marie Cole (Nat's second wife), Harry Belafonte, Freddie Cole, Oscar Peterson and Ella Fitzgerald. Most of the film clips are brief although there are tantalizing excerpts from Cole's

The Nat King Cole Trio with guitarist Oscar Moore appeared in many shorts and films in the '40s.

appearance on **This Is Your Life** and the 1955 semi-fictional short **The Nat King Cole Story**.

Nat King Cole and Joe Adams's Orchestra
(1951, 15 minutes)

Nat King Cole sings "Destination Moon," "Too Young" and "That's My Girl" with backing by an orchestra, guitarist Irving Ashby, bassist Joe Comfort and Jack Costanzo on bongo.

The Nat King Cole Musical Story
(1955, 18 minutes)

This oddity was an attempt at telling the Nat King Cole story with Cole himself singing and playing "Sweet Lorraine," "Route 66," "Pretend," "Straighten Up and Fly Right" and "Darling, Je Vous Aime Beaucoup." It gives listeners a rare chance to hear Cole in a trio format (with guitarist John Collins and bassist Charlie Harris) this late in his career even if the storyline is partly fictional.

 ### Nellie *(1981, 60 minutes)*

Nellie Lutcher, a fine pianist and an eccentric singer who had some hit records in the late '40s for Capitol, is well showcased during this hour special. Joined by both John Collins and Ulysses Livingston on guitars, trumpeter Bobby Bryant (who plays muted), bassist Billy Hadnott and drummer Gene Washington, Lutcher treats the set as a live performance even though it was filmed in a studio. She is briefly interviewed on a few occasions but mostly is seen performing a fairly definitive program ("Imagine You," "Hurry on Down to My Place," "Mack the Knife," "A Chicken Ain't Nothin' but a Bird," "This Can't Be Love," "The Entertainer," "The Lady's in Love with You," "Fine Brown Frame," "He's a Real Gone Guy") with plenty of spirit and swing.

 ### New Orleans Blues *(1943, 15 minutes)*

The Louis Prima Big Band, with ex–Glenn Miller vocalist Ray Eberle, performs "All or Nothing at All," "That Old Black Magic" (long before Prima and Keely Smith had a hit with the song), "So Good Night" and "Way Down Yonder in New Orleans."

New Year's Eve Jazz Celebration
(1985, 120 minutes)

On December 31, 1985, a lengthy all-star jazz party held at singer Ethel Ennis's club in Baltimore was televised on PBS. An opening version of "It's a Wonderful World" features all of the musicians and singers. Pianist Cedar Walton with Ray Brown and drummer Mickey Roker perform "Satin Doll" and then the trio becomes a quartet with the addition of Milt Jackson ("In a Sentimental Mood," "Things Ain't What They Used to Be," "Take the 'A' Train"). Gerry Mulligan is in top form on "Georgia on My Mind" and "St. Louis Blues," interacting with harmonica wizard Toots Thielemans on "Line for Lyons"; Toots takes "Sophisticated Lady" as his feature. Ethel Ennis sings "Blue Skies" and "Do What You Wanna Be" and Joe Williams brings in the New Year with "I Want a Little Girl," "Alright, OK, You Win," "Close Enough for Love" and "Hold It Right There." Phil Woods plays three numbers (an original, "Goodbye Mr. Evans" and "Willow Weep for Me"), Toots returns for "Bluesette," Ennis sings "Lover Man" and Mulligan closes the show with "Broadway." Hopefully someday this excellent and extensive concert will be made available on DVD.

Newport Jazz '88
(1988, 60 minutes)

Some of the highlights from the 1988 Newport Jazz Festival are included on this hour performance film. Grover Washington plays alto on a soulful original and soprano on "Stella by Starlight." Carmen McRae, joined by a group that includes tenor saxophonist Clifford Jordan, performs "Old Devil Moon," "'Round Midnight" and "Straight No Chaser." The Herbie Hancock Trio (with bassist Buster Williams and drummer Al Foster) plays two numbers including "Just One of Those Things," Montgomery, Plant and Stritch (two female singers and a male vocalist who also plays

Take That Away from Me," "Lullaby of Birdland" and "A Night in Tunisia," duets with Joe Pass on "I'm Just a Lucky So and So" and is joined by Oscar Peterson for a closing "Perdido."

 ### On Stage at Wolf Trap: Gunther Schuller and the New England Ragtime Ensemble
(1986, 60 minutes)

Gunther Schuller and the New England Ragtime Ensemble perform an entertaining hour of early music on this PBS special. In their repertoire are Scott Joplin rags ("Maple Leaf Rag," "Sunflower Slow Drag," "The Entertainer"), James Scott's "Hilarity Rag," Arthur Marshall's "Swipesy," Zez Confrey's "Dizzy Fingers," a pair of Jelly Roll Morton jazz numbers ("Smoke House Blues" and "Grandpa's Spells") and a delightful and authentic-sounding version of James Reese Europe's "Castle House Rag."

 ### The Opry House
(1929, 9 minutes)

The Mound City Blue Blowers (with Red McKenzie on comb and Eddie Lang playing rhythm guitar) perform "I Ain't Got Nobody," "Let Me Call You Sweetheart" and "My Gal Sal" on this very valuable short. There are also vocals from Lew Hearn and Doris Walker.

 ### Oscar Peterson: Words and Music
(1983, 60 minutes)

During this documentary from the Canadian Broadcasting Corporation, pianist Oscar Peterson talks about his early life and performs with bassist Niels Pedersen, drummer Martin Taylor and (on one uptempo number) Joe Pass. The best moments musically are during an unaccompanied uptempo blues. Along the way Peterson's sister Daisy, former bandleader Johnny Holmes and producer Norman Granz reminisce a bit. Peterson is not only seen onstage but playing various keyboards at home, fishing, relaxing and on the road.

 ### Outside in Sight: The Music of United Front
(1986, 29 minutes)

The San Francisco–based quartet United Front (consisting of percussionist Anthony Brown, bassist Mark Izu, saxophonist Lewis Jordan and trumpeter George Sams) is seen rehearsing, performing before an audience and discussing the jazz life and their struggles.

Ovoutie O'Rooney (1946, 16 minutes)

See: **The Small Black Groups** (page 119)

 ### Ozzie Nelson and His Orchestra
(1939, 10 minutes)

Although he would become famous for the situation comedy **Ozzie and Harriet**, Ozzie Nelson was a decent singer who led a fine swing band in the 1930s and '40s. This short has an amusing look at his life as a bandleader ("Wave-a-Stick Blues"), a medium-tempo version of "Begin the Beguine" and a heated rendition of "Put on Your Old Grey Bonnet."

 ### Ozzie Nelson and His Orchestra
(1943, 9 minutes)

Ozzie Nelson led one of the most underrated bands of the swing era. During this short, his band sounds excellent on a riffing blues, and "Chinatown, My Chinatown," backing the leader on the comedy number "Come on, Get Up" and "I'm Dancing with the Mamma with the Moola."

 ### Parade of the Bands
(1955, 29 minutes)

This British short features six bands that were popular in England during the mid-'50s, including Michael Mitchell (with singer Liza Ashwood), Eric Jupp, Frank Weir (with singer Rusty Harran) and Francisco Caves. Of strongest interest from the jazz standpoint are trumpeter Freddy Randall's group and Johnny Dankworth's orchestra with Cleo Laine.

Paramount Pictorial Magazine No. 837: The World at Large
(1933, 10 minutes)

This entry in a series of general-interest news shorts has Irving Mills during a four-minute section introducing Baron Lee's Blue Rhythm Band ("Ridin' in Rhythm") and the big bands of Duke Ellington ("Sophisticated Lady" and "Creole Rhapsody") and Cab Calloway ("The Scat Song"); Cab's hot chorus steals the show. All of the performances are very brief excerpts with only "Creole Rhapsody" being over a minute long (and just barely) and Duke's band not being seen. Ellington's section of **Paramount Pictorial No. 889** is included in **Duke Ellington 1929–1943**.

Passing It On *(1985, 23 minutes)*

See: **Three Piano Portraits** (page 133)

 Pete's Place
(1966, 17 minutes)

This brief film features clarinetist Pete Fountain during Mardi Gras in New Orleans.

 Pie, Pie Blackbird
(1932, 9 minutes)

The plot of this short is a bit nonsensical as Nina Mae McKinney, with her "sons" the Nicholas Brothers, bakes a blackbird pie. Inside the pie are Eubie Blake and his orchestra (the second pianist is George Rickson and all of the personnel is obscure) performing in chef's outfits. McKinney sings "Blackbird Pie," Blake's band performs "Memories of You," backs McKinney on "Everything that I Got Belongs to You" and romps on "I'll Be Glad When You're Dead You Rascal You." Blake, who was already 48, had more than a half-century to go. Finishing the film, the Nicholas Brothers dance on a heated "China Boy." Despite the silliness of it all, the music is enjoyable.

 Pity the Poor Rich *(1935, 22 minutes)*

The entertaining British trumpeter/vocalist Nat Gonella performs "Georgia on My Mind," "I'm Gonna Wash My Hands of You," "Troublesome Trumpet" and "Tiger Rag" with his Georgians. The sextet also includes tenor saxophonist Don Barrigo and altoist Eric Ritty.

 Playback *(1963, 5 minutes apiece)*

In 1963, Columbia Records filmed some of its top-selling jazz artists talking briefly about their new records and playing short excerpts from some of the selections. Of strongest interest are the segments by André Previn with his trio (bassist Red Mitchell and drummer Frank Capp), the Dave Brubeck Quartet (which includes "Blue Rondo à la Turk"), Duke Ellington's orchestra (playing part of the "Nutcracker Suite") and Teddy Wilson ("Tea for Two").

 Portrait of a Bushman
(1966, 8 minutes)

This Danish short features pianist Dollar Brand (a few years before he renamed himself Abdullah Ibrahim) at the Montmartre performing with bassist Johnny Gertze and drummer Makaya Ntshoko.

 Queen of the Boogie
(1947, 10 minutes)

Pianist/singer Hadda Brooks is featured on an all-Black short named after her title.

 Radio Melodies
(1943, 15 minutes)

The early Stan Kenton Orchestra performs "Artistry in Rhythm" (under the name of "Production on Theme"), "Reed Rapture," "Ride On" and "Hip Hip Hooray." Dolly Mitchell is the vocalist, and the band includes trumpeter Buddy Childers, tenor saxophonist Red Dorris, baritonist Bob Gioga and Kenton on piano.

Rambling 'Round Radio Row No. 1
(1932, 9 minutes)

A reporter who is writing an article on radio goes to a radio station where he hears the Boswell Sisters rehearse "We've Got to Put the Sun Back in the Sky." He also sees Abe Lyman and watches Kate Smith perform.

 Ray Anthony and His Orchestra
(1947, 11 minutes)

The nostalgic swing trumpeter Ray Anthony and his big band perform "I'll Close My Eyes," "Let's Go Back and Kiss the Boys Again" and "Finiculi, Finicula." This short is from the **Thrills of Music** series.

 Ray Anthony and His Orchestra
(1950, 14 minutes)

In addition to playing their usual swing music, Ray Anthony and his orchestra back the Starlighters and a tap dancing xylophonist (Jimmy Vey). The songs include "Toot Toot Tootsie Goodbye" and "Come to the Fair."

 Ray McKinley and His Orchestra
(1942, 8 minutes)

The otherwise undocumented Ray McKinley big band of 1942 swings well on "St. Louis Blues," "Big Boy," "Yank, Yankee Doodle" and an exciting "Jive Bomber." All these songs except "Yank, Yankee Doodle" have been reissued on **Meet the Bandleaders** (Swingtime Video 110).

 Ray McKinley and His Orchestra
(1946, 10 minutes)

The drummer's underrated band performs "Hoodle Addie," "Tabu" and "Comin' Out."

Readin,' Ritin' and Rhythm
(1939, 10 minutes)

The Lucky Millinder Orchestra (with trumpeter Frankie Newton and tenor saxophonist Don Byas) is featured two years before it made its recording debut. The highlight of the short is "Ride Red Ride."

Record Hop *(1957, 15 minutes)*

The Charlie Barnet Orchestra functions as a house band on some numbers behind singers Ella Mae Morse, the Lancers, Tex Williams and Alan Copeland. The selections include "Redskin Rhumba," "Every Night," "Claude Reigns" (featuring pianist Claude Williams), "Will You Still Be Mine," "Accentuate the Positive" and "Myra."

 Record Party
(1947, 15 minutes)

This short features Connie Haines and the Pied Pipers plus the Page Cavanaugh Trio (with guitarist Al Viola).

 Red Nichols and His Five Pennies
(1929, 9 minutes)

This very valuable (but rarely seen) short features cornetist Red Nichols's Five Pennies (with Eddie Condon on rhythm guitar) playing "Ida, Sweet as Apple Cider," "Who Cares" and "China Boy."

Red Nichols and His Five Pennies
(1950, 15 minutes)

Cornetist Red Nichols's Dixieland group (a sextet also including trombonist King Jackson, clarinetist Rosy McHargue, the great bass saxophonist Joe Rushton, pianist Bob Hammack and drummer Rollie Culver) play "Three Blind Mice" and "The Entry of the Gladiators," also backing June Hutton, the Skylarks and some tap dancers on "Do It Again," "Vaudeville Is Back" and "I Got Tookin'."

Red Nichols and His World Famous Pennies
(1936, 9 minutes)

The Red Nichols big band along with singer Bob Carter and the Wallace Sisters are featured during this fairly straightforward short. Nichols's big band was never as interesting as his Five Pennies, but this film has its moments. Nichols performs "Wail of the Winds" (his theme song), "Get Happy," "Cryin' for the Carolines," "Sleepy Time Down South," "Troublesome Trumpet," "Can't You Hear Me Calling" and "Carolina in the Morning."

 Redskin Rhumba *(1948, 15 minutes)*

The big band era might have been over by 1948, but Charlie Barnet's orchestra was still playing fairly regularly and the bandleader was just beginning to open his music a little toward bop. At the time of this short, his orchestra included trumpeter/arranger Neal Hefti, altoist Bud Shank and pianist Claude Williamson, plus singers Clark Dennis and Virginia Maxey. Barnet's band is in fine form on "Redskin Rhumba," "Skyliner," "Jeepers Creepers," "Peg of My Heart," "Jealousy" and "Pompton Turnpike." Four of the six numbers (the instrumentals) were reissued on **Swing: Best of the Big Bands, Vol. 1 and 2**.

Rhapsody in Black and Blue *(1932, 10 minutes)*

A very stereotyped and tasteless but valuable short featuring Louis Armstrong (in a leopard skin) performing "I'll Be Glad When You're Dead, You Rascal You" and "Shine." Victoria Spivey has a small role as an angry wife.

Rhapsody in Wood *(1947, 9 minutes).*

This particular George Pal Puppetoon has Woody Herman interacting with animated puppets. He plays clarinet throughout (backing is by members of the First Herd who do not appear on-screen), explains the origin of the music and discusses his grandfather's life.

Rhythm in a Riff *(1946, 45 minutes)*

See: **Things to Come** (page 133)

Riot in Rhythm *(1957, 15 minutes)*

The Harry James Orchestra is mostly used in support of singers (Johnny O'Neill and the De Castro Sisters) and

dancers on this program. The James band performs "Teach Me Tonight," "Heartbreak Hotel" and "Jericho."

 Rob McConnell: Brass Goes Silver *(1993, 54 minutes)*

This Canadian film pays tribute to valve trombonist/ arranger Rob McConnell's Boss Brass, featuring such players as trumpeter Guido Basso, Moe Koffman and Rick Wilkins on reeds, guitarist Ed Bickert and pianist Don Thompson.

Rosemary Clooney: With Love *(1981, 60 minutes)*

Rosemary Clooney, who was 53 at the time, is heard at her peak on this hour-long PBS television special. What makes this set of particular interest is that Clooney is joined by the Concord All-Stars: tenor saxophonist Scott Hamilton, cornetist Warren Vache, pianist Dave McKenna, guitarist Cal Collins, bassist Bob Maize and drummer Jake Hanna. The singer performs an excellent program ("Tenderly," "Hey There," "I Will Wait for You," "Just the Way You Are," "Our Love Is Here to Stay," "Strike Up the Band," "But Beautiful," "She's Funny that Way," "I Can't Get Started," "As Time Goes By," "I'm Checkin' Out Goombye," "The Way We Were"). There is solo space along the way for the other players, with particularly heated playing on "Strike Up the Band" and "I'm Checkin' Out Goombye."

 Rufus Jones for President *(1933, 16 minutes)*

This short is absurd and full of outrageous racial stereotypes, but it is of interest because it features Sammy Davis, Jr., as a child (his face was already familiar), singing "I'll Be Glad When You're Dead, You Rascal You" and tap dancing. Ethel Waters plays his mother, singing "Am I Blue" and "Underneath the Harlem Moon." The plot, a dream about Davis becoming president, is too ridiculous to even repeat!

St. Louis Blues *(1929, 16 minutes)*

See: **The Blues** (page 26)

Salute to Louis Armstrong
(1972, 25 minutes)

This film is a tribute to Louis Armstrong, celebrating his legacy on what was believed to have been his 70th birthday (July 4, 1970) at the Newport Jazz Festival. Among the notables featured are Dizzy Gillespie, Ray Nance, Bobby Hackett, Tyree Glenn and Mahalia Jackson. Satchmo was under doctor's orders not to play trumpet, but he is featured singing. Among the numbers are "Pennies from Heaven," "Blueberry Hill" and "Mack the Knife."

Salute to Dizzy Gillespie
(1988, 90 minutes)

During a special concert at Wolf Trap on June 6, 1987, a remarkable group of all-stars paid tribute to Dizzy Gillespie, who turned 70 that year. There are some vintage clips, some summaries of Gillespie's life and comments from many of the principals including the trumpeter himself. Dizzy's playing is in better-than-usual form for this late period. "Birks' Works" features Wynton Marsalis, J.J. Johnson, Benny Carter, pianist Hank Jones, bassist Rufus Reid and drummer Mickey Roker. "Fiesta Mojo" includes percussionists Candido, Mongo Santamaria, Ignacio Berroa and Nickey Marrero in a large group with saxophonists Sam Rivers and Arnie Lawrence, flutist Dave Valentin, trombonist Steve Turre, David Amram on pennywhistle, trumpeter Jimmy Owens and pianist Walter Davis, Jr. "Tanga" features Valentin, Freddie Hubbard, singer Flora Purim and percussionist Airto Moreirao. But those numbers are just warm-ups for the next four performances. A lengthy "Ooo-Pop-A-Da" has remarkable scat singing by Dizzy, Jon Hendricks and James Moody plus solos from trumpeter Jon Faddis, trombonist Slide Hampton

and baritonist Cecil Payne. "All the Things You Are" is a duet by Gillespie and Oscar Peterson. On an uptempo blues, Dizzy interacts with Sonny Rollins and "This Is the Start of a Beautiful Friendship" has Gillespie dueting with Carmen McRae who not only sings but plays effective piano. There are some touching moments along the way and virtually everything works.

A Salute to Duke
(1981, 89 minutes)

Seven years after Duke Ellington's death, he was paid tribute on this PBS television special by Sarah Vaughan, Joe Williams, Max Roach, dancer Harold Nicholas and an orchestra led by Billy Taylor. Unfortunately, most of the musicians are not identified other than violinist Joe Kennedy, Jr., and surprisingly there are no alumni from his band. Vaughan is typically outstanding on "I Let a Song Go Out of My Heart" and "I've Got It Bad"; Joe Williams is fine on "Do Nothing Till You Hear from Me" and "Lush Life" and does his best to keep up with Sassy on "It Don't Mean a Thing" although that is impossible. The Billy Taylor Orchestra performs "Take the 'A' Train," "Caravan" (featuring Kennedy), "C Jam Blues" and "Battle Royal," Nicholas dances to "Come Sunday" and Roach has a drum solo on "What Am I Here For." There are also a few comments (but no music) from Ella Fitzgerald.

Salute to Duke Ellington
(1950, 16 minutes)

This Universal short features the 1950 Duke Ellington Orchestra performing "Things Ain't What They Used to Be," "Hello, Little Boy" (with singer Chubby Kemp), the intriguing "A History of Jazz in Three Minutes," "She Wouldn't Be Moved" and "Violet Blue" (on which Kay Davis takes the vocal). Among the key players featured at least briefly are Ray Nance, trumpeter Nelson Williams, altoist Russell Procope, Tyree Glenn, bassist Wendell Marshall and Sonny Greer.

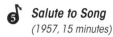

Salute to Song
(1957, 15 minutes)

This Universal short has appearances by a variety of musical guests, including Cal Tjader's quintet and Freddy Martin's orchestra.

Sarah Vaughan and Herb Jeffries
(1950, 15 minutes)

Sarah Vaughan sounds as wondrous as always on memorable versions of "Don't Blame Me" and "I Cried for You"; both of these numbers have been made available on **Swing—Best of the Big Bands, Vol. 2**. Kid Ory's band (with trumpeter Teddy Buckner, clarinetist Joe Darensbourg, pianist Lloyd Glenn, bassist Ed Garland and drummer Minor Hall) plays "Muskrat Ramble," and there are features for Herb Jeffries and the Treniers.

Satchmo *(1979, 86 minutes)*

This is a delightful compilation of some of the most exciting filmed performances by Louis Armstrong from throughout his career. There is no real narration (nor is any needed) other than some comments by Armstrong himself about his career. Quite a few classic movie and television clips are included. Among the many highlights are a version of "Back O'Town Blues" from 1965, some of the best moments from the documentary **Satchmo the Great** (including "Black and Blue" from 1956, "C'est Si Bon" and part of an interview with Edward R. Murrow), "Mack the Knife," "Nobody Knows the Trouble I've Seen," the 1933 performances of "I Cover the Waterfront" and "Dinah," "That's My Desire" (with Velma Middleton in 1951), a remarkable version of "St. Louis Blues" with Leonard Bernstein and the New York Philharmonic (clarinetist Edmond Hall's first long note in his solo is unforgettable), "Rockin' Chair" with Jack Teagarden, and clips from the 1970 Newport Jazz Festival (with spots for Bobby Hackett, Wild Bill Davison, Dizzy Gillespie and Mahalia Jackson). Shown on

television in the early '80s, this is a show well deserving of being made available on DVD.

Satchmo the Great
(1957, 63 minutes)

Louis Armstrong's worldwide travels of the 1950s (including a visit to Africa), his appearance on Edward R. Murrow's **See It Now** television show, and a remarkable version of "St. Louis Blues" with the New York Philharmonic and Leonard Bernstein (with W.C. Handy in the audience) are all in this wonderful documentary, which celebrates his role as America's goodwill ambassador. Armstrong's All-Stars at the time included Trummy Young, Edmond Hall, Billy Kyle, Jack Lesberg or Dale Jones on bass, Barrett Deems and Velma Middleton. Claude Luter's orchestra is also briefly seen. There is a lot of good humor throughout this film and quite a bit of music, including "The Saints," "When It's Sleepy Time Down South," "That's My Desire," "Blueberry Hill," "Kokomo," "Mop Mop," "C'est Si Bon," "Ole Miss," "Struttin' with Some Barbecue," "Mack the Knife," "The Bucket's Got a Hole in It," "Sly Mongoose," "Royal Garden Blues," "Black and Blue," "Mahogany Hall Stomp" and that very special version of "St. Louis Blues."

The Saturday Night Swing Club
(1938, 9 minutes)

A filmed version of the popular **Saturday Night Swing Club** radio show has announcer/actor Paul Douglas hosting Leith Stevens's orchestra ("Dipsy Doodle" and "Bob White") and a Dixieland septet led by Bobby Hackett that includes Pee Wee Russell, trombonist George Brunies, Eddie Condon and drummer Chauncey Morehouse playing "At the Jazz Band Ball."

The Sauter-Finegan Orchestra
(1955, 18 minutes)

The unusual orchestra, co-led by arrangers Eddie Sauter and Bill Finegan, performs "Doodletown Pipers,"

"Doodletown Races," "Hold Back Tomorrow," "Midnight Sleigh Ride," "John Henry" and "Thunderbreak." Considering its popularity in the mid-'50s, it is surprising how little film exists of the Sauter-Finegan Orchestra.

🎵 Save the Children
(1973, 123 minutes)

In 1972 Jesse Jackson's PUSH sponsored the Black Exposition in Chicago. This extensive filmed concert mostly features soul and R&B performers. Among the few exceptions were the Cannonball Adderley Quintet ("Country Preacher"), Quincy Jones ("On a Clear Day" and "Killer Joe") and Ramsey Lewis.

🎵 Saxophone Diplomacy
(1984, 28 minutes)

In 1983, before the fall of communism and the end of the Soviet Union, the Rova Saxophone Quartet visited Russia, performing concerts in Moscow, Riga and Leningrad. This informal documentary has comments from each of the saxophonists (Larry Ochs, Bruce Ackley, Jon Raskin and Andrew Voigt), impressions of the country and the people, and various Russians commenting on Rova's avant-garde music, which was met with strong approval. Despite difficulties with bureaucracy and the challenge of working around the repression, Rova had a successful tour and good feelings resulted from this visit. There are excerpts from four forbidding numbers ("Terrains," "The Throes," "Flamingo Horizons," "Paint Another Toke of the Shootpop") during this well-conceived documentary.

🎵 Scandals of 1933
(1933, 10 minutes)

The Mills Blue Rhythm Band, under the direction of Lucky Millinder and featuring vocals by Putney Dandridge, perform "It Don't Mean a Thing," "Dinah," "I Ain't Got Nobody," "Please" and "Nagasaki" in spirited fashion.

🎵 Scott Joplin, King of Ragtime Composers
(1977, 15 minutes)

A couple of years after **The Sting** made Scott Joplin a household name (by using a few of his songs prominently on its soundtrack), this short documentary paid tribute to Joplin. Eartha Kitt does the narration, there is a brief appearance by Eubie Blake (who knew Joplin) and bits of Joplin's music are utilized including part of "Treemonisha."

🎵 See the Music
(1970, 23 minutes)

This West German documentary features altoist Marion Brown and trumpeter Leo Smith playing some free improvisations (with other local musicians on "little instruments") and talking about their lives.

🎵 Seger Ellis and His Embassy Club Orchestra
(1929, 9 minutes)

The nasal-voiced singer heads a band that includes trumpeter Fuzzy Farrer, Tommy Dorsey, Jimmy Dorsey, pianist Arthur Schutt, Eddie Lang, violinist Al Duffy and drummer Stan King on "How Can I Love Again," "Am I Blue" and "I've Got a Feeling I'm Falling."

🎵 Shepherd of the Night Flock
(1977, 57 minutes)

Father John Gensel constantly helped out the jazz community in New York and this documentary tells his story. There are some excerpts from Duke Ellington's last concert and trumpeters Joe Newman and Howard McGhee, tenor saxophonist Zoot Sims and Billy Taylor make appearances.

🎵 Sing Bing Sing
(1932, 19 minutes)

Bing Crosby, playing a radio crooner (not much of a stretch for him), elopes with Florine McKinney with the help of a gorilla. He sings "In Your Hideaway," "Between the Devil and the Deep Blue Sea," "Lovable" and "Snuggled on Your Shoulder."

Sing, Helen, Sing
(1943, 11 minutes)

Helen O'Connell, who had recently left Jimmy Dorsey's orchestra, entertains American servicemen while backed by Joe Venuti's big band.

 Sissle and Blake's Snappy Songs
(1923, 7 minutes)

This and **Eubie Blake Plays** may very well be the earliest examples of Black musicians in a sound film. In 1923, producer Lee De Forest filmed some of vaudeville's top headliners for posterity; it was four years before **The Jazz Singer**. Pianist Eubie Blake and singer Noble Sissle perform "Affectionate Dan," "All God's Chillun Got Shoes" and an unidentified song. The sound quality is primitive, but the performers' enthusiasm still comes through.

 Smash Your Baggage
(1933, 9 minutes)

This interesting short features a group led by banjoist Elmer Snowden (listed as Small's Paradise Entertainers) that never recorded. The plot is about a group of train porters deciding to have a benefit. The band plays an instrumental version of "Bugle Call Rag," backs some acrobatic dancers on "Tiger Rag," "My Man's Gone" and "Concentrating on You," and accompanies an unknown female singer on "Stop the Moon, Stop the Sun." Snowden's band consists of trumpeters Roy Eldridge (three years before he made his recording debut) and Leonard Davis, trombonist Dickie Wells, the reeds of Otto Hardwicke, Wayman Carver and George Washington, pianist Don Kirkpatrick, Dick Fullbright on bass and tuba, Big Sid Catlett and Snowden. Eldridge is prominent on "Tiger Rag" and has a couple of lines as do some of the other band members.

 Smith, James O. Organist USA
(1965, 97 minutes)

This little-known German documentary features organist Jimmy Smith during a European tour.

 Smoke Rings *(1943, 15 minutes)*

Glen Gray and his Casa Loma Orchestra are heard a little bit past their prime on this short. They perform "That's My Affair," "Little Man with the Hammer" (trombonist Pee Wee Hunt takes the vocal), "Can't Get Stuff in Your Cuff" (featuring the Pied Pipers) and "I'm Sorry."

 Song Hits on Parade
(1936, 10 minutes)

Fred Rich led a first-class dance band during the late '20s and throughout the 1930s, one that worked steadily on radio. This short has his orchestra (which includes future comedian Jerry Colonna on trombone, bass saxophonist Adrian Rollini and drummer Chauncey Morehouse) performing "Happy Days Are Here Again," "Cross Patch," "I Can't Escape from You," "Those Foolish Things" and "Tiger Rag." However the most significant selection is "Until Today," for it features Bunny Berigan, on what is likely his only appearance on film, taking the vocal and a brief trumpet solo a little reminiscent in format to "I Can't Get Started." Three of these selections (including "Until Today") have been reissued on 1984's **Meet the Bandleaders** (Swingtime Video 105).

 A Song Is Born *(1939, 9 minutes)*

The Larry Clinton Orchestra, an underrated big band, performs five songs during this short. Bea Wain sings "Love Doesn't Grow on Trees" and "Heart and Soul," Ford Leary is the vocalist on "I Fell Up to Heaven," and the band also performs "The Devil with the Devil" and a brief "Dipsy Doodle." Unfortunately the orchestra never really has a chance to cut loose or show off its jazz abilities. All of these selections except "The Devil with the Devil" were reissued on **Meet the Bandleaders** (Swingtime Video 105).

 Sonny *(1968, 11 minutes)*

Former Duke Ellington drummer Sonny Greer is portrayed during this brief film.

Sonny Dunham and His Orchestra
(1944, 10 minutes)

The underrated trumpeter Sonny Dunham leads his big band (plus singer Angela Greene and the Pied Pipers) on swinging versions of "Sweet Georgia Brown," "Annie Laurie," "Memories of You," "Bob White," "Liza" and "Someday I'll Meet You Again."

 ### Soul to Soul
(1971, 96 minutes)

To celebrate Ghana's 14th anniversary, a concert filled with rock, soul and jazz stars was presented and filmed. The plot behind the film traces the roots of American soul to Africa. Les McCann, Eddie Harris, Cannonball Adderley and Willie Bobo are the jazz acts.

 ### Sounds of Summer: The Concord Jazz Festival
(1970, 60 minutes)

Highlights from an early Concord Jazz Festival are featured during this hour film. Featured are the Bola Sete Quartet, Carmen McRae, the big bands of Stan Kenton and Don Ellis, the Cal Tjader Quintet and Willie Bobo.

 ### Sous-Sol
(1953, 14 minutes)

Trumpeter Peanuts Holland and pianist Lil Armstrong make brief appearances in a French short that has glimpses of several cafes and cabarets.

 ### Southern Crossing
(1981, 92 minutes)

This documentary has the highlights of a five-day jazz festival from January, 1980 held in Sydney, Australia. The stars include the Dave Brubeck Quartet, Herbie Mann, Les McCann's group, Toshiko Akiyoshi and Lew Tabackin leading an all-star Australian band and a few local combos.

 ### The Sportsmen and Ziggy Elman's Orchestra
(1951, 15 minutes)

For this Universal International short, trumpeter Ziggy Elman's big band backs several performers including the Sportsmen and the Knight Sisters (a dancing duo). In addition Mel Henke's trio plays "In a Little Spanish Town" and Elman is featured on the umpteenth revival of his lone hit, "And the Angels Sing."

Stage Entrance *(1951, 7 minutes)*

See: **Celebrating Bird: The Triumph of Charlie Parker** (page 222)

 ### Stan Kenton and His Orchestra: Artistry in Rhythm
(1945, 9 minutes)

The Stan Kenton Big Band was coming into its own in 1945, featuring trumpeter Buddy Childers, altoist Boots Mussulli, tenors Vido Musso and Bob Cooper, bassist Eddie Safranski and most importantly singer June Christy. On this excellent short, Kenton's orchestra plays "Artistry in Rhythm," "If I Could Be with You," "Somebody Loves Me," "Fine, Fine Deal," "I Been Down in Texas" and "Don't Blame Me."

 ### Stars and Violins
(1944 , 15 minutes)

The Jack Teagarden big band, five years into its struggle and two years away from going bankrupt, sticks to swing music and ballads on this obscure short. They perform "Stars and Violins," "A Dream Ago," "Basin Street Blues" (with Teagarden on the vocal), "Sunday" (featuring the Pied Pipers), "Let's Live Again" and "Fort Knox Jump."

Stephane Grappelli and His Quintet *(1946, 14 minutes)*

See: **Stephane Grappelli: A Life in the Jazz Century** (page 125)

♪ *Stompin' for Mili*
(1955, 9 minutes)

This brief documentary was shot by photographer Gjon Mili (who a decade earlier had filmed **Jammin' the Blues**) and George Avakian's brother Aram at a Dave Brubeck recording session in 1954. Apparently Mili was unimpressed by Brubeck's music and told him so, which inspired Brubeck to swing very hard on the title piece, showing Mili what he could really do. The quartet at the time also included altoist Paul Desmond, bassist Bob Bates and drummer Joe Dodge.

♪ *Stop for Bud*
(1963, 12 minutes)

This odd Danish short focuses on Bud Powell. He is seen playing a little in Copenhagen with bassist Niels-Henning Orsted Pedersen and an unidentified drummer (the music does not quite match the picture), but is mostly featured walking around Copenhagen while Dexter Gordon narrates.

♪ *The Story of a Jazz Musician*
(1962, 26 minutes)

Paul Horn is portrayed in his early pre–new age days when he was an up-and-coming bopish altoist and flutist. He is interviewed, seen at a rehearsal of his quintet and performs at Shelley's Manne Hole.

♪ *Studio Live with Freddie Hubbard*
(1981, 59 minutes)

This documentary covers trumpeter Freddie Hubbard's recording sessions of July, 1981, which resulted in the album **Ride Like the Wind**. Though Hubbard plays well, the music is actually dull, as was the rather commercial finished product for Elektra Musician. The large band playing with Hubbard includes altoist Bud Shank and tenor saxophonist Bill Perkins with the featured tunes "Birdland," "Ride Like the Wind" and "This Is It."

♪ *Sugar Chile Robinson/Billie Holiday/ Count Basie and His Sextet*
(1950, 15 minutes)

This short is valuable for it features Billie Holiday singing "God Bless the Child" and "Now, Baby or Never" while backed by the Count Basie Septet (with Clark Terry, clarinetist Marshall Royal, tenor saxophonist Wardell Gray, Freddie Green, bassist Jimmy Lewis and drummer Gus Johnson). Basie's combo also plays "One O'Clock Jump," and the child star Sugar Chile Robinson plays heated boogie-woogie piano on "Numbers Boogie" and "After School Boogie." The two Billie Holiday numbers have been reissued a couple of times including on **Swing: The Best of the Big Bands, Vol. 1** while Robinson's "Numbers Boogie" is on **Vol. 2** in that series.

♪ *Sweet Serenade* *(1950, 15 minutes)*

Tex Beneke's nostalgia orchestra, playing in a style similar to Glenn Miller's, performs "Moonlight Serenade," "You Turned the Tables on Me," "Swing Low, Sweet Chariot," "Pin-Striped Pants," "Tuxedo Junction" and "St. Louis Blues." The Moonlight Serenaders take the vocals.

♪ *Sweet Swing* *(1944, 15 minutes)*

The Eddie Miller Big Band, which had a similar sound to Bob Crosby's, did not last long but fortunately made this one short. The tenor saxophonist is well-featured along with singer Ray Eberle on "Once in a While," "Comin' Through the Rye," "Put Your Arms Around Me Honey," "Just a Step Away from Heaven," "I Surrender Dear," "Boogie Woogie Maxie" and "I've Got Sixpence."

♪ *Swing Cats Jamboree*
(1938, 9 minutes)

Louis Prima's sextet with clarinetist Meyer Weinberg and singer Shirley Lloyd perform "Way Down Yonder in New Orleans," "I Can't Give You Anything but Love," "If You Love Me," "You're an Education in Yourself" and "Loch Lomond."

🎵 ***Swing High, Swing Sweet***
(1945, 15 minutes)

This **Universal Name Band** musical features Jan Savitt and his orchestra (Savitt's violin is showcased on "Caprice"), singer Ella Mae Morse ("Cow Cow Boogie" and "All I Do Is Dream of Me") and the Delta Rhythm Boys ("What a Difference a Day Makes").

Swing Hutton Swing *(1937, 10 minutes)*

See: **All Girl Bands** (page 19)

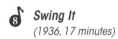 ***Swing into Spring*** *(1958, 52 minutes)*

This is the first of two all-star **Swing into Spring** jazz specials for NBC. It aired on April 9, 1958, with Dave Garroway as the host. Featured is a specially assembled version of Benny Goodman's big band (with trumpeters Billy Butterfield, Buck Clayton and Harry James, trombonists Lou McGarity, Urbie Green and Eddie Bert, five saxophonists including altoist Hymie Schertzer and tenors Zoot Sims and Al Klink, pianist Hank Jones, guitarist Kenny Burrell, bassist George Duvivier and drummer Roy Burns), the Benny Goodman Quintet/Sextet (Goodman, Red Norvo, Teddy Wilson, Arvell Shaw, Roy Burnes and sometimes Harry James), Ella Fitzgerald and Jo Stafford. The repertoire might be predictable ("Let's Dance," "Riding High," "Sometimes I'm Happy," "Don't Be That Way," "Rachel's Dream," "King Porter Stomp," "Spring Rhapsody," "Gotta Be This Or That," "Goodbye," and a medley of seven numbers by the sextet and the two singers), but the playing is consistently inspired. Also, this show gives one a rare opportunity to see Harry James reunited with his former boss.

🎵 ***Swing into Spring*** *(1959, 52 minutes)*

For the second **Swing into Spring** special, which aired on April 10, 1959, the Benny Goodman Orchestra (Buck Clayton and three trumpeters, Urbie Green and Buster Cooper among the three trombonists, a sax section with Hymie Schertzer, Herb Geller on tenor and Pepper Adams, Hank Jones, Kenny Burrell, bassist Jack Lesberg and Roy Burnes), the BG Quintet (with Lionel Hampton, pianist André Previn, Jack Lesberg and drummer Shelly Manne), Ella Fitzgerald, Peggy Lee and the Hi-Lo's are featured. The music includes "Let's Dance," "Swing into Spring," "'S Wonderful," "Things Are Swingin'," "Theme from Mozart Clarinet Quintet," "Bach Goes to Town," "Swing Low, Sweet Clarinet," "Air Mail Special," "Why Don't You Do Right," "Like Young," "Mountain Greenery," "Ah Men, Ah Women," "I Must Have That Man," "I'm Just Wild about Harry," "Sweet Lorraine," "The Gentleman Is a Dope," "When a Woman Loves a Man," "The Glory of Love," "A String of Pearls," "Goody Goody," "You Turned the Tables on Me," "One O'Clock Jump," and "Goodbye." The repertoire is the equal of the first show even if some corny dance numbers are distracting and Goodman's narration in spots could have been improved. One wishes that Fitzgerald was featured more, but overall this show is a near-classic.

🎵 ***Swing It***
(1936, 17 minutes)

Louis Prima and his Gang (a drumless quintet that features clarinetist Pee Wee Russell) perform exciting versions of "Way Down Yonder in New Orleans," "Isle of Capri," "Basin Street Blues," "Up a Lazy River" and "Dinah."

🎵 ***Swing Styles***
(1939, 10 minutes)

In addition to features for organist Milt Herth, Tito and the Frazee Sisters, the Adrian Rollini Trio (with the leader on vibes) is showcased on one number.

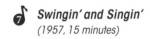 ***Swingin' and Singin'***
(1957, 15 minutes)

This Universal short features the Maynard Ferguson Orchestra (with altoist Herb Geller and drummer Mel Lewis) on "Wailing Boat" and "Birth of the Blues." The musicians also back dancers and singers (Russ Arno, the Sabres and the DeCastro Sisters).

Swingin' the Blues *(1981, 30 minutes)*

This half-hour program, hosted by Billy Taylor, features Count Basie at the time of his 75th birthday in 1979. Basie and his orchestra (which includes tenor saxophonist Eric Dixon, Freddie Green, bassist John Clayton and drummer Duffy Jackson) are seen performing in Kansas City, and Basie is interviewed briefly by Taylor. His band performs a fine version of "All of Me," "I Can't Stop Loving You," "Everyday I Have the Blues" (with singer Dennis Rowland), "Whirly-Bird" and "Things Ain't What They Used to Be."

 Swingtime Holiday *(1944, 15 minutes)*

The Gus Arnheim Orchestra, a minor-league band by the 1940s, plays swing with a guest spot from the Delta Rhythm Boys. Performed are "Pagan Love Song," "You're My Dish," "Shake Well Before Using," "Do Nothin' Til You Hear from Me," "Jersey Bounce" and "Rhythm Rhapsody."

Symphony in Black *(1935, 9 minutes)*

See: **Duke Ellington 1929–1943** (page 47)

 Symphony in Swing *(1949, 15 minutes)*

For this short, the Duke Ellington Orchestra is featured on a brief "Take the 'A' Train," "Suddenly It Jumped" (which has dancing from the Edwards Sisters), "On a Turquoise Cloud" (featuring Kay Davis's semi-operatic singing) and an excellent version of "Frankie and Johnny" with Tyree Glenn in the late Tricky Sam Nanton's old position. The latter two songs are available on **Swing: The Best of the Big Bands, Vol. 1**. In addition, the Delta Rhythm Boys perform "Knock Me a Kiss." This particular edition of the Ellington big band includes trumpeters Al Killian, Shorty Baker, Frances Williams, Shelton Hemphill and Ray Nance, trombonists Lawrence Brown, Tyree Glenn and Quentin Jackson, a reed section comprised of Johnny Hodges, Russell Procope, Jimmy Hamilton, Ben Webster and Harry Carney, bassist Wendell Marshall and Sonny Greer.

 Symphonie Sous le Soleil *(1952, 21 minutes)*

Sidney Bechet was such a major celebrity in France in the 1950s that this film was made of his wedding. Clarinetist Claude Luter and his band play a little.

 Tailgate Man from New Orleans *(1956, 12 minutes)*

Made in France but in English, this film short features Kid Ory with his Creole Jazz Band (trumpeter Alvin Alcorn, clarinetist Phil Gomez, guitarist Julian Davidson, probably pianist Cedric Haywood, bassist Wellman Braud and drummer Minor Hall) performing "Blues for Jimmie Noone," "C'est L'Autre Can-Can" and "Muskrat Ramble." Ory also talks a little about his early life.

 Teddy Powell and His Band *(1942, 9 minutes)*

Teddy Powell had a solid swing band, but this short mostly finds his orchestra backing singers Allan Courtney, Peggy Mann and Tommy Taylor. They perform "Sans Culottes," "My Little Cousins" and "Joltin' Joe DiMaggio."

 Teresa Brewer and the Firehouse Five Plus Two *(1951, 16 minutes)*

A bit of a grab bag, this short features the pop singer Teresa Brewer, the popular Dixieland group the Firehouse Five Plus Two, violinist Joe Venuti, harmonica player Leo Diamond and a dance duo on "Music, Music, Music," "Old Man Mose," "Everybody Loves My Baby," "Johnson Rag," "Hot Canary," "Fantasy in Blue" and "When You Bump into Someone You Know."

 Tex Beneke *(1948, 18 minutes)*

Tex Beneke had split from the Glenn Miller estate by this time, leading an orchestra under his own name. However, the repertoire and arrangements are very much in the Miller manner: "Moonlight Serenade," "In the Mood,"

"Don't Be that Way," "Five Minutes More," "Serenade in Blue," "American Patrol" and "Some Other Time."

Tex Beneke and His Orchestra
(1948, 15 minutes)

The Tex Beneke Orchestra is joined during this short by Garry Stevens and the Moonlight Serenaders. The program consists of "Moonlight Serenade," "Over the Rainbow," "Too Late" and "Kalamazoo."

Tex Beneke and His Orchestra
(1948, 15 minutes)

Disc jockey Martin Block tells the story behind the Tex Beneke Orchestra. The band plays a few short numbers, most notably "Makin' Love Mountain Style."

Tex Beneke and the Glenn Miller Orchestra
(1946, 17 minutes)

Tex Beneke leads the Glenn Miller ghost band during this short from 1946, an expanded outfit that has a full string section and singing from the Crew Chiefs. It was a nice try, but no band under the name of Glenn Miller would be allowed to evolve after Miller's death in 1944. Still at this early point, the spirit was still there. Beneke sings and plays a little tenor on "Chattanooga Choo Choo," "Meadowlands," "Cynthia's in Love," "Little Brown Jug" and "Hey! Ba-Ba-Re-Bop." "Chattanooga Choo Choo" and the last number have been released as part of **Swing: The Best of the Big Bands, Vol. 2** while "Little Brown Jug" is on **Vol. 4.**

That's the Spirit
(1933, 12 minutes)

The racial stereotypes are a bit overwhelming at times in this short but worth sitting through for the music. Miller and Moreland play a pair of cowardly night watchmen in a haunted music store who nevertheless enjoy the music played by Noble Sissle's orchestra. Sissle dances and conducts the band (which includes clarinetist Buster Bailey,

trombonist Wilbur DeParis and three violins) on a country swing version of "St. Louis Blues." The Washboard Serenaders (comprised of kazoo, guitar, piano and washboard with a couple of the musicians scatting) romps through a brief hot number and Cora LaRedd (in blackface) sings a song. Best is a rapid (if at times silly) version of "Tiger Rag" with Bailey taking a particularly hyper solo.

Theater for a Story *(1959, 30 minutes)*

See: **Vintage Collection, Vol. 2 1960–61** (page 136)

Those Blues
(1932, 9 minutes)

Vincent Lopez's dance band performs a few songs, including "St. Louis Blues" and "Those Blues."

Timex All-Star Jazz Show #1
(1957, 55 minutes)

Although a bit overcrowded and aimed at a general rather than jazz audience, the four **Timex All-Star Jazz Shows** of 1957–59 (which were organized by writer George Simon) are filled with timeless moments. They have not been made widely available yet on video although some can be found in collector's shops. All four shows aired on NBC and the first was shown on December 30, 1957. Hosted by Steve Allen, this program features Woody Herman's Third Herd ("Apple Honey," "The Preacher" and backing June Christy on "I Want to Be Happy"), Louis Armstrong's All-Stars ("Mahogany Hall Stomp," "Blueberry Hill," "Rockin' Chair" with guest Jack Teagarden and "Up the Lazy River"), the Dave Brubeck Quartet ("St. Louis Blues"), Duke Ellington's orchestra ("Ballet of the Flying Saucers" and a very short excerpt from "Such Sweet Thunder"), Carmen McRae ("A Foggy Day" and "They All Laughed"), the Gene Krupa Trio with Charlie Ventura and pianist Bobby Scott ("Dark Eyes") and the Bobby Hackett All-Stars (with Teagarden) on "Struttin' with Some Barbecue," plus many of the above on a closing version of "The Saints." Among the sidemen seen along the way are tenors Al Cohn, Zoot Sims and Paul Quinichette, trombonist Trummy Young, clarinetists Edmond Hall and Peanuts Hucko, altoist Paul Desmond, pianist Ray Bryant and drummer Cozy Cole.

Timex All-Star Jazz Show #2
(1958, 55 minutes)

The second Timex special aired on April 30, 1958, and was hosted by Garry Moore. Featured are Lionel Hampton ("Hamp's Boogie Woogie," "I Like Jazz," "Moon Glow" and "Real Gone and Crazy"), Louis Armstrong's All-Stars ("When It's Sleepy Time Down South," "Muskrat Ramble," "On the Sunny Side of the Street" and "Jeepers Creepers"), the George Shearing Quintet ("Lullaby of Birdland," "Cuban Fantasy" and "September in the Rain"), the Dukes of Dixieland ("September in the Rain" and "Over the Waves"), Jaye P. Morgan (singing "My Baby Just Cares for Me" and "The Lady Is a Tramp"), a group with Ruby Braff, Jack Teagarden and Tony Parenti ("Basin Street Blues"), the Gerry Mulligan Quartet with Art Farmer, bassist Henry Grimes and drummer Dave Bailey ("Night Walk") and many of the participants on "St. Louis Blues." The other musicians seen include Randy Hall on tin whistle, drummer Cozy Cole, guitarist Toots Thielemans with Shearing, Trummy Young and Edmond Hall with Armstrong, and trumpeter Frank Assunto leading the Dukes.

Timex All-Star Jazz Show #3
(1958, 50 minutes)

This time around, the Timex special (which aired November 10, 1958) was co-hosted by Bob Crosby and Hoagy Carmichael. Gene Krupa and Lionel Hampton (on drums) sit in with Les Brown ("One O'Clock Jump"), Louis Armstrong performs "I Love Jazz" and Hampton (back on vibes) jams on "How High the Moon" and "Hamp's Boogie Woogie." The other participants include Anita O'Day ("Let Me Off Uptown" and "Four Brothers"), the Les Brown Orchestra ("The Continental"), the

Bobcats ("Royal Garden Blues" and joined by Armstrong on "South Rampart Street Parade"), the Chico Hamilton Quintet ("Sleep" and "The Morning After"), singer Jane Morgan ("You Do Something to Me" and "The Day the Rains Came") and the duo of Bob Haggart and Gene Krupa ("Big Noise from Winnetka"). A medley of 11 Hoagy Carmichael songs (only one is longer than 33 seconds) is sung by Carmichael, Morgan, O'Day, Crosby and Armstrong before "Two O'Clock Jump" gives Krupa, Hamilton and Hampton a chance to have a brief drum battle. Among the sidemen are Trummy Young, clarinetist Peanuts Hucko, bassist George Morrow, Eric Dolphy on alto (with Hamilton), trumpeters Yank Lawson, Pee Wee Erwin and Chris Griffin, tenor saxophonist Bud Freeman and pianist Ralph Sutton.

Timex All-Star Jazz Show #4:
The Golden Age of Jazz
(1959, 59 minutes)

The fourth and final Timex jazz special (not counting the one from 1972) aired on January 7, 1959, and has the most famous performance of these shows, Louis Armstrong and Dizzy Gillespie teaming up for their only filmed joint appearance ever on "Umbrella Man." Jackie Gleason hosts and the program also features Duke Ellington and his orchestra ("Satin Doll," "Take the 'A' Train," "Rockin' in Rhythm," "Sophisticated Lady," "Things Ain't What They Used to Be"), the Armstrong All-Stars ("Now You Has Jazz," "Tiger Rag," "Ole Miss"), singer Barbara Dane ("Old Fashioned Love"), the Dukes of Dixieland ("Ory's Creole Trombone," "Just a Closer Walk with Thee"), Dizzy Gillespie's quintet ("St. Louis Blues"), Ruth Olay ("I Let a Song Go Out of My Heart"), Dakota Staton ("The Thrill Is Gone," "I Hear Music"), the George Shearing Quintet ("Easy to Remember"), Barbara Dane and Dakota Staton together on "Body and Soul" with a sextet also including Roy Eldridge, Coleman Hawkins and Vic Dickenson, and a final jam on "Perdido." There was way too much underutilized talent on this show (which also had Gene Krupa, Jo Jones, Bobby Hackett and Junior Mance) and the series in general, but at least this was a noble attempt to get some jazz on television.

♪ Timothy Leary's Wedding
(1964, 12 minutes)

One cannot imagine this short having wide circulation! The LSD guru's wedding film includes a very brief appearance by Charles Mingus on piano.

♪ Tommy Dorsey and His Orchestra
(1951, 15 minutes)

By the time this short was made for Universal, Tommy Dorsey was playing nostalgia swing with few surprises other than the occasional outbursts of trumpeter Charlie Shavers. His orchestra performs "You Left Your Brown-Eyed Baby," a spirited rendition of "Opus No. 1," "Diane," "The Hucklebuck" and "Boogie Woogie." Frances Irvin and Bob London have vocals but do not make much of an impression. "Opus No. 1" and "Boogie Woogie" are included in the videotape **Swing: The Best of the Big Bands, Vol. 1**.

♪ Trumpet Serenade
(1942, 13 minutes)

This musical short features Harry James and his big band performing "Nobody Knows The Trouble I've Seen," his hit "You Made Me Love You," "He's 1-A in the Army" (featuring Helen Forrest), "James Session" and "Concerto for Trumpet."

♪ Tumbleweed Tempos
(1946, 15 minutes)

Ella Mae Morse was famous for singing "Cow Cow Boogie" with Freddie Slack's orchestra. During this short she is joined by Spade Cooley's Western swing orchestra for "The Campbells Are Coming," "The Life of the Party," "Turn My Picture Upside Down," "Crazy 'Cause I Love You" and "Don't Move."

♪ Two Plus Fours
(1930, 17 minutes)

This very obscure short comedy, which was recently rediscovered, features Bing Crosby and the Rhythm Boys (Harry Barris who has a key role and Al Rinker) singing two versions of "The Stein Song."

♪ Vitaphone Varieties
(1936, 10 minutes)

Several different performers are featured during this brief film, most notably Louis Prima's band with clarinetist Pee Wee Russell on a humorous rendition of "Chinatown, My Chinatown." Other selections include "Full Steam Ahead," "Lonely Gondolier," "Sleepy Time Down South," "Are You from Dixie" and "Smile."

♪ V.S.O.P. II
(1983, 60 minutes)

The Public Broadcasting System in Chicago filmed and broadcast this one-hour performance from Herbie Hancock's **V.S.O.P. II**. The quintet consists of Hancock on acoustic piano, Ron Carter, Tony Williams, Wynton Marsalis and Branford Marsalis on tenor and soprano. There are times when the group is similar in style to the Miles Davis Quintet of the mid-'60s (of which Hancock, Carter and Williams were members), with Wynton sounding like Miles Davis might have if he had had loads of technique. The group performs a pair of Hancock originals, "Well You Needn't," Tony Williams's "Sister Cheryl" and a closing romp through the chord changes of "I Got Rhythm."

♪ The Wildest
(1957, 15 minutes)

This rare short features Louis Prima, Keely Smith, Sam Butera and the Witnesses during a performance in Lake Tahoe shortly after this combination began to really click.

♪ Wingy Manone and the Climax Jazz Band
(1976, 16 minutes)

Filmed June 10, 1976, trumpeter Wingy Manone (76 and near the end of his career) plays and sings with the

Climax Jazz Band, a hot sextet from Canada. Manone still had plenty of spirit and is in good form on "Way Down Yonder in New Orleans," "Basin Street Blues," "Oochi Chornaya," "We Ain't Givin' Nothin' Away" and "On the Sunny Side of the Street," taking jivey good-humored vocals along with some hot solos.

The Wizard of Waukesha
(1979, 60 minutes)

This is an excellent documentary on Les Paul and his diverse career, telling stories about his life as a guitarist, inventor, innovator and player of everything from swing-oriented jazz to country music. Paul was extensively interviewed and some old film clips are utilized, including a couple from the television show that he had with Mary Ford. Although a bit dated (since Paul has continued playing up to the present time), the hour does a solid job of summing up his life.

Woman's a Fool *(1947, unknown length)*

See: **The Blues** (page 26)

Woody Herman and His Orchestra
(1938, 9 minutes)

The early Woody Herman orchestra performs "Carolina in the Morning," "Holiday," "You Must Have Been a Beautiful Baby," "The Shag" and "Doctor Jazz." Herman, whether singing or playing clarinet, is the main star throughout. The most intriguing aspect to this short is what is missing. Although singer Lee Wiley is listed in the credits, she is nowhere to be seen, and thus far no film of her has ever turned up.

Woody Herman and His Orchestra
(1948, 15 minutes)

Although one wishes this short were several times longer, it gives viewers a valuable sampling of Woody Herman's Second Herd. After Herman's theme "Blue Flame," the classic orchestra performs "Sabre Dance," "Caldonia," features

for the Modernaires and a dance duo ("Jingle Bell Polka" and "Cane Walk") and a heated rendition of "Northwest Passage." The soloists are mostly Herman on clarinet, tenor saxophonist Stan Getz and trumpeter Shorty Rogers, while the orchestra at the time includes tenors Zoot Sims and Al Cohn, baritonist Serge Chaloff, the cheerleading bassist Chubby Jackson and drummer Don Lamond. The two hottest numbers, "Caldonia" and "Northwest Passage," were reissued as part of **Swing: Best of the Big Bands, Vol. 2.**

Woody Herman's Varieties
(1951, 14 minutes)

Woody Herman's Third Herd is often relegated to backing other performers on this short including singers, dancers and even acrobats. However the fine band is featured on "99 Guys" and "Apple Honey" with the soloists including tenors Bill Perkins and Dick Hafer.

A World of Beauty
(1955, 18 minutes)

This little-known news short mostly deals with the Miss Universe contest of 1955. There is a cameo appearance by June Christy with Pete Rugolo's orchestra.

The Yacht Party
(1932, 15 minutes)

The Roger Wolfe Kahn Orchestra with the young Artie Shaw as a key soloist is featured on "Way Down Yonder in New Orleans," "Crazy People" and "Dinah." Gertrude Niesen sings one number with the band, Melissa Mason dances on "Dinah" and there are two vocals from the quartet the Kahn-A-Sirs. Kahn's band also includes trumpeter Charlie Teagarden and drummer Chauncey Morehouse.

You Made Me Love You: A Tribute to Harry James
(1985, 60 minutes)

Billy Taylor is the host of this nostalgic PBS television special. The Harry James ghost band (James died two years earlier) was being fronted by trumpeter Joe Graves at the time, and the band actually sounds dull as it runs through some of its repertoire ("Ciribiribin," "Don't Be That Way," "Sweet Georgia Brown," "On a Clear Day," "Sleepy Lagoon," "Just a Gigolo") before a dancing audience in Omaha, Nebraska. However, some old clips are shown of James and a 67-year-old Helen Forrest sounds good guesting with the band ("Almost Like Being in Love," "I'm Beginning to See the Light," "I Don't Want to Walk Without You," "I Cried for You," "More Than You Know," "I've Heard That Song Before," "You Made Me Love You"). But easily the best performance is when Billy Taylor sits in on piano and jams on a heated version of "Give Me the Simple Life" with the rhythm section.

 ### Young Artists: In Performance at the White House
(1982, 60 minutes)

This special White House concert (which has an opening speech from Nancy Reagan) introduces trumpeter Jon Faddis (who was already well known in jazz) and the then-unknown singer Dianne Schuur. The proceedings begin with a fine version of "Groovin' High" from Dizzy Gillespie, Stan Getz, Chick Corea, bassist Miroslav Vitous and drummer Roy Haynes. The trio of Corea, Vitous and Haynes performs a medley that includes a free improvisation, "Autumn Leaves" and "Rhythm-A-Ning," and Stan Getz plays an original with his trio of the period (pianist Jim McNeely, bassist Marc Johnson and drummer Adam Nussbaum). Gillespie introduces Faddis and the two trumpeters jam on "And Then She Stopped" with the Corea trio. Finally, on "Summertime," in addition to solos by Faddis, Getz and Gillespie, Diane Schuur gets a chance to sing, making a strong impression on Nancy Reagan and many viewers. In fact, Schuur's contract with GRP, which led to her fame, was the direct result of her appearance on this telecast.

 ### Yours Truly *(1943, 10 minutes)*

Johnny Long led an underrated orchestra during the swing era, one that had a lone hit in "A Shanty in Old Shanty Town." This short features his band and singer Marilyn Day on "One Dozen Roses," "Don't Worry," "If You Please," "Minute Waltz" and "One O'Clock Jump."

Review Section Four:

Miscellaneous Items of Interest

The Adventures of Hajji Baba *(1954, 86 minutes)*

John Derek and Elaine Stewart star in an adventure film. Nat King Cole sings the theme song on the soundtrack.

Alfie *(1966, 114 minutes)*

This popular British comedy has a film score by Sonny Rollins.

Alfie Darling *(1975, 102 minutes)*

A less interesting second installment of Alfie has Annie Ross in an acting role.

Assault on a Queen *(1966, 106 minutes)*

Duke Ellington wrote the score for this Frank Sinatra/Virna Lisi thriller. His orchestra appears on the soundtrack, but none of the pieces had an independent life beyond the film.

Autumn Leaves *(1956, 107 minutes)*

This late-period Joan Crawford movie has Nat King Cole singing the title song on the soundtrack.

Awakenings *(1990, 120 minutes)*

Dexter Gordon has a small and inconsequential part in this sad Robin Williams story about coma victims given a drug that temporarily wakes them up.

The Black Godfather *(1974, 96 minutes)*

Jimmy Witherspoon has an acting role in this blaxploitation film about Black gangsters.

Blowup *(1966, 111 minutes)*

This British mystery film features a memorable soundtrack by Herbie Hancock that includes some prominent playing by Freddie Hubbard.

The Bridges of Madison County *(1995, 135 minutes)*

Photographer Clint Eastwood becomes involved with a married Iowa housewife (Meryl Streep) in this tearjerker romance movie. Very effective use is made on the soundtrack of the recordings of Johnny Hartman, Dinah Washington and Irene Kral, with the original pieces scored by Lennie Niehaus.

Buddy Traps in Sound Effects *(1929, 7 minutes)*

Eleven-year-old Buddy Rich is featuring singing, dancing and playing "The Stars and Stripes Forever" on drums. Unfortunately, the film is lost although the soundtrack has survived.

But Not for Me *(1959, 105 minutes)*

This entertaining Clark Gable/Carroll Baker film has Ella Fitzgerald singing the title cut on the soundtrack.

Carib Gold *(1955, 72 minutes)*

Ethel Waters is one of the stars in this drama about shrimp fishermen and sunken treasure.

Change of Mind *(1969, 98 minutes)*

Duke Ellington wrote the score for this ambitious movie about a White racist's brain being transplanted into a Black man's body. Songs include "Black Butterfly,"

"Wanderlust," "What Good Am I Without You" and a remake of "Creole Rhapsody."

Chappaqua *(1969, 82 minutes)*

Ornette Coleman wrote the original score for this eccentric film. However, it was rejected and replaced with one by Ravi Shankar instead. Coleman has a brief nonspeaking role.

The Children of Sanchez *(1978, 126 minutes)*

Chuck Mangione wrote the score for this Anthony Quinn film about a Mexican family.

The Cool World *(1963, 105 minutes)*

A Black teenager from Harlem dreams of owning his own gun and leading a gang. Mal Waldron's score features the Dizzy Gillespie Quintet with James Moody, pianist Kenny Barron, bassist Chris White and drummer Rudy Collins.

Le Depart *(1966, 91 minutes)*

Polish writer Krzysztol Komeda's score for this film about a hairdresser includes some playing from Don Cherry, Gato Barbieri, pianist Rene Urtreger and guitarist Philippe Catherine.

Desperate Characters *(1971, 87 minutes)*

The soundtrack for this look at two days in the life of a New York couple includes playing from altoist Lee Konitz, guitarist Jim Hall and bassist Ron Carter.

Doctor Rhythm *(1938, 81 minutes)*

Louis Armstrong recorded "The Trumpet Player's Lament" for this Bing Crosby/Beatrice Lillie film, but it was deleted before the movie's release. Considering the studio recording that resulted, it was no great loss.

Elevator to the Gallows *(1957, 87 minutes)*

This excellent French suspense film (which was released in France as **Ascenseur Pour L'Echafaud**) depicts a "perfect crime" (a man and woman planning and carrying out the murder of her husband) that is foiled by a stuck elevator. Miles Davis and the quintet he led for a few months in France that year (tenor saxophonist Barney Wilen, pianist Rene Urtreger, bassist Pierre Michelot and drummer Kenny Clarke) are featured prominently throughout the soundtrack. This worthy film is available through New Yorker Video.

The Emperor Jones *(1933, 89 minutes)*

Billie Holiday appears as an extra in a crowd scene in this Paul Robeson film although no one seems to have ever seen her.

Ex-Flame *(1930, 68 minutes)*

This melodrama is believed to have included Louis Armstrong's first film appearance. Unfortunately, the movie is long lost and even the soundtrack does not exist.

Des Femmes Disparaissent *(1959, 85 minutes)*

The soundtrack to this French film which features Art Blakey's Jazz Messengers (trumpeter Lee Morgan, tenor saxophonist Benny Golson, pianist Bobby Timmons and bassist Jymie Merritt) is much better known than the movie itself.

Freaky Friday *(1976, 100 minutes)*

Jack Sheldon has an acting role in this original version of the fantasy comedy about a quarrelling mother and teenage daughter who switch personalities for a day.

The French Connection *(1971, 104 minutes)*

Don Ellis wrote the memorable score to this famous action film.

The French Connection II *(1975, 119 minutes)*

Don Ellis also wrote the score for this superior follow-up.

From Here to Eternity *(1953, 114 minutes)*

In this famous movie, Montgomery's Cliff's bugle playing is ghosted by Manny Klein.

Girl's Town *(1959, 90 minutes)*

This odd juvenile film has a major acting role for Ray Anthony.

The Good for Nothing *(1917, unknown length)*

No relation to the 1914 Charlie Chaplin film of the same name, this obscure and probably lost movie has an appearance by the Original Dixieland Jazz Band, which is considered the earliest appearance of a jazz band on film, even if it is a silent movie.

Heartbeat *(1979, 109 minutes)*

The lives of beat poets and novelists Jack Kerouac and Neal Cassady inspired this story. Art Pepper's alto is prominent throughout the soundtrack.

High School Confidential *(1959, 85 minutes)*

This juvenile rock 'n' roll high school drama has a role for Ray Anthony.

Higher and Higher *(1943, 91 minutes)*

Somewhere in this early Frank Sinatra movie Charles Mingus appears as an extra.

Hurry Sundown *(1966, 146 minutes)*

Actor Michael Caine is occasionally shown playing alto sax in this film; Ronnie Lang actually ghosts his solos.

In Town Tonight *(1935, 78 minutes)*

This plotless British revue, named after the popular radio series, originally had the great Coleman Hawkins featured on "On the Sunny Side of the Street" and "Sweet Sue." Unfortunately, no print has survived that includes that segment.

Is Everybody Happy *(1929, 74 minutes)*

One of the major lost films, this feature stars cornball singer/clarinetist Ted Lewis and his band, which at the time included cornetist Muggsy Spanier, trombonist George Brunies and clarinetist/baritonist Don Murray; the latter died before the movie was completed. Among the numbers are "St. Louis Blues," "Tiger Rag," "In the Land of Jazz," "Start the Band," "Wouldn't It Be Wonderful," "I'm the Medicine Man for the Blues," "New Orleans" and "Samoa." There was also a later movie titled **Is Everybody Happy** (1943, 73 minutes) that is a semifictional biography of Lewis with Michael Duana playing the lead, but it includes no real jazz.

Jack Johnson *(1970, 88 minutes)*

This documentary on the early Black heavyweight champion is very well done. However, the soundtrack by Miles Davis's fusion band (Steve Grossman on soprano, Herbie Hancock, John McLaughlin, electric bassist Mike Henderson and drummer Billy Cobham) is out of place in depicting events of 1910.

Jazz Is Our Religion *(1972, 50 minutes)*

Valerie Wilmer's photographs are seen throughout this film and, although there is music (by Johnny Griffin, Jon Hendricks and the Kenny Clarke/Francy Boland big band) and lots of talking (from Rashied Ali, Art Blakey, Marion Brown, Bill Evans, Jimmy Garrison, Dizzy Gillespie, Jo Jones and Dewey Redman, among others), no musician is shown live on camera.

The Jungle Book *(1967, 78 minutes)*

Disney's popular full-length cartoon features Louis Prima speaking and singing as King Louie of the Apes.

Legion of the Condemned *(1928, 83 minutes)*

This Gary Cooper/Fay Wray melodrama about the French Air Legion and spies during World War I is silent and lost. Mutt Carey's band with clarinetist Joe Darensbourg appears in one scene.

Let's Do It Again (1975, 113 minutes)

Bill Cosby and Sidney Poitier star in this comedy (the sequel to **Uptown Saturday Night**), which has small roles for Billy Eckstine and Med Flory.

Make Mine Music (1945, 75 minutes)

This series of ten Disney animated cartoons features music prominently. One of the best has the Benny Goodman Quartet (with Teddy Wilson, bassist Sid Weiss and drummer Cozy Cole) providing the music for "After You've Gone" and "All the Cats Join In."

The Marrying Kind (1952, 93 minutes)

In this Judy Holliday comedy, tenor saxophonist Georgie Auld has a small acting role as Spec the mailman.

Mary Lou (1948, 65 minutes)

Percussionist Jack Costanza appears as a dancer in this film about a stewardess who becomes a nightclub singer.

Member of the Wedding (1953, 89 minutes)

This somewhat tedious Julie Harris movie has Ethel Waters in one of her better nonmusical roles.

Midnight in the Garden of Good and Evil (1997, 155 minutes)

James Moody is briefly seen twice in this eccentric murder mystery, walking an imaginary dog and speaking a couple of lines.

The Moonshine War (1970, 100 minutes)

Singer Joe Williams, who would later have an occasional role on *The Bill Cosby Show*, proves to be an effective actor in this Alan Alda/Richard Widmark tale about moonshiners in the South in the early '30s.

A New Kind of Love (1963, 109 minutes)

Erroll Garner wrote part of the film score for this light-hearted Paul Newman film and is heard throughout the movie's soundtrack.

New York Eye and Ear Control (1964, 34 minutes)

This short film is very difficult to locate, but legendary for its avant-garde soundtrack featuring tenor saxophonist Albert Ayler, cornetist Don Cherry, altoist John Tchicai, trombonist Roswell Rudd, bassist Gary Peacock and drummer Sunny Murray.

No Sun in Venice (1957, 90 minutes)

John Lewis wrote the soundtrack for this obscure French/Italian film. The Modern Jazz Quartet (with Milt Jackson, bassist Percy Heath and drummer Connie Kay) is heard throughout the soundtrack.

Odds Against Tomorrow (1959, 96 minutes)

This superior crime drama about a robbery that goes wrong features a score by John Lewis and prominent playing on the soundtrack by the Modern Jazz Quartet. Lewis's "Skating in Central Park" is memorable.

O.K. End Here (1963, 30 minutes)

Sue Graham Mingus appears as the female lead in this short drama about a couple's relationship. Ornette Coleman wrote the soundtrack.

The Pink Panther (1963, 114 minutes)

Henry Mancini used jazz as a strong flavor in many of his film scores. Plas Johnson's tenor playing throughout the soundtrack of **The Pink Panther** is memorable. Later films in this series have Tony Coe featured on tenor.

Pinky (1949, 102 minutes)

Ethel Waters has a highly rated dramatic role in a story about racial prejudice.

Remember My Name *(1978, 94 minutes)*

The plot of this Geraldine Chaplin movie is partly based on the songs written by 83-year-old classic blues singer Alberta Hunter. Hunter performs on the soundtrack with a small band that includes Doc Cheatham, trombonist Vic Dickenson, tenor saxophonist Budd Johnson and pianist Gerald Cook.

The Sandpiper *(1965, 117 minutes)*

This Elizabeth Taylor/Richard Burton film is forgettable overall, but the Johnny Mandel song "The Shadow of Your Smile" is haunting and memorable. It features Jack Sheldon's trumpet on the soundtrack throughout the movie.

School Daze *(1988, 121 minutes)*

Spike Lee's film about a Black college and the different approaches to gaining an education has an acting role for Branford Marsalis.

See Here, Private Hargrove *(1944, 101 minutes)*

Singer Bob Crosby had a short and unsuccessful career as an actor. He is one of the characters in this story about a reporter in the Army during World War II.

Shadows *(1958, 81 minutes)*

This film from director John Cassavetes is mostly improvised, and shows it. The aimless story (filmed with a very low budget) has some interesting statements about race relations, but mostly looks amateurish and the acting (from unknowns) is erratic. The soundtrack features Shafi Hadi's tenor, some bass interludes from Charles Mingus and brief playing from trombonist Jimmy Knepper and pianist Phineas Newborn.

The Singing Sheriff *(1944, 63 minutes)*

Bob Crosby does his best as the lead in this Western B movie comedy.

Snow White *(1933, 6 minutes)*

This Betty Boop cartoon has a soundtrack that features Cab Calloway and his band performing "St. James Infirmary" and "Tiger Rag."

The Sting *(1973, 129 minutes)*

The use of Scott Joplin's songs (particularly "The Entertainer" and "Solace") throughout this Paul Newman/Robert Redford classic by Marvin Hamlisch (who also plays piano on the soundtrack) helped launch the comeback of ragtime, with "The Entertainer" making the best seller charts more than a half century after Joplin's death. Never mind that the film was set in the 1930s when ragtime was largely extinct!

Tales of Manhattan *(1942, 118 minutes)*

This drama about the many owners of a coat has a stereotyped acting role for Ethel Waters.

The Three Little Bops *(1956, 8 minutes)*

This classic Warner Bros. cartoon has the Three Little Pigs forming a jazz band that the Big Bad Wolf, a poor trumpeter, wants desperately to join. Shorty Rogers composed the music, his band provides the soundtrack, and the story is hilarious.

Throw Mamma from the Train *(1987, 86 minutes)*

Branford Marsalis and Annie Ross have acting roles in this offbeat Billy Crystal/Danny DeVito comedy.

Who's Crazy *(1965, 83 minutes)*

This odd movie, which was mostly made up as it went along, has the Ornette Coleman Trio (with bassist David Izenzon and drummer Charles Moffett) improvising the soundtrack.

The Wild One (1953, 79 minutes)

Marlon Brando's famous motorcycle gang movie has a dramatic soundtrack by Leith Stevens that effectively uses Shorty Rogers and his Giants, an all-star group of West Coast jazz greats.

Yamekraw (1930, 9 minutes)

It is a bit frustrating that no musician appears on-screen during this rendition of James P. Johnson's "Yamekraw." There is no dialog, and the story, which is full of stereotypes, tells the clichéd tale of idyllic life in the country, a youth going to the city, having trouble in a nightclub and returning home safe. The soundtrack is played by Hugo Marianni and his Mediterraneans.

Interviews:

Three Jazz Film Collectors

Mark Cantor

Owner of one of the largest jazz film collections in the world, Mark Cantor (based in the Los Angeles area) has been a music film archivist for 30 years. He frequently presents jazz film shows as special events and parts of festivals. He can be reached at markcantor@aol.com.

How did you originally become interested in jazz?

I've been listening to music ever since I was a toddler; it was always around the house. Back in those days when one bought a phonograph, two or three high-fidelity LPs were included along with the purchase. When my father got a hi-fi set, it came with the Benny Goodman 1938 Carnegie Hall concert, an Artie Shaw record and something by Stan Getz. Since my parents did not buy many records, that was the only music that I knew for years, and it pushed me in the direction of jazz.

How did you become a film collector, since that is much different from being a record collector?

I had been collecting 78s for many years. One Saturday as I was prowling through secondhand stores and the Salvation Army, I made a stop at Don Brown's Jazzman Records. Up on a shelf was something that was just labeled Jazz Movies. It was pretty expensive, ten dollars, which was two weeks' allowance at the time. I bought it anyway and took it home although I could not play it because it was a 16-millimeter sound film. It sat on the shelf until I went to college. At that time, a buddy of mine got hold of a projector, we watched it, and it turned out to be **Jammin' the Blues** with Lester Young, Harry "Sweets" Edison and some

of my other musical heroes. It made me wonder what other films were available. That is how it all began.

Typically, through the years, how have you run across and acquired films?

It is like any hobby. You learn where things might be lurking and then you lurk there yourself. If you're lucky, there is something special waiting for you.

Do any particular adventures come to mind about your search for films?

Before eBay, you could buy Soundies and short subjects for next to nothing. Quite often there were great surprises. There was a magazine called *The Big Reel* where one could buy films. It was always a bit chancy because what was offered was not always what one got. One time I wanted to upgrade a film I have of the Slim Gaillard Trio so I ordered another copy. Instead, I got sent a Spanish language drama. There were other things spliced onto the film so it would equal the length that was advertised. I watched it through and in the middle it suddenly switched to three performances by the Erroll Garner Trio and some Tony Bennett backed by Bobby Hackett. So I ended up getting the better of the deal!

About how many films do you own?

I've never counted, but if you include films, videos, DVDs and laser discs, I'd say close to 5,000.

What are some of your prized possessions, things that are not available elsewhere?

There is some Miles Davis from 1957, a concert in Germany. He had finished a European tour and was getting ready to come back to the States. As a last minute gig, he flew to Germany and played with a big band that supported him as the soloist. I also have some Billie Holiday from local Los Angeles television and a few Black short subjects that were not known before. And then there is the Clifford Brown clip.

Tell us the story behind the Clifford Brown film.

Back in the mid-1950s, Soupy Sales had a regular comedy/variety show in Detroit. The producer of the program, with Soupy's full support, had an arrangement with the local nightclubs where the clubs would send over the featured artist and they would play on the show. The clubs and the artists did not get paid, but it was good publicity. Clifford Brown was in town with the Max Roach group. He came down to the studio, played great on "Lady Be Good" and "Memories of You" and talked about the upcoming engagement. The series was live and, since there was no syndication of the program, there were no kinescopes. Soupy thought that it would be nice to have a copy of what he was doing, so he had a kinescope shot, and it just happened to be that program. Soupy kept the kinescope and many years later had it transferred to VHS. It was fortunate he did that because he apparently lost the kinescope. I arranged to get the VHS, had it worked on in the lab and transferred it back to film so it could be shared in my programs. It is the only known footage, so far, of Clifford Brown.

Do you know anything about a film called The Good for Nothing from 1917 that is supposed to have an appearance by the Original Dixieland Jazz Band?

There was such a film, but I doubt that it still exists. It is one of those things that many of us have been looking for for years. I've yet to hear of a copy turning up.

I know that one of the earliest jazz-related sound shorts is of the Van Eps Trio. What year is that from and what songs do they play?

It is probably the earliest existing jazz sound film although it is possible that other ragtime bands were filmed during the era. It is called **A Bit of Jazz**. The songs are "Love Nest," "Japanese Sandman," "Whispering," "Swanee" and "Listen to the Mockingbird" and that suggests that it's from 1920 or '21.

Do you know of other jazz sound films from before 1927, other than the Noble Sissle and Eubie Blake shorts?

Around 1923 an all-female band, Helen Lewis and Her Jazz Syncopators, was filmed. There is another DeForest film featuring Ben Bernie in addition to the clip of "Sweet Georgia Brown" from 1925. It is amazing because the film has the band playing "Lady Be Good," "Indian Love Call," "Tea for Two" and "Fascinating Rhythm," songs that are being played as pop songs of the day. Little did they know that those tunes would become standards. There are other peripheral things, including the Roy Smeck clip from 1926, depending on how one defines jazz.

If you could name two or three lost films that you would love to see, which would they be?

Number one would be a film from 1938 called **Policy Man** that featured Count Basie and his orchestra. There is **Ex-Flame** from 1930 with Louis Armstrong. There is also some indication that there was a whole series of experimental films made in the 1920s that might have included Bix Beiderbecke, King Oliver, Bessie Smith and Paul Whiteman. If those were actually made and it's not just a big rumor, obviously I would love to see those turn up.

Are there any films at all of Lee Wiley or Mildred Bailey?

Lee Wiley made television appearances, but none seem to have survived. With Mildred Bailey, there are indications of a Vitaphone short and possibly a Universal short, but they have not been discovered yet.

What have been some of the more recent discoveries of jazz films?

I love modern jazz as much as the older stuff. There have been discoveries of new clips of Thelonious Monk, Rahsaan Roland Kirk, Dexter Gordon, Chet Baker and quite a few others. Many American jazz musicians toured Europe in the 1960s and '70s and appeared on European television, so a great deal of unavailable film exists. It is hard to get that stuff out of the European archives.

With the Clifford Brown film showing up after so many years, anything is possible.

I've learned over the years that if there are rumors, it often turns out that the films do exist somewhere.

Ken Poston

An important force in the jazz scene of Los Angeles, Ken Poston organizes major jazz festivals and conventions that are frequently three or four days long. Among his many successes have been Jazz West Coast, Jazz West Coast II and reunions of the Stan Kenton Orchestra (including most notably *Back to Balboa*). He is also an occasional disc jockey and a longtime jazz recording and film collector. Several years ago he founded the Los Angeles Jazz Institute and he serves as its director. Ken can be reached at (562) 985-7065 and kpostjwc@earthlink.net.

How did you originally become interested in jazz?

I played trumpet when I was in junior high school, so I bought records of trumpet players. I began with records by Miles Davis and Shorty Rogers, trying to play along with them and becoming more and more interested in the music. By the time I got to high school and college, I was very interested in the historical aspect of jazz.

When did you start collecting jazz films?

I bought a VCR while I was in college, around 1982. I relentlessly taped everything that came on TV. I also started finding sources where one could buy films on videotape although it was expensive at the time; that's where my money went. Even the blank tapes were $12–15 at the time. I was cramming six hours of music on each tape.

Tell us about the Los Angeles Jazz Institute.

I started it four or five years ago. When doing a radio show, I might need to find a specific recording. Quite often I would discover that it was tucked away in someone's garage or had been thrown away or lost; it took a lot of digging at times. I realized that there were no organized archives on the West Coast, so I had to create my own research facility by buying all the stuff myself. The idea was to create a place where all of the valuable jazz recordings and films could be housed and would be accessible. I used my own collection as the basis and then we started gathering other collections, including some from musicians. We are housed at Cal State Long Beach and it is working out the way that we envisioned it. It is accessible to the public by reservation. The emphasis is on Los Angeles–based musicians although we do cover a much wider span of jazz history.

How many recordings does the institute have?

About 75,000 recordings in all the formats combined.

About how many films?

Most of our jazz films are on videotape. Roughly there are between three and four thousand hours of footage.

What are some of the more exciting films in the archives?

Some of the television programs of the 1950s and '60s in particular are exciting and unique, such as episodes of *The Stars of Jazz* and *Frankly Jazz*. We have some home movies, including some from Howard Rumsey in which he and Lee Morgan are out on Howard's sailboat. There are a lot of film outtakes from Stan Kenton's **Bound to Be Heard** raw footage. On video we have a lot of films that are not commercially available, situations where I borrowed films from people's collections and transferred them to video. The collection is broken down into television, documentaries, live performances, feature films, Soundies and shorts.

How many of The Stars of Jazz shows do you have?

We just acquired the Jimmy Baker collection, which has all of the 16-inch transcriptions of the audio. Altogether we have around 20 different shows on video. UCLA has 35 or 40 shows and, other than a couple of programs, our shows are duplicated by their archives. Out of the 170 shows that were aired, I doubt that more than 40 or 50 at best still exist. Most of the surviving shows are from 1958 although there are a few titles from 1956, including the Billie Holiday show. Unfortunately, the Chet Baker program has not shown up yet.

How many Frankly Jazz programs do you have?

We have around 14. That series was only on for a year with possibly 26 shows in all. We turned up a video recently of the Victor Feldman Trio with Sammy Davis, Jr., as a guest. He doesn't sing on that show, but surprisingly he plays the vibes very well.

What are some of the other television shows in the collection?

The *Jazz 625* shows from England are great. They put most of those programs out in England, but they are in different formats and one had to spend money to get them transferred to the machines used in the U.S. *The Subject Is Jazz* is another really good series, but those haven't come out yet. We have three or four episodes. We also have some of the *Dial M for Music* shows and a bunch of the Tommy and Jimmy Dorsey *Stage Shows* from the mid-'50s.

Do any of the Eddie Condon shows exist from the late 1940s?

We have the audio to all of them, but I don't think any of the video has ever shown up. That was probably too early for kinescopes.

What about the Jerry Lewis telethon that Charlie Parker played on?

No sign of that. Speaking of Jerry Lewis, he produced a half-hour special that featured the Terry Gibbs Dream Band around 1959 or '60. We've been trying to track that down for years. We've written a lot of letters, but Jerry Lewis hasn't written back. Terry thinks that Jerry probably has it somewhere.

What have been some of the most exciting film discoveries of the past few years that you know about?

There are all kinds of oddball things that are regularly being discovered. The 1960 Newport Jazz Festival for some reason was filmed by an arm of the government, maybe the Treasury Department. I have the Gerry Mulligan Concert Jazz Band and Maynard Ferguson big band sets. I have no idea why it happened to be filmed. Miles Davis's appearance on the *Steve Allen Show* from 1964 with Wayne Shorter has surfaced in recent times. One time when I was at Steve Allen's office, my jaw just hit the floor because there were a lot more jazz artists' appearances from his shows that have survived than I thought. He always said that a lot of the shows were erased by the network, but I was amazed by the stuff he still had.

In the mid-1950s, the Lighthouse All-Stars made two appearances on a couple of national shows. One was Dave Galloway's *Wide Wide World* in 1956, and the other was the year before when *Monitor* did a simulcast for the premiere of their radio show that was also on television. In both cases, the shows were shot in Hermosa Beach. Those are the kind of things that are not easily accessible because the networks charge a huge amount of money per second to use them in documentaries, like $100 a second. So it is kind of frustrating that there is important jazz footage that no one will see.

What are some of the shows that you wish would show up?

One is the Joe Adams show that was done in the early 1950s, having a house band with Buddy Collette and Art Farmer, the later Central Avenue guys. The other one is a show that Gene Norman hosted called *Face the Music* that featured jazz guests all the time. We have the audio from one of those shows that had the Lighthouse All-Stars with Art Pepper instead of Jimmy Giuffre, from around 1952.

I've always thought that there was more footage from the Norman Granz **Improvisation** film than has been released. One time I was with Norman Granz in his office and he just didn't want to be bothered with it. This is before the film on **Improvisation** had been discovered. I asked him if it was really lost. He said, "No, it's not lost. I know where it is, it's downstairs. I just have no interest in it." I didn't bug him too much because he wasn't the type of guy that one wanted to push. At some point someone from Japan was able to work something out with him and release that material. Norman said that it was incomplete and, I swear, when I did the interview, he said that he had filmed Bird and Lester Young together. So maybe someday that will show up too.

John Altman

It would not be an overstatement to say that the British-born John Altman has accomplished a great deal in his overlapping careers. He has written the music for scores of films (including the ship orchestra's music for **Titanic**), countless television shows and thousands of commercials in addition to acting in movies. He has been a saxophonist since the age of 13, working at his first gig literally the day after he first blew into a sax. Altman has played with a bewildering assortment of bands (includ-

ing blues, funk, rock, folk, reggae and punk groups) and served as Van Morrison's musical director, although his first love is jazz. And he is a notable jazz film collector.

How did you originally become interested in jazz?

I grew up in a family that was filled with bandleaders. My uncle was Britain's leading clarinetist, Sid Phillips, my mother's brothers were all musicians, and one of my uncles was the conductor at the Palladium, working with Sinatra, Judy Garland and Nat King Cole. I discovered my parent's 78 collection early on and, rather than smashing them up, I treasured them. At the age of five I was memorizing Jack Teagarden's solos; not a bad way to start! My life was always involved in music.

How did you become interested in collecting jazz films?

While working on a movie in Germany, I went to the hotel room, turned on the television and I was surprised to see the Berlin Jazz Festival being broadcast. The next day I mentioned to the director that I saw some jazz on television, which was becoming a rarity in England. He told me that they have jazz on TV in Germany all the time and that he'd tape some for me. He was a bit indiscriminate so I would be sent the most horrendous things sandwiched between real gems. Then a very good friend of mine, an accountant who travels a lot in Europe and is a big jazz fan, had a great idea. We thought that if we could get a pool of people (say one in every country) to tape and send us jazz that was on television, we could get a giant swap going. It was successful, and it just grew and grew, with both new and vintage performances being swapped. Among the people involved in the swapping was a director from Swedish television who had access to a lot of archival material that he had at home, including concerts from the Duke Ellington band in the 1950s, Charles Mingus, Bill Evans rehearsing and Stan Getz playing "Focus" with Eddie Sauter. It got to the point where tapes by the hundreds were arriving.

How many people altogether are involved in this trading?

At its peak, we had at least one person from virtually every country in the world. We were getting things from Australia, New Zealand, United States, Canada, all the Scandinavian countries, Germany, France, Italy, Switzerland, Ireland and Yugoslavia. We received films from nearly every country that had television stations.

About how many films and tapes of jazz do you now own?

Upwards of 4,000–5,000 videos.

What are some of the real treasures in your collection, some of the film clips you never thought you'd see?

Certainly Stan Getz playing "Focus" with Eddie Sauter's orchestra. I have a jam session at the Cannes Jazz Festival with Stan Getz, Coleman Hawkins, Don Byas, and Barney Wilen all playing together, some conversations between Charles Mingus and Eric Dolphy which are fascinating, Bud Powell performing a blistering 45-minute set in the late 1950s (smiling and playing magnificently) and Duke Ellington's orchestra at its best during a 90-minute concert from 1956. One show has Roy Eldridge playing drums with Sidney Bechet on "Sweet Georgia Brown," trading fours with him! There is Lars Gullin playing his compositions with a choir, Gerry Mulligan's 1960 Concert Jazz Band at the Newport Jazz Festival, Jack Teagarden with strings, Scott LaFaro performing with Richie Kamuca and Frank Rosolino from the *Stars of Jazz* television series, Booker Little playing for 20 minutes with Max Roach's group, a lot of Lee Morgan and a half-hour set of the John Coltrane Quartet at Antibes in 1965. It is shocking how much film there is out there. The holy grail

is that there is supposedly a video of the Miles Davis Quintet in 1959 with Stan Getz substituting for Miles, playing with John Coltrane, Wynton Kelly, Paul Chambers and Jimmy Cobb.

Do you think there's any chance that some of those films will become available eventually to the general public?

There are some problems. As the people discovered who put together **The Miles Davis Story** documentary, a lot of the television stations do not necessarily have the stuff that survived, and there is a question over who actually owns it and how much they should charge. Just for the 30-second excerpt of Miles playing in 1957 with a European big band, they had to spend an absolute fortune. The cost of using film clips runs into so much money, which is why most of the documentaries have people talking over the music, which is terribly frustrating.

There is another problem. In the past I've had Gil Evans, Al Cohn and Art Farmer watching films of themselves and they loved them. But some of the other guys are miffed at the existence of some of the films because they were never paid for their appearances on television. There is a big question over who owns the rights: the record labels that the musicians were signed to at the time, the television stations, or the musicians themselves? And how much should it cost to lease these shows so the general public can see them? With all of the programs that are in the archives of European television stations, nobody has much of a clue over what is available and what it would cost to release the performances commercially. I hope they get it straightened out eventually because the films are so valuable, allowing today's jazz fans and musicians the opportunity to see as well as hear the legends of the past who are no longer with us.

Top-Rated Films

Films That Received a Perfect 10 Rating

Section 1

🎵 Bix—Ain't None of Them Play Like Him Yet *Playboy Home Video*

🎵 Calle 54 *Miramax*

🎵 Charles Mingus Sextet *Shanachie*

🎵 Jazz Band Ball *Shanachie*

🎵 John Coltrane—The Coltrane Legacy *VAI Artists International*

🎵 Miles Davis Quintet: Live in Sweden *Columbia/Legacy*

🎵 The Sound of Jazz *Vintage Jazz Classics*

🎵 Stephane Grappelli: A Life in the Jazz Century *Music on Earth*

🎵 Talmage Farlow *Rhapsody Films*

🎵 Thelonious Monk: Straight No Chaser *Warner Home Video*

Section 3

🎵 Artie Shaw: Time Is All You've Got

🎵 Jazz Jamboree

Films That Received a 9 Rating

Section 1

🎵 Alberta Hunter: My Castle's Rockin' *View Video*

🎵 Art Blakey: A Jazz Messenger *Rhapsody Films*

🎵 The Art Ensemble of Chicago: Live from the Jazz Showcase *Rhapsody Films*

🎵 The Blues *Storyville*

🎵 Buck Clayton All-Stars *Shanachie*

♪ Buddy Rich: At the Top   *Hudson Music*

♪ Count Basie: Whirly-Bird   *Vintage Jazz Classics*

♪ David, Moffett & Ornette: The Ornette Coleman Trio 1966   *Rhapsody Films*

♪ Duke Ellington: 1929–1943   *Storyville*

♪ Dynasty: The Jackie McLean Quintet   *Triloka Video*

♪ Eddie Jefferson: Live from the Jazz Showcase   *Rhapsody Films*

♪ Eddie "Lockjaw" Davis: Volume One   *Storyville*

♪ Erroll Garner: In Performance   *Kultur Films*

♪ Harlem Roots Vol. 1: The Big Bands   *Storyville*

♪ Harlem Roots Vol. 2: The Headliners   *Storyville*

♪ Jazz Alley Vol. 1   *Storyville*

♪ Jazz at the Smithsonian: Alberta Hunter   *Kultur Films*

♪ Jazz Casual: Sonny Rollins   *Rhino Home Video*

♪ Jazz on a Summer's Day   *New Yorker Video*

♪ Jazz Scene USA—Cannonball Adderley Sextet/Teddy Edward Sextet   *Shanachie*

♪ Les McCann & Eddie Harris: Swiss Movement   *Rhino Home Video*

♪ Louis Jordan and His Tympany Band   *Storyville*

♪ Louis Prima: The Wildest   *Image Entertainment*

♪ Memories of Duke   *A*Vision*

♪ One Night with Blue Note   *Blue Note*

♪ Sarah Vaughan: The Divine One   *BMG Video*

♪ The Small Black Groups   *Storyville*

♪ The Snader Telescriptions: The Small Jazz Groups   *Storyville*

♪ Steve Lacy: Lift the Bandstand   *Rhapsody Films*

♪ Tenor Legends: Coleman Hawkins & Dexter Gordon   *Shanachie*

♪ Things to Come   *Vintage Jazz Classics*

♪ Vintage Collection Vol. 2: 1960–61   *A*Vision*

Section 2 *(for the Jazz)*

♪ The Big Broadcast

♪ Bird

♪ Birth of the Blues

♪ Cabin in the Sky

♪ The Five Pennies

♪ Round Midnight

♪ Stormy Weather

♪ Sun Valley Serenade

Section 3

♪ All Star Swing Festival

♪ Celebrating Bird: The Triumph of Charlie Parker

♪ Close Farm-ony

♪ Duke Ellington: Love You Madly

♪ The Great Rocky Mountain Jazz Party

♪ The Long Night of Lady Day

♪ Salute to Dizzy Gillespie

♪ Satchmo

♪ Satchmo the Great

Addresses of Film Labels

Here are the majority of the labels represented in the first review section. Mailing and e-mail addresses change often so some of these may already be out of date. Fortunately there are many ways to acquire jazz videotapes and DVDs, particularly on the Web, so have fun!

30N-90W Records c/o Jazz Crusade, 585 Pond Street, Bridgeport, CT 06606, www.jazzcrusade.com

Advance Music, www.advancemusic.com

Aix Records, www.aixrecords.com

Arbors, 2189 Cleveland Street, Suite 225, Clearwater, FL 33765, www.arborsrecords.com

Banjou Productions, www.banugibson.com

Basin Street Records, 4130 Canal St., New Orleans, LA 70119, www.basinstreetrecords.com

Blue Note Video, 150 Fifth Avenue, 6th Floor, New York, NY 10011, www.bluenote.com

BMG Video, 1540 Broadway, 43rd Floor, New York, NY 10036, www.bmg.com

Caravan of Dreams Productions, Dream Distributors, 7 Silver Hills Road, Santa Fe, NM 87508

Chesky Records, 355 W. 52nd Street, 6th Floor, New York, NY 10019, www.chesky.com

Columbia/Legacy Video, 550 Madison Avenue, 31st Floor, New York, NY 10022-3211, www.sony.com

Concord Records, 100 N. Crescent Drive, Suite 275, Beverly, Hills, CA 90210, www.concordrecords.com

Cuneiform Records, P.O. Box 8427, Silver Spring, MD 20907-8427, www.cuneiformrecords.com

DCI Music Video, 541 Avenue of the Americas, New York, NY 10011

Direct Cinema Limited, P.O. Box 10003, Santa Monica, CA 90410-1003, www.directcinema.com

Eagle Vision, 22 W. 38th Street, 7th Floor, New York, NY 10018, www.eaglevisionusa.com

EMI Music Canada, 3109 American Drive, Mississauga, Ontario, Canada, L4V 1B2, www.emimusic.ca

Euro Arts Entertainment, Hohenzollerndamm 150, 14199 Berlin, Germany, www.euroarts.com

Forest Farm Music, P.O. Box 5816, Santa Barbara, CA 93150

GOAL Productions, 2623 East Foothill Boulevard, Suite 101, Pasadena, CA 91107-3466, www.goalproductions.com

GRP Video, 555 West 57th Street, New York, NY 10019, www.grp.com

Guitarchives Music Inc., Box 360, Ganges, British Columbia, Canada V8K 2W1, www.guitarchives.com

Hudson Music, 311 West 34th St., Suite 9D, New York, NY 1001, www.hudsonmusic.com

Hyena Records, 250 W. 57th St., Suite 725, New York, NY 10107, www.hyenarecords.com

Icarus Films International, 32 Court Street, Suite 2105, Brooklyn, NY 11201, www.icarusfilmsinternational.com

Image Entertainment, 20525 Nordhoff St., Suite 200, Chatsworth, CA 91311-6019, www.image-entertainment.com

Inakustik, www.in-akustik.com

Jezebel Productions, P.O. Box 1348, New York, NY 10011, www.jezebel.org

JSL Records, c/o The AudioWorks Group, Ltd., 245 W. 25th St., New York, NY 10001, www.jslrecords.com

K2B2 Records, 1748 Roosevelt Avenue, Los Angeles, CA 90006, www.K2B2.com

Kultur Films, 195 Highway 36, West Long Branch, NJ 07764, www.kulturvideo.com

Leisure Video, P.O. Box 56757, New Orleans, LA 70156-6757

Lightyear Entertainment, 434 Avenue of the Americas, 6th Floor, New York, NY 10011, www.lightyear.com

Marsalis Music, 323 Broadway, Cambridge, MA 02139, www.marsalismusic.com

Music on Earth, 42 Barnfield Road, Ealing, London W51QT, England, www.musiconearth.co.uk

Music Sweethearts Inc., 18310 Heather Ave., Cerritos, CA 90703, www.dvdjazz.com

Music Video Distributors, P.O. Box 280, Oaks, PA 19456, www.musicvideodistributors.com

Mystic Fire, P.O. Box 422, New York, NY 10012, www.mysticfire.com

N Coded Music, 133 W. 25th Street, 9th Floor, New York, NY 10001

The National Center for Jewish Film, Brandeis University, Lown Building #102, Waltham, MA 02454, www.brandeis.edu/jewishfilm

New Yorker Video, 16 W 61st Street, New York, NY 10023, www.newyorkerfilms.com

NJN Public Television, P.O. Box 777, Trenton, NJ 08625-0777, www.njn.net

Passport Entertainment, 10520 Magnolia Boulevard, North Hollywood, CA 91601, www.passportproductions.com

PBS Home Video, www.pbs.org

Playboy Home Video, www.playboy.com

Polygram Video, 1755 Broadway, 3rd Floor, New York, NY 10019, www.polygram.com

Proscenium Entertainment, Dept. 7, Box 909, Highstown, NJ 08520

Quantum Leap Group Limited, 1A Great Northern Street, Huntingdon, Cambs PE29 7HJ England, www.qleap.co.uk

Rendezvous Productions, P.O. Box 4605, San Clemente, CA 92674

Rhapsody Films, 46-2 Becket Hill Road, Lyme, CT 06371, www.cinemaweb.com/rhapsody

Rhino Home Video, 3400 W. Olive Avenue, Burbank, CA 91505, www.rhino.com

Rosetta Records, 115 West 16th Street, #267, New York, NY 10011

Rounder Video, 1 Camp Street, Cambridge, MA 02140, www.rounder.com

Shanachie Entertainment, 37 E. Clinton Street, Newton, NJ 07860, www.shanachie.com

Song of the Spirit, P.O. Box 444, Willernie, MN 55090

Sony Music Video, www.sonymusicvideo.com

Storyville Records, Dortheavej 39, 2400 Copenhagen NV, Denmark, www.storyville-records.com

TDK Mediactive, www.tdk-mediactive.com

Triloka Video, 23852 Pacific Coast Highway #745, Malibu, CA 90265, www.triloka.com

Upstream Productions, 420 First Avenue West, Seattle, WA 98119

Vestapol, Stefan Grossman's Guitar Workshop, P.O. Box 802, Sparta, NJ 07871, www.guitarvideos.com

Video Artists International, 109 Wheeler Avenue, Pleasantville, NY 10570, www.vaimusic.com

View Video, 34 East 23rd St., New York, NY 10010, www.view.com

Warner Reprise Video, 3300 Warner Boulevard, Burbank, CA 91505, www.warnerbros.com

Winstar Video, 419 Park Avenue South, New York, NY 10016

Yazoo Records, c/o Shanachie, Dept. WWW, 37 E. Clinton Street, Newton, NJ 07860, www.yazoorecords.com

Bibliography

Artie Shaw: A Musical Biography and Discography, by Vladimir Simosko (2000, Scarecrow Press)

Benny Goodman: Listen to His Legacy, by D. Russell Connor (1988, Scarecrow Press)

Benny Goodman: Wrappin' It Up, by D. Russell Connor (1996, Scarecrow Press)

Deep in a Dream: The Long Night of Chet Baker, by James Gavin (2002, Alfred A. Knopf Publishers)

Duke Ellington: Day by Day and Film by Film, by Dr. Klaus Stratemann (1992, JazzMedia ApS)

Jazz in the Movies, by David Meeker (1981, Da Capo Press)

The Kenton Kronicles, by Steven Harris (2000, Dynaflow Publications)

Louis Armstrong on the Screen, by Dr. Klaus Stratemann (1996, JazzMedia ApS)

The New Grove Dictionary of Jazz, ed. by Barry Kernfield (1988, St. Martin's Press)

Pee Wee Speaks: A Discography of Pee Wee Russell, by Robert Hilbert and David Niven (1992, Scarecrow Press)

Sidney Bechet: The Wizard of Jazz, by John Chilton (1987, Oxford University Press)

The Soundies Distributing Corporation of America, by Maurice Terenzio, Scott MacGillivray and Ted Okuda (1991, McFarland & Company)

Space Is the Place: The Lives and Times of Sun Ra, by John Szwed (1997, Pantheon Books)

Stars of Jazz, by Ray Avery (1998, JazzMedia ApS)

Those Swinging Years, by Charlie Barnet and Stanley Dance (1984, Louisiana State University Press)

Index